THE MODERNITY OF TRADITION

Lloyd I. Rudolph
Susanne Hoeber Rudolph

THE MODERNITY
OF
TRADITION

Political Development in India

THE UNIVERSITY OF CHICAGO PRESS, CHICAGO & LONDON

ISBN: 0-226-73134-0 (Clothbound); 0-226-73135-9 (Paperback)
Library of Congress Catalog Card Number: 67-25527

The University of Chicago Press, Chicago 60637
The University of Chicago Press, Ltd., London

To Johannes and Elfriede Hoeber and Bertha Rudolph

PREFACE

We have been influenced in the writing of this book not only by the discipline of particular disciplines but also by the discipline of particular problems. Our approach and idiom have been varied to meet the requirements of those problems with which we have dealt here, drawing on the relevant insights, methods, and languages of sociology, anthropology, and psychology in our examination of the nature and course of political development in India.

The character of this book has been affected, too, by particular people. Here we would like to acknowledge the influence of those who have mattered most for this book. We have come to share the concern of Louis Hartz, Samuel H. Beer, and Carl J. Friedrich for comparative analysis oriented as much to historical problems as to the requirements of disciplinary theory. At a time when the relevance and respectability of new nations as objects of scholarly inquiry and scientific investigation were not yet established, Rupert Emerson's, Milton Singer's, and Edward Shils's work and interests suggested new possibilities and directions. We have profited from the professional wisdom of our friend and colleague W. H. Morris-Jones. Erik H. Erikson's capacity to relate psychological processes to social and cultural change informed our effort to analyze political development and the course of modernization in India. David Riesman's example of humanistic and responsible social science helped shape our view of the professional enterprise, and his friendship has lent zest to our work over the years.

We are grateful for financial support to the Foreign Area Training Program of the Ford Foundation, the United States Educational Foundation in India, and, at the University of Chicago, the Committee on Southern Asian Studies, the College, and the Social Sciences Research Committee. Our colleagues in the Committee on Southern Asian Studies and in the Committee for the Comparative Study of

Preface

New Nations have provided a stimulating environment for the development of this book.

We thank the following journals for permission to use in altered form material that appeared in their pages: *Pacific Affairs, World Politics, Comparative Studies in Society and History, American Political Science Review, American Scholar, Conspectus* (New Delhi), and *Economic and Political Weekly* (Bombay).

Papers presented at the Conference on Social Structure and Social Change in India, University of Chicago, June 3–5, 1965, and so cited in this book, will appear in Milton Singer and Bernard S. Cohn, eds., *Structure and Change in Indian Society,* to be published in 1968 under the auspices of the Viking Fund by the Aldine Publishing Co., Chicago.

We are indebted for the index to Mrs. Joan Landy Erdman.

The independent and efficient manner with which, at various stages of completion, Mrs. Mary Akenson and Mrs. Karen Capps prepared the typescript of the manuscript gave us considerable comfort.

Barnard, Vermont
1967

viii

CONTENTS

Contents

PART THREE

LEGAL CULTURES AND SOCIAL CHANGE:
PANCHAYATS, PANDITS, AND PROFESSIONALS 251

x

THE MODERNITY
OF
TRADITION

INTRODUCTION

Modernity has generally been opposed to tradition in contemporary analyses of social and political change. In this book we analyze variations in the meaning of modernity and tradition and suggest how they infiltrate and transform each other. The roots of the opposition of modernity and tradition go back at least as far as the Enlightenment. Condorcet's unilinear vision of progress found nothing of value in the past and saw the hope of mankind in the future. His perspective is still to be found in the assumptions of those concerned to understand the course of modernization in new nations. So, too, is Marx's variant of the Enlightenment attitude. The idea of dialectical conflict denigrates the past in its assumption that "theses" will be consumed in the fires of revolutionary change. Building on such assumptions, theorists of social change in new nations have found a dichotomy between tradition and modernity. Useless and valueless, tradition has been relegated to a historical trash heap. Modernity will be realized when tradition has been destroyed and superseded.

The assumption that modernity and tradition are radically contradictory rests on a misdiagnosis of tradition as it is found in traditional societies, a misunderstanding of modernity as it is found in modern societies, and a misapprehension of the relationship between them.[1] There is a striking contrast between the image of modern

[1] Despite our reservations concerning models of tradition and modernity, we find certain contrasts heuristically useful: "modernity" assumes that local ties and parochial perspectives give way to universal commitments and cosmopolitan attitudes; that the truths of utility, calculation, and science take precedence over those of the emotions, the sacred, and the non-rational; that the individual rather than the group be the primary unit of society and politics; that the associations in which men live and work be based on choice not birth; that mastery rather than fatalism orient their attitude toward the material and human environment; that identity be chosen and achieved, not ascribed and affirmed;

3

society developed by scholars whose purview is Europe and America and the image drawn by those whose aim is to compare such modern Western societies with traditional non-Western ones.

Scholars who confine their attention to their own or other modern societies have in our generation increasingly stressed traditional survivals. Studies of American political behavior suggest the persistence of such traditional forces as local history, ethnicity, race, and religious community. American sociologists studying the fate of the melting pot emphasize the importance of ethnic and religious solidarities and structures. The literature on organization reveals that the modern corporation attempts with considerable success to create diffuse affective bonds among not only its employees but also their wives, families, and neighbors. Corporate concerns and private interest become inextricably entangled. Economic relations among and between employers and employees take on affective dimensions and assume aspects of traditional patron-client relationships. The new urban sociology tells us that the metropolis produces collectivities of urban villagers. In sum, the literature focusing exclusively on so modern a society as America tends to contradict the notion that tradition and modernity are dichotomous. It suggests instead that there may be certain persistent requirements of the human condition that tradition, as it is expressed in the past of particular nations, can and does satisfy.

When we turn, on the other hand, to the image of modern society that emerges from much of the literature comparing it to traditional society, we find that its traditional features have either disappeared from view or are pictured as residual categories that have failed to yield, because of some inefficiency in the historical process, to the imperatives of modernization. In this literature, tradition lives on today only in new nations that stand at or near the beginning of a

---

that work be separated from family, residence, and community in bureaucratic organizations; that manhood be delayed while youth prepares for its tasks and responsibilities; that age, even when it is prolonged, surrender much of its authority to youth and men some of theirs to women; that mankind cease to live as races apart by recognizing in society and politics its common humanity; that government cease to be a manifestation of powers beyond man and out of the reach of ordinary men by basing itself on participation, consent, and public accountability.

historical process that modern Western nations have already traversed.

The misunderstanding of modern society that excludes its traditional features is paralleled by a misdiagnosis of traditional society that underestimates its modern potentialities. Those who study new nations comparatively often find only manifest and dominant values, configurations, and structures that fit a model of tradition and miss latent, deviant, or minority ones that may fit a model of modernity. All civilizations and complex cultures, predominantly traditional or modern, encompass a range of sentiments, psychological predispositions, norms, and structures that "belong" with an ideal type other than their own. Analyses that aim to validate heuristic theories may obscure or ignore these deviations, but theories concerned to encompass social change do so at their peril.

Comparative stratification studies, for example, have tended to use a reified conception of the Indian caste system as an approximation of the ideal type of traditional stratification: a system in which rigidly ascribed and closed status groups whose superordinate and subordinate relationships are legitimized by a comprehensive sacred ideology block social mobility and change. Much of that image has always been correct. But we are now beginning to recognize that earlier interpretations based on sacred texts took too literally their descriptions of social organization and assumed too readily the social validity of their legitimizing values. These texts' Brahmanic ideology in fact masked considerable mobility and social change. Conquest and novel economic opportunities often enabled alien or subordinate peoples or castes to establish themselves within the traditional system. These groups were provided with names, symbols, genealogies, and ritual rank appropriate to their newly won power and status. By the time British ethnographers got to work, these events and processes had disappeared from view; castes who might have established themselves in the fifteenth or seventeenth century were presented in terms of Vedic social structure, with the clear implication that they had been in place since time immemorial. Subsequent interpretations of the caste system based on sacred texts and deductions from an ideal-typical model of a traditional stratification system led to systematic inattention to the evidence of mobility and social change.

Psychological theories of entrepreneurship provide another example of how potentially modern features of traditional Indian society have been hidden from view. Entrepreneurship in the modern West has often been linked to a character structure associated with Protestantism or early liberalism, both conspicuous in India by their absence. Yet new historical and anthropological research suggests that the ethic and character of traditional merchant castes could be channelled into behavior appropriate to capitalist entrepreneurship within the framework of continuing familial and community obligations. Even more recently, new studies have revealed how Brahmans, socialized as a literary and priestly class but blocked by contemporary events from occupying such roles or their modern equivalents, have harbored recessive capacities for economic enterprise. And Gandhi's this-worldly asceticism translated a variant of traditional merchant entrepreneurship into political terms.

The cumulative effect of the misdiagnosis of traditional societies and the misunderstanding of modern societies has been to produce an analytic gap between tradition and modernity. We find the literature speaking of an abyss between them; stressing incompatibilities between their norms, structures, and personalities; and describing the hollowness of men and institutions in midpassage. Because they are seen as mutually exclusive, to depart from one is disorienting and traumatic, to enter the other alienating and superficial. Nor does the notion of transitional society escape the preoccupation with the dichotomy between tradition and modernity, for it assumes rather than challenges it. If the two systems are taken to be fundamentally different and incompatible, then social engineers working with new blueprints and new materials are required. Change takes on a systemic rather than adaptive character.

The opposition of modernity and tradition is also a natural consequence of the comparative method of analysis. Students of American society who examined it in isolation tended to stress the importance of class differences and conflict, whereas those who did so comparatively tended to stress class homogeneity and the absence of ideological conflict. To some extent, the one-sided view of traditional and modern societies that emerges from the comparative view of new and old nations arises out of similar differences of assumptions and perspectives. We recognize how modern we are by examining how traditional they are. One of the great attractions of comparative analysis has been to correct excessively narrow perspectives and the parochial judgments they produce by placing any particular instance in the context of plausible alternatives. But comparative analysis can also mislead if the questions that are built into the terms of comparison are a product of unproved assumptions.

Interest in comparison has not always been combined with knowledge of and sensibility toward particular non-Western nations. The strongest impulse for comparative work has come from those familiar with Western comparative politics and political sociology. They have, characteristically and understandably, been influenced by categories of analysis and historical possibilities fashioned in their own familiar context. It is in this sense that the comparative approach has found it hard to avoid an imperialism of categories and historical possibilities. Comparison becomes a way of measuring, and the standards of measure have a way of carrying normative implications. Has a particular new nation approximated the standards of the context out of which the comparison and the comparativist arose? One result has been comparative inquiry aimed at discovering whether the non-West has or can have such characterological, structural, or philosophic features as an achievement ethic, modern bureaucracy, individualism, or an attitude of mastery toward the physical and human environment. Because Western nations have realized certain objective conditions such as industrialization, urbanization, and literacy before political democracy, they are often assumed to be requisites of it. Such assumptions and inquiries have the effect of limiting the models of modernity and the processes and sequences of modernization to the experience of Western nations. The myths and realities of Western experience set limits to the social scientific imagination, and modernity becomes what we imagine ourselves to be.

The difficulties that can arise from the use of ideal-typical concepts in empirical investigation have often been recited. They can screen out perceptions of the particular and the exceptional that contradict dominant trends and motifs. Such theoretical screening is especially inimical to the analysis of social change because it eliminates from consideration latent, deviant, and minority alternatives. With some

7

alteration in historical circumstances, such alternatives may become the source of new or transformed identities, structures, and norms. Social change and the new realities it creates arise not only from the impact of objective, exogenous, or revolutionary forces on established systems but also from alternative potentialities within such systems. Marxist theory brilliantly stresses this insight when it emphasizes the creative possibilities of historical contradictions. Ideal-typical or heuristic analyses of modernity and tradition in particular historical and national settings are likely to miss these creative possibilities in so far as they assume that the characterological, structural, and ideological components of each are absent in the other and thereby place modernity and tradition in a dichotomous rather than a dialectical relationship. Such a divorce of modernity and tradition can be and sometimes is compounded by deducing a model of tradition from a model of modernity and proceeding, in the study of modernization in particular traditional societies, on the assumption that the deduced model provides the point of departure for change.

Probably there was no better way to begin the comparative enterprise than with the ideal-typical categories suggested by Western experience. But if we are right in believing that tradition and modernity are internally varied, then research and findings that proceed on the assumption of a dichotomous relationship between internally relatively consistent models are serious obstacles to understanding social change and modernization. Systematic social science schemes fed by non-contextual behavioral data selected with a view to filling in the outlines of ideal types may ignore, obscure, or falsify more than they reveal.

The separation of tradition and modernity has not been alleviated by those on speaking terms with the particulars of traditional societies. Area scholars have rarely exhibited strong predilections for comparative theory. Their strength has lain in a concern for the integrity, the autonomous meaning, and the inner logic of their subjects, civilizations, institutions, religions, philosophies, and individuals. They have appreciated the way chronology, by excluding some possibilities and including others, shapes consciousness and the subsequent course of historical events. The strength of historical particularism lies in aesthetic and philosophic empathy, in the sensitivity

8

for process in time and context, and in the discipline, not of a discipline, but of the experience of mastering and understanding a subject from within as well as from without.

An exclusive preoccupation with historical particularism is, of course, inimical to the growth and refinement of theory, particularly theory arising from comparative studies and knowledge. On the other hand, it possesses the resources for exposing and correcting the biases and limitations of theory whose origin lies in other historical contexts. By insisting on the independent significance of alien particulars, making clear that they are not always or merely the source of instances and illustrations, the small Arabic numerals to be ordered (or excluded) beneath the Roman in an imported conceptual scheme, historical particularism can suggest the inappropriateness of dichotomies and ideal types derived from Western historical experience and normative concerns. Properly attended to, they can, of course, provide insights and instances for new and more valid general theory.

The separation of tradition and modernity may arise from still another source, from the distortions that influence the view held by historically ascendant classes, races, or nations of those that are or were subject to them. Dominant classes, races, and nations attribute causal potency to those attributes associated with their subjection of others. The mirror image of others as the opposite of oneself becomes an element in civilizational, national, and personal esteem. Africans, including American Negroes, long appeared to Americans as black, lazy, cannibalistic, chaotically sexual, childish and incapable of social organization and government. We liked them that way because it strengthened the mirror image we had of ourselves as white, industrious, self-controlled, organized, orderly, and mature. India seen as a mirror image of the West appears otherworldly, fatalistic, unegalitarian, and corporate. It is as though we would be less ourselves, less this-worldly, masterful, egalitarian, and individualistic if they were less what they are. Occasionally one comes away from a colleague's work with the impression that he is reassuring himself and his readers of the uniqueness of the Western achievement, a uniqueness that would be endangered by recognition of the cultural, functional, and structural analogues to be found in non-Western, traditional societies.

If there have been false starts and enthusiasms in the exploration of tradition and modernity and their relation, there have also been promising beginnings. Greater familiarity and appreciation of non-Western traditional societies have already acted as correctives in lay as well as scholarly circles. So, too, has the changing power relationship between old and new states. Non-Western scholars who command the attention and respect of their Western colleagues have helped disabuse them of an overly simple and Occident-centered view of the relation between tradition and modernity. The too easy equation of Western and modern has become increasingly apparent in the face of studies that focus on the varieties of modernity, including the Japanese and Russian cases, and the ways in which the traditions of particular modern nations, Western and non-Western alike, have made them as unlike as like each other. Renewed attention to economic, political, and social modernization in Western nations has led to a more differentiated view of the conditions and processes involved and has drawn attention to the parallels and analogues between the past circumstances of modern nations and those of contemporary traditional societies.

Our concern in this book is to accord tradition a higher priority in the study of modernization than has often been the case in previous analyses of it. By placing Indian manifestations of tradition in the foreground of observation, we are better able to explore its internal variations and potentialities for change. The examination of internal variations within traditional and modern societies draws attention to those features of each that are present in the other. If tradition and modernity are seen as continuous rather than separated by an abyss, if they are dialectically rather than dichotomously related, and if internal variations are attended to and taken seriously, then those sectors of traditional society that contain or express potentialities for change from dominant norms and structures become critical for understanding the nature and processes of modernization. Classes and castes, religions and sects, statuses and roles that represent deviations from dominant motifs; stresses within dominant ideologies; and recessive themes in cultural patterns and psychological makeup that can be mobilized by somewhat changed historical circumstances become grist for the mill of social change. The components of "new" men may exist among the "old"; it is not always necessary for new men to be the progenitors or creators of a modern economy or polity. Cultural patterning is rarely homogeneous nor does it always command total compliance among social groups and individuals. Those qualities of groups or individuals or structures that produce incongruence and strain in relation to a society's dominant motifs, or those points at which socialization creates friction or conflict rather than integration and control, can become at critical historical moments the sources of incremental or fundamental social change.

Gandhi's leadership, which we explore in one of the parts of this book, illustrates some of these observations. It would be difficult to place him with either the new or old society, although his symbolism was traditional. His ideology and tactics stressed non-violence, asceticism, compromise, and consensualism, themes that are as susceptible to a fatalistic and otherworldly interpretation as to an activist and this-worldly one. Whether one or another of these interpretations is valid depends upon the meaning with which they are infused and the purposes to which they are put. In fact, Gandhi harnessed them to the requirements and purposes of a modern mass movement whose goals were national independence, coherence, and self-esteem. The potential for activism and mastery of the environment had always been there; changed historical circumstances provided an opportunity for its expression.

The introduction of new ideas and objective forces that followed British conquest and rule mobilized latent, deviant, or minority qualities within traditional Indian society that were like or compatible with them. For example, in Part One we examine how horizontal solidarities and interests latent in the caste system have been used in its structural, functional, and cultural transformation. In its transformed state, caste has helped India's peasant society make a success of representative democracy and fostered the growth of equality by making Indians less separate and more alike. Traditional law, another subject of later detailed analysis, was characterized by simultaneous conflict and integration of parochial customary law and an overarching pattern of sacred law that was cultivated and interpreted by Brahmans. The need for more uniform law that followed the introduction of the British raj strengthened the second at the expense of the first. For some time in a variety of ways, indigenous high-culture law aided in establishing a national legal framework.

Increased attentiveness to the variations and potentialities of traditional society not only yields insights into the connections between it and "modernity" but also, when combined with attentiveness to "traditional" aspects of modern societies, raises questions about the meaning of modernity. The modernization of traditional new nations has begun to suggest that established notions of modernity may have to be amended and revised. Our study of Indian law suggests how and why Indians, still closer to the consensual and face-to-face procedures of traditional law, might choose, even as modern Western law of late has, to incorporate such "traditional" aspects into their legal system. The persistence of caste communities in contemporary Indian politics and ethnic and religious ones in modern American politics, which we examine below, suggests that political modernity, contrary to broadly shared assumptions, may involve ascriptive and corporate features. Paracommunities, associations combining traditional and modern features, are not merely transitional phenomena but a persistent feature of modernity.

Our argument concerning the modernity of tradition and its correlate, that modernity incorporates traditional aspects, is based on a rather different view of historical processes, sequences, and end products than many comparative analyses of modernization in new nations. The latter are often expressed in terms of requisites or conditions, certain levels of industrialization, urbanization, literacy, mass communications, and so on, which must be realized before modern behavior and structures in the economic, social, and political realms can be independently and effectively established. By relating such factors, through multivariate analysis, to aggregate characteristics of systems, these theories attempt to establish when and under what conditions such aspects of modernity as political democracy or social mobilization are possible and viable. Although there is no mention of necessity or inevitability in such theories, they do tend to assume that some processes and sequences are related in predictable ways to certain historical end products, including political democracy. But must we assume, as such theories tend to, that because in modern Western nations particular conditions preceded the emergence of modern societies and democratic politics they will or must be replicated in our own era to produce the same results? Will the muse of history, having prescribed a particular historical sequence for the Atlantic nations, suffer a failure of imagination and repeat herself endlessly into future historical time?

Although certain historical reiterations and coincidences are surely to be expected, there are compelling reasons to believe that different processes, sequences, and relationships are probable. Knowledge of what has happened in history, of what is available from the political, economic, and administrative experience of "modern" nations, and of what is transferable from the accomplishments of science and technology creates new historical possibilities. Scenarios of modernization have been repeated often enough for their significance and lessons to become part of elite world consciousness. The muse may be susceptible to feedback. To be sure, nations and their leaders do not always learn, nor are they always receptive to such knowledge. But certain possibilities, certain alternatives that were not available to seventeenth and eighteenth century Europeans and Americans, are today not only available but taken for granted in many new nations.

Western observers often view the aspirations and ambitions of new nations in the spirit of the father who finds his son taking for granted the birthright that he has labored long and arduously to produce. He mistrusts the son's assumption that he can take as a starting point what his father has made available without experiencing in considerable measure similar trials and tribulations. There is, however, another side to such historical moments. The techniques and methods, the values and structures, the character and behavior for satisfying the aspirations of new generations and new nations, are known and available. They can be used or abused. New nations do not find themselves in the situation that Europeans did two hundred years ago. The world knows how to build a steel mill, both in the narrow technical sense and, to some extent, in the wider social sense. It knows the capacities of scientific agriculture even though poor and ignorant Indians, like poor and ignorant Tennesseeans, may take some time to use them effectively. Experience with cultural and technical innovation has made it abundantly clear that we cannot expect lessons that history has to teach to be easily or happily learned. At the same time, there is no doubt that the environment of change and innovation in the mid-twentieth century is radically different from that of the eighteenth: many historical processes and sequences have been telescoped or eliminated.

Some have also been reversed. What was in one context a culmination may in another be a cause. Because modernity has been realized in history, it is possible to imagine, anticipate, and produce reversals in the order of its achievement as well as modifications in its form and meaning. The initial act of creation may require different social and psychological qualities than adaptability to its fruits. The presence of models, the fact that a certain kind of history has already been experienced and that this experience is susceptible of vicarious meaning for others, means that the history of modernization will not be the same for all nations and for all time.

There is of course nothing natural or inevitable about modernization that connects congenial elements of the old society to the needs of the new. Nothing may happen; tradition and modernity may not connect. There must be apparent incentives on the side of adaptation, innovation, and change before some kind of dialogue between the new and the old arises. Such situations have not been established in all new nations. In what follows we explore the modernity of tradition in India.

PART ONE

Traditional Structures
and Modern Politics: Caste

Like Marx a century ago, contemporary social scientists tend to see the objective conditions of modernity—critical levels of industrialization, urbanization, per capita income, and education—as requisites for the conduct of modern democratic politics. Political democracy, they believe, must await its time. The objective conditions of tradition—poverty, low levels of education and mass communication, and a predominantly peasant economy—render unlikely the appearance, much less the success, of political democracy. Modernity and tradition, in this view, are dichotomous. Marx's *The Eighteenth Brumaire of Louis Napoleon* and *The British Rule in India,* written over a century ago, present the classic statement of this view.

Marx, Modernity, and Mobilization

Peasant nations, Marx observed in the *The Eighteenth Brumaire of Louis Napoleon,* are formed "by simple addition of homologous magnitudes, much as potatoes in a sack form a sackful of potatoes."[1] Objectively, peasants form a class; the mode of life, interests, and culture that flow from their productive circumstances separate peasants from other classes and place their class in opposition to others. But subjectively and practically, peasants form a vast mass "the members of which live in similar conditions, but without entering into manifold relations with one another." They are isolated from one another by their mode of production, poor communications, and

[1] Karl Marx, "The Eighteenth Brumaire of Louis Napoleon," *Selected Works* (New York, n.d.), II, 415.

poverty. The small holding, because it cannot support division of labor or the application of science, lacks multiplicity of development, diversity of talents, and a variety of social relationships. Peasant society consists of self-sufficient peasant families; "a few score of these make up a village, and a few score villages a Department."[2]

Peasants do not form a class, Marx argued, because their relations are "strictly local." They know each other only parochially. Because the "identity of their interests begets no unity, no natural union and no political organization, [they] . . . cannot represent themselves, they must be represented. . . . Their representative," he continued, "must at the same time appear as their master, as an authority over them, as an unlimited governmental power that protects them against other classes and sends them the rain and the sunshine from above. The political influence," he concludes, "of the small peasant, therefore, finds its final expression in the executive power subordinating society to itself."[3]

Much contemporary social science tends to agree with the Marxian view that the early stages of economic development and social and political modernization in peasant societies are likely to produce popular authoritarian or revolutionary ideological regimes that subordinate society to themselves. The circumstances of mid-twentieth century India bring these possibilities into sharp focus and provide the basis for an assessment of the general validity of this view.

At independence Indian society encompassed active but receding feudal classes, a growing, vigorous but divided bourgeoisie, a visible, important but still immature industrial economy, and a massive peasantry.[4] Despite increasing fragmentation and debt Indian peas-

---

[2] *Ibid.*, 414–15.   [3] *Ibid.*, 415.

[4] For a discussion of feudal classes, see Howard L. Erdman, *The Swatantra Party and Indian Conservatism* (Cambridge, 1967). For its business classes, see Helen B. Lamb, "Indian Business Communities and the Evolution of an Industrial Class," *Pacific Affairs*, XXVIII (June, 1955), 101–16; and D. R. Gadgil, *Origins of the Modern Indian Business Class* (New York, 1959).

For India's social and political development, see B. B. Misra, *The Indian Middle Classes: Their Growth in Modern Times* (London, 1961); Charles Heimsath, *Indian Nationalism and Hindu Social Reform* (Princeton, 1964); and Bruce T. McCully, *English Education and the Origin of Indian Nationalism* (New York, 1940). For industrial development, see Vera Anstey, *The Economic*

ants, like peasants elsewhere,[5] have not, as Marx thought they would, parted with their attachment to the small holding or provided that "chorus without which the solo song [of the urban proletariat] in all peasant nations becomes a swan song."[6] Instead of surrendering themselves to a political master in the hope of protection and benefits or recognizing their "natural ally and leader" in the industrial proletariat, Indian peasants have found in traditional social arrangements some of the means to represent and rule themselves.

The leading and most pervasive natural association of the old regime, caste, has responded to changes in its political and economic environment by transforming itself from below and within. Hierarchy, privilege, and moral parochialism no longer exhaust its secular significance. Caste has become a means to level the old order's inequalities by helping to destroy its moral basis and social structure. In doing so, caste has helped peasants to represent and rule themselves by attaching them to the ideas, processes, and institutions of political democracy.[7]

Development of India (4th ed.; London, 1952); H. Venkatasubbiah, *Indian Economy since Independence* (Bombay, 1961); and Charles A. Myers, *Labor Problems in the Industrialization of India* (Cambridge, Mass., 1958). Myron Weiner's *The Politics of Scarcity* (Chicago, 1962) provides a useful analysis of interest groups in Indian politics.

For particulars on the distribution of national income among sectors of the economy, see the Government of India, Central Statistical Organization, Department of Statistics, *Statistical Abstract of the Indian Union, 1961* (Delhi, 1961). Agriculture, not including forestry and fishing, accounted for 46.8 per cent of national income in the period 1959–60 (p. 21).

[5] See, for example, David Mitrany, *Marx against the Peasant: A Study in Social Dogmatism* (New York, 1961).

[6] Marx, *Selected Works*, II, 419.

[7] For the idea that traditional institutions may be adaptive to modern society and politics, see also the work of Harold Gould—for example, "The Adaptive Functions of Caste in Contemporary Indian Society," *Asian Survey*, III (September, 1963). See also Joseph Gusfield, "Political Community and Group Interests in Modern India" (mimeographed, July, 1964). Ann Willner has pursued somewhat similar lines of argument with respect to Indonesia: "The Underdeveloped Study of Political Development," *World Politics* (April, 1964), and "Neotraditionalism as the Condition for Modernization: The Case of Indonesia" (mimeographed, 1966).

The weakness and failure of revolution and reaction are also closely related to the relative weight in traditional Indian society of micro-
as against macro-institutions. India's old regime, particularly at the
time it confronted British power and ideas in the eighteenth and
nineteenth centuries, was diffuse and decentralized, dominated by
micro- rather than macro-institutions. With the disintegration of the
Moghul empire and the weakening of Indian regional and local rule
by British policy and administration, the traditional society of villages, castes, and families had assumed a considerable measure of
self-regulation.[8] Social integration and control were given form and
substance by the high culture—by Hindu metaphysics, morals, and
social organization—but the high culture was widely varied in its
practical expression and increasingly dilute as it approached the
lower reaches of society and its little traditions.[9] The predominance
of micro-institutions deflected and contained the extremes of organized change through political action.[10] India's traditional macro-

[8] See Romila Thapar, "Seminar on Ideas in the 18th and 19th Centuries—a
Report," *Enquiry*, N.S. I, No. 3 (O.S. No. 9) (Winter, 1964), 114–30. "The
18th century," she writes, "saw the decay of empire at the political level and
the more wide-spread break-up of social organizations at a basic level. Village
economy became more localized, communities tended to develop into self-
sufficient centres. This was to become the prototype of Britain's picture of
India . . ." (p. 115).
Not only may the British have been misled in their estimate of the relative
weight and importance of micro- as against macro-institutions by forming their
estimates after, rather than before, the collapse of the Moghul empire, but
also, she suggests, there were periods over the long course of Indian history
when one or the other has been to the fore (p. 116).
See also Bernard S. Cohn, "Political Systems in Eighteenth Century India:
The Banaras Region," *Journal of the American Oriental Society*, LXXXII (July–
September, 1962), and "From Indian Status to British Contract," *Journal of
Economic History*, XXI (December, 1961).

[9] For a discussion of the structures, processes, and rules that link the society
and culture of the locality in India with those of its civilization, see Milton
Singer, "The Social Organization of Indian Civilization," *Diogenes*, XLV
(Spring, 1964), 84–119. It surveys and integrates the relevant monographic
literature, particularly the work of Singer himself, M. N. Srinivas, Bernard S.
Cohn, and McKim Marriott.

[10] "The fact . . . remains," Irawati Karve writes, "that while the more centrally organized societies of the west succumbed to political and religious domi-

20

institutions were difficult to attack or defend nationally: When Marx wrote, the most recent empire existed in name only; Hinduism had no church, no hierarchy, no orthodoxy; the nobility of the sword like that of the robe lacked institutional means to give it political standing or effectiveness as an estate of the realm; nor was India's third estate organized or represented as such.[11]

The strength and importance of micro-institutions also affected the capacity of British rule to change Indian society. British imperialism in India, like the revolutionary ideological regimes of Russia and China, manufactured and induced change from outside and above in order to establish new values and some aspects of a modern economy. But British imperialism was less sweeping in its impact not only because it was less eager for apocalyptic moral and material realization and less prone to coercive and total methods but also because in its tasks of destruction and reconstruction it was constrained by the greater strength in India of the traditional society's micro-institutions.

In 1853, Marx saw the coming of modernity in India in terms of the destruction of the objective conditions of tradition and their replacement by the objective conditions of modernity, that is, replication of Western history and social relations. "England *has broken down the entire framework of Indian society, without any symptoms of reconstruction yet appearing."*[12] It has, however, "a double mission to fulfill . . . one destructive, and the other regenerative—*the annihilation of the old Asiatic society,—*and the *laying of the material*

---

nation to a degree intensive enough to change radically their structure, the Hindu society has survived over 2000 years of continuous pressure from foreign conquerors and new religions. The survival became possible through its very structural looseness" (*Hindu Society: An Interpretation* [Poona, 1961], p. 127). The relationship between macro- and micro-institutions in ancient India is discussed by Rushton Coulborn in "The State and Religion: Iran, India and China"; by J. A. B. van Buitenen in "Comment on Coulborn's Iran, India and China"; and in Coulborn's "Reply to the Critics," in *Comparative Studies in Society and History,* I (1958–59), 44–57, 385–87, and 387–93.

[11] For India's modern constitutional history, see Reginald Coupland, *The Indian Problem: Report on the Constitutional Problem in India* (London, 1944).

[12] Karl Marx, "The British Rule in India," *Selected Works,* II, 652 (italics added).

foundations of Western society in Asia."[13] It had begun the latter[14] by imposing political unity, now (1853) to be strengthened and perpetuated by the electric telegraph; by introducing the first free press in Asia, "a new and powerful agent of reconstruction"; by creating private property in land; by educating Indians and thereby producing "a fresh class . . . endowed with the requirements for government and imbued with European science"; by connecting India through steam navigation with itself and the world, thereby breaking the isolation "which was the prime law of its stagnation"; and by gifting India "with the means of irrigation and of internal communication (railroads) which will, when completed, liberate her productive powers by revitalizing agriculture and enabling her to exchange what she produces."[15]

The railroads along with the multiplication of roads, he argued, will destroy village isolation and its accompanying "self-sufficient inertia" by supplying that intercourse with other villages without which *"the desire and efforts indispensable to social advance"* are absent. By introducing foreign and domestic manufactured goods, modern transportation and communication will "put the hereditary and stipendiary village artisanship of India to full proof of its capacity, and then supply its defects."[16] Because the railway system requires industrial processes for its support and because Indians have the aptitude and are getting the requisite training to man it, the railway system "will become the forerunner of modern industry." Modern industry, in turn, "will dissolve the hereditary divisions of labour, upon which rest the Indian *castes, those decisive impediments to Indian progress. . . ."*[17] When the Indian people appropriate the material civilization the English bourgeoisie has created they will be able to emancipate themselves and mend their social condition. For Marx, modern India would be both Western and socialist.

[13] *Ibid.*, 658 (italics added).

[14] "The work of regeneration hardly transpires through a heap of ruins," he observes. "Nevertheless it has begun" (*ibid.*, 658).

[15] *Ibid.*, 658–60.

[16] Marx quoting Chapman, *The Cotton and Commerce of India,* in *ibid.*, 661 (italics added).

[17] *Ibid.*, 661–62 (italics added).

England's mission of destruction, "the annihilation of old Asiatic society," was not yet complete in 1853. "We know," he writes, "that the municipal organization [village and caste *panchayats,* or councils] and the economical basis of the village communities have been broken up, but their worst feature, the dissolution of society into stereotype and disconnected atoms [that is, the Indian villages and castes], has survived . . ." the revolutionary impact of British imperialism.[18] Marx expected this feature too would disappear. He believed that Indian development would follow the classical pattern alleged to characterize Western history, the atomization of traditional corporate structures and their supersession by classes and national communities based on individuals, whose ills, exploitations, and alienations would in turn be repaired by communism's voluntary corporate structures. A new historiography may want to investigate whether traditional Western corporatism was ever so effectively destroyed as this theory holds. In any case, India has shown a strong propensity to transform rather than supersede traditional corporate structures, to move imperceptibly from traditional to modern corporatism without so marked an intervening individualist phase as the West is said to have experienced.

The raj did indeed undermine the "self-sufficient inertia" of village and caste and release "the desires and efforts indispensable to social advance."[19] Improved communications, particularly the railroads, did further this process. But what form and purpose did those desires and efforts for social advance assume? Marx left this question unanswered because unnoticed, concentrating his attention instead on the development of the material bases for a modern economy and society, which he expected would destroy traditional corporatism and be appropriated by the people for their emancipation and well-being. Caste, that most pervasive and, for most students of Indian society, Marxian and non-Marxian alike, most retrograde of India's social institutions has not only survived the impact of British imperialism but also transformed and transvalued itself. In doing so, it has helped to dissolve what Marx called the "village system,"[20] in-

[18] *Ibid.,* 660.

[19] *Ibid.,* 661.

[20] *Ibid.,* 654–55.

cluding a caste-based social hierarchy, and contributed to the success of political democracy by helping India's mass electorate to participate meaningfully and effectively in it.[21]

There is a variety of ways in which caste has affected political life in contemporary India. Some have been inimical to the realization of political democracy. Others, however, as demonstrated by extensive and weighty evidence, have contributed more to its realization than to its inhibition. Critical to this result has been the interaction of its transformed expressions with political parties, particularly with that now venerable political structure, the Indian National Congress. It is the relatively even balance between the integrating and modernizing structures of the Congress and other political parties, on the one hand, and independent, traditionally familiar institutions such as caste, on the other, that has given rural people some means to represent and rule themselves.

The relationship that caste bears to politics can best be understood in terms of three types of political mobilization, each suggestive of different phases of political development: vertical, horizontal, and differential. Vertical mobilization is the marshaling of political support by traditional notables in local societies that are organized and integrated by rank, mutual dependence, and the legitimacy of traditional authority. Notables reach vertically into such social systems by attaching dependents and socially inferior groups to themselves through their interests and deference. The community of the locality defines the boundaries of the system and contains its structural dimensions. The social discipline and leadership that Tocqueville found in the "natural" associations of aristocratic societies and Burke found in Britain's "little platoons" invoke the conditions under which vertical mobilization can be effectively practiced. Vertical mobilization remains a viable strategy for dominant classes and castes until dependents, tenants, and clients become sufficiently politicized to be mobilized by ideological appeals to class or community interests and sentiments. In Britain local traditional elites were characteristically territorial aristocracy and gentry. As their role in

[21] An earlier version of this argument appeared in Lloyd I. Rudolph and Susanne Hoeber Rudolph, "The Political Role of India's Caste Associations," *Pacific Affairs,* XXXIII (March, 1960), 5–22.

representative institutions began to involve them in processes of popular participation and consent, they turned traditional loyalty and economic dependence to good account by mobilizing dependents and inferiors.[22] In India traditional elites were characteristically the leaders of locally dominant castes. They, too, responded to representative government and popular politics by mobilizing what local notables in Britain called their "interest."

Horizontal mobilization involves the marshaling of popular political support by class or community leaders and their specialized organizations. Ignoring the leaders and members of natural associations or little platoons, they make direct ideological appeals to classes or communities. Horizontal mobilization of solidarities among class or community equals introduces a new pattern of cleavage by challenging the vertical solidarities and structures of traditional societies. Differences between European and Indian political modernization are found primarily in the character of horizontal mobilization. In India a central structure for this purpose has been a transformed version of caste, although class, too, has played a part and is increasingly doing so, whereas in Europe horizontal mobilization has been more marked by the development of class interest, consciousness, and

---

[22] For political development in Britain generally see Samuel H. Beer, *British Politics in the Collectivist Age* (New York, 1965) (published in Britain as *Modern British Politics: A Study of Parties and Pressure Groups* [London, 1965]). Beer examines structural and normative changes. See "Part One: Five Types of Politics [Old Tory, Old Whig, Liberal, Radical, Collectivist]" for variations in methods of mobilization. For the shift from vertical to horizontal mobilization, see Lloyd I. Rudolph, "The Meaning of Party: From the Politics of Status to the Politics of Opinion in Eighteenth Century England and America"(Ph.D. thesis in government, Harvard University, 1956).

The work of Sir Lewis B. Namier and those influenced by him provides a detailed but dynamic picture of the nature of vertical mobilization in eighteenth century Britain and relates it to the political patterns established by traditional elites in the context of Britain's changing constitutional order. Herbert Butterfield's *George III and the Historians* (London, 1957) presents not only an important framework within which to judge the work of the "Namier school" but also a brilliant analysis of political development as seen through the lens of historiography. Richard Pares' *George III and the Politicians* (Oxford, 1953) states a third persuasive perspective of the period. Norman Gash's *Politics in the Age of Peel* (London, 1953) remains the best analysis of vertical mobilization during the first half of the nineteenth century in Britain.

organization.[23] Even though the Indian National Congress' mobilization of modern and neotraditional middle classes and, to a lesser extent, peasants and workers was, of course, more than an "exception," it yet remains true that the mobilization of caste communities helps to distinguish Indian from European horizontal mobilization.

Differential mobilization involves the marshaling of direct and indirect political support by political parties (and other integrative structures) from viable, but internally differentiated, communities through parallel appeals to ideology, sentiment, and interest. The agent of mobilization in this case is the political party rather than the local notable or community association, and its strategies of mobilization vary. This is most apparent in the factors that are considered in the nomination of candidates, a process that sums up decisions con-

---

[23] See Beer, *British Politics in the Collectivist Age,* and Rudolph, "The Meaning of Party," for general treatments of vertical mobilization. The latter examines the emergence of associations specializing in politics and of organized public opinion as a dynamic and legitimizing element in government and politics.

The politics of class in a "popular" context of horizontal mobilization dates at least from the seventeenth century. Michael L. Walzer portrays the rise of the professional revolutionary in *The Revolution of the Saints: A Study of the Origins of Radical Politics* (Cambridge, 1965), and Christopher Hill emphasizes the role of class in his *Puritanism and Revolution; Studies in Interpretation of the English Revolution of the Seventeenth Century* (London, 1958). The existence and political importance of class mobility and decline are at the center of the argument between Lawrence Stone and Hugh R. Trevor-Roper. For the mob as an early form of horizontal mobilization see Lloyd I. Rudolph, "The Eighteenth Century Mob in America and Europe," *American Quarterly,* XI, No. 4 (1959).

For the horizontal mobilization characteristic of early radical politics see George Rude, *Wilkes and Liberty: A Social Study of 1763 to 1774* (Oxford, 1962); and I. Christie, *Wilkes, Wyvill and Reform: The Parliamentary Reform Movement in British Politics, 1760–1785* (London, 1963); Herbert Butterfield, *George III, Lord North and the People, 1779–1780* (London, 1949); and Eugene C. Black, *The Association: British Extraparliamentary Political Organization, 1769–1793* (Cambridge, 1963). They provide variegated analyses of the circumstances, structures, and purposes that characterized horizontal mobilization through popular appeals and political associations. The best single work on horizontal mobilization of the "proletariat" is Edward P. Thompson's *The Making of the English Working Classes* (New York, 1964).

cerning approaches to mobilization.[24] Parties may appeal to voters directly as individuals or indirectly through the organized groups to which they belong. Direct appeals to individual voters may stress ideology or issues, on the one hand, or community identification through caste, on the other. These appeals may be contradictory or complementary. Whether or not they are in conflict is in considerable measure dependent upon the size of the constituency and the number, homogeneity, and cohesiveness of its community components. At the level of the state assembly constituency, they are often complementary and at the village and ward level frequently so. In constituencies in which one caste community is numerically predominant or socially dominant, all parties, regardless of ideological, cultural or interest orientation are more likely to choose candidates from it.

Political parties in India must also mobilize political support indirectly from independently organized and directed classes, communities, and interests. In so far as they are independent and command the support of those whom they purport to represent, their members are less rather than more accessible to direct party appeals. The range of issues on which members of a caste community in India are accessible to direct party appeals and the degree of accessibility depend in considerable measure on the extent of the community's internal differentiation on class and interest lines. When an organized caste community is relatively homogeneous and cohesive and its common interests are still diffuse and varied, it is likely to form a partisan attachment to a particular political party and even to form and operate a political party of its own. As it becomes differentiated by class interest and by differences in education, income, occupation, and cultural style and as the range of its members' *common* interests narrows in consequence, it is likely to move from a strategy of partisan attachment to a non-partisan strategy of relations with all parties in which political calculations that relate its interests to political possibilities predominate.

The analysis that follows rests on our own investigations as well as evidence provided by the growing literature on caste and politics. We shall focus initially on horizontal mobilization of caste communities

[24] For a systematic discussion of such factors, see Ramashray Roy, "Selection of Congress Candidates," I–V, *Economic and Political Weekly,* I (December 31, 1966); II (January 7 and 14; February 11 and 18, 1967).

by caste associations. Horizontal mobilization illustrates most clearly how the cultural and structural transformation of a traditional institution contributes to political modernization and democracy, including political participation and representation. The subsequent analysis of differential mobilization will suggest how the role caste plays in politics depends on external factors—its historical, social, and political environment—and on internal factors—the caste's readiness and capacity for common consciousness, mobilization, and organization. Caste changes its character over time and so does the environment with which it interacts. The "entry" of any particular caste into the political arena and the strategies it pursues there are affected by the circumstances it confronts in the environment and by its inner life and state of development.[25]

The considerable variety in reports on caste associations suggests how both they and their political and social environment change through time. The entry problems of the Nadars and the Vanniyars in the early and mid-nineteenth century were different from those of the Jatavs and Noniyas in the late nineteenth and early twentieth centuries and different again from those of the castes involved in the Gujarat Kshatriya Sabha in the period after independence and two general elections. The mid-nineteenth century conditions which Nadars and Vanniyars encountered were dominated by the administrative structure and alien cultural impact of the British raj, on the one hand, and the high saliency of ritual rank for social standing, on the other. The Jatavs and Noniyas, too, were caught up in some of these social and political forces but were affected earlier in their careers as mobile castes by the secular forces of a modern economy and society and by considerations of competitive democratic politics, including the influence of class and ideology. In the case of the Gujarat Kshatriya Sabha, secular political and social forces outweigh but do not eliminate sacred and traditional ones in shaping the structural and cultural character of caste entry into the political system. These changing environmental circumstances not only influence

[25] For an example of the analytic use of the idea of "entry" as a way of thinking about strategy in relation to the political, ideological, and social environment facing *nouveau arrivé* political actors, see Warren Ilchman, "Political Development and Foreign Policy: The Case of India," *Journal of Commonwealth Political Studies,* IV (November, 1966).

the internal and external environment of a caste during its period of entry but also significantly shape the strategy it adopts at that time and subsequently.

Paracommunities: The Sociology of Caste Associations

Caste associations are paracommunities that enable members of castes to pursue social mobility, political power, and economic advantage. The characteristics of the paracommunity resemble in many ways those of the voluntary association or interest group familiar to European and American politics. On the other hand, the paracommunity is distinguishable in a number of important respects not only from the voluntary association but also from the natural association such as caste out of which it has developed.

The local subcaste, or jati, established by ascription the group within which a person might marry and, more broadly, the social, economic, and moral circumstances of his life. He could not, in so far as caste was embedded in social structure and cultural norms, change his social identity.[1] Social reality was never so rigid as this theoretical statement of it suggests: radical alterations in political or economic circumstances and the short- and long-run consequences of great religious movements enabled entire jatis to change their rank and standing; more prosperous sections of jatis separated themselves from their former kin and distinguished themselves by new names and

[1] Alternative status systems that parallel that of caste are emerging rapidly in contemporary India, and we shall take them into account below. An early study noting these was S. C. Dube, *Indian Village* (London, 1956), pp. 161–66; see also our discussion of aspects of this problem in "Indian Political Studies and the Scope of Comparative Politics," *Far Eastern Survey*, XXVII (September, 1959), 134–38, where accounts of village statuses by Sushil Dey, Baij Nath Singh, Evelyn Wood, John T. Hitchock, Henry Orenstein, Alan Beal, and Edward B. and Louise G. Harper are analyzed. Their articles appeared in Richard L. Park and Irene Tinker (eds.), *Leadership and Political Institutions in India* (Princeton, 1959).

practices; war, famine, and opportunity altered caste; and much more rarely, extraordinary individuals transcended the system.[2] Comparatively, however, the norm appeared to be rigorously ascriptive with endogamy, summation of roles, and congruence among social, religious, economic, and political structures characterizing the system. Jati norms and culture shaped character and prescribed ritual, occupational,[3] commensal, marital, and social conduct, and jati organization and authority enforced them.

Such social homogeneity resulted in a sense of exclusiveness and identity that tended to subsume all social roles to that of jati membership. The unit of action and location of caste has been, until recently, the jati in the village or group of villages. Traditionally, it had been concerned with settling problems at the village level, both within the caste and in relation to other castes. At most, its geographic spread took account of the reach of intracaste (endogamous) marriages, which often extended to other villages, but the village unit was crucial. Leadership was hereditary, generally exercised by the senior members of a specific lineage group. Social integration, the relationship of a caste to other castes, was governed, at the level of social ideology, by dharma, the sacred and traditional prescriptions of duty that permeate Hindu life, and, at the level of local interaction, interpreted and enforced for the most part by the local "dominant caste."[4] Finally, the organization of caste was latent—governed by generally understood customary relations—rather than manifest— rationalized in explicit legal structures.

The emergence of caste associations capable of effecting structural and cultural change was associated with many of the objective changes that Marx saw. Particularly important for the spread of new ideas and systems of interaction were improved means of communication, Western education, and the subjective and objective effects of

[2] See pp. 118–19 (n. 24) for a more extended discussion.

[3] The materials of the older caste ethnographers indicate that the breakdown of social and occupational homogeneity was apparent in the nineteenth century. Both Edgar Thurston, *Castes and Tribes of Southern India* (Madras, 1909), and William Crooke, *The Tribes and Castes of the North West Provinces and Oudh* (Calcutta, 1896), bear this out.

[4] See M. N. Srinivas, "The Dominant Caste in Rampura," *American Anthropologist,* LXI (February, 1959).

new economic opportunities associated with the growth of a market economy and the penetration of state economic activity.[5] On the one hand, these forces undermined the hold of the traditional culture and society as it was organized in relatively autonomous units; on the other hand, they created the conditions under which local sub-castes (jatis) could be linked together in geographically extended associations. Opportunities outside the local *jajmani* (patron-client) economy[6] provided the material bases and new sensibilities that enabled jatis, or sections of them, to raise themselves. Caste associations linking the more advanced sections of similar jatis undertook to upgrade the position of the caste in the social hierarchy. They pressed for the extension of privileges and rights by adopting the attributes and emulating the behavior of higher castes and by turning to the state for recognition of their claims.

Rising castes have tended to assimilate the norms and symbols of the twice-born castes, whether Brahman, Kshatriya, or Vaishya,[7] that

[5] See M. N. Srinivas' seminal articles, "A Note on Sanskritization and Westernization," *Far Eastern Quarterly*, XV (August, 1956), and "Caste in Modern India," *Journal of Asian Studies*, XVI (August, 1957). These articles appear as the first and second chapters in *Caste in Modern India, and Other Essays* (Bombay, 1962). William L. Rowe's "The New Cauhans: A Caste Mobility Movement in North India," in J. Silverberg (ed.), "Social Mobility in Caste in India" (a forthcoming special issue of *Comparative Studies in Society and History*), provides a detailed picture of how such changes affected a particular caste.

[6] The original work on the *jajmani* system was by W. H. Wiser, *The Hindu Jajmani System* (Lucknow, 1936). A more recent critical and comparative account can be found in Thomas O. Beidelman, *A Comparative Analysis of the Jajmani System* (Locust Valley, N.Y., 1959). Also notable are Harold Gould, "The Hindu Jajmani System: A Case Study of Economic Particularism," *Southwestern Journal of Anthropology*, XIV (Winter, 1958), and more recently, Pauline Mahar Kolenda, "Toward a Model of the Hindu Jajmani System," *Human Organization*, XX (Spring, 1963), 11–31.

[7] The priests, warrior-rulers, and merchants respectively of the four-fold varna hierarchy described in sacred texts and constituting an important component of traditional social ideology. Brahmans, Kshatriyas, and Vaishyas are twice-born in that they have experienced spiritual rebirth at the time (age nine to twelve) of the *upanayana* ceremony when they don the sacred thread symbolizing their twice-born status. The twice-born castes (varnas) are distinguished from the Sudra varna. Sudras are barred from knowledge of the

loomed largest on the cultural and social landscape of their region. More often than not they "rediscovered" their Kshatriya origins and history. Frequent, too, was the adoption of Brahman and Vaishya practices of vegetarianism, teetotalism, and the prohibition of remarriage by widows. To pay a dowry rather than a bride price; to arrange marriages before puberty; to practice Vedic ceremonies and rituals and have the services of Brahman priests at them; to wear the sacred thread, symbol of twice-born ritual rank; to ride a horse or be carried on a palanquin at ceremonial occasions; to dress in ways appropriate to high caste standing—these were the signs of twice-born culture and rank that mobile castes pursued and that caste associations initiated and managed.[8]

When the caste associations turned to the state for furthering their purposes, their initial claims were aimed at raising caste status in terms of the values and structure of the caste order. But as liberal and democratic ideas penetrated to wider sections of the population, the aims of the caste association began to shift from sacred to secular goals. Instead of demanding entry into temples, prestigious caste names, and "honorable" occupations and histories in the Census, the associations began to press for places in the new administrative and educational institutions and for political representation. Independence and the realization of political democracy intensified these new

---

sacred texts, into which the twice-born varnas are initiated. This ideal social formulation of the sacred texts was never a faithful representation of social reality; to the extent that it was, it has declined dramatically over the last two hundred years.

[8] The caste association has not been alone in this type of activity. More parochial village caste groups have also pursued emulation as a vehicle for improving status, sometimes successfully. See, for example, the progress of the Boad Distillers, in F. G. Bailey, *Caste and the Economic Frontier* (Manchester, 1957). But McKim Marriott has pointed out that any caste group operating in an intimate local setting, where relative status positions are well understood and jealously protected, might have trouble advancing itself by emulation: "A mere brandishing of Brahmanical symbols by a well-known village group can scarcely hope to impress a village audience in its own parochial terms. . . ." See his "Interactional and Attributional Theories of Caste Ranking," *Man in India,* XXXIX (April–June, 1959), 105. Conversely, the caste association, operating in the wider, and more impersonal, setting of a district or a state, may encounter less resistance to its emulative claims because in the wider setting there is no clear standard for assessing its "true" position.

concerns. Caste associations attempted to have their members nominated for elective office, working through existing parties or forming
their own; to maximize caste representation and influence in state
cabinets and lesser governing bodies; and to use ministerial, legislative, and administrative channels to press for action on caste objectives in the welfare, educational, and economic realms.[9] Perhaps the
most significant aspect of the caste association in the contemporay
era, however, has been its capacity to organize what appears to be a
politically illiterate mass electorate. Doing so enabled it to realize in
some measure its new formed aspirations and to educate its members
in the methods and values of political democracy.

The caste association is a paracommunity. It is no longer an
ascriptive association in the sense in which caste taken as jati was and
is. It has taken on features of the voluntary association. Membership
in caste associations is *not* purely ascriptive; birth in the caste is a
necessary but not a sufficient condition for membership. One must
also "join" through some conscious act involving various degrees of
identification—ranging from providing financial support to an association's educational, welfare, or commercial activities, to attending
caste association meetings, to voting for candidates supported by
caste association leaders. The caste association has generally both a
potential and an actual membership; when it speaks, it often claims
to speak for a much wider group than its active followers. Although
the purposes of caste are wide-ranging and diffuse, affecting every
aspect of members' life paths, the functions and interests of caste
associations have become increasingly specialized. The traditional
authority and functions of the jati are declining, but the caste association's concern to control or influence those who hold political power
and thereby allocate resources, opportunity, and honor has revived
and extended caste loyalties in new and larger contexts. At the same
time, its followers tend in the early phases of the caste association to
retain the more intense and exclusive loyalties and identities characteristic of ascriptive associations and to be, as a consequence, less subject to the crosscutting pressures that affect members of more strictly

[9] See, for example, Selig Harrison, "Caste and the Andhra Communists,"
American Political Science Review, L (June, 1956); M. L. P. Patterson, "Caste
and Politics in Maharashtra," *Economic Weekly,* VIII (July 21, 1956), as well
as the various studies cited on p. 62, n. 57.

voluntary associations.[10] With the passage of time and internal differentiation within the association, however, loyalties are diluted and the membership becomes more amenable to political mobilization from without.

Since modern means of transportation and communication have had the effect of broadening caste consciousness and structures, binding together jatis that had been relatively autonomous into geographically extended associations, caste associations today usually parallel administrative and political units—states, districts, taluks (subdistricts), and municipalities—whose offices and powers of legislation or decision-making are the object of caste association efforts. Some caste associations have even reached toward substantial cross-regional constituencies.

Leadership in the caste association is no longer in the hands of those qualified by heredity—the senior or more able members of the lineage, which traditionally supplied jati leadership. The availability of association leaders is conditioned by their ability to articulate and represent the purposes of the caste association, and for this purpose they must be literate in the ways of modern administration and the new democratic politics. Men whose educational and occupational backgrounds assure these skills helped form caste associations, and the more "democratic" of them occupy leadership positions. The new leaders stand in a more accountable and responsible relationship to their followers because their authority depends to a great extent on their capacity to represent and make good the association's purposes.[11]

[10] For the most influential contemporary analysis of multiple group memberships and the crosscutting pressures that arise from them, see David Truman, *The Governmental Process* (New York, 1951).

[11] The 1967 general election seems to have brought these considerations to a head. For example, a senior minister of the defeated Congress government in Madras, who was himself standing for Parliament, attributed his defeat in part to the inability of the older generation leaders of the largest caste in his constituency to command the electoral following they had been able to in previous elections. Younger generations in the caste community led by younger men repudiated the directives of the established leaders by voting DMK rather than Congress. Caste solidarity, he reported, remained high but the failure of older leaders closely identified with Congress rule to represent and speak for

Finally, at the organizational level, the caste association abandons the latent structure of caste for the manifest structure characteristic of the voluntary association. It has offices, membership, incipient bureaucratization, publications, and a quasi-legislative process expressed through conferences, delegates, and resolutions. On the other hand, the shared sense of culture, character, and status tends to create solidarity of a higher order than is usually found among more strictly voluntary associations where a multiplicity of social roles and the plurality of members' values and interests tend to dilute the intensity of commitment and identification.[12]

The paracommunity contributes to fundamental structural and cultural change by providing an adaptive institution in which tradi-

---

caste interests resulted in their repudiation and replacement by a new generation of younger leaders better able to do so.

[12] Marc Galanter illuminates the complexities for policy and law of the nature of group membership in a time of rapid social change in "The Problem of Group Membership: Some Reflections on the Judicial View of Indian Society," *Journal of the Indian Law Institute,* IV (July–September, 1962), 331–58. He reminds us that the Indian Constitution "set forth a general program for the reconstruction of Indian society. . . . It clearly sets out to secure to individuals equality of status and opportunity, to abolish invidious distinctions among groups, to protect the integrity and give free play to voluntary associations, the widest freedom of association to the individual and generally the widest personal freedom compatible with the public good. Without pursuing all of these in detail, it is clear that the following general principles are consistently in evidence: (1) a commitment to the replacement of ascribed status by voluntary affiliations; (2) an emphasis on the integrity and autonomy of groups within society; (3) a withdrawal of governmental recognition of rank ordering among groups."

In tracing with great skill two lines of cases dealing with group membership, Galanter finds that "the pragmatic approach [as against the 'fictional'] seems more congenial to the constitutional design. Its emphasis on the actual conduct of the individual and the actual acceptance by members of the group gives greater play to the voluntary principle. . . . The fictional approach, on the other hand, severely limits the voluntary principle and the autonomy of the group by giving conduct unintended consequences on theoretical grounds and by determining the question of membership without consulting the views of the relevant groups. It gives, if unwillingly, legal effectiveness to the notions of rank order among groups and mutual exclusiveness among them. The appearance and persistence of such an approach at this time," he concludes, "should be regarded as an anachronism . . ." (pp. 357–58).

tional and modern social features can meet and fuse. The caste association, a crucial paracommunity for Indian society, is both leveling the sacred and hierarchical caste order and replacing it. By initiating, managing, and encouraging the efforts of lower castes to become twice-born, to don the sacred thread symbolizing high ritual rank and culture, it in effect if not in intention drains the caste hierarchy of meaning by homogenizing and democratizing it. When most men can wear the sacred thread or achieve power and status without it, it will have lost its capacity to divide and distance them from each other. And by providing a structure for the pursuit of political power, social status, and economic interest, the paracommunity based on caste sentiment and interest makes secular concerns and representative democracy comprehensible and manageable to ordinary Indians.

Horizontal Mobilization

The Nadars

Kamaraj Nadar, formerly the chief minister of Madras State, president of the ruling Congress party and, for a time after the death of Jawaharlal Nehru, one of the dominant figures in Indian public life, is the descendant of a caste whose recent history illustrates the process of social change and modernization from within and below. At the time Marx wrote, Shanans were toddy tappers, an occupation considered polluting by the canons of Hindu orthodoxy. Over the past century, the caste has transformed itself by creating new units of consciousness, organization, and action. By appealing to the common identity of caste brethren, it mobilized horizontal solidarity against the subjection of caste hierarchy. Today, by successfully changing its caste culture and having this change recognized by the state and by Madras society, it, like other castes which have participated in similar processes, occupies a new and higher place in a changed social order.[1]

The modern history of the Shanans begins with the final defeat in 1801 of the Poligars by British forces and the subsequent establishment early in the nineteenth century of radically improved conditions of law and order and communications.[2] These changed circumstances affected the areas where Shanans were concentrated—what soon came to be the southern portions of the Madras Presidency and the southernmost portion of what was then the princely state of Travancore. They are today the Tirunelveli and Kanyakumari districts of Madras State. In these areas Shanans frequently lived in villages in which they were the sole inhabitants or the majority. During the six-month palmyra palm season, most climbed and tapped the trees of the abundant palmyra forests and groves, converting the sap into jaggery (unrefined sugar) or distilling it into sweet (unfermented) and hard (fermented) toddy. During the rest of the year they worked if they could as agricultural laborers.

[1] A preliminary description and interpretation of the ways in which the history of the Nadar caste association contributes to an understanding of social change and political modernization in India appeared in L. I. Rudolph, "The Modernity of Tradition: The Democratic Incarnation of Caste," *American Political Science Review*, LIX (December, 1965). Since then Robert L. Hardgrave, Jr., has completed his field work on an analysis of the Nadars. Some of this is available in two short preliminary studies, "Organization and Change among the Nadars of Tamilnad" (Madurai, March, 1965 [mimeographed]) and "Varieties of Political Behavior among Nadars of Tamilnad" (University of Chicago, April, 1966 [mimeographed]). The latter study was given as a paper at the Association for Asian Studies meeting, New York, April 5, 1966. His "The Nadars: The Political Culture of a Community in Change," was submitted as a Ph.D. dissertation to the Department of Political Science, University of Chicago, in June, 1966. Through diachronic and synchronic cultural, social, and political analyses of a caste community, Hardgrave establishes the importance for understanding social change and political modernization of focusing on the middle sector between the village and locality and the larger societies and polities of state and nation. In doing so, he has provided students of Indian society and politics and those interested in the comparative study of political development with a wealth of new and important empirical and theoretical findings. We have added descriptive material and modified our interpretation at certain points in the light of his various studies of the Nadars.

[2] This and the next three paragraphs draw on Hardgrave, "Organization and Change among the Nadars of Tamilnad," pp. 5, 7–9.

The trees and the land on which they stood were typically controlled by a small endogamous section of the community known as Nadans, lords of the *nads* (country or locality). Although exercising economic and political power over their kinsmen and tenants, and demanding and receiving deference from them, they were regarded by the larger Hindu society as part of the Shanan community and treated accordingly.

Because the community's customary occupation included the manufacture of an alcoholic drink, it was classified by the Brahmanically-dominated sacred order as polluted and polluting and placed in the ritual hierarchy of Hindu society below the Sudras but above other even more defiling castes. Typically, Shanans were not allowed to enter the compounds of temples consecrated to Brahmanical deities such as Shiva or to use wells of higher castes. At least in Travancore, they were expected to maintain a prescribed physical distance between themselves and Brahmans. In multicaste villages, barbers and washermen would not ordinarily serve them.

Two forces associated with British rule, Christian missionary activities and new economic opportunities, began to affect Shanan life profoundly. In the second and third decade of the nineteenth century, large numbers of Shanans became Christian converts in what has sometimes been described as a mass movement.[3] Many of those not converted were nevertheless deeply influenced. Those Shanans who had traded in local markets began to trade more widely. These early Shanan traders began by carrying northward jaggery, dried fish, and salt, at first trading itinerantly from *pettais* (fortified enclosures) and later from towns that grew up around these trading posts. In time, Shanans came to settle in appreciable numbers in such major trading centers. Their numbers and the scope of their activities grew until Shanans had come to occupy an important place in the commercial life of Madras.[4]

[3] See J. Waskom Pickett, *Christian Mass Movements in India* (New York, 1933); Church Missionary Society, *The Mass Movements in the Telugu Area* (n.p., 1926).

[4] The Iravas of Travancore were also originally toddy tappers. Changed economic opportunities appear to have affected them in a manner similar to the Nadars. The Travancore census of 1931 lists the following occupations (per thousand) among Iravas: toddy drawers, 38; cultivators, owners, and tenants,

One of the first evidences of Shanan aspirations for greater equality and dignity is found in the homely story of the breast cloth controversy. In southern Travancore, dress, like forms of speech, customarily symbolized inferior and superior status and the subjection and domination that accompanied them. One mark of respect to superiors was a bare chest. Priests honored deities in this way as did men caste superiors.[5] Lower caste women, including Shanan women, did not customarily wear apparel above the waist. These arrangements did not long go unaffected by the Victorian Christian preference for covered limbs, not to mention torsos, which was transmitted through missionary education. By 1829, under pressure from missionaries and from the practice of Hindu as well as Christian Shanan women, and goaded by the disorder that resulted from clashes between Shanans and higher castes over this issue, the government of Travancore ordered that "native Christian" women might cover their breasts in the manner of Syrian Christians and Moplah Muslims but not in the manner of higher caste Hindu women. Shanan women continued to emulate the dress of the locally dominant Nair caste. Threats and disturbances provoked by this practice culminated in the Travancore riot of 1858. The question of whether Shanan women would or would not give up the practice of going about without an upper cloth had become sufficiently serious to require state intervention.[6] The next year, Sir Charles Trevelyan, the governor of Madras, granted them permission to wear a cloth over their breasts and shoulders, and the Mararaja of Travancore, in whose princely state the riot had occurred, found no objection to Shanan women's putting on a jacket, tying themselves round with coarse cloth, or "covering their bosoms in any manner whatever, but not like the women of higher castes."[7]

316; field laborers and woodcutters, 160; industries (mainly production of coir yarn), 223; transport, 34; trade, 76; lawyers, doctors, and teachers, 13; domestic servants, 12; others, 128 (cited in A. Aiyappan, *Iravas and Culture Change* [Madras, 1945], p. 106).

[5] Aiyappan, *Iravas and Culture Change,* p. 34.

[6] Edgar Thurston, *Castes and Tribes of Southern India* (Madras, 1909), VI, 365.

[7] *Ibid.*

Soon after these events, pamphlets setting out the caste's claims to Kshatriya (warrior-ruler) status appeared. Members began to claim the right to wear the sacred thread, symbol of the spiritually twice-born Brahman, Kshatriya, and Vaisya varnas, and to be carried on palanquins at their wedding ceremonies, another custom previously confined to the highest castes. "Kshatriya" academies, open to all, but designed particularly for the education of Shanan boys, were started, marriage rules tightened, Brahmans "of a less particular kind" induced to act as priests, and "a sort of incomplete parody of the ceremony of investiture with the sacred thread" symbolizing twice-born status practiced.[8] "We humbly beg," a group of Shanan petitioners addressed the census commissioner in 1901, "that we are the descendants of the Pandya or Dravida Xatra race who . . . first disafforested and colonized this land of South India" and presented him with a historical volume entitled *Short Account of the . . . Tamil Xatras, the Original but Downtrodden Royal Race of Southern India.*[9] Shanans gave as evidence such claims as the following: that coins called Shanans proved they long ago had the authority to strike coinage; that Shanan was a corruption of *Shandror* (nobleman); and that the honorific "Nadar," by which leaders of the caste were addressed, proved they were Kshatriyas because it meant ruler of a locality. In 1891 the census commissioner observed that the Shanans were "usually placed a little above the Pallas and Paraiyans, and are considered to be one of the polluting castes, but of late many have put forward the claim to be considered Kshatriyas, and at least 24,000 of them appear [that is, gave their caste to the census enumerator] as Kshatriyas in the caste tables." To the learned commissioner's essentialist assumptions and archetypical perspective, this was "of course, absurd";[10] to the Shanans and other mobile castes throughout the country it was not.[11]

The Shanans continued to press for recognition and legitimation from Hindu society of their new sense of self-esteem. At the moral and ritual center of Hindu society lay religion and its most visible and accessible target, the temple. In 1874, Shanans tried unsuccessfully to establish their right to enter the great Minakshi Temple at

[8] *Ibid.*, pp. 365–66.   [9] *Ibid.*, p. 367.   [10] *Ibid.*, p. 369.

[11] For other castes producing "synthetic" histories, see p. 62, n. 57.

Madurai.[12] Other efforts in Madurai and elsewhere to establish Shanan claims to enter or share in the government of temples also failed. On May 14, 1897, fifteen Shanans, despite the efforts of temple custodians to prevent them from doing so, entered the Minakshi Sundareswara Temple at Kamudi and worshipped there. The temple's hereditary trustee, the Raja of Ramnad, Raja M. Bhaskara Sethupethi, natural leader of the Maravan community and dedicated enemy of Shanan "pretensions," brought suit against the offenders, asking that they compensate the temple for the purification ceremonies undertaken after its defilement and that it be established that neither by sacred law nor by custom did Shanans have a right to enter the temple.

In the Kamudi Temple case the Shanans, through the legal system of the British raj, made a major effort to cross the pollution barrier of Hindu society and establish their claim within it to twice-born status.[13] They hoped to win through the legal processes and sanctions of the alien and secular political order what they had been unable to gain from the religious institutions of traditional society—sacred legitimacy for their claims to a greater measure of equality. Their hopes were dashed by the courts. The District Court at Madurai and, on appeal, the High Court of Madras and the Privy Council agreed that neither custom nor *sastras* (sacred texts) sanctioned their entering the temple at Kamudi. "There is no sort of proof," the High Court held, "that even suggests a probability that the Shanans are descendants from Kshatriya or warrior castes of Hindus, or from the Pandiya, Chola, or Chera race of kings." Nor did the honorific appellation Nadar entitle them to claim higher status or greater rights; it in no way changed their ritual status. From time immemorial, the Shanans had cultivated the palmyra palm and collected and distilled its juice, an occupation that placed them in general social estimation "just above that of . . . Pariahs . . . who are on all hands regarded as unclean, prohibited from the use of Hindu temples and below that of the . . . Maravans [the caste directly concerned] and other classes admittedly free to worship in Hindu

[12] Thurston, *Castes and Tribes of Southern India,* VI, 355.

[13] Sankaralinga Nadan v. Rajeswara Dorai, Indian Law Reports, 31 Madras 236 (1908). The quotations below are all drawn from this report of the case.

temples." Further, the court held, there were no grounds whatsoever for regarding them as of Aryan origin; their worship, said the court, was a form of demonology.

The court was not unaware of the radical changes in Shanan circumstances. "No doubt," it observed, "many Shanans have abandoned their hereditary occupation, and have won for themselves by education, industry, and frugality respectable positions. . . . In the process of time, many Shanans took to cultivating, trade, and money lending, and today there is a numerous and prosperous body of Shanans who have no immediate concern with the immemorial calling of their caste. In many villages they own much of the land, and monopolize the bulk of trade and wealth." The court recognized that these *de facto* changes created difficulties: the Shanans have "not unnaturally sought for social recognition, and to be treated on an equal footing in religious matters." It was also "natural to feel sympathy for their efforts . . . but such sympathy," the court warned, "will not be increased by unreasonable and unfounded pretensions, and, in the effort to rise, the Shanans must not invade the established rights of other castes."

The court invoked Brahman written and edited law and the testimony of Brahman witnesses concerning local custom to sustain its interpretation.[14] "According to the Agama Shastras which are received as authoritative by worshippers of Siva in the Madura district," the court found, "entry into a temple, where the ritual prescribed by these Shastras is observed, is prohibited to all those whose profession is the manufacture of intoxicating liquor and the climbing of palmyra and cocoanut trees." Plaintiffs' thirty-four witnesses were unanimous in testifying that Shanans did not enter the temple at Kamudi. "Most of them [the witnesses] are Brahmans," the court observed, "who, being in a position of acknowledged superiority to both contending parties [Shanans and Maravans], are less likely than others to be swayed by personal bias or self-interest." Although there were some Brahmans among the Shanans' twenty-eight witnesses, they were, in the judgment of their lordships of the Privy Council, generally "men of much lower standing and respectability,

14 For a discussion of the critiques of the Madras High Court, particularly its Brahmanic bias, see below, "Legal Cultures and Social Change: Panchayats, Pandits, and Professionals," pp. 251–93.

and are to a large extent in the pay or under the control of the Nadars. . . ."

The court's allegations concerning the susceptibility of non-Brahmans to Nadar persuasion, including monetary inducements, were given unexpected support when the Raja of Ramnad, the head of the Maravan community, trustee of the temple, and original plaintiff, agreed, after winning the case in the district court, to "compromise" in the face of the Shanans' appeal to the High Court by allowing them to enter the Kamudi temple and worship there. "A very sordid motive for this surrender," their lordships of the Privy Council observed, "was specifically asserted and has not been disproved." When the High Court joined other plaintiffs to the original plaintiff so that the suit could be heard on appeal, the raja's confidence in the justice of his case "convalesced."

In the court's judgment, birth, not achievement, defined social identity. Rights were rooted in Brahmanically-defined custom and Brahmanically-edited sacred texts, not in general ideas of treating equals equally or in "right reason." Only Aryans, not Dravidians, could be Kshatriyas; the pollution of the fathers followed the sons into commerce, the professions, and agriculture. The court advised the Shanans, in phrases reminiscent of the U.S. Supreme Court's doctrine in *Plessy* v. *Ferguson* with respect to Negro claims to equality,[15] to use their own temples and thus to be equal though separate. Shanans were "numerous and strong enough in wealth and education to rise along their own lines . . . without appropriating the institutions or infringing the rights of others."

Civil war in the form of the Tirunelveli Riots of 1899 followed close on the heels of the Kamudi temple case. "The pretensions of the Shanans to a much higher position in the religio-social scale than the other castes are willing to allow," the inspector-general of police

[15] 163 U.S. 537 (1896). "If one race," the Court observed, "be inferior to the other socially, the Constitution of the United States cannot put them on the same plane. . . . We consider the underlying fallacy of the plaintiff's argument [that by enforcing segregation between whites and Negroes the states were denying the equal protection of the laws assured by the Fourteenth Amendment] to consist in the assumption that the enforced separation of the two races stamps the colored race with a badge of inferiority. If this be so, it is not by reason of anything found in the act, but solely because the colored race chooses to put that construction upon it" (p. 551).

43

wrote in his administration report for that year, were the cause of extensive civil disorder and violence.[16] High on the list of Shanan "pretensions" was their claim to entry of temples. When the manager of the Visvanatheswara temple at Sivakasi closed it rather than give in to the pressure of a massive Shanan agitation for entry (an act again reminiscent of American events in the early phases of the struggle for integration), Shanans and their enemies agreed that they had gained at least a partial victory. Most opposed to Shanan mobility were the Maravans, their near neighbors in space and status. A "clean" caste, the Maravans could enter the temple at Sivakasi. To share it with the Shanans, a polluting caste according to the ritual definitions of traditional society, seemed intolerable. More generally, Maravans, with the sympathetic support of other higher castes in the area, wanted retribution for the wrongs they had suffered at Shanan hands. Through the use of force and violence, the Maravans hoped to so punish and intimidate the Shanans as to pre-empt further Shanan efforts to rise. The Maravans launched attacks on Shanan villages and sections, burning, looting, and sometimes killing. On June 6, 1899, Maravans marched on Sivakasi where Shanans, who had been expecting the attack, succeeded at the cost of sixteen lives in driving them away from the town. The inspector-general of police summed up the struggle in the following statistics: 23 murders, 102 robberies, and many cases of arson; 1,958 arrests and 552 convictions including 7 death sentences.

The Shanans who had moved north into Ramnad district and beyond organized the community for self-improvement as well as self-government by forming *uravinmurai* (community councils).[17] The councils in turn levied *mahimai* ("betterment" tax) on Shanan households. *Mahimai* funds were used to build public facilities such as wells and temples, to invest in Shanan enterprises, and to establish schools.[18] In 1895, prominent members of the community attempted

[16] Thurston, *Castes and Tribes of Southern India,* VI, 364.

[17] Hardgrave, "Organization and Change among the Nadars of Tamilnad," pp. 10, 11.

[18] The Virudhunagar *uravinmurai* in 1889 founded the Kshatriya High School. It was open to all castes and was one of the first free schools in the Madras Presidency (*ibid.,* p. 11).

to organize a caste association, the Kshatriya Mahajana Sangam, but the effort was still-born. Fifteen years later, in 1910, Rao Bahadur T. Rattinasami Nadar, a wealthy liquor manufacturer of Porayar, Tanjore District, revived the earlier association as the Nadar Mahajana Sangam. It held two conferences in that year, the latter attended by 750 delegates, but it was not until 1917 that its conferences became annual functions.[19] The official purposes of the organization are

> to promote the social, material, and general welfare of the Nadars; to protect and promote the interests and rights of the community; to take practical measures for the social, moral, and intellectual advancement of the Nadars; to start schools and colleges for imparting western education to Nadar children and to help poor but deserving pupils belonging to the community with scholarships, books, fees, etc.; to encourage and promote commercial and industrial enterprise among the members of the community; the raising of funds by subscription, donation or other means for the above objects, and the doing of all such other things as are incidental and conducive to the attainment of the above objects or any of them.[20]

In 1921, the Shanans succeeded in officially changing their name. Their metamorphosis was wrought neither by the institutions of traditional society nor by findings of the legal system of the British state that custom or the sacred texts of traditional society justified Shanan claims. It was the government of Madras that wrought this important symbolic change, and its reasons for doing so were in considerable measure political. Nadars had brought increasing political pressure to bear on government to recognize the changes in self and social esteem resulting from a century of social change and mobility. At the same time, the government of Madras was confronted with the prospect of sharing the reins of government with elected

---

[19] There are two Nadar caste associations, the Nadar Mahajana Sangam of Madurai and the Dakshina Mara Nadar Sangam of Tirunelveli. The Nadar Mahajana Sangam, the larger and more influential of the two, has organized Nadar conferences since 1910.

[20] *Rules and Regulations of the Nadar Mahajana Sabha, Madurai* (Madurai: Nadar Mahajana Sangam, 1919), pp. 12–13, as cited by Hardgrave, "Organization and Change among the Nadars of Tamilnad," p. 21.

45

Indian ministers under the dyarchy provisions of the Montagu-Chelmsford reforms of 1919. There were those among its officers who believed it necessary to mobilize and secure the political support of those classes and castes that viewed the most prominent aspirant for power and legitimacy, the Indian National Congress, as an instrument not of nationalism but rather of Brahman political domination.[21]

"The Shanar of 1911," Census Commissioner G. T. Boag wrote in 1921, "now appears as a Nadar; this is done under orders of the Government of Madras, that the word Shanar should cease to be used in official records."[22] The Shanans' secular and official social transformation extended to occupation as well as name. The government, "in deference to the wishes of the Nadar community," decided

[21] For the context of Madras politics during this period, see Eugene F. Irschick, "Politics and Social Change in South India: The Non-Brahmin Movement and Tamil Separatism, 1916–1929" (Ph.D. dissertation, Department of History, University of Chicago, 1964). Irschick points out that there were those within official British circles in Madras concerned about Brahman dominance in administration and politics. Their sympathy for the grievances and goals of the anti-Brahman political movement arose not only out of a concern for justice and democracy but also from a desire to foster and use the anti-Brahman movement as a countervailing force to Brahman power. It can be surmised that it was out of such motives that government issued its order concerning the Nadars. Irschick makes clear, it should be noted, that the Justice party, the organized political expression of anti-Brahmanism, failed to keep the support of the depressed classes, particularly the untouchable castes. It was the Madras government in the context of a labor dispute in 1921 that defended their rights and security against the threats to them by non-Brahman caste Hindus (see pp. 228–32).

[22] *Census of India,* 1921, Vol. XIII, *Madras,* Pt. I ("Report" [Madras, 1922]), p. 153 n. The relevant Government Orders are Government of Madras, Law (General) Department, G.O. No. 56, 8 April 1921, and Government of Madras, Law (General) Department, G.O. No. 785, 7 July 1921. Circulars No. 4 and No. 5 of the Nadar Mahajana Sangam contain the instructions of the caste association to its followers concerning the responses to be given to census enumerators. Census Commissioner Boag's description and analysis of changes in caste names generally on pp. 153–55 of Vol. XIII is particularly instructive for the shift from Shanan to Nadar. We wish to thank Robert L. Hardgrave, Jr., for his help in obtaining the texts of the relevant G.O.'s and the Sangam's circulars, and the Nadar Mahajana Sangam for its courtesy in making its archives available to him.

to list in the census actual rather than traditional occupations. The census superintendent observes that neither common name nor common traditional occupation is a "safe guide" to the definition of caste or the identification of a particular caste. The Nadars, for example, who were in earlier censuses shown as toddy tappers or drawers, "now claim that they are by tradition and inheritance lords of the soil and that toddy-drawing was the occupation only of comparatively degenerate members of the caste. . . . In deference to the wishes of the representatives of the Nadar community," he continues, "the Madras Government have decided on this occasion not to show traditional occupations in the census tables. . . ."[23]

For several generations Shanans have increasingly shared the public indentity Nadar and are today recognized as an "advanced," prosperous community. Sections of it, living in more remote villages, still tap the palmyra palm, make jaggery, and distill toddy; they tend to know themselves and to be known by others as Shanans. Nadars, however, have breached the pollution barrier, changed their rank within traditional society, and occupy an important place in the modern society of Madras and India.[24]

[23] *Census of India,* 1921, Vol. XIII, *Madras,* Pt. I, p. 154.

[24] See *Man in India,* XXXIX (April–June, 1959), particularly McKim Marriotts' "Interactional and Attributional Theories of Caste Ranking," for discussions of the relationship between caste mobility and caste ranking. Marriott is critical of M. N. Srinivas for being too "attributional." For Srinivas' views, see his *Caste in Modern India, and Other Essays* (Bombay, 1962), particularly Chaps. I and II, and his more recent *Social Change in Modern India* (Berkeley, Calif., 1966). Milton Singer in ". . . Indian Civilization . . . ," *Diogenes,* XLV (Spring, 1964), tries to accommodate both views but suggests that Marriott may have overstated the case against attributional ranking. See particularly the sections on "Sanskritization and Culture Mobility," ". . . Attributes vs. Interactions in Caste Mobility," and "Westernization and Sanskritization," pp. 99–108.

It is not yet entirely clear how much and in what ways the Shanans' changing social standing has been reflected over time in village consciousness and behavior. Because their rise was accompanied by increasing wealth and education, decreasing pollution, and the emulation and appropriation of higher caste and class behavior and symbols, the Shanans' change of name and status was in considerable measure recognized at the local level *over time* by appropriate changes in the evaluations and behavior of non-Shanans of all ranks and castes. Most dramatic evidence of such changes is found in the analysis of the breast

In the period after World War I Nadars began to abandon the social, legal, and administrative pursuit of twice-born status. They turned to a new sector to increase their status and influence— politics. In the context of the narrow franchise and notability politics that characterized public life in the 1919–35 period of the Montagu-Chelmsford reforms, politically self-conscious and active Nadars associated themselves for the most part with the anti-Brahman Justice party and its non-nationalist, loyalist, and co-operative politics. W. P. A. Soundrapandian Nadar, a leading figure in the Nadar Mahajana Sangam during this period, was recommended in December, 1920, by P. T. Rajan of the recently formed and victorious Justice party, for membership in the Madras Legislative Council. Upon the governor's subsequent nomination, he became its first Nadar member. The Nadar Mahajana Sangam abandoned its practice of inviting prominent Brahmans to preside over its annual conferences. It substituted in their stead luminaries of the anti-Brahman movement, including the Raja of Ramnad, son of their late adversary at Kamudi and Sivakasi.[25] Even more radical was W. P. A. Soundrapandian Nadar's effort to associate the community with E. V. Ramasami Naicker's Self-Respect Movement. In contrast to the Justice party, it attacked Brahman domination more on the front of religion and culture than politics. Anti-clerical, "rationalist," and Dravidian in its ideological orientation, it found its most dramatic expression in Self-Respect marriages. These dispensed with Brahman priests by substituting in their stead lay luminaries of the Self-Respect Movement, particularly E. V. Ramasami Naicker himself.[26]

---

cloth controversy, 1829–59, p. 39 above. Conspicuous too has been the marked change in Nadar-Maravan relations; see p. 94 for the Ramnad situation. On the other hand, the Nadar Mahajana Sangam, in representing the community's interest before the Backward Classes Commission, held that 90 per cent of the community was still backward, that is, illiterate, poor, and discriminated against by other castes. More light on this point is available in Robert L. Hardgrave, Jr., "The Nadars: The Political Culture of a Community in Change."

[25] Hardgrave, "Organization and Change among the Nadars of Tamilnad," p. 26.

[26] For the Dravidian orientation in Madras politics, see L. I. Rudolph, "Urban Life and Populist Radicalism: Dravidian Politics in Madras," *Journal of Asian Studies*, XX (May, 1961).

The year 1937 marked a watershed in the social and political orientation of the Nadar community: its anti-Brahman inspired drive toward de-Sanskritization waned markedly in the face of more clearly secular, economic, and political concerns. Its non-nationalist, pro-British political orientation began to alter in a Congress direction. Under the 1935 Government of India Act, the franchise was expanded and provincial governments put wholly under the charge of Indian ministers. In Madras, a Brahman, C. Rajagopalachari, formed a Congress government. Unlike the Justice party governments of the twenties and thirties, he acted to remove the civil and social disabilities that affected lower castes. Particularly important was the Temple Entry Authorization and Indemnity Act of 1939. It provided the conditions under which all castes might enter temples. The actual opening of the great Meenakshi Temple at Madurai, a major center of Nadar population, also influenced Nadar opinion. The pro-government orientation of the merchant leaders of the community, mounting nationalist fervor for independence from Britain, shifts within the Madras Congress organization in the preceding decade that gave greater weight to non-Brahman leadership, and the election of Kamaraj Nadar as its president in 1940 aided and abetted the trend toward Congress preference among the politically active sections of the Nadar community.[27] When independence, and with it universal franchise and self-government, came to India, the Nadars had already a well-established interest in politics and acted in fairly unified ways with respect to it.

The Vanniyars

The Vanniyars, or Vanniya Kula Kshatriyas, are primarily a caste of agricultural laborers, although also included are substantial numbers of cultivator-owners and petty landlords in Madras State. The caste makes up slightly less than 10 per cent of the population of Madras, but in the four northern districts of the state (North Arcot,

---

[27] Hardgrave, "Organization and Change among the Nadars of Tamilnad," p. 37. After a short-lived split in the Sangam between 1940 and 1942, when the National Nadar Association was organized, pro-Congress officers established their ascendancy over the Justice party faction. The Sangam did not meet between 1943 and 1946. With independence in 1947, the organization was headed by leaders who were at that time pro-Congress.

South Arcot, Chingleput, and Salem) where they are concentrated, it constitutes about a fourth of the population.[28] As early as 1833, the Pallis, as they were then called, had ceased to accept their status as a humble agricultural caste and tried to procure a decree in Pondicherry that they were not a low caste.[29] In anticipation of a census-taking in 1871, they petitioned to be classified as Kshatriyas. By 1891 the community had established seven schools for its members, and an enterprising Palli who had risen to the status of a High Court vakil (lawyer) produced a book, a caste history. Ten years later he wrote another. Both supported the caste's claim to be Kshatriyas and connected Pallis by descent with the great Pallava dynasty.[30] Oral histories simultaneously were stressing descent from the traditional "fire races," which Kshatriyas both north and south often claim as ancestors.

Such radically revisionist history has characteristically accompanied efforts by caste associations to establish new identities and statuses. The symbiosis linking subject and dominant social groups seems to require for its dissolution the re-examination of the past and the reconstruction of myth and history. The Vanniyars, like the Nadars and other mobile castes, sought independence, equality, and dignity through such means. The twice-born, against whom revisionist history is directed, share with established social orders at other times and places and with some scholars of social change an essentialist view of identity that, by ignoring ways in which the past is a human creation in which power and artifice play a part, finds the

[28] These figures are necessarily tentative because they are based on the 1931 census, the last Indian census to enumerate caste. At that time, the Vanniyars numbered 2,944,014, and almost all of the Vanniyars were located in those parts of Madras that remained with the state after Andhra was detached in 1953. Presumably the Vanniyar population has increased substantially since then at a rate not too different from the average population increase. In Chingleput, North Arcot, Salem, and South Arcot, there were 2,349,920 Vanniyars in 1931 in a total population for these districts of 8,810,583. See *Census of India*, 1931, Vol. XIV, *Madras*, Pt. II ("Imperial and Provincial Tables").

[29] On this and some of the material that follows, see Thurston, *Castes and Tribes of Southern India*, I, 1–28.

[30] T. Ayakannu Nayakar, *Vannikula Vilakkam: A Treatise on the Vanniya Caste* (n.p., 1891), and *Varuna Darpanam* ("Mirror of Castes") (n.p., 1901).

self and social definitions of such rising castes amusing and hypocritical if not dangerous and immoral. There is some tendency among ethnographers to believe Kshatriyas are "real" if their assimilation to the varna system is ancient and undocumented history and "false" if it is recent and may be documented.[31]

By 1901 the Pallis had not won any battles, but everyone was aware of their efforts. The Madras census commissioner noted that "they claim for themselves a position higher than that which Hindu society is inclined to accord them" and added that they were attempting to achieve this status via "a widespread organization engineered from Madras."[32] The organization's sporadic seventy-year activities to make Pallis conscious of their dignified and glorious history were bearing fruit. Instead of giving the old name, Palli, many were beginning to refer to themselves as Agnikula Kshatriyas or Vannikula Kshatriyas (that is, Kshatriyas of the fire race). The associations of the caste were spreading and becoming increasingly effective in various districts, enforcing a higher "Sanskritized" standard of social conduct:

> They have been closely bound together by an organization managed by one of their caste, who was a prominent person in these parts . . . and their *esprit de corps* is now surprisingly strong. They are tending gradually to approach the Brahmanical standard of social conduct, discouraging adult marriage, meat-eating, and widow remarriage. . . . In 1904 a document came before one of the courts which showed that, in the year previous, the representatives of the caste in 34 villages in this district had bound themselves in writing, under penalty of excommunication to refrain (except with the consent of all parties)

[31] The significance of history as a way of coming to grips with other issues of changing social status and identity is suggested by Maureen Patterson, who points out that a great burgeoning of Chitpavan Brahman family histories follows and appears to be related to the rise of anti-Brahmanism in Maharashtra. M. L. P. Patterson, "Chitpavan Brahman Family Histories," (paper delivered at the Conference on Social Structure and Social Change, Wenner-Gren Foundation, University of Chicago, June 3–6, 1965), p. 19.

[32] *Census of India*, 1901, *Madras*, Pt. I ("Report"), p. 171.

51

from the practices formerly in existence of marrying two wives, and of allowing a woman to marry again during the lifetime of her first husband.[33]

Mr. J. Chartres Moloney, of the Indian civil service, having survived the decennial onslaught of petitions from castes who wanted to be reclassified, remarked in the census of 1911:

> The last few years, and especially the occasion of the present census, have witnessed an extraordinary revival of the caste spirit in certain aspects. For numerous caste *sabhas* have emerged, each keen to assert the dignity of the social group which it represents.[34]

The Vanniyars, like the Nadars, persuaded their members to give a new name to the census enumerators, asked the census commissioners to list this new name when the old one bore some odium, and urged the census officers either to revise or to drop the description of traditional caste occupations. It was as a result of these pressures and favorable political circumstances[35] that the Madras census dropped caste occupations in 1921. The effectiveness of the Pallis in influencing the official recorders, on the one hand, and their own members, on the other, was considerable. By 1931 the Pallis had disappeared altogether from the census, and only the Vanniya Kula Kshatriyas remained.

The explicit organization of the Vanniya Kula Kshatriyas in an association called the Vanniya Kula Kshatriya Sangam dates back at least thirty years in some districts, although the 1901 census commissioner indicated that some organizational stirrings were visible then and the Pondicherry petition of 1833 indicates even earlier (probably sporadic) activity. The Vanniya Kula Kshatriya Sangam of North Arcot District held its thirty-fourth annual conference in 1953, and the South Arcot Sangam held its tenth in 1954.[36] For the

33 W. Francis in *Gazetteer of South Arcot District,* cited in Thurston, *Castes and Tribes of Southern India,* VI, 12.

34 *Census of India,* 1911, *Madras,* Pt. I ("Report"), p. 178.

35 See n. 21 above, where the work of Eugene F. Irschick on Madras political history is brought to bear on this question.

36 *Hindu* (Madras), June 18, 1953; *Mail* (Madras), June 21, 1954.

Vanniya Kula Kshatriya Sangam, the district unit was initially more important than the larger, Madras-wide organization that developed somewhat later. In 1952, the Vanniya Kula Kshatriyas published a volume whose introduction expressed the Sangam's efforts to heighten caste solidarity and effectiveness:

> The Vanniya Kula Kshatriyas who till now were proverbially considered to be backward in education have made long strides in a short space of time and have come almost on a level with other communities . . . , [but] the community has not realized its deserving status in society. . . . A cursory view of the book will show every reader how many a desirable fruit of the community was veiled by the leaves . . . , will stimulate the younger generation to greater deeds and will fill the hearts of the older with just pride in the achievements of the community. . . .[37]

That the Sangam still had some work ahead may be inferred from the fact that it listed 298 names, or about .01 per cent of the community, as holders of degrees or diplomas.[38]

Democratic politics spurred on the development of caste associations. Just after World War II when the electorate had been expanded but had not yet reached the adult suffrage level of the first general election in 1952, the Vanniya Kula Kshatriya Sangam pressed two demands on the Congress party state ministry: it wanted the appointments to the civil services (which are based on competitive examinations) to reflect the Vanniyars' percentage in the population,[39] and it wanted Congress itself, through party nominations, to assure the election of Vanniyars on a population basis to all elected bodies—municipal corporations, district boards, and the state legislature. The demands were Jacksonian in their optimism concerning the universal distribution of the capacity to hold administrative and

[37] *Graduates and Diploma Holders among the Vanniya Kula Kshatriya* (Triplicane, Madras, 1952).

[38] A diploma holder is about the equivalent of an American high-school graduate; a graduate is one who has finished college.

[39] This issue has deep roots in Madras political and administrative life. For its background and previous efforts to cope with the conflicting claims of merit and efficiency as against those of social justice and equalization of opportunity, see Irschick, "Politics and Social Change in South India," Chap. VII.

elective office. But they were not altogether unreasonable in view of constitutional, statutory, and administrative provisions at the central and the state levels that were designed to give special consideration to scheduled castes (untouchables) and backward classes in the public services and educational institutions and in view of the Congress' known disposition to give some special consideration in candidate selection to "depressed" elements in the population.[40] The demands assumed that the authority of caste depended less on traditional rank and more on numbers in the context of democratic authority. The Congress ministry of Madras did not respond favorably to the Vanniyar demands, however, nor did the nominating bodies of the Congress party. From that time, the Vanniyars decided that they could rely only on themselves, dropped the attempt to work through the Congress or any other party, and began to contest for public office as independents.

Their first major electoral efforts were exerted in district board elections in the districts where their greatest strength lay. The district boards became one of their main targets, not only because they represented geographic and "system" boundaries within which caste influence could be maximized, but also because the subjects falling under their competence, especially educational and medical facilities and road building, were of the greatest local interest. (The equivalent unit of political attention in most states in the 1960's was the *panchayat samiti* or union.) In 1949, the Vanniyars did well in the

[40] For programs dealing with the scheduled castes and backward classes, see Lelah Dushkin, "The Backward Classes, I: Special Treatment Policy," "The Backward Classes, II: Removal of Disabilities," and "The Backward Classes, III: Future of Special Treatment," *Economic Weekly*, October 28, November 4 and 18, 1961. See also Andre Beteille, "The Future of the Backward Classes: The Competing Demands of Status and Power," *Perspectives*, Suppl. to the *Indian Journal of Public Administration*, XI (January-March, 1965); Marc Galanter, "Equality and 'Protective Discrimination' in India," *Rutgers Law Review*, XXI (Fall, 1961), 42–74; and Galanter, "Law and Caste in Modern India," *Asian Survey*, IV (November, 1963), 544–59. We have preferred to characterize the policy as progressive rather than protective discrimination. By progressive we mean the kind of principle involved in the progressive income tax, that is, a means to equalize the allocation of resources and opportunities. If protective is too patronizing a word, progressive may be too ideological a characterization of the goals and policies involved, but we are unable to find a more neutral word.

district elections, capturing, for example, 22 of the 52 seats in the South Arcot District Board, defeating many Congress party candidates, and almost succeeding in electing its president.[41]

In 1951, with the prospect of the 1952 elections before them, the Vanniyars convened a major conference of the Vanniya Kula Kshatriya Sangam on a state-wide basis. The conference resolved that the Vanniyars should contest the elections "in cooperation with the toiling masses," and a political party called the Tamilnad Toilers' party was formed. The leading spirits in the conference were men with modern and cosmopolitan qualifications rather than hereditary and traditional ones. Two of the most significant were N. A. Manikkavelu Naicker, a lawyer with experience in earlier state-wide party activities, notably the Swarajya party, and S. S. Ramaswami Padayachi, a young man (thirty-three in 1951) who was a high-school graduate, chairman of the Cuddalore Municipal Council, member of the South Arcot District Board, and the candidate narrowly defeated for the board's presidency in 1949.[42] The names of Padayachi and Naicker, especially the former, provided an effective signal for caste solidarity in voting. Padayachi's youth is an interesting commentary on leadership patterns in castes coming to political self-consciousness; older members of lower castes generally do not command the necessary modern skills to be effective in the larger contexts of district and state affairs.

Organizationally, the conference represented a capstone in the expansion of the association, since it mobilized the Vanniyars on a state-wide basis. It sought at once to centralize control and to bring about a proliferation of operating subunits, working toward a more rationalized campaign organization capable of maximum mobilization of potential membership. A central election committee, of which Padayachi was elected chairman, was established to supervise Vanniyard candidate selections throughout the state, along with twelve district election committees.[43]

Subsequently, the more "modern" state-wide effort represented by

[41] See interview with S. S. Ramaswami Padayachi, a prominent Vanniyar leader, in *Mail* (Madras), April 27, 1954.

[42] *Mail* (Madras), April 13, 1954; *Indian Express* (Madras), April 14, 1954.

[43] *Mail* (Madras), October 13, 1951.

the conference broke on the rock of more "traditional" local loyalties; the caste *sabhas* of North and South Arcot districts failed to agree and formed rival organizations. The Tamilnad Toilers as a party remained strong in South Arcot and Salem under Padayachi's guidance, while the North Arcot and Chingleput Vanniyars rallied to a second caste party, the Commonweal party, under Naicker.

During the campaign, the caste *sabhas-cum*-parties utilized the established village social organization, mobilizing Vanniyar village leaders to gain support for their parties. This means of mobilization was effective despite widespread illiteracy and the absence of mass media because it was able to define and translate electoral issues at the grass roots in meaningful terms: government services for production and welfare, particularly roads, credit, education, and health, could surely be better and more firmly secured for poor Vanniyars if men familiar with their plight, that is, other Vanniyars or their friends, were elected to office. Observers more familiar with theory than with these experiences and processes might suppose from watching, for example, national leaders speak to vast and apparently uncomprehending throngs that there is an unbridgeable gap between the ordinary Indian voter and his government. Others watching village election meetings in which caste headmen engage in running debate with aspiring legislators and state and national candidates huddle in endless conferences with representative village and local leaders are likely to come to quite different conclusions: behind these meetings and private negotiations there lies more discourse than distance, more dialogue than domination. They are part of a chain of communication, access, and influence that links the purposes of village, caste, and locality to the political systems of state and nation.[44] Common caste background is not essential to such exchanges,

[44] For an example of an influential contrary point of view, see Lucien Pye, "The Non-Western Political Process," *Journal of Politics,* II–III (August, 1958), 468–86. Here and elsewhere in this chapter our analysis suggests that Pye's analysis may have treated a heuristic dichotomy, Western–non-Western, as an empirical one. In any case, the following generalizations are not valid for India: "(6) The non-Western political process is characterized by a lack of integration among the participants, and this situation is a function of the lack of a unified communications system in the society" (p. 474); "(10) In non-Western societies the intensity and breadth of political discussion has little rela-

but the fact that candidate and local leaders share a common caste culture and interest or are linked by those who do provides a context in which discourse and dialogue are natural and easy.

The Commonweal party, representing the older caste *sabha* of North Arcot and Chingleput, made few electoral appeals or commitments. It won six seats in the state legislative assembly. The Tamilnad Toilers, speaking for the younger South Arcot *sabha* projected a leftist image and expounded socialist ideas. It captured 19 seats. This gave the Vanniyars 25 of the 190 seats in the legislature of post-1953 Madras, or 13 per cent as against their 10 per cent of the population.

In the same 1952 general elections, the Congress party failed to win a majority in the Madras State legislature. In its search for enough legislative support to form a government, it persuaded the six Commonweal party members to support a Congress ministry, but it could not persuade them to join the Congress. In return, Naicker, the Commonweal leader, was given a seat in the cabinet, an event that delighted many Vanniyars but won him public catcalls from the Tamilnad Toilers, who decided to remain in opposition.[45]

---

tionship to political decision-making" (p. 478); "(12) In the non-Western political process there are relatively few explicitly organized interest groups with functionally specific roles" (p. 480). Pye goes on to support this generalization with the observations that "in many cases groups, such as . . . peasant associations that in form would appear to represent a specific interest, are in fact agents of the government or a dominant party or movement. . . . In situations where the associations are autonomous, the tendency is for them to act as protective associations and not as pressure groups. . . . They do not seek to apply pressure openly on the government in order to influence positively the formation of public policy" (p. 480). "(13) In the non-Western political process the national leadership must appeal to an undifferentiated public" (p. 482); and "(17) The non-Western political process operates largely without benefit of political 'brokers'" (p. 485). In support of this generalization he observes that "in most non-Western societies, the role of political 'broker' has been partially filled by those who perform a 'mediator's' role, which consists largely of transmitting the views of the elite to the masses. . . . They do not find it essential to identify and articulate the values of their public. . . . As a consequence, they have not acted in a fashion that would stimulate the emergence of functionally specific interest groups" (pp. 485–86). This model reappears in Chapter 2 of Pye's *Politics, Personality and Nation-Building* (New Haven, 1962).

[45] *Indian Express* (Madras) and *Hindu* (Madras), May 13, 1952.

Shortly thereafter, the Tamilnad Toilers also opened "negotiations" with Congress, presumably to see what offices might be offered in return for support.[46] The negotiations came to nothing until 1954 when C. Rajagopalachari, a Brahman statesman with a long and distinguished history in the nationalist movement, resigned as chief minister. He was replaced by the shrewd and competent but less cosmopolitan Kamaraj Nadar, from the successfully mobile Nadar community, who had made his reputation as chief of the Madras Congress party over more than a decade.[47]

The Tamilnad Toilers decided to support Kamaraj's ministry, and Padayachi joined the cabinet. Naicker, too, remained in the cabinet, with the result that the Vanniyars could now call two of the eight cabinet seats their own. Padayachi reported to the press that he was happy to see that this ministry was so much more representative of backward classes than any previous one. With two ministers in the cabinet and cordial relations with Congress assured, the Commonweal and the Tamilnad Toiler parties were dissolved, their members joining the Congress.[48]

Throughout this period, both before and after the dissolution of the two caste parties, the demands of the Vanniya Kula Kshatriya Sangam continued to find active expression. The *sangam* had three

[46] *Mail* (Madras), October 21, 1952.

[47] See p. 49 above.

[48] *Mail* (Madras), July 30, 1956. The parties were in fact dissolved before 1956. At that time, the election commission merely recognized their dissolution officially.

The procedure followed by the Vanniyars is not unusual. In Rajasthan the Kshatriya Mahasabha (of Rajputs) pursued an almost identical tactic in 1952, campaigning successfully for the legislature, extracting not cabinet offices but concessions on land reform from Congress, and then joining the party, which needed members to strengthen its precarious majority. The Jat caste *sabhas* in Rajasthan very nearly did the same when in 1950 many members considered converting the Rajasthan branch of the Krishikar Lok party into a Jat branch. But the Jats, with politically literate leaders and a self-conscious and effectively mobilized following, saw the expediency of infiltrating the weak Rajasthan Congress; they gave up the idea of a separate party and contested the elections for the most part under the Congress party label. For a more detailed discussion of these developments, see Lloyd I. Rudolph and Susanne Hoeber Rudolph, "From Princes to Politicians in Rajasthan" (forthcoming).

primary objectives. The first was educational services. At stake were scholarships that would allow a village student to pay for a room at the hostel of a distant secondary institution, fee concessions at institutions that still charged tuition, and the reservation of seats for Vanniyars in institutions of higher learning. The second objective was places in the civil service (which conferred status as well as a job). The third was winning Congress "tickets" (that is, nominations) for seats in lower governing boards as well as in the legislature and for places in the cabinet. The *sangam* was also interested in various economic services affecting Vanniyars. That they could hope for government help in several respects was clear from the fact that they had been officially classified as a backward class, that is, a caste above the untouchable level but one whose status and condition were nevertheless so weak that it deserved special consideration under the policy of "progressive discrimination" that has been a central feature of Indian social policy.[49]

The way these demands were pursued and the responses of the two ministers to them are apparent from the proceedings of *sangam* meetings and conferences. Shortly after his appointment in 1954, Padayachi explained to a *sangam* conference why he had joined the Kamaraj ministry when he had not joined the earlier one of Rajagopalachari; the Vanniyars' demands for educational facilities and representation in the civil services, he said, had not been met by the Rajagopalarchari ministry, but a more generous attitude was expected from the Kamaraj ministry.[50] At a North Arcot conference in 1955, he could report that the government had been doing its best to give school fee concessions, scholarships, and employment preference to the Vanniya Kula Kshatriyas.[51] At that time, five out of every twenty seats in the state civil service were reserved for "qualified candidates of the backward classes," in addition to the reservations for scheduled castes and tribes. These reservations were established by administrative order in co-operation with the Public Service Commission. Padayachi apparently paid close attention to such matters, and presumably his and Naicker's views on how this diffi-

[49] See n. 40 above.

[50] *Indian Express* (Madras), April 28, 1954; *Mail* (Madras), May 30, 1954.

[51] *Mail* (Madras), January 5, 1955.

cult problem might be handled were always available to the government. The frequency with which both men reported to Vanniyar meetings indicates that they considered themselves to some extent special agents of Vanniyar interests; drawing a line between this role and their role as cabinet members responsible for the formulation and administration of public policy is of course difficult.

The quality of the *sangam*'s economic demands is illustrated by another North Arcot conference, in 1953, which was addressed by Naicker. The resolutions present a striking illustration of the Vanniya Kula Kshatriya Sangam as an economic interest group—one might expect similar resolutions from western farm groups in the United States. They urged better irrigation in North Arcot district, electricity for agricultural areas, better roads, expansion of the Krishna Pennar multipurpose water project, relief to tenants for rain failure, and (recalling the fact that many Vanniyars were tenants and laborers) ownership of the soil by the tillers.[52]

Negotiations with the Congress concerning the number of nominations that would be given to the Vanniyars in local board elections became very lively late in 1954, just before the district board elections. One result of the negotiations concerning seats in North Arcot was the promise given by the officers of the state Congress party that, once the district board was elected, it would choose a Vanniyar chairman. This promise came in response to Vanniyar pressure to extend to district boards the principle of "communal rotation" in the selection of officers, a principle that had long been recognized in the Madras municipal corporation presidency. In this case, the promise placed the state party in a difficult situation: the non-Vanniyar Congress party members of the North Arcot District Board, many of whom belonged to the higher caste of Reddiars, saw no reason why they should be bound at the district level by negotiations carried on by the state party with the Vanniyars. They accordingly decided not to vote for a Vanniyar and, in co-operation with non-Congress members of the board, elected a Reddiar president. The Madras Congress party, knowing that it might not be able to count on Vanniyar support in the general elections in 1957 if it did not keep faith with the Vanniyars, took strict disciplinary action and sus-

[52] *Hindu* (Madras), June 18, 1953.

pended a number of recalcitrant Reddiar members from the party. According to the newspaper report:

> Sri Karayalar (President of the state Congress organization) said that indiscipline in Congress ranks should not be tolerated as it would weaken the organization. . . . In the North Arcot case, Sri Karayalar said, the idea was that the Presidentship this time should go to a member of the Vanniyar community as in South Arcot. All along the Reddiars had been presidents there. The Vanniyar community had supported the Congress in the Board elections and the understanding all along had been that the Congress nominee for the Presidentship should be a member of the Vanniyar community. . . .[53]

Throughout this period, the *sangam*'s organizational structure was being elaborated and expanded. Local branches sprang up in many places, often at the level of smaller administrative units such as taluks and towns. Usually one of the ministers graced the occasion with his presence.[54] At all these sessions, the ministers and others sought to strengthen the *sangam*'s solidarity, to increase the sense of unity and of mission. Padayachi reminded a conference that his ministership was the result of the united efforts and sacrifices of the community over a long period, and at the thirty-fourth annual conference of the *sangam* at North Arcot, the caste flag was ceremonially unfurled.

The cases of the Shanans who became Nadars and the Pallis who became Vanniyars suggest that the study of caste mobility and ranking in India and social mobilization and political participation in premodern settings have not taken sufficient account of middle level structures and analysis. The caste association, operating in the social space defined by village and jati, on the one hand, and by varna and

[53] *Mail* (Madras), November 20, 1954.

[54] As they did at the first conference of the North Madras Vanniya Kula Kshatriya Sangam, the conference of the Uttiramerur sub-taluk *sangam,* the tenth annual meeting of the South Arcot *sangam,* the second annual conference at Perambur, and a conference at Ayyumpet. See *Hindu* (Madras), May 23, 1953; *Mail* (Madras), June 21, 1954, and January 10, 1956; *Indian Express* (Madras), July 23, 1956.

social class, on the other, takes several generations to establish itself at the regional or state level and to work its effects locally. Behavioral studies of caste rank in one locality at one point in time may miss such changes.[55] So, too, may analyses that seek to make social mobilization, political development, and stable democracy dependent on high levels of income, media exposure, literacy, urbanization, or industrialization.[56] The historical, social, and cultural analyses of these two caste associations illustrate in some measure general processes of social change and political modernization in India. Political man in democratic India has been wrought out of traditional materials; he is not a new man. Acting through such means as caste associations, he is capable at various levels and in the context of various systems of calculating political advantage in the pursuit of moral and material ends and of establishing or maintaining countervailing power.

Castes, described by Marx over a century ago as "stereotype and disconnected units" that had survived the breakup of the village economy and government and that were to be dissolved by the effects of industrialization, have not yet been so. Instead, they seem, in good Hindu fashion, to have been reincarnated in various modern forms—one of the most striking, the caste association. It has become a vehicle for internal cultural reform and external social change in all parts of India, not only in Madras.[57] The caste association enables middle and

[55] See McKim Marriott, "Interactional and Attributional Theories of Caste Ranking," for an example of an influential analysis in this genre. Marriott emphasizes caste mobility in a later analysis, "Multiple Reference in Indian Caste Systems," in James Silverberg (ed.), "Social Mobility in Caste" (a forthcoming special issue of *Comparative Studies of Society and History*).

[56] See, for example, Seymour M. Lipset, "Some Social Requisites of Democracy: Economic Development and Political Legitimacy," *American Political Science Review*, LIII (March, 1959), and Karl W. Deutsch, "Social Mobilization and Political Development," *American Political Science Review*, LV (September, 1961), 493–514. Deutsch, however, has recognized the role that more ascriptive loyalties—linguistic attachments—play in political mobilization.

[57] Other caste associations that have performed such functions as well as the political are the following: the Yogis and Namasudras of Bengal (Nirmal Kumar Bose, "Some Aspects of Caste in Bengal," in Milton Singer [ed.], *Traditional India: Structure and Change* [Philadelphia, 1959]); the Shri Rajput Pacharni Sabha of the Noniyas of U.P. (William Rowe, "The New Cauhans: A Caste Mobility Movement in North India," in James Silverberg [ed.], "Social

lower castes to establish the basis of self-esteem under circumstances in which they have begun to feel the inferiority rather than the necessity of their condition and to win social esteem, first from the state, then from the macrosociety, and last and most slowly from the microsociety of village and locality.

A vehicle of consciousness and organization, the caste association has enabled lower castes to emulate twice-born castes' norms and practices and to appropriate some of their charisma and prestige for themselves. In doing so they have not only socially upgraded themselves but also contributed to structural change in society by helping to level the ritually based social hierarchy of the caste system.

By mobilizing similar but dispersed and isolated jatis of village and

Mobility in Caste"); the Ahir Kshatriya Mahasabha of the Ahirs of U.P., the Gopi Jatiya Sabha (1912) for Ahir Jatis from throughout North India, and the All India Yadav Mahasabha for herding castes throughout India (M.S.A. Rao, "Caste and the Indian Army," *Economic Weekly,* August 29, 1964; M. N. Srinivas, *Social Change in India,* p. 100); the Jatav Vir Mahasabha (1917), the Jatav Pracharak Mandal (1924), and the Jatav Yuvak Mandal (1930) of the Chamars of U.P. (Owen W. Lynch, "The Politics of Untouchability: A Caste Study from Agra, India" [a paper presented at the Conference of Social Structure and Social Change, University of Chicago, June 3–6, 1965], and G. S. Bhatt, "The Chamars of Lucknow," *Eastern Anthropologist,* VIII [September, 1954]); the Mahar conferences in Maharashtra (Nagpur, 1920) leading to the Independent Labor party, mainly a Mahar party (Eleanor Zelliot "The Mahar Political Movement," in Rajni Kothari [ed.], "Caste and Politics in India" [forthcoming], MS p. 30); the Nair Service Society and the Sri Narayana Dharma Paripalana Yogam of the Nairs and the Iravas of Kerala (Aiyappan, *Iravas and Culture Change*); the Kayastha associations of North India (William Rowe, "Mobility in the Caste System" [a paper delivered at the Conference on Social Structure and Social Change, University of Chicago, June 3–6, 1965]); the oilmen of Orissa (F. G. Bailey, "Traditional Society and Representation: A Case Study in Orissa," *Archive of European Sociology,* I [1960], 128); the Kshatriya Mahasabha of the Rajputs and the Jat Kisan Sabhas of Rajasthan (L. I. Rudolph and S. H. Rudolph, "From Princes to Politicians" [forthcoming]); the Gujarat Kshatriya Mahasabha of the Rajputs, Bariyas, and Bhils of Gujarat (Rajni Kothari and Rushikesh Maru, "Caste and Secularism in India," *Journal of Asian Studies,* XXIV [November, 1965]); a series of caste associations of Brahmans, Khatris, Kayasthas, Vaishyas, barbers, and sweepers in Kanpur (P. K. Nandi, "A Study of Caste Organizations in Kanpur," *Man in India,* XLV [January–March, 1963], 84–99); and the Berwa Mahasabha of the Rajasthan Berwa untouchables resident in Delhi (Ruth Simmons, Berkeley, Calif., personal communication, fall, 1966).

locality in horizontal organizations with common identities, caste associations have contributed significantly to the success of political democracy by providing bases for communication, representation, and leadership. They have taught illiterate peasants how to participate meaningfully and effectively in politics. Lower castes, whose large numbers give them an advantage in competitive democratic politics, have in many areas gained influence, access, and power in state and society. With these at their command, they can change in their favor the allocation of resources, privileges, and honors. Rather than providing the basis for a reaction, caste has absorbed and synthesized some of the new democratic values. Ironically, caste associations have become one of the factors that link the mass electorate to the new democratic political processes and make these processes comprehensible in familiar terms to a population still largely illiterate.

The Politics of Caste

Nationalist elites in new states tend to be deeply suspicious of tribal, linguistic, religious, regional, and caste loyalties and structures. More often than not they perceive them as a threat to the incipient nations and fragile states that they govern. Such concerns have frequently led to attempts to dispense with rather than integrate them. Their view is often shared by statesmen and scholars in old states, who believe that powerful ascriptive structures are a threat to liberal democratic or socialist societies and states—that the individual must precede associations, in time and in importance, if the contractual civil society or the ideological collective is to have practical and moral validity.

Such a critique is based on a misapprehension of the nature of modern society and politics. In India, the blurring of lines between natural and voluntary structures has placed her associational life on a footing not too different from that of modern nations. Natural associations based on religion, language, ethnicity, and locality have not been assimilated or dissolved in modern nations; in fact they continue to play important, sometimes decisive, roles in their societies and politics.[1] Indeed, the crosscutting forces that arise in modern pluralist societies have not prevented their formally voluntary structures from taking on ascriptive features; bureaucratic organizations can and often do assume familial qualities in ways that approximate the experiences of those living within transformed primary groups.[2]

[1] For America, see Will Herberg, *Protestant, Catholic, Jew: An Essay in American Religious Sociology* (Garden City, N.Y., 1960); Nathan Glazer and Daniel Patrick Moynihan, *Beyond the Melting Pot: The Negroes, Puerto Ricans, Jews, Italians, and Irish of New York City* (Cambridge, Mass., 1963); and Milton M. Gordon, *Assimilation in American Life: The Role of Race, Religion and National Origins* (New York, 1964).

[2] For a recent critical view of social pluralism as it has hardened and subordinated itself to bureaucratic leadership, see Henry Kariel, *The Decline of American Pluralism* (Stanford, 1961). Kariel is so concerned that he "would have us move . . . from the much celebrated ideal of Tocqueville toward the still unfashionable one of Rousseau."

Milton Gordon in *Assimilation in American Life* mounts an impressive case for the rigid compartmentalization of American communal life at the rank and file level. Seymour M. Lipset, Martin Trow, and James Coleman, in *Union Democracy: The Inside Politics of the International Typographical Union* (Glencoe, 1956), examine the rigidities and bureaucratic domination of unions and professional associations by analyzing the exception. Everett C. Hughes, in *Men and Their Work* (Glencoe, 1958), suggests how occupational associations in America, like castes in India, upgrade themselves by changing their names and histories and purify themselves and their rituals by emulating "higher" occupational groups in the matter of educational requirements, licensing standards, and ceremonial niceties. John R. Murphy's "Professional and Occupational Licensing: A National Problem with State Control" (a term paper in Government 155a: Government Regulation of Industry, at Harvard University, 1959–60), along with Hughes's analyses, suggested these comparisons with caste mobility in India.

Kariel and Lipset, Trow, and Coleman emphasize the inability of members of formally voluntary associations, like peasants in Marx's analysis, to represent and rule themselves; therefore, they fall victim to the executive power (the bureaucracy). William H. Whyte, Jr., in *The Organization Man* (New York, 1956), although not ignoring structural factors, emphasizes the ways in which formally voluntary organizations absorb and tend to monopolize the affective life and identities of their members and their families. For a similar perspective, see Amitai Etzioni, *A Comparative Analysis of Complex Organizations* (New York, 1961).

Heuristic efforts to distinguish traditional from modern society must guard against the danger of taking formal structural and normative features as exhaustive and, as a consequence, ignoring a more indeterminate reality in which one blends into the other and varies with the play of contextual forces and events in time.

Even if the persistence of ascriptive and neo-ascriptive structures and norms were not so prominent a feature of modern societies, a concern to contain the disruptive effects of modernization by helping such structures play productive rather than counterproductive roles in the process should direct sympathetic attention to their study and use. Those national leaders who have not felt this concern and who have tried to dispense with natural associations by directing their attention, programs, and ideological appeals solely to embryonic modern classes and incipient nations have tended to produce unstable and ineffective autocratic regimes. A strategy more likely to achieve modernization with stability, effectiveness, and liberty is one that provides those who represent natural associations with conditions and incentives that enable them to foster the interests of their groups in ways and contexts that also lead toward modernity.[3]

At the same time, the intractability of powerful and independent natural associations, rooted in the soil and the heart, cannot be underestimated. They led to the partition of the Indian subcontinent and to charges of genocide in Ruanda,[4] and they fuel the political instability and civil wars of African, Near Eastern, Asian and some modern Western states.[5] When natural associations are too few, when they are socially and morally independent of each other, and when they

[3] For a somewhat similar perspective on Africa's ethnic groups, see Aristide Zolberg, "Mass Parties and National Integration: The Case of the Ivory Coast," *Journal of Politics*, XXV (February, 1963), 36–48.

[4] See Jacques J. Maquet, *The Premise of Inequality in Ruanda* (London, 1961). For the genocide charge, see *Keesing's Contemporary Archives*, XIV (1963–64), 20085–86.

[5] For Walloon-Flemish differences in Belgium, see Ernest Mandel, "The Dialectic of Class and Region in Belgium," *New Left Review*, No. 20 (Summer, 1963), 2–31; *Keesing's Contemporary Archives*, XIII (1961–62), 17968, 18391, 18623, and 18941, and XIV (1963–64), 19601. For the differences in Canada between the French Catholics and the English Protestants, see the *Preliminary Report* of the Royal Commission on Bilingualism and Biculturalism (Ottawa, 1965). The commission warned that Canada was undergoing "the greatest crisis in its history" (p. 13). See also Edmund Wilson, *O Canada* (New York, 1965).

lack a limited but critically important identification with leaders, values, and institutions capable of sustaining national politics and a modern state, they destroy the viability of a civil society that transcends them.

Overcoming the tendency of ascriptive associations to formulate separate political identities and establish separate political structures requires powerful integrative forces. Strong leadership, nationalist ideology, and viable state structures may not be enough. Extended and socially penetrating experience of modern political culture and institutions along with broadly recognized economic interdependence can be critical. So, too, can the capacity to maintain a balance between the claims of the nation-state and those of ascriptive solidarities. Nkrumah's Ghana represented a pathology of national integration, the pursuit of unity without regard for ascriptive local pluralism, whereas Balewa's Nigeria represented the pathology of diversity, a nation-state with too limited a sense of citizenship.

Castes do not pose the same kind of potential threat to the nation-state that tribes, religious communities, and linguistic groups do. In India, the latter have made successful claims to separate political identities; for Muslims, this meant partition and the creation of the sovereign state of Pakistan, and for others, recognition within the framework of the federal system.[6] Castes have not demanded separate political identities. As parts of a larger society, they are symbioti-

[6] Many religious groups (the Christians and, after independence, the Muslims) and many tribal groups (the Bhils, for example) have not in fact posed such problems of integration. But others have, at various levels: before independence Muslims sought their political identity in the nation-state of Pakistan; the various Indian linguistic groups succeeded, through the formation of Andhra (1954), the States Reorganization Act of 1956, and the bifurcation of Bombay into Maharashtra and Gujarat (1960), in establishing separate political identities and some measure of autonomy within the federal system; the Naga tribes won recognition as a separate state through rebellion (Marcus Franda, "The Naga National Council: A Study of Group Politics" [M.A. thesis, University of Chicago, 1960]); and the Sikhs found a measure of political identity first in the compromise achieved in the Punjab legislature whereby two intrastate regional committees with broad recommendatory powers were established for Sikh and Hindu legislators respectively (see Joan V. Bondurant, *Regionalism versus Provincialism* [Berkeley, Calif., 1958], pp. 114–24) and then in Punjabi Suba, granted in 1966. See Kushwant Singh, *A History of the Sikhs, Volume 2, 1839–1964* (Princeton, N.J., 1966).

cally related to each other, and as participants in Hindu culture, this relationship is integrated and legitimized. When castes come to mobilize themselves politically, they are concerned with the distribution of values, status, and resources within a political system, not with the realization of nationhood although such a demand is not beyond the bounds of possibility, however unlikely it may be. A caste like the Jats of Rajasthan, Punjab, and Uttar Pradesh, which spreads across present state boundaries, has a contiguous territorial base, and possesses a viable political history (for the Jats, conquests as recently as the eighteenth century), might develop "national" aspirations.[7]

India's political parties, particularly the governing Congress party, have played an indispensable part in brokering and integrating diverse social forces. On the whole, they have been able to subsume castes to their larger ideological and programmatic purposes, but they have been notably less successful with other natural associations. In the former bilingual state of Bombay, for example, the Samyukta Maharashtra Samiti and the Maha Gujarat Parishad, associations of Marathi and Gujarati linguistic nationalism respectively, subsumed national and other regional parties in their drives for separate political identities.[8] The politics of partition, states reorganization, and the realization of Punjabi Suba in 1966 make abundantly clear that the quest for linguistic-cultural and religious-political autonomy cannot easily be accommodated or contained by parties. The program and patronage demands of castes, on the other hand—because the political role of castes is more akin to that of interest and ethnic groups[9]

[7] For a visual statement of the 20–30 per cent concentration of Jats in a determinable geographic area, see the excellent map, helpful in many other ways to social scientists, by Joseph Schwartzberg, in "The Distribution of Selected Castes in the North Indian Plain," *Geographical Review,* LV (Winter, 1965), 477–95.

[8] See Marshall Windmiller, "The Politics of States Reorganization in India: The Case of Bombay," *Far Eastern Survey,* XXV (September, 1956), 129–43; and Phillips Talbot, "The Second General Elections: Voting in the States" (India, PT–6–1957; American Universities Field Staff, New York, 1957); Selig Harrison, in *India, the Most Dangerous Decade* (Princeton, N.J., 1956), provides a provocative and pessimistic account of the role of language in national politics.

[9] For a discussion of interest groups and their political role in India, see Myron Weiner, *The Politics of Scarcity* (Chicago, 1962). For a study of a particular

in American politics than to that of other natural associations in India—are more amenable to party management through legislation, policy implementation, and ticket balancing. As a general rule, then, caste is more likely to be subsumed and integrated by leadership and policies of parties than it is to threaten established political communities and structures.[10]

Because castes are ordinarily bounded by language, they have affected Indian political life more at the state and local levels than at the national level. In the south, where efforts have been made to draw linguistic and state boundaries congruently, castes do not usually reach beyond the state. In the north, along with Hindi, castes can be found in more than one and sometimes in all four Hindi-speaking

---

interest group, see Leon V. Hirsch, *Marketing in an Underdeveloped Economy: The North Indian Sugar Industry* (Englewood Cliffs, N.J., 1961).

[10] The role of caste and language in Indian politics is engaging the interest of Indian political scientists as they turn their attention from constitutional, national, and international politics to the state level. In December, 1965, the University of Rajasthan at Jaipur sponsored a seminar on state politics. A report on the conference by K. P. Karunakaran, a leading Indian political scientist, cautions those who wish to apply "American" theory and methods to Indian problems. ". . . One of the questions," he writes, "which often came up was to what extent the foreign models and tools of research could be applied to India. There was general appreciation of the fact that the impact of American education and American political scientists on India was at first healthy because it allowed Indian political science to disentangle itself from the narrow path of constitutionalism laid down by the British. But it was also feared that there was an almost mechanical attempt on the part of many Indian political scientists to try and fit in Indian politics with an American model; . . . this approach did considerable harm by misleading the public. Americans, as a rule, failed to grasp the main forces at work in the Indian political field. They rarely understood the meaning of the word 'caste.' To them the movement for linguistic provinces was an attempt at fragmentation of the country. . . . But there were others who challenged these concepts and maintained that very often what was referred to as 'fragmentation' by Americans was a step towards strengthening the political unity of the country, because by fulfilling the aspirations of the people and democratising the politics of a region, that region could be made a willing and enthusiastic partner in the new India that was shaping" ("Politics at State Level," *Now,* February 4, 1966, p. 13).

states.[11] Despite the possibilities that the northern situation creates, castes there, with the exception of attempts to lobby the census commissioner for more dignified names or classifications, have not as yet mobilized politically across state boundaries.

The relationship of caste to social and political change and to the conduct of government and politics varies more than the examples of the Nadars and Vanniyars suggest. Some of the factors that effect its role include (1) the number and size of other caste actors; (2) regional differences and their effect on the caste profile of particular states; (3) differences in the level and characteristics of relevant political systems; (4) the relative significance of dominant and subject castes and the related propensities toward vertical and horizontal mobilization; (5) changes over time in the social and political environment in which particular castes operate; (6) the degree of self-consciousness and cohesion that characterize particular castes; and (7) the countervailing power of other castes, interest groups, and integrative forces, particularly political parties.

The number and size of caste actors within a state political system shape the nature of its politics. The situation in most states recalls one of Madison's conditions for republican liberty: that there be too many "interests" to establish a "tyranny" based on a permanent majority. For example, in Rajasthan, Jats are the largest caste with 9 per cent of the population, and in Madras Vanniyars are most numerous with almost 10 per cent. Even at the district level, where caste percentages climb as high as 20 or 30, it is uncommon to find a permanent majority. Ordinarily, castes must find common ground with each other in order to share in government, and it is rare for those who do to remain united for a sufficiently long period and on a sufficiently broad range of men and measures to establish a tyranny over the rest. And of course, castes are not the only political actors in state political systems nor are they immune from the impact of crosscutting and integrative political forces.

11 Schwartzberg, "The Distribution of Selected Castes in the North Indian Plain." His maps show that among the non-twice-born castes, Kurmis, Chamars, and Ahirs are located throughout the North Indian plain; Jats also are distributed across several states. Belgaum District, Mysore, is a notable exception to the typical South Indian pattern. See Myron Weiner, *Party Building in a New Nation* (Chicago, 1967).

Caste pluralism is not, however, characteristic of all states. In Mysore, for example, Lingayats constitute approximately 20 and Okkaligas approximately 15 per cent of the population. Rivalry between these two castes has been the source of destabilizing factionalism within the Congress party government, biased administration, and a finding by the Supreme Court that the state's system for reserving seats in educational institutions for backward classes was a "fraud on the constitution."[12] In Kerala, religious or caste communities or coalitions of them have tended to shape party strategy and political behavior: Iravas (or Ezhavas) and scheduled castes, 34 per cent of the population; Christians, 24 per cent; Nairs and Namboodiri Brahmans, 19 per cent; and Muslims, 20 per cent.[13] The inability of Kerala to govern itself has been, in considerable measure, attributable to these rather special social conditions. Political parties—in their appeals, electoral support, and to a somewhat lesser extent, candidate selection—tended in the 1950's to be dependent on the major ascriptive communities: the Communist Party of India (CPI) on the Iravas and scheduled castes, the Congress on Christians and Nairs, the Socialists on Nairs, and the Muslim League on Muslims.[14]

[12] Balaji v. State of Mysore, All India Reporter, 1963 Mysore 649.

[13] Kathleen Gough, "Village Politics in Kerala—I," *Economic Weekly,* February 20, 1965, p. 365.

[14] Michael St. John, "The Communist Party and Communal Politics in Kerala" (Senior honors thesis, Department of Social Relations, Harvard University, 1962), particularly pp. 72–81. In describing the Communist-Irava relationship, St. John observes that "the dominant theme of the Ezhavas [Iravas] activity throughout the years has been reform. . . . Today the reform which the Ezhavas want is economic, and they have become convinced during the last decade [1952–62] that it is only through the K.C.P. [Kerala Communist Party] that they will secure it. The Ezhavas are a politically conscious group, aware of the issues, and not easily swayed by slogans. For this reason they have been willing to support the K.C.P. in spite of the Congress orientation of their caste associations leaders. . . . Thus between the Ezhavas and the Communists there has been no fundamental meeting of minds, but rather a fortunate confluence of program and action. . . . The Communists, for their part, do not really think of the Ezhavas as the 'proper' class for their support . . ." (pp. 149–51). At the same time, St. John argues that the KCP is the "*only* autonomous political party, for the others, as brokers for communal interests, are little more than the sum of their parts. The Communists do appeal to different castes, as we have seen

The period between 1957 and 1959, when the Communists gained and lost power, may have marked a watershed for this pattern of Kerala politics. The very success of the CPI in gaining power under the banner of class ideology and in governing, for the most part, in the interests of the poor and dispossessed crystallized class tendencies

---

in the case of the Ezhavas, but their appeal is germane to their program, and their program is within the framework of an overriding plan. . . . The members have a commitment to the theory and the party which is deeply engrained. . . . They rise and fall with the relative success of the Party much as other persons in Kerala rise and fall with the vacillations in fortune of their community" (pp. 158–59). One of the critical tests of the nature of the relationship between Communist ideology and the need for community support was the party's effort to drop caste as a test for backwardness, substituting in its stead income. "Immediately a howl of protest went up from the Ezhavas, who are classified as backward. . . . Fearing for their electoral support, the Communists for once gave in to communal sentiment . . ." (p. 174).

E. M. S. Namboodiripad, the pre-eminent leader of the CPI in Kerala and one of the party's handful of major national leaders, writes that caste associations were "the first form in which the peasant masses rose in struggle against feudalism." Today, however, "it is easy enough to see . . . that these caste organizations are not the class organizations of the peasantry; they do, on the contrary, consolidate the caste separatism of the people in general and of the peasantry in particular, so that the grip of these caste organizations on the peasantry has to be broken if they are to be organized as a class" (*The National Question in Kerala* [Bombay, 1952], pp. 102, 106).

St. John tested the relationship between party and community in electoral behavior by correlating the votes of those supporting the United Front (made up of the Congress party, Praja Socialist party, and Muslim League) and the CPI in the 1960 election when voting choice was as polarized as it has ever been. He hypothesized that there should be a positive relationship between the district vote of the two party groupings and the community proportions of the population of each district said to be in support of the United Front and the CPI; that is, Christians, Nairs, and Muslims versus Iravas and scheduled castes. Excluding Kozhikode District because of its peculiar community distribution, St. John performed a rank correlation for the remaining eight districts of the state, producing a .60 measure (the result with Kozhikode was .38). This is the most precise evidence to date on the relationship between community and party in electoral behavior at the state level. When the studies of the 1965 election in Kerala by Samuel J. Eldersveld and Rajni Kothari become available, we may have more precise indications. See also n. 21 below. A table prepared by Anthony J. Fernandez (Appendix, Table 1) indicates the leadership ties of parties to communities.

within the various communities and helped free their members for mobilization by party rather than community appeals.

The 1959 "liberation" struggle against the Communist government and the 1960 mid-term election that followed obscured for a time the dimensions of the shift in Kerala politics from community to class.[15] The liberation struggle led by Christian bishops and Mannath Padmanabhan, for almost two generations the political strategist of the Nair Service Society,[16] and Congress' success in returning to power at the head of a coalition of the community and party forces that came together in the liberation struggle, seemed to reverse the trends made visible by the period of Communist rule. In 1962, however, the Congress, under the guidance of the party's High Command, began an effort to free itself from dependence on the leaders of the Nair, Christian, and Muslim communities by giving greater scope to Irava leadership and support and by attempting to emphasize class mobilization from below rather than community mobilization from above.[17] The coalition chief minister, Nair and Socialist P. T. Pillai, was replaced by R. Shanker, a leader of the progressive faction in the Congress and a former official of the Irava caste association, and the Muslim speaker of the assembly was replaced by a Congressman. One of the consequences of the new strategy became apparent thirty months later when Nair and Christian members of the Congress crossed the aisle, brought down the Shanker government, and formed

[15] Christians, Nairs, and Muslims joined forces in 1960 behind a party coalition of the Congress, Socialist, and Muslim League parties to defeat the CPI; they had become convinced that the protection of their class interests (Christians and Nairs) or religious convictions and institutions (all three communities) overrode the differences they had previously translated into partisan political conflict (see K. P. Baghat, *The Kerala Mid Term Election of 1960* [Bombay, 1962]).

[16] See Bashiruddin Ahmed, "Communist and Congress Prospects in Kerala," *Asian Survey*, VI (July, 1966), 393–95, for a synoptic view of the strategies and kaleidoscopic alliances not only of the Nair Service Society (NSS) but also of the Irava caste association (the Shri Narayana Dharma Paripalan Yogam, or SNDP), the Syrian Christian Church, and the Muslims.

[17] The attempts of the Congress High Command, particularly under the influence of Kamaraj Nadar, to broaden the party's social base in an Irava direction are summed up in Robert L. Hardgrave, Jr., "Caste and the Kerala Elections," *Economic Weekly*, April 17, 1965.

the rebel Kerala Congress party to contest the ensuing 1965 mid-term election.[18] That election proved to be an inconclusive test of the strategy of class mobilization under Irava leadership.[19] No party or coalition of parties was able to form a government, and the state remained under president's rule until the general election of 1967.

In anticipation of that election E. M. S. Namboodiripad, the astute leader of the CPI-Marxist party in Kerala, forged a seven party coalition that swept to a decisive victory, reducing Congress to a mere 9 seats in an assembly of 133.[20] This debacle was associated with

[18] The disintegration of this coalition and the subsequent split of the Congress party can be traced to the conflict generated by class differences within communities and the larger and more general conflict between community and class appeals and organizations. Poor Muslims saw little reason to support a coalition government that, on the one hand, denied them in the name of secular democracy a place in its cabinet and, later, the speakership of the assembly and, on the other, stumbled and procrastinated in pressing for progressive economic and welfare measures to which it was pledged. Within the Congress, those who wished to implement programs to help the poor and the dispossessed, most of whom were Muslim, Irava, or scheduled caste, did battle with the representatives of the Christian and Nair establishments.

[19] This was not the view of sources sympathetic to the CPI. They believed that the loose alliance it had formed captured over 52 per cent of the vote and enough seats to form a government if only the CPI-Marxist M.L.A.'s jailed by Union Home Minister Nanda were released. On the other hand, Bashiruddin Ahmed, a careful scholar of Kerala politics, concludes his analysis of the Congress and Communist prospects after the 1965 election by remarking that "it seems possible that the Communist Party will no longer constitute a state-wide contender for power . . . . [It] may well become no more than a party of pressure in the politics of the State . . ." ("Communist and Congress Prospects in Kerala," p. 393). ". . . The deep thrust and penetration of [Congress'] organization, and its success in weaning away Nair and Christian support from the N.S.S. and the Church along with the deep inroads it has made into pockets of Communist support among Ezhavas [Iravas], ensures Congress a dynamic focal position in Kerala politics" (ibid., p. 399). However, Ahmed's condition for this outcome, healing of the split between the Congress and the Kerala Congress, was not fulfilled.

[20] Congress and the Kerala Congress together won 14 seats and polled 43 per cent of the vote (Congress, 35.4 per cent; Kerala Congress, 7.6); the United Front parties won 113 seats (CPI-Marxist, 52; CPI, 19; SSP, 19; Muslim League, 14; RSP, 6; KTP, 2; and KSP, 1) and polled 51.4 per cent of the vote (CPI-Marxist, 23.5 per cent; CPI, 8.5; SSP, 8.4; Muslim League, 6.7; RSP, 2.7; KTP,

Congress' return to a strategy of community mobilization from above.[21] The leaders of the Nair and Christian communities, having failed to persuade the Kerala Congress to merge with the official Congress, deserted the Kerala Congress to assume a decisive role in the direction of the Congress campaign. The political fickleness of the Nair and Christian leaders not only proved the undoing of both the Congress and the Kerala Congress but also seems to have accelerated the decline of political cohesiveness among Nairs and Christians. Even though the political base of the CPI-Marxist party remains in the poorer section of the Irava community, it demonstrated in the 1967 election that it had enhanced its capacity to mobilize from below a wide spectrum of classes through electoral alliances and direct appeals to ideology and interest.[22] Whether Kerala has left be-

---

1.1; and KSP, 0.5). Government of India, Press Information Bureau, "Kerala Assembly Results, Analysis I" (New Delhi, February, 1967; mimeographed). See also M. V. Pylee, "The Congress Debacle in Kerala," *Economic and Political Weekly*, II (March 4, 1967), 483–84.

[21] Congress, which stood alone in 1967, fared much worse than did the CPI when it stood alone against a united opposition in 1960 in part because the Kerala Congress so split the Nair and Christian vote that Congress lost up to 50 seats to the United Front candidates in the six Travancore and Cochin districts where these communities are concentrated. The *Hindustan Times'* special correspondent wrote on March 4, 1967 that "a study of the voting figures shows that if these parties had put up a joint battle against the United Front they could have improved their position, possibly to the extent of winning about 50 seats." See also M. V. Pylee, "The Congress Debacle in Kerala" (p. 484), where he estimates the loss as high as 60 seats. The United Front won 67 and the Congress and Kerala Congress together 14 of the 85 seats in the six districts located in Travancore and Cochin. Government of India, Press Information Bureau, "Kerala Assembly: An Analysis-3; Seats Won District Wise" (New Delhi, February, 1967; mimeographed).

Another important reason for Congress' defeat was the fact that, having sacrificed in the name of secularism what little influence remained to it among Muslims, it was unable to win any of the 48 seats located in the three Malabar districts where the Muslim vote is located. All the candidates put up by the Samastha Kerala Muslim League, formed by Muslims identified with Congress to counter Muslim League and United Front electoral influence in Malabar, lost their deposits.

[22] Kathleen Gough discusses what she calls the Communist cross-caste strategy in two villages in "Village Politics in Kerala—II," *Economic Weekly*, February 27, 1965, pp. 415–16. A. Aiyappan, in *Social Revolution in a Kerala Village;*

hind the political instability and incapacity to govern itself that arise from the existence of too few, too large, and too impenetrable communities remains to be seen.

Beyond the structural and cultural differences that characterize state caste constellations lie more general regional differences. Caste profiles change as one moves from the Gangetic heartland, where Aryan peoples and Sanskritic culture made their most deep penetration, toward the south and the rimlands. Most striking is the relative absence of twice-born castes, other than Brahmans, in the southern states and the smaller percentage of Brahmans there.[23] The movement of Aryan people and their Sanskrit culture toward the south does not seem to have brought within its fold regionally and locally dominant castes. Such castes in the south performed Kshatriya and Vaishya functions and occupied equivalent social (but not ritual) statuses to those of their northern counterparts but remained Sudras.[24] As a result, Brahmans in the south have tended to be more separated from the rest of the population than Brahmans in the north. In the south they are the only representatives of twice-born religion and ritual status, whereas in the north they blend into the large twice-born population of other significant and powerful castes. The range of social distance between the top and the bottom of the

---

A Study in Culture Change (Bombay, 1965), writes from a lifetime of study and a recent investigation of a Kerala village that "the horizontal consolidation of caste . . . is an ongoing process, but a parallel trend which splits each caste vertically and thus weakens it is also now in the process of development. Within the Irava caste, as also within other castes, there is class formation. . . . Class interests cut across caste. The Communists in Kerala are the least caste-minded among the political parties there. . . . Fission on party lines of cleavage has already taken place in the S.N.D.P.Y. [the Irava caste association], and the Irava leaders are now making an effort to keep the Association above party politics. Whether and how far these efforts will succeed remains to be seen" (p. 169).

[23] Less than 3 per cent in Madras, as against over 8 per cent in the plains of Uttar Pradesh.

[24] The Vellalas, Mudaliars, Reddiars, Chettiars, Naidus, and Kammas, prosperous Madras and Andhra castes often high in social rank, are all Sudras. So are the Nairs of Kerala, who rank immediately after the Namboodiri Brahmans.

caste structure is greater in the south than it is in the north, where pollution is conveyed by touch, not proximity, as in the south.[25]

Regional caste profiles affect the nature of political cleavage and mobilization. The wide ritual gulf, for example, between the tiny Madras Brahman elite (less than 3 per cent) and other castes contributed to and was compounded by their domination of modern political, administrative, and professional life. Their initial control of the nationalist movement in Madras led those castes who by education, income and political sophistication felt themselves the equal of Brahmans and yet found themselves excluded from leading positions in political and professional life to oppose traditional and modern Brahman domination by forming the anti-Brahman, anti-nationalist Justice party.[26] The elimination of Brahmans from positions of political leadership that Justice party governments represented did not still the anti-Brahmanical impulse in Madras politics; after independence the Dravida Kazhagam and the Dravida Munnetra Kazhagam deepened and broadened their political appeal by linking it to themes of northern domination and Hindi hegemony.[27] In Maharashtra, too, the relative absence of non-Brahman twice-born castes has helped to make Brahmans the target of movements directed against their social and political dominance. Many Marathas, like Vellalas and Mudaliars in Madras, first entered politics in response to anti-Brahman slogans.[28] Their mobilization has been followed in turn, as was the case in Madras, by that of castes like the untouchable Mahars still lower in the ritual hierarchy.[29]

[25] For the harshness of social distance in Kerala, see A. Aiyappan, *Iravas and Culture Change* (Madras, 1945), and McKim Marriott, *Caste Ranking and Community Structure in Five Regions of India and Pakistan* (Deccan College Monograph Series, No. 23; Poona, 1960), pp. 26–31. For Brahman "distance" in Madras, see Andre Beteille, *Caste, Class and Power: Changing Patterns of Stratification in a Tanjore Village* (Berkeley, Calif., 1965).

[26] See Eugene F. Irschick, "Politics and Social Change in South India" (Ph.D. dissertation, Department of History, University of Chicago, 1964).

[27] See L. I. Rudolph, "Urban Life and Populist Radicalism: Dravidian Politics in Madras," *Journal of Asian Studies,* XX (May, 1961).

[28] See M. L. P. Patterson, "Caste and Politics in Maharashtra," *Economic Weekly,* VIII (July 21, 1956).

[29] For the Mahars, see Eleanor Zelliot, "The Mahar Political Movement," in Rajni Kothari (ed.), "Caste and Politics in India" (forthcoming).

Opposite tendencies have characterized Uttar Pradesh. There a relatively large proportion of the population is made up of twice-born castes.[30] Their ritual and social proximity creates greater continuity in the scale of ritual rank. Along with Brahmans, other twice-born castes had access to modern professional and political structures. Instead of tension between them and a Brahman ritual and modern elite, there has been a general sharing of social status and political power. Nor has Uttar Pradesh witnessed that massive mobilization of lower-level Sudra or advanced untouchable castes that status-deprived upper-level Sudra castes inaugurated in Madras and Maharashtra against the established social structure and the legitimacy of its norms.

In general, regional variations in caste profiles seem to be associated with differences in the kind and rate of political mobilization and with the nature of the political conflict they produce. Anti-Brahmanism seems to have flourished in regions characterized by steep and discontinuous traditional social hierarchies, and it in turn seems to have fostered the political mobilization of castes still lower in the ritual hierarchy.[31] At the other extreme, regions with relative-

[30] In the plains part of U.P., Brahmans formed 8.7 per cent of the total population, according to the 1931 census. Rajputs formed more than 5 per cent of the population in most U.P. districts at that time (Schwartzberg, "The Distribution of Selected Castes in the North Indian Plain," p. 485 and map). Prominent also among the political leadership are Kayasthas. Whether they should or should not be classified as twice-born has been a matter of litigation as well as sociological and historical argument. Whichever status they are said to occupy, it is not as distinct, in the north, from Brahmans as are Sudras in parts of the south.

[31] Mysore and Andhra have not been immune to anti-Brahmanism, but it has been much less virulent and politically significant than that found in Madras and Maharashtra. Kerala has not experienced much anti-Brahmanism either, but this may be in part because of the links of blood and kinship that unite Nairs and Namboodiri Brahmans, and in part because of strong Brahman leadership of the Communist party. The Telugu Brahmans of Andhra may have escaped the experience of the Tamil Brahmans of Madras because of the history of the Telugu linguistic area. Andhra became aware of a distinct regional identity that differentiated her from Tamilnad—with which she shared a single political identity in the Presidency of Madras—early in the twentieth century. Telugu Brahmans were able to join with other Andhra castes in protest against "Tamil domination," which turned out, incidentally, to be mostly Tamil Brahman domination, at a time when the Brahman–non-Brahman conflict was joined

ly higher proportions of twice-born castes and more gradual and continuous social landscapes seem to be less susceptible to horizontal
mobilizations from below of ritually deprived castes seeking opportunities, status, and political power. The tendency for castes to spread
across state boundaries in the north and to be bounded by them in
the south also affects political mobilization. Ahirs and Kurmis,
peasant castes, are distributed along the massive Gangetic valley and
beyond; numerous in Uttar Pradesh, Bihar, and Madhya Pradesh,
they can also be found in Orissa and the Punjab.[32] Among such widely scattered caste populations, the sheer magnitude of the distances
and the difficulties of communication and organization involved
(there are eighty million people in Uttar Pradesh alone) inhibit the
creation of a sense of community and common interest.[33]

It is likely that these differences in regional caste profiles will yield
to more homogenous patterns, partly in consequence of politics. In
Madras and Maharashtra, anti-Brahmanism has declined as other
castes have won access to power and resources. That Madras' previously anti-Brahman Dravida Munnetra Kazhagam (Dravidian Progressive Federation [DMK]) has become sufficiently self-confident
and politically pragmatic to solicit Brahman support, and that Brahmans have been willing to reciprocate these advances suggests the
gradual transformation of extreme superordinate-subordinate relations among communities into more equal ones.

The politics of caste varies with context and level. Disparate
though interacting political systems of village, block, district, state

---

in Madras. But it is also true that Indian and English observers at the beginning
of this century, in contrasting Madras and Andhra, noted that Telugu "Brahmans
were less concerned with pollution and more willing to attend ceremonies
of other castes" (Carolyn Elliott, "Caste and Faction in Andhra Pradesh" [paper
delivered at the Association for Asian Studies, New York, April 4–6, 1966], p. 9).

[32] See p. 70, n. 11.

[33] The relationship of caste profiles and caste distribution to political boundaries is, of course, only one among many variables influencing differences in
political mobilization among regions. Differences in literacy, education, communication, and length and depth of experience with imperial rule would also
count for much.

legislative assembly and national parliamentary constituencies, and state affect the form and force of caste factors in politics. Who a man is, the manners he uses, the kinds of help or co-operation he can command, depend upon whether he is in the world of the village, the world of the state capital, or the worlds that lie between them. He may act more or less in terms of his own and others' caste or be guided in his behavior by the norms of shared citizenship, depending upon the system of action in which he finds himself.[34] Politicians on tour employ democratic manners; at home in arranging marriages or in social intercourse with neighbors, they are likely to observe caste differences.

It is easier in the face-to-face political community of the village and the immediate locality than in more distant and impersonal settings for dominant castes to use traditional patterns of respect and obedience for political purposes. Village Chamars in Uttar Pradesh confront ritual and economic disabilities that leave them subject to the command of local notables, whereas urban Chamars in Agra play a leading role in the city's political life.[35] More recently, particularly

[34] See Harold Gould, "The Adaptive Functions of Caste in Contemporary Indian Society," *Asian Survey*, III (September, 1963), for a discussion of a sample of fifty riksha drivers in Lucknow in their urban and rural contexts: "They really have two social structural models inside them simultaneously and utilized each in its appropriate place" (p. 435).

[35] Harold Gould found, for example, that in Faizabad constituency scheduled caste "landless menials are still too economically dependent upon the Thakurs ..." to vote independently. "Many scheduled caste people were gathered together in little groups by their Thakur overlords and marched to the polls under Thakur supervision in order to ensure that they voted for the Jan Sangh. They were able to impose their will in this way, by threatening these impoverished folk with such economic sanctions as the denial of opportunities for field labour, withdrawal of sharecropping privileges and the calling in of loans" ("Traditionalism and Modernism in U.P.," in Myron Weiner and Rajni Kothari (eds.), *Indian Voting Behaviour* [Calcutta, 1965], p. 175). In contrast, Owen W. Lynch describes the ability of Jatavs (formerly Chamars) to elect the vice-chairman of the Agra municipality through an alliance with the Jan Sangh ("The Politics of Untouchability: A Case Study from Agra, India" [a paper presented at the Conference on Social Structure and Social Change, University of Chicago, June 3–6, 1965]).

with the introduction of the secret ballot in village elections, the capacity of dominant castes to mobilize subject castes has declined. As traditional loyalties and discipline dissolve, lower caste independence and cohesion, especially among those castes aspiring to village-wide influence or power, tend to increase.[36] At the same time that intracaste cohesion may be on the rise in the village, it may be on the decline in higher level political systems. Vanniyars in a Madras village, for example, acted in a corporate manner toward rival castes after the discipline of Vanniyar caste associations in district and state contexts had been penetrated by the mobilizing efforts of political parties.[37] Depending on the political system, castes exhibit different levels of politicization, independence, and cohesion.

In the more impersonal settings of higher level systems, the mobilization of large numbers begins to defy the capabilities of vertical integration. Local notables who can still mobilize their interest for political purposes by commanding the support of dependents, kin, and neighbors may or may not have the political skills required to create appropriate and effective factional combinations to meet the exigencies of various political systems. At higher levels of politics, politicians must have recourse to the representation of independent interests and to ideological and programmatic appeals through more manifest and specialized political structures, particularly the political party. At these levels, independent political calculations begin to split, combine, or fuse castes of all ranks. Upper castes may need the numerical strength that lower castes' support can supply; lower castes or communities may want access to resources and opportunities that support for upper caste leadership can yield; and previously dispossessed castes and communities may want to secure independent access to political power through parties that challenge established norms and structures. As the conduct of politics moves from the vil-

---

[36] See Ralph Retzlaff, *Village Government* (Bombay, 1962), for an extended examination of changes in village leadership and electoral behavior, including evidence of high cohesion among lower castes after the political control of dominant castes has been broken.

[37] Joan Menscher, comment in the course of discussion, Conference on Social Structure and Social Change, University of Chicago, June 3–6, 1965.

lage to the state capital, political perceptions, motives, and organizations become more differentiated, independent, and powerful.[38]

The relative significance of dominant and subject castes in the politics of particular states affects their patterns of political mobilization.[39] Both vertical mobilization by dominant castes and horizontal

[38] In Modasa assembly constituency of Gujarat, Rajni Kothari and Ghanshyam Shah found that "politics is the great leveller of social distances and dominance positions found in peasant society. . . . Baniyas, Patidars and Kshatriyas were indeed the significant categories of Modasa politics, but they operated not as traditional communal groups but as political groups, in the process passing over important social gradations or creating new ones" ("Caste Orientation of Political Factions: Modasa Constituency," in Weiner and Kothari [eds.], *Indian Voting Behaviour*, p. 161). And in Baroda East, a Gujarat urban assembly constituency, Kothari and Tarun Seth found that while "castes and communities constitute effective bases for political organization and mobilisation" they are split or united on political lines ("Extent and Limits of Community Voting: The Case of Baroda East," in Weiner and Kothari [eds.], *Indian Voting Behaviour*, p. 24).

Paul Brass's analysis of polling station data for the 1962 election in Aligarh assembly and parliamentary constituencies reveals massive community voting, but of a complex sort. Muslims voted as a community for what they believed to be their community's interest, but that did not necessarily lead them to support a Muslim. They supported a Muslim and a non-Muslim, identifying their community's interest with a political party. The successful Republican party Legislative Assembly candidate, a Muslim, Dr. Abdul Bashir Khan, "polled between 83.7 and 95.4 percent of the total vote in his ten best polling stations, which covered 26 *mohallas* (neighborhoods) in the town. The median percentage of Muslim residents in these *mohallas,* according to the 1951 census, was 89.6 percent. . . . In contrast, in the Aligarh town component of the Aligarh *parliamentary* constituency, the Congress candidate (Jarrar Haider, a Muslim) won a plurality of the votes in only 1 of 96 polling stations. The remaining 95 polling stations were divided between the winning Republican candidate (B. P. Maurya, a Chamar) and the Arya Samaj candidate (Shiv Kumar Shastri, a Hindu). Nine out of 10 of B. P. Maurya's best polling stations (between 81.8 and 95.2 per cent of the vote) were the same as the Republican [party's Muslim] candidate's best" (*Factional Politics in an Indian State: The Congress Party in Uttar Pradesh* [Berkeley, Calif., 1965], pp. 109–10, n. 47).

[39] The idea of a dominant caste has been used in village studies, notably by M. N. Srinivas but also by others. It refers to those castes that dominate particular villages or localities by virtue of their ritual rank, numbers, or economic power. See M. N. Srinivas, "The Dominant Caste in Rampura," *American Anthropologist,* LXI (February, 1959). We are more concerned with regional

mobilization by subject castes alter traditional power relationships, the first when the formality of consent through voting replaces obedience based on traditional authority and dependence, the second by enabling subject castes to be politically independent of their former masters.[40] In Andhra politics, for example, vertical mobilization by Reddis is a central feature.[41] A traditionally dominant landlord caste, they are also the state's largest caste, with 12 per cent of the population. In 1965, 28 per cent of the seats in the Andhra legislature and 40 per cent of the places in the Congress cabinet were held by Reddis. They also held the presidencies of the Congress, Communist, and Independent parties. In the 1967 election, they accounted for 25 per cent of all legislative assembly candidates. Reddi dominance of state politics is the result of local and regional dominance based on vertical mobilization by Reddi notables, not horizontal solidarity, mobilization, or formal organization.[42] The more enterprising and

---

dominance, which can express itself in a state context. For one discussion of regional dominance, see Adrian C. Mayer, "The Dominant Caste in a Region of Central India," *Southwestern Journal of Anthropology*, XIV (1958), 407–27.

[40] A fascinating account of the shift from vertical to horizontal mobilization at the village level and the role of the secret ballot in culminating a series of longer developments is Harold Gould's "The Incident of the Fish," in Robert Sakai (ed.), *Studies in Asia* (Lincoln, Neb., 1966). The account combines a sensitive humanism with social science. The attempt by some American Negro leaders to mobilize Negroes on a horizontal (race) basis in the summer of 1966 was defended precisely on the ground that only in this way could they be freed of dependence on white politics.

We have stressed the ties of deference and economic dependence in vertical mobilization. But physical coercion is also part of the pattern. Beteille, *Caste, Class and Power,* draws a vivid picture of a Kallan Panchayat president who uses "brief" methods to enforce his views. Cohn (p. 135, n. 12, below) and Rowe and Bailey (p. 32, n. 8, above) all document straight coercion.

[41] Our analysis in this paragraph draws on Carolyn Elliott's paper, "Caste and Faction in Andhra Pradesh." Her Harvard Ph.D. thesis, "Participation in an Expanding Polity: A Study of Andhra Pradesh" (Fall, 1967), provides additional materials.

[42] Except for a short while, and for mainly non-political purposes, when a Reddi caste association prosecuted educational activities after a state-wide meeting in 1923 (John Leonard, "Politics and Social Change in South India: A Study of the Andhra Movement" [typescript]). For the figure for the 1967 election, see *The Statesman* (Delhi), February 15, 1967.

able among them have concerted with others to form factional alliances capable of capturing power at the district and state levels. At the same time, the state's politics have been characterized by considerable fluidity as factional alliances have split and factions decomposed.

In Uttar Pradesh, too, the relative significance of dominant castes has produced a politics of vertical mobilization, faction and personalism, although in this state it has created higher levels of instability than it has in Andhra.[43] Local notables, still relatively free from the challenges that horizontal mobilization of caste, community, or class can mount, concert to form factions and factional alliances designed to control political systems ranging from Legislative Assembly constituencies to Pradesh Congress committees and state governments. Ahirs, Chamars, and possibly Kurmis (if they were able to mobilize horizontally) have a numerical potential to modify or upset this political pattern.[44] The Chamars in alliance with the Muslims, with the help of rebel Congressmen, have shown some sign of doing so; under the aegis of the Republican party, they succeeded in 1962 in electing B. P. Maurya to Parliament from an Aligarh constituency.[45] Outside U.P. but still in the Hindi heartland, developments in Haryana in 1967 after the general election suggested the potential influence of these castes when a Jat-Ahir-scheduled caste alliance resigned from Congress to form a new government under the leadership of Chief Minister Rao Birender Singh.[46] Similarly in Bihar, the influence of the powerful Ahir Congressman Lakhan Singh Yadav was critical in deciding the leadership of the Congress opposition after that election.[47]

[43] Brass, *Factional Politics in an Indian State: The Congress Party in Uttar Pradesh* (Berkeley, Calif., 1965).

[44] Schwartzberg, "The Distribution of Selected Castes in the North Indian Plain," pp. 482–83 (map). The Ahirs have from 5–20 per cent in a majority of U.P. districts, the Chamars 10–20 per cent, the Kurmis 2.5–10 per cent in about half the districts.

[45] For Chamar politics, see Lynch, "The Politics of Untouchability." Brass observes of the Chamar-Muslim alliance that "the maintenance of such an alliance is difficult to imagine" (*Factional Politics in an Indian State,* p. 110).

[46] *Link* (Delhi), IX (February 26, March 5 and 26, 1967).

[47] *Link* (Delhi), IX (March 12, 1967).

Madras politics, on the other hand, has been characteristically that of horizontal mobilization by subject castes. The state's traditionally dominant Brahman caste was early and successfully challenged by Sudra castes, prosperous, educated, and ambitious Vellalas, Mudaliars, Naidus, and Chettiars, who formed the Justice party in 1916.[48] Brahmans were too few (less than 3 per cent of the population), too isolated ritually and socially, and too fastidious to withstand this and subsequent attacks by Dravidian ideological movements on their religious, cultural, and political dominance. Recently, Andre Beteille found that even at the village level Brahmans were less effective than dominant non-Brahman castes at building and holding through vertical mobilization the political support of lower castes.[49]

Individual castes and state political systems are not necessarily characterized by only one pattern of mobilization, nor is vertical mobilization necessarily confined to dominant castes and horizontal mobilization to subject ones. Carolyn Elliott points out that in Andhra Reddi landed notables are prone to mobilize their interests vertically, whereas Reddi (and other) middle peasant castes are more likely to try to mobilize their caste fellows through horizontal appeals and structures.[50] In Rajasthan, Rajputs, who had ruled the state as princes and jagirdars before independence, developed, in the early 1950's, considerable horizontal solidarity and organizational capability in the face of proposed land reforms and the desire to return to power under democratic auspices. The Jats, a large, prosperous peasant caste of Rajasthan, organized horizontally to challenge and counter Rajput dominance even while mobilizing their dependents through vertical means in localities where they were dominant.

At the level of state political systems, the effectiveness of castes as political actors depends upon a variety of internal and external conditions. Internally, critical variables include the number and geographic distribution of caste members available for politicization and

[48] Irschick, "Politics and Social Change in South India."

[49] Beteille, *Caste, Class and Power,* p. 167.

[50] Elliott, "Caste and Faction in Andhra Pradesh," p. 8.

mobilization; levels of political consciousness, literacy and cohesiveness at particular historical periods; the effectiveness of available leadership; and relative ritual rank, social status, and economic independence. Externally, they include the number and power of countervailing interest-group forces; the effectiveness and reach of party organization and leadership; the effectiveness with which local notables of dominant castes are able to mobilize their interests and to concert with others at the state level; the degree to which the size of a state and regional differences within it facilitate or inhibit communication, organization, and the growth of common consciousness and purpose.

Thus, in Rajasthan, formerly part of princely India, the early and persistent political influence of the Jats, the state's largest caste, with 9 per cent of the population, may be explained by the particular constellation of these factors.[51] After the 1962 general election, 13 per cent of the seats in the Rajasthan Legislative Assembly were held by Jats, the politically influential Speaker of the Assembly was a Jat, and two of the cabinet's most powerful members were drawn from Jat ranks. Jats are not only numerous but also relatively highly politicized. They were the first caste in the state to organize caste associations for purposes of self-help, mobility, and interest representation and have not as yet lost the advantage they gained as "first-comers" over those now benefitting from their example and techniques. Rajasthan remains a relatively backward state socially and economically, despite its rapid rate of economic development. As a result, Jat interests do not yet confront the powerful countervailing interest-group forces that are likely to arise in the not too distant future. Because some sections of the caste were prosperous peasants, Jat notables, particularly after land reform had reduced local Rajput influence, have been able to reap the political advantages of vertical mobilization. That numbers alone do not suffice in winning political influence and power is evidenced by contrasting the Jats' situation with that of Rajasthan's Chamars. Almost as numerous as the Jats, their poverty, subjection, low levels of political consciousness and

[51] See Rudolph and Rudolph, "From Princes to Politicians," for a more detailed treatment of Rajasthan politics, including the role of caste associations.

organization, and paucity of effective leaders have inhibited the realization of political power inherent in their numbers.

Although the Jats are the most numerous and best mobilized caste in Rajasthan politics, internal cleavages, countervailing interest-group forces, and the capacity of party politics to assimilate and constrain assertions of caste political identity and power have prevented them from gaining that measure of political ascendency over public life that the Rajputs held under princely rule. Region and personality coincide to divide the politically advanced sections of the caste into competing factions. So, too, do generational differences; when these have coincided with class differences, internal cleavages have not been easily susceptible to repair by appeals to community interest or sentiment. The most formidable of the countervailing forces opposing the growth of Jat power is the Rajput interest. At its head stand former maharajas and jagirdars to whose command of regional and local support have been added the organizational and ideological capabilities of modern politics and the glamor that royalty and nobility can evoke in the mundane world of competitive democratic politics. Rajputs, however, are also divided by class, region, and personality. It is these divisions that have provided grist for the mill of party appeals.[52] Before the 1967 general election, the most severe challenge to governmental stability in Rajasthan, whose Congress chief minister has held office the longest of any in India, came from a political faction within the governing party led by a Jat and a Rajput former maharaja. These developments reflect not only the growing differentiation of caste communities on class and interest lines and the ways such differences can unite members of various castes but also the growing independence of politics. Political commitments and loyalties, political rewards and sanctions, are not merely the building blocks of faction; they are also the means through which parties can fraction, combine, and assimilate caste identities and lead them toward the more general goals of a political community.[53]

[52] See *ibid.*, for a detailed discussion of these factors.

[53] *Ibid.* will provide a more comprehensive and detailed analysis of the course of political development in Rajasthan.

Differential Mobilization:
Fission, Fusion, and Decompression

Membership in a caste association is based both on birth and on choice: one must be born into a particular jati to qualify, but one must then choose to identify oneself with the association. The ascriptive element strongly suggests that there is a natural limit to the paracommunity's capacity to approximate a voluntary association. It can be argued that however far it may lead those who identify with it from the narrow confines of the traditional face-to-face community it cannot lead them beyond ascriptive boundaries. The individual can never be fully free to define himself, to make his own destiny, nor can he, as a result, act politically in ways that are untainted by primordial group parochialism and selfishness.

Recent developments challenge this view. Ascription may not be so immutable; for India the choice may not be confined to having a society with or without some form of caste sentiment and structure. To be born with a social identity whose boundaries, norms, and culture are changing suggests that ascription is mutable. The changes that caste has and is undergoing are carrying it beyond traditional ascriptive definitions. These changes include internal differentiation (fission) and the operation of integrative institutions upon it; federation of castes (fusion) into larger associations that express shared interests, symbols, and norms; and decompression of caste's village home.

These processes of change are illustrated by the Vanniyars of Madras. In 1952, as the largest single caste in Madras, they capped a history of internal reform and organizational modernization by contesting with considerable success the first general election under the banner of two caste parties, the Tamilnad Toilers (TNT) and the Commonweal party; the first was strongest in South Arcot although reaching into Salem and Tiruchirapalli, the second in North Arcot. By 1957, the Vanniyars seemed to have perfected the technique of caste representation. Solidly entrenched in Kamaraj's Congress party, they were nominated in large numbers and helped it gain an impressive victory in the 1957 general elections. In the process of establishing themselves in the governing Congress party, however, they had given up something: their political autonomy in caste parties. At the same time they retained within the Congress a visible level of cohesion and common purpose.

By 1962, radical changes in the Vanniyar's social and political circumstances had taken place. Internal differentiation along economic, cultural, and social lines and rivalry among the community's leaders were articulated and mobilized from without by political parties competing for Vanniyar support. The result shattered Vanniyar corporate power. After having been subsumed by Congress, a voluntary and integrative institution, Vanniyar solidarity began to dissolve in the current of party competition.

This effect is most sharply etched in South Arcot District, over half of whose 2.5 million people are Vanniyars and where the TNT in 1952 captured thirteen of the district's nineteen legislative Assembly seats.[1] The first crack in Vanniyar solidarity appeared in 1954, when that party's chief led his followers into Kamaraj Nadar's government and became a minister. A splinter TNT group under A. Govindaswami, MLA, opposed the merger and joined the leading opposition party, the DMK (Dravida Munnetra Kazhagam [Dravidian Progressive Federation]).

In 1957, when the Congress party gave tickets to (nominated) former TNT members in preference to old-time Congressmen, K. S. Venkatakrishna Reddiar, along with other higher-caste landowning notables from his own caste (Reddiar) and the Naidu, Vellala, and Mudaliar castes and with the support of dissident or still dependent sections of the Vanniyars, helped form the Congress Reform Committee (CRC; later the Indian National Democratic Congress, INDC). Despite the fact that the leadership of the CRC was drawn from castes that had been and in some measure still were the masters and sometimes the oppressors and exploiters of their Vanniyar ten-

[1] *Express* (Chittoor) March 7, 1962. We should like to acknowledge the very helpful, extensive, and detailed articles of the *Express'* special correspondent, Mr. M. Mohan Ram, on the 1962 election in North Arcot, Salem, Tiruchirapalli, Tanjore, and South Arcot districts, upon which much of the analysis below is based (see the *Express* (Chittoor) for March 7, 15, 17, 20, and 21, 1962).

ants and laborers, the party was able to rally considerable numbers to its cause and gain a modest electoral success. By 1962, however, the CRC, now the INDC, had evaporated, some members having made their peace with the Congress, others having joined the DMK or the Swatantra party. In 1960, a year after the Swatantra party was created, S. S. Ramaswami Padayachi, the creator and leader of the TNT, began to move in its direction; by 1961, he had joined it and become its head in South Arcot District.

The once monolithic Vanniyar political front was divided at the time of the 1962 general elections into three contending groups—one supporting the Congress under Srinivasa Padayachi; the second owing allegiance to the DMK, led by Govindaswami; and the third under Swatantra influence, loyal to Ramaswami Padayachi.[2] All three major parties in South Arcot District were now under Vanniyar leadership. In the elections for the district's fifteen non-reserved seats (four seats were reserved for scheduled caste candidates), thirteen were won by Vanniyars, eight as Congress and five as DMK candidates. S. S. Ramaswami Padayachi and a number of other Swatantra candidates lost, however, some by close margins.

The 1967 elections witnessed the complete collapse of the Vanniyar community's capacity to operate as a political party. Padayachi revived the Taminad Toilers party in anticipation of the election, but his efforts to enter the United Front organized by the DMK and Swatantra were rejected by DMK leaders on the ground that they already had the support of the community and gave it adequate representation.[3] An influential and knowledgeable member of the community estimated that Vanniyars won sixteen to eighteen of the DMK's one hundred thirty-eight seats and six to eight of the forty-nine Congress seats in the state legislature, at least 10 per cent of the Legislative Assembly seats.

The external boundaries of the Vanniyar community began to collapse as pressure from outside became stronger than pressure from within. The internal forces generated by shared community interest and sentiment and guided by political calculation and organization

[2] *Express* (Chittoor), March 21, 1962.

[3] *Hindu* (Madras), October 11, 1966, and interviews with Vanniyar and DMK notables in February, 1967.

were weakened by differentiation along class and ideological lines. Political parties mobilized those emergent differences in their efforts to aggregate and integrate electoral and interest-group support. The result vitiated the community's solidarity and political power by further weakening caste's ascriptive hold on social identity and behavior. By freeing Vanniyars from the constraints of caste, differentiation enabled them to approach in their norms and conduct the more universal and functionally specific characteristic associated with models of modern society and democratic politics.

The effects of differentiation are also visible among the Rajputs of Rajasthan. Before independence, Rajputs were the rulers, feudal lords, and court retainers of princely states and jagirdari estates. Their caste association, the Kshatriya Mahasabha, spoke initially for all ranks within the community. The formation in 1954 of a new caste association, the Bhooswami Sangh, brought into the open the conflict between the "small" Rajputs, whose modest landholdings had to be supplemented by income from service under princes or jagirdars, and the jagirdars, who had dismissed most of them from service with the advent of land reform.[4] When it became apparent in the course of the negotiations and bargaining over land reform that the Rajput magnates were not prepared to use the Kshatriya Mahasabha to protect the interests of small Rajputs, the Bhooswami Sangh took up the task of doing so. Political parties were quick to capitalize on these class and ideological differences within the Rajput community. Rajput magnates opposed the Congress "revolution" in the first general election of 1952 by identifying with the reactionary Ram Rajya Parishad and the politically active Maharaja of Jodhpur or standing as independents. When the Congress government, after very nearly losing the election to the Rajput-led opposition, met some of the "large" Rajput demands in framing land reform legislation, many crossed the aisle. Later, following the 1957 general election and the formation of the conservative Swatantra party in 1959, those who felt their influence in the Congress to be incommensurate with their political strength joined or supported the new party. Small Rajputs tended to identify with the Jan Sangh.

[4] Rudolph and Rudolph, "The Political Modernization of an Indian Feudal Order: An Analysis of Rajput Adaptation in Rajasthan," *Journal of Social Issues* (forthcoming), MS pp. 21 ff.

Its Hindu revivalism, nationalism, and defense of small-scale property interests spoke to those who wished to defend their precarious respectability and economic position from the inroads of a bureaucratized and secular society and state.

By 1967, and prior to the general election of that year, community differentiation led to the defection from Congress of a section of the Rajputs under Maharaja Harishchandra of Jhalawar together with a section of the peasant Jats under Kumbha Ram Arya. They joined together to oppose the Congress (in alliance with the Swatantra and Jan Sangh parties) in part as a maneuver to enhance their political power, in part in defense of landed interest, a common concern sufficiently compelling to override traditional community antagonisms.

The distribution of Rajput legislators among the parties summarizes the degree of differentiation: In 1952, Rajputs held 37 per cent of the seats in the Rajasthan Assembly. All of them were concentrated in the reactionary or conservative parties, that is, independents, Ram Rajya Parishad, Jan Sangh, Swatantra (after 1959), and Hindu Mahasabha. In 1957 and 1962, Rajputs declined to 15 per cent of all legislators and were increasingly distributed over the political spectrum: 9 per cent were Congressmen in 1957 and 12 per cent in 1962; at the same time Rajput percentages in reactionary or conservative parties fell from 84 in 1952 to 48 in 1957 to 22 in 1962.[5]

Differentiation has also affected the Nadar community. Since independence the political orientation of the Nadar Mahajana Sangam, its leading caste association, has become more specialized and less partisan. The sangam's executive council in 1957 voted down, just before the general elections, a motion that the association commit itself to supporting Nadar candidates. What had come naturally to earlier generations was rejected in favor of a policy that called upon Nadars to vote as individuals and the sangam to refrain from identifying itself with any community or political party.

Class interest and ideology have led Nadar businessmen and professionals to support the conservative Swatantra party and Nadar industrial workers to support the "revolutionary" Communist party.

[5] Rudolph and Rudolph, "From Princes to Politicians" (forthcoming).

92

Young Nadars, particularly students, and some among the older generations, particularly the more militant former Justicites who do not support the Dravida Kazhagam have been attracted by the anti-Brahmanism, Dravidian cultural revivalism, and regional nationalism of the Dravida Munnetra Kazhagam (DMK).[6]

The Nadar establishment remained, on the whole, pro-Congress. Its commercial interests pointed in the direction of having good relations with government, whatever its complexion. Congress ideology, programs, and command of resources gave it an electoral advantage and made it easier to mobilize interest-group support. Whether the Nadars' affinity for Congress will persist after the party's defeat by the DMK in Madras in 1967 only time can tell. Most Nadars found it difficult to forget that the Congress was the party of Kamaraj Nadar, the community's most illustrious son.[7] When Kamaraj fell victim to the DMK sweep in Madras—a result to which the Nadars of his home town, Virudhanagar, may have contributed —his political influence in Madras and the country at large was diminished but not destroyed.[8] Under his leadership Congress mobilized the community from below by its appeals to the poor and disadvantaged as well as from above by the implicit attraction of shared community identity. And Kamaraj's informal alliance with E. V. Ramaswami Naicker's anti-Brahman, Dravidian-fundamentalist Dravida Kazhagam (DK) has attracted support from those at all levels who are susceptible to such appeals.

Caste sentiment and interest continue to shape in varying degrees and ways Nadar political behavior and organization. In areas such as Tirunelveli District, where Nadars are the most numerous caste in several Legislative Assembly constituencies and, generally, have supported the Congress party, political differences tend to be expressed

---

[6] Robert L. Hardgrave, Jr., "Varieties of Political Behavior among Nadars of Tamilnad" (University of Chicago, April, 1966 [mimeographed]), p. 6; Myron Weiner, "Madurai," in *Party Building in a New Nation* (Chicago, 1967), p. 420.

[7] Although his commitment to Congress at an early age aroused at that time the enmity of his caste fellows and although he never relied upon or directly courted Nadar support, his power and fame have attracted such support.

[8] For an analysis of this campaign, see *Home Rule* (Madras), March 19, 1967.

through Nadar-led or -dominated factions. Nevertheless intraparty factional differences have made inroads into Nadar political dominance by extending across community boundaries. For example, the Maravan speaker of the Madras Assembly, with Kamaraj's backing and the support of one Nadar faction, wrested control of the Tirunelveli District Congress Committee and the important Tiruchendur Taluk Committee from a second Nadar faction, led by an ambitious and powerful Nadar who had challenged Kamaraj's authority at the state level.[9] In Ramnad District, where Nadars are typically in a minority within Legislative Assembly constituencies, the caste has remained relatively cohesive politically, aligning itself with the party controlled by that faction of the more numerous Maravans most likely to support its interests. This has meant, ironically, that it has for over a generation supported the descendants of the Nadars' opponent in the Kamudi temple case, the late Raja of Ramnad.[10]

In the more urban, commercial, and industrial setting of the city of Madurai, Nadar electoral behavior at the Legislative Assembly level and above is more influenced by class, economic interest, and ideology than in Tirunelveli and Ramnad districts. However in municipal elections, Nadar candidates are nominated by all parties contesting in the two city wards where Nadars are concentrated. And at the parliamentary constituency level, non-Communist Nadar

[9] In 1963, Kamaraj successfully intervened against Nadar district leader Kosalram. Kosalram had directly challenged Kamaraj's authority by attempting to have a factional colleague elected president of the Madras Congress Committee. Kamaraj supported a factional ally of Kosalram's rival, the Maravan speaker of the Madras Assembly. In 1965, an ally of the speaker was elected head of the Tiruchendur Taluk Committee, Kosalram's home organization (Hardgrave, "Varieties of Political Behavior among Nadars . . . ," p. 8).

[10] In Ramnad constituency, which includes Kamudi, the leader of the dominant Maravan faction, until his death in 1964, was Mathuralinga Thevar. The late Raja of Ramnad led the minority faction. In a constituency in which candidates of all parties are typically Maravans, Nadars have backed the Maravan candidates sponsored by the Raja of Ramnad. Before independence, he and the Nadars supported the Justice party against the Thevar-backed Maravan candidates of the Congress party. In 1947, Thevar shifted to the Boseist Forward Block and the Nadars, following the lead of the Raja of Ramnad, changed their allegiance to the Congress. In 1964, after Mathuralinga's death, a Congress-backed Maravan candidate, with Nadar support, won the by-election to fill his vacant seat (*ibid.*, p. 9).

94

voters helped elect an able Nadar Communist party candidate in the 1957 general election rather than support a weak, non-Nadar Congress candidate.[11] Madras' cosmopolitan, highly differentiated setting makes it difficult to trace specifically caste patterns of electoral behavior at the state level and above. But here, too, as in Madurai, in the smaller, more intimate setting of municipal corporation ward politics, community representativeness and interest remain highly salient.[12]

Generally, the pattern of differential mobilization for electoral behavior varies with the quality of issues, candidates, and party organizations in particular settings and at particular times. The smaller the political system, and the more homogeneous its social components, the more likely it is that caste considerations will loom large. Whether Nadars are a plurality or a minority—and if a minority, whether they are a large and cohesive minority—affects, at one and the same time, political strategy and tactics and the saliency of caste for electoral behavior.

Nadars participate in politics indirectly through representational processes as well as directly through elections. In the face of internal differentiation and elongation of the community on a socioeconomic continuum, its principal caste association, the Nadar Mahajana Sangam, has increasingly adopted a non-partisan strategy in the representation of the community's less diffuse, more specialized interests. Political parties, endeavoring to represent and aggregate group interests, have found in the community and its leaders sources of ideas and support even as the community, gradually gaining in wealth, status, and power has turned inward for programs, resources, and administrative means to serve its needs.

The sangam has represented the interest of the community to government with respect to the welfare of the palmyra palm climbers, or toddy tappers, and access to educational opportunities. After independence, it opposed the tax imposed on palmyra palms in Tirunelveli and Ramnad districts. When prohibition legislation in 1948 threatened to displace not only those who manufactured hard

[11] *Ibid.*, p. 10.

[12] We do not have for the city of Madras the kind of detailed polling station data Paul Brass assembled for Aligarh.

toddy but also those who produced sweet toddy and jaggery, it fought successfully to ease the regulations so that the latter would not be left without a means of livelihood. And it fought successfully over a ten-year period to qualify the less advanced sections of the Nadar community for places and scholarships for backward classes established under the aegis of the post-independence Backward Classes Commission.[13]

The sangam and the community as a whole have made their greatest and most determined effort in the field of education. From 1889, when the sangam founded its first school, it has used *mahimai* funds and has raised other sums to insure that through them and the additional state aid they generate educational opportunities would be available. Substantial allocations have been made to educational loans and scholarships.[14] In 1947, the first Nadar college was founded. Since then the community has established two additional colleges, including one for women, and founded a polytechnic. The sangam also supports reading rooms and libraries.

The sangam also plays an entrepreneurial role, actively supporting the commercial and industrial life of the community through local financial institutions and the Nadar, now Tamilnad, National Bank.[15] It also keeps nine agents in the field. They approach Nadars who are outside the fold and organize them into either local *uravinmurai* or sangam branches. Participation in such a group makes it possible for the backward and less self-conscious Nadars to help

[13] Hardgrave, "Organization and Change among the Nadars of Tamilnad," (Madurai, 1965 [mimeographed]), p. 28.

[14] Hardgrave reports, on the basis of the Report of the Nadar Mahajana Sangam, Fifty-fifth Annual Meeting, Coimbatore, that between 1921 and 1964, 3,024 students received Rs. 400,000 worth of scholarships ("Organization and Change among the Nadars . . . ," p. 29).

[15] Although Hardgrave has opened up the subject of the role of caste associations in economic development in his analysis of the various ways the local *uravinmurai* and the Nadar Mahajana Sangam have served the economic life of the community, this fertile field of study remains relatively untouched. Economists and other social scientists might well study enterprising commercial communities such as the Nadars (note that Nadars *became* a modern commercial and industrial community) to understand the nature of the entrepreneurial character and the sources, past, present, and future, of economic innovation and capital investment.

themselves by raising *mahimai* funds and qualifies them for a variety of services from the parent organization. Services include access to education, business loans, advice and assistance in local disputes with other communities, and arbitration of internal disputes.

Having passed through ideological phases stressing Sanskritization and anti-Brahmanical de-Sanskritization, the community now teaches the equality of all castes. The sangam's self-image is that of a community, not a communal, organization. In 1952 it disavowed the creation of "caste feeling" even while affirming that it meant to raise "the Nadar community and the country along with it."[16] At its annual meeting in 1964 it resolved "to have cordial relations with other communities"; the Nadar community ought to allow other communities to use the schools, tanks (artificial ponds), temples, and wells started or established by Nadars.[17]

The Nadars have, over one hundred thirty years, learned to associate for self-improvement and social mobility; to mobilize for politics through horizontal appeals to caste fellows; and after experiencing a dilution of caste identity and a narrowing of common interests, to pursue what remains of each through electoral, representational, and self-governmental processes. Under such circumstances caste retains a diminished but persistent saliency for partisan politics and considerable vigor in the non-partisan representation of community interests.

The consequences of differentiation for Vanniyars, Rajputs, and Nadars suggest a paradox: the establishment of political democracy and competitive partisan politics helped to reinvigorate caste by giving it new functions and structures. Yet it is political parties that weaken caste organizations by articulating and mobilizing divisions within them and by translating these divisions into extracaste norms and structures. It is in this sense that modern politics appears to be an instrument for both the revival and the supersession of traditional society. It seems likely that this paradoxical situation will persist rather than be resolved: the need for mediating collectivities and

[16] *Nadar Mahajana Sangam: 42 Years of Service* (Madurai, 1952), as cited by Hardgrave, in *ibid.*, p. 33.

[17] *Report of the Nadar Mahajana Sangam, 55th Annual Meeting,* Coimbatore, May 31, 1964, as cited and translated from Tamil by Hardgrave, in *ibid.*, p. 33.

adaptive structures based on birth and integrated by primary group sentiment and interest transcends the imperatives of modernity in politics and society not only in India but also in advanced industrial nations.[18] In so far as this is so, caste identities and structures retain a future.

The ascriptive and particularistic qualities of paracommunities based on caste are being affected by higher levels of integration (fusion) as well as by differentiation (fission). A recent federation of three castes provides an example. Although folklore suggests a relationship among the Kallan, Maravar, and Agamudiar castes of central and southern Madras, they have been defined and separated historically by ritual rank, social distance, and endogamy.[19] Recently their caste associations and leaders, under the influence of the continuing dialogue between democratic institutions and processes and those of traditional society, have begun to create new and larger forms of consciousness, organization, and action.[20] Experience in the Madras Legislative Assembly, the lessons of party and electoral politics, a growing sense of common purpose, and the importance of

[18] See also Harold Gould's "The Adaptive Functions of Caste in Contemporary Indian Society," *Asian Survey*, III (September, 1963).

[19] For the Parumali-nadu Kallans, see Dumont's *Une Sous-Caste de L'Inde du Sud: Organisation Sociale et Religieuse des Pramalai Kallar* (Paris, 1957). Edgar Thurston's *Castes and Tribes of Southern India* (Madras, 1909) contains information about the Kallans (III, 53–91), the Maravans (V, 22–48), and the Agamudiars (I, 5–16). The link among these castes is older than the present beginnings of political federation. They share common mythological ancestors (see Thurston, *Castes and Tribes of Southern India,* I, 7, for two versions of the Agamudiar creation myth) and a common mobility pattern in traditional society. "There is a Tamil proverb," Thurston writes, "to the effect that a Kallan may become a Maravan. By respectability he may develop into a Agamudiyan, and, by slow degrees, become a Vellala, from which he may rise to be a Mudaliar" (I, 7). Vellalas and Mudaliars are traditionally ranked above Agamudiars.

[20] W. H. Morris-Jones' analyses of the "languages of politics" and the "dialogue" between government and political forces have been helpful for the formulation and statement of the argument here. See his *The Government and Politics of India,* Chap. 2, "Politics and Society," and Chap. 6, "The Ordering Framework," for these two ideas.

numbers for realizing political objectives contributed to this result.[21] The three castes have styled themselves "Mukkulator" (literally, "three castes") and have begun to represent themselves in terms of this common name; the organization and leadership that brought the association into being contribute to its growing importance and strength. The bases of Mukkulator social and political identity remain ascriptive social and cultural communities within specific geographic locations, but just as the caste association attenuated the importance of these factors by upgrading and extending the jati, so this federation of caste associations has further attenuated their importance by the addition of choice. Paracommunities may be placed along a continuum. The self and public definitions of the Mukkulators and their organization and political role approach even more closely than those of the caste association the qualities, form, and functions of voluntary associations with political objectives. By further blurring the line between natural and voluntary association and ascription and choice, the caste federation seems to break down the dichotomy between tradition and modernity. What appeared to be an absolute division in theory if not in practice between traditional and modern society has become, in the Indian context, increasingly relative. At the theoretical level, a continuum that bridges the two rather than a dichotomy may be a more appropriate characterization of both the practical and the theoretical issues involved.

Two recent studies of a caste federation in Kaira District, Gujarat, by Rajni Kothari and R. M. Maru and by Myron Weiner, confirm and deepen these observations.[22] The Kshatriya Sabha of Gujarat includes a more diverse range of communities than the federation of Mukkulators: a marginal peasant and landless laborer caste (Bariyas) and a depressed tribal community (Bhils) have combined under the leadership of twice-born Rajputs. The *sabha* has artic-

[21] The discussion below is based in part on an interview with T. Ramachandran, M.L.A., chief whip of the Congress party in the Madras Assembly. He is in no way responsible for the judgments found in the analysis.

[22] Rajni Kothari and R. M. Maru, "Caste and Secularism in India," *Journal of Asian Studies*, XXV (November, 1965); Myron Weiner, "Segmentation and Political Participation: Kaira District," in *Party Building in a New Nation* (Chicago, 1967).

ulated their "common economic interests and a growing secular identity born partly out of past folklore but more out of a common resentment against well-to-do castes. . . ."[23] Over time, the *sabha* has helped the lower communities to become Kshatriyas in their own and, increasingly, society's eyes.

The Kshatriya Sabha's socially and politically democratic character can be explained, Kothari and Maru argue, by the motivation that lay behind its formation. Caste consciousness played a part, but not for the purpose of preserving caste traditions and customs but rather of transforming them through political power.[24] It is this transformation, including its effect on consciousness, that the authors call "secularization." They relate it to Sanskritization (emulation of high caste norms and practice) of lower castes and modernization (social reform and ideological change) of higher. Both low and high castes can agree on social leveling and articulation of group purposes, the first to improve, the second to preserve, their status through political action.[25] Political considerations fuse them together. The higher castes need numerical strength to sustain their power and status; the lower need access to resources and opportunities that support of the higher can yield. Lower castes may agree to be led and even governed by higher castes, but their agreement to do so is "increasingly conditioned by norms of accountability and notions of interest and right."[26]

The federation's use of traditional Kshatriya symbolism and culture has united members of these diverse ascriptive communities into a voluntary association. By doing so, it has dramatically portrayed how secularization replaces ritual with achievement norms and structures. "Many people ask me who was a Rajput [Kshatriya varna]. I told them a Rajput was one who was willing to serve and die for his country. . . . It is not a question of blood but of spirit and action," said one of the leaders of the *sabha*.[27] "The Kshatriyas are a class, not a caste,"[28] said another. "We say," adds one of the group's

[23] Kothari and Maru, "Caste and Secularism in India," p. 35.

[24] *Ibid.*, p. 130.

[25] *Ibid.*, pp. 35–36.   [26] *Ibid.*, p. 49.

[27] Weiner, *Party Building in a New Nation,* pp. 96 and 99.

[28] *Ibid.*, p. 97.

Rajput leaders, "that if the Bhils [tribal people] are brave enough we will call them Kshatriyas."[29] This social development from caste (and tribe) to varna to class transforms ascriptive ritual rank from a relatively closed to a relatively open status category: members of a variety of ascriptive communities (although only certain ones are eligible) may choose to identify with and participate in the Kshatriya Sabha. Nor is the transformation of status merely rhetorical: within the *sabha,* Bariyas now sit on charpoys (rope beds) on an equal level with Rajputs, whereas previously they had symbolized their ascribed status difference by sitting on the ground.[30] And the *sabha* uses its collective electoral strength to further the interests of all its members by bargaining with the parties for access to political power and the governmental allocation of resources.[31]

The Kshatriya Sabha is located even farther than the Mukkulator federation along that continuum that links natural to voluntary associations and modernity to tradition.

Decompression too has altered the traditional meaning of caste for the lives and fortunes of village Indians. Accompanying the fission and fusion of differentiation and federation has been a dilution and diffusion of affective and structural bonds. As the block and district headquarters, the extravillage enterprise and the market town, the local school, cinema, and radio set, have become increasingly relevant for village lives, they have created alternative environments for profit, prestige, and self-esteem. By enlarging the reach of empathy, broadening horizons, and multiplying reference groups, they have helped to deparochialize the intimate and closed world of the village. New opportunities, sentiments, and ideas have reduced and dispersed the

---

[29] *Ibid.*, p. 99.

[30] *Ibid.*, p. 100.

[31] When the Congress failed to provide adequate recognition to *sabha* demands it shifted its support to the Swatantra party, helping to elect that party's general secretary, Minoo Masani in a prestige by-election in 1963. Recently, in anticipation of the 1967 general elections, its leader, Narendra Singh Mahida, withdrew his support from Swatantra in what appears to be a move to enhance the *sabha*'s bargaining position (see *ibid.*, Chap. 4, and *Link* (Delhi), November 7, 1965).

concentration of affect, power, and economic dependence at the local level.[32]

By pursuing the goals of social mobility, self-help, and political power, caste associations and federations have played a major role in the decompression of village life. Reaching out toward state and national legislative constituencies, community development blocks and *panchayat samitis,* state secretariats and assemblies, and even the government in Delhi and the politics of the nation has educated and elevated caste consciousness. In attempting to share power and shape decisions in such contexts caste structure and norms have broadened. If the pursuit of political power has engaged the ambition of those enveloped in village and caste parochialism, it has also aroused their imaginations, led them to larger and more inclusive identities, and placed them in contexts of action that are structurally more specific but affectively less intense. The drift of power, profit, and honor away from the locality is not likely to make Indian villages into bedroom suburbs, but it is breaking their ancient monopoly on all aspects of life.

There is an increasing indeterminacy in the boundaries separating ascriptive and voluntary, parochial and cosmopolitan, traditional

[32] The caste association can be viewed as both an independent and dependent variable in the process of decompression and deparochialization. A few studies that highlight these processes are those by F. G. Bailey, who describes how the extension of the economic and political frontier (by which he means primarily the state administration) has liberated several castes, particularly the Boad Outcastes, from the social, cultural, and governmental authority of the village of Bisipara (*Caste and the Economic Frontier* [Manchester, 1957]); T. Scarlett Epstein, who shows how in the "dry" village of Dalena (but not in the wet one of Wangala) in Mysore radical economic change led to its integration into the regional economy, undermined the principle on which its society was organized (p. 325), and replaced ritual with economic aspects of prestige (p. 334) (*Economic Development and Social Change in South India* [Manchester, 1964]); and William L. Rowe, who has shown how the Noniyas, an aggressively upward mobile caste of Senapur, loosened the hold of the village's dominant caste by building a school with tiles purchased outright from a potter's village adjacent to Banaras twenty-five miles away ("Changing Rural Class Structure and the Jajmani System," *Human Organization,* XXII [Spring, 1963]). For the concept of empathy, its role in modernization, and its relation to communication, see Daniel Lerner, *Modernizing the Middle East: The Passing of Traditional Society* (Glencoe, Ill., 1958), particularly Chaps. 1 and 2.

and modern. Caste is losing the functions, norms, and structure once associated with it and acquiring new ones. It is serving the ritual and occupational goals of traditional society less, the mobility and participation goals of modern society more.[33] In doing so, it helps to substitute in the lives of ordinary Indians choice for birth, equality for hierarchy, and opportunity for fate.

The Future of Equality: The Social Conditions of Political Integration

---

Changes in the culture, structure, and public functions of caste are necessary but not sufficient conditions for its democratic incarnation. A profound change in the nature of human sensibility is also required. The universalization of power that accompanied the imposition from above of political democracy must be paralleled in some measure by another characteristic of modernity, the universalization of fellow feeling. Traditional society patterns the emotional universe narrowly, confining the range of permissible affect to the primary group and territorial community, whereas modern society extends the boundaries of the emotional universe beyond the locality to nation and mankind.[1] Tocqueville found that "real sympathy can exist only between those who are alike, and in aristocratic ages men

---

[33] For an excellent sociological discussion of the role of caste in modern society, see Doris Leventhal, "A Parsonian Approach to the Analysis of Change in the Indian Caste System" (Senior honors thesis, Department of Social Relations, Harvard University, 1961). The thesis, which accepts the dichotomy between traditional and modern society more than we are inclined to do, comes to somewhat different conclusions. In his article, "Resiliency and Change in the Indian Caste System: the Umar of U.P.," *Journal of Asian Studies,* XXVI (August, 1967), Richard G. Fox found that the local jatis and their regulatory structures (panchayats) were defunct but that the Umar caste association, a more modern structure, was active and effective (pp. 580–86).

[1] For a suggestive essay on the patterning of affect, see Hilda Geertz, "The Vocabulary of Emotion," *Psychiatry,* XXII (August, 1959).

acknowledge none but the members of their own caste to be like themselves." But "when all the ranks of a community are nearly equal, as all men think and feel in nearly the same manner, each of them may judge in a moment of the sensations of all the others; he casts a rapid glance upon himself and that is enough."[2] The change from aristocratic to democratic sensibilities confronts severe moral and structural difficulties in a country like India where men have been profoundly separated from one another by traditional social arrangements. "The survival of the caste system," Edward Shils writes, "cuts human beings off from each other. It inhibits the growth of sensibilities which are required for the perception of the moral quality of other human beings. . . . It is the caste system which helps deaden the imagination to the state of mind of other human beings."[3]

Because fellow feeling helps men to share perceptions, "rationality," symbols, and a sense of common destiny, it contributes substantially to the creation of the bonds that unite citizens in a nation. In India political democracy, the moral equality and structural unity of universal citizenship, was established in official ideology and constitutional arrangements before fellow feeling became a widely felt reality. Of course political democracy has helped to foster fellow feeling, as have a variety of forces and processes to be discussed below. Whether or not they will continue to provide that minimal level of affective support essential for the survival of the democratic state and the incipient democratic society remains for the future to say. Here we analyze and assess the contributions of the diffusion of power, the increasing homogeneity of culture wrought by the expansion of ascriptive boundaries, the downward spread of the culture of the twice-born varnas, and the effects of Westernization and secularization. After doing so we turn to an examination of the most severe test for the future of fellow feeling in India, the 15 per cent of the population known by the administrative euphemism, the scheduled castes.

[2] Alexis de Tocqueville, *Democracy in America* (Anchor ed.), II, 173, 175–76.

[3] Edward Shils, *The Intellectual between Tradition and Modernity: The Indian Case* (The Hague, 1961), p. 70.

The spread of political power to lower, more numerous castes, which we have discussed at length above, has had important effects on human perceptions and relationships. The redistribution of wealth and the shifts in the command of productive resources that accompany as well as occur independently of these changes are of great importance, too, in the creation of the new sensibility. We are primarily concerned here, however, with the association between spread of fellow feeling and the growing equality in the access to and use of political power.

Our interviews with former princes and noblemen of Rajasthan in 1956, 1963 and 1967 captured the dynamics of this process. These men were Rajputs, the warrior-ruler caste whose social and economic domination of Rajasthan's princely states invested them with that sense of superiority which birth, honor, privilege, and wealth inspire. In 1956 our Rajput informants normally could give only the names, and sometimes not even the names, of their opponents in the first general election of 1952. Their best efforts at description produced such faceless phrases as a "no-account man" or, for those who had the benefit of an education at an English-style public school, "some scallywag." Two general elections later, in 1963, their electoral opponents, sometimes the same men who had stood against them in 1952, had taken on names, faces, and distinctive qualities. We were now told, for example, that "he was a Jat who served in the army. When he came back to his village he started to tell his kinsmen (caste fellows) that their children should have education so that they could hold jobs and that he would get it for them if they supported his election to the assembly. His father is a rich agriculturalist and gives him money; so does his uncle. He looks like an army man; he is a big fellow." Their opponents became human beings with comprehensible biographies.

In 1956 our Rajput acquaintances heatedly discussed what to do about their invitations to attend the wedding of the daughter of a very prominent Congress politician. The wedding obviously had important latent political functions. It would be attended by the leading figures of the ruling Congress party, men who, although of lower caste, were the new holders of power. Having won the first general election, they were settling the pattern of land reform, a matter in which Rajput noblemen were vitally interested. By the conventions of the old order, the invitation was an affront; judged in modern terms, attendance was the essence of political-economic prudence. Those who went were shamed by those who did not for their lack of honor and integrity. In 1963, the first major social event of our return visit was the wedding of a socially prominent and politically important Rajput nobleman's daughter. Present were many of the state's major political figures, Congressmen and opposition leaders representing many hues of the social spectrum. Few Rajputs thought the event extraordinary, and little was said about it. The new distribution of power, confirmed in three general elections, was legitimized in the broad acceptance of the idea and institutions of the new political culture. Those who, before they won power, fell outside the ambit of human perception or sympathy except as the inferior dependents of local notables now became part of a common universe of emotion and calculation.

Cultural homogenization and the broadening or elimination of structural boundaries that parallel it also foster fellow feeling. As men come to share values, life styles, and manners and are included within or cross what previously appeared as structural boundaries to social intercourse, they find it easier and more natural to recognize each other's humanity.

The future of ascriptively-based structural boundaries and cultural differences in India can only be estimated by examining what has happened to them in more modern societies such as America. There are those who foresee, sometimes on scientific grounds, sometimes on normative, the disappearance of all ascriptively-based cultural differences and structural barriers in the face of the objective forces of modernization and the progressive realization of equality. The commitment to modernity's radical individualism and universalism, embedded in liberal and Marxist thought and the scientific culture, assumes that as men are released from traditional corporate structures and self-definitions and liberated from prescientific ideas they will become at once more individual and alike. The heuristic properties of modernity are taken not only as desirable but also as fully realizable; modernizing societies ought to become what modern societies are assumed to be. The great categories for examining the problems of modern man, the individual and the mass, autonomy and conformity, do not accord a place to ascriptive structures and identities; they do not admit the possibilities of man rooted in and, in some measure, defined by paracommunities, ascriptively created cultural and social categories. That these assumptions, which are common in much contemporary analysis of modernity and modernization, are problematic is suggested by the fate of cultural homogenization and structural fusion in America.

In America, the creed of the melting pot united conformity to Anglo-Saxon language and culture and the fusion of cultural and structural heterogeneity. That the ethnic and religious communities involved in both processes should have proved so durable even in "modern" America suggests that individualism and homogeneity may not be inevitable consequences of modernization. The *public* ideology of the melting pot (the fusion of cultural and structural differences) and the practice of assimilating the "dominant" Anglo-Saxon culture and language were paralleled in America by *private* commitments to maintaining ethnic or religious natural associations. The strength of such private commitments can be measured by the ethnic and religious patterns of suburban and intra-urban migration, by the high levels of ethnic and religious endogamy that continue to characterize American marriages, and by voting patterns that demonstrate the persistence and independence of ethnic and religious identities. Despite impressive "objective forces" such as a common language and political culture, a relatively homogeneous class structure, national mass media, and unprecedented rates of residential mobility[4] the hold of ethnicity and religious community on social and political norms and behavior remains significant. As of 1950, ethnic endogamy, although declining, remained between 40 and 75 per cent, depending on the ethnic group and city,[5] and religious community endogamy was even higher, between 78 and 96 per cent,

[4] Donald J. Bogue, *The Population of the United States* (Glencoe, Ill.), p. 375.

[5] Ruby Jo Reeves Kennedy, "Single or Triple Melting Pot? Inter-Marriage Trends in New Haven, 1870–1950," *American Journal of Sociology,* LVIII, (July, 1952), 56–59. She reports the rate of Italian in-marriage in New Haven as declining from 97.71 per cent in 1900 to 76.70 per cent in 1950. Irish in-marriage was 50 per cent in 1950, and Polish 41 per cent.

depending on the faith and locale.[6] Patterns of urban settlement suggest that, far from being solvents of ascriptive ties, great American cities provide contexts in which ethnic and religious communities retain their identities and structures.[7]

Paralleling continued residential segregation and the persistence of community structures is the significance at the national as well as the municipal level of voting preferences based on community solidarities.[8] It is not so surprising that in the early stages of social

[6] A survey by the Bureau of the Census of a national sample of existing marriages showed that Jews contracted 93 per cent endogamous marriages and Catholics 78 per cent; cited in Milton Gordon, *Assimilation in American Life: The Role of Race, Religion, and National Origin* (New York, 1964), pp. 181–82, 215. An earlier study by Ruby Jo Reeves Kennedy showed the following trends in levels of religious community endogamy: Catholic stocks marry Catholics 95.35 per cent, 1870; 85.78 per cent, 1900; 82.05 per cent, 1930; 83.71 per cent, 1940. Protestant stocks marry Protestants 99.11 per cent, 1870; 90.86 per cent, 1900; 78.19 per cent, 1930; 79.72 per cent, 1940. Jews marry Jews 100 per cent, 1870; 98.82 per cent, 1900; 97.01 per cent, 1930; 94.32 per cent, 1940 (Kennedy, "Single or Triple Melting Pot? Intermarriage Trends in New Haven, 1870–1940," *American Journal of Sociology*, XLIX [January, 1944]), 331–39. For the sociology of religious communities generally, see Will Herberg, *Protestant, Catholic, Jew* (Garden City, N.Y., 1960).

[7] See Gordon, *Assimilation in American Life*, and Glazer and Moynihan, *Beyond the Melting Pot: The Negroes, Puerto Ricans, Jews, Italians, and Irish of New York City* (Cambridge, Mass., 1963), for recent evidence on these points. The Glazer and Moynihan conclusions may well not apply to all American cities. New York City evidently provides large enough concentrations of ethnic communities that each community can be "self-sufficient." This may not be true in some other cities. William S. Rowe has discussed parallels in Bombay: "Caste communities [have] retained their internal structure in the city environment [as] is attested to by the historical references to panchayats and headmen." Rowe also found castes being received into particular residential wards of the city, "almost as though the map of the North Indian District had been reproduced within the wards of the city," and this in a dense industrial slum ("Caste, Kinship and Association in Urban India" [unpublished MS, 1964], cited by Harold A. Gould, "Discussion of Lynch's Study of the Agra Yatavs" [a paper delivered at the Association for Asian Studies, San Francisco, April, 1965]). Gould says Lynch produced somewhat similar findings for Agra.

[8] For a recent analysis supporting this view, see Raymond E. Wolfinger, "The Development and Persistence of Ethnic Voting," *American Political Sci-*

mobility and cultural assimilation, which American Negroes are now experiencing, electoral behavior should be affected by ethnic and religious considerations. In the 1964 presidential election, with relatively little tension between class and community orientations, northern urban Negroes played an important role in Lyndon Johnson's victory by their almost unanimous opposition to Barry Goldwater.[9] It is more surprising that community considerations, particularly religious community affiliation, should affect electoral behavior after the communities involved have been integrated into the national society and have been differentiated internally. In 1960 upper class Catholics returned from the Republican fold to vote for a Catholic candidate, John F. Kennedy, when that community's polit-

---

ence Review, LIX (December, 1965). Focusing primarily on Italian Catholics in New Haven, Wolfinger shows that despite class characteristics that point in a Democratic direction, Italian Catholics in New Haven have retained the Republican orientation that the community acquired when it entered politics under the leadership of an Italian Catholic candidate for Mayor. Wolfinger's analysis raises Robert Dahl's doubts concerning the "third stage," in which communities become so differentiated that they lose any meaningful political orientation based on community per se, to a level that puts the stage itself in jeopardy (see Robert Dahl, *Who Governs?* [New Haven, Conn., 1961]).

[9] For Negro mobilization and politics, see Harold R. Isaacs, *The New World of Negro Americans* (New York, 1963); William Brink and Louis Harris, *The Negro Revolution in America* (New York, 1964); James Q. Wilson, *Negro Politics* (Glencoe, Ill., 1962); M. Elaine Burgess, *Negro Leadership in a Southern City* (Chapel Hill, N.C., 1962); and Angus Campbell *et al., The American Voter* (New York, 1964), particularly pp. 149–53.

Since World War II Negro votes have become increasingly critical for presidential victory since they are concentrated in the major northern industrial cities (and in the South). Percentages are as follows: Washington, 53.9; Baltimore, 34.8; Detroit, 28.9; Cleveland, 28.6; Philadelphia, 26.4; Chicago, 22; New York, 14; and Los Angeles, 13.5 (James W. Vander Zanden, *American Minority Relations* [New York, 1963], p. 215). In 1960, 52 per cent of the Negro population lived in the South but only 38 per cent were registered to vote (62 per cent are registered outside the South). Their potential impact on the politics of southern states can be seen from the following percentages: Mississippi, 42; South Carolina, 35; Louisiana, 32; Alabama, 30; Georgia, 28; North Carolina, 24; Arkansas, 22; Virginia, 21; Florida, 18; Tennessee, 17; and Texas, 12 (Brink and Harris, *The Negro Revolution in America,* pp. 82–83).

ical legitimacy and identity were under attack.[10] Jewish voting, too, in the face of marked internal differentiation, has been characterized by high levels of cohesion in that community's support of Democratic and liberal candidates.[11] The third generation revives what the first and second devalued through flight and assimilation. If ascriptive diversity remains characteristic of so modern and integrated a nation as America, we must certainly expect it to remain so for India, a nation whose cultural life and social structure have been shaped by a morally segmented ancient civilization, a structurally segmented traditional society, local parochialism, and regional nationalism.[12]

The saliency and weight of these considerations in India are affected, as they have been elsewhere, by growing differentiation between primary and secondary relationships, between beliefs and manners that govern relations among individuals and roles within primary groups and those that prevail outside in the public realm. In India, relations in the public realm are being profoundly affected by an official ideology of equality, by the legal and practical effects of political democracy, and by the slow but discernible homogenization of the symbols used in speech and dress. If public manners re-

[10] For Catholic political behavior, see Campbell *et al.*, *The American Voter*, pp. 164–71, 175–77; William V. Shannon, *The American Irish* (New York, 1963), pp. 409–13. The Irish, too, have been and still are a critical component of presidential victory. They have dominated and to a considerable extent continue to dominate the political organizations of many of the states in which the Catholic population runs between 20 and 60 per cent. These states in turn control a large segment of the total electoral college vote. This was made dramatically apparent to the country when the memorandum drawn up by Theodore Sorenson for John F. Kennedy when he made a bid for the vice-presidential nomination in 1956 became public knowledge. Shannon, citing the Sorenson memorandum, gives the following Catholic percentages: Rhode Island, 60; Massachusetts, 50; Connecticut, 49; New Jersey, 39; New York, 32; Wisconsin, 32; Illinois, 30; Pennsylvania, 29; Michigan, 24; Minnesota, 24; California, 22; Montana, 22; Maryland, 21; and Ohio, 20 (p. 409).

[11] See Campbell *et al.*, *The American Voter*, pp. 92, 164–71; Lawrence H. Fuchs, *The Political Behavior of American Jews* (Glencoe, Ill., 1956), pp. 99–120.

[12] For an effort to compare the role of ascriptive communities in India and America, see Vincent C. Watson, *Communal Politics in India and the United States: A Comparative Analysis* (School of Arts and Sciences, Georgia State College, Research Paper No. 10; Atlanta, 1965).

quire that a southern white address a southern Negro by his proper name rather than as "boy" and if a Kerala Irava ceases to refer to himself as "slave" when addressing a Namboodiri Brahman, changes conducive to the consolidation of a democratic society and polity have taken place. Ascriptive heterogeneity in India, as in America, may not be incompatible with a democratic society and state and with political integration if political leaders and issues strengthen rather than vitiate public manners appropriate to democracy.

Given the difficulties that confront India in her efforts to reduce cultural differences rooted in structural segmentation and to realize national integration, it is the degree of success that she has achieved along these lines rather than the failures that is remarkable. Four processes are making Indians more alike and, in doing so, are laying the necessary but not sufficient conditions for national integration: ascriptive boundaries are expanding; the culture and status of the twice-born varnas are spreading to the Sudra castes; Westernization is affecting the ideas and occupations of broader sections of society; and secularization is dismantling ritual barriers and disarming sacred sanctions.

The formation and purposes of caste associations and federations have expanded the jati's boundaries and the ambit of caste fellowship. These developments have been accompanied by the propagation and spread by caste associations of norms that challenge the validity of established endogamous boundaries, most commonly by calling for their expansion to other hitherto endogamous groups within the jati, similar jatis, or fellow varna members, rarely by calling for their destruction. For example, the caste association of potters in Maharashtra passes a resolution that subcastes among the potters should be abolished and the unity of the caste "restored" by intermarriage; the Kayasths in Bombay, Bengal, and Uttar Pradesh attempt to create a comprehensive north Indian endogamous caste; the journal of a Bengal weaver caste presses for the abolition of endogamous divisions within.[13] It is as though Indians meant to form their notions

[13] Irawati Karve, *Hindu Society: An Interpretation* (Poona, 1961), p. 159. She is troubled by the exclusion of less well-off and advanced potters from these arrangements, and the resentment and bitterness that such invidious distinctions create. Though not wishing to deny or minimize developments in this direc-

of common citizenship and common humanity by expanding rather than destroying the natural associations of birth and locality. A somewhat similar development has characterized cultural homogenization on the American scene, where the "triple melting pot" phenomenon suggests that ethnic groups have found it easiest to step beyond ethnic endogamy by remaining within some larger, still

---

tion, we are impressed that the net result of this and like developments elsewhere is to make more inclusive the definition of fellow humanity.

William L. Rowe, in his survey of caste-history materials for northern India, reports that one of the three main areas toward which the Kayasthas of Bombay, Bengal, and the United Provinces, in their efforts to attain Kshatriya status, directed their considerable literary and organizational talents was the "creation of a powerful All-India high-status endogamous caste of Kayasthas." More generally, he found that "an important theme which appears in many caste publications is the attempt to create the widest possible caste endogamy, to effectively extend the boundaries of the marriage network. . . . To the extent that state-wide resolutions on caste reforms have been uniformly translated into custom over time, the possibility exists for broadening the area of the marriage network and hence the solidity of a caste on a regional or national basis" ("Mobility in the Caste System" [a paper presented at the Conference on Social Structure and Social Change, University of Chicago, June 3–6, 1965], pp. 3, 9).

Nirmal Kumar Bose, reporting on Priti Mitra's work on Bengal caste histories, observes that "some articles published in . . . [-Yogi Sakha, the journal of the Yogis, a "clean" caste of weavers that claimed in 1931 that it was Brahman] advocated the liquidation of endogamous subdivisions within the caste" ("Some Aspects of Caste in Bengal," in Milton Singer [ed.], Traditional India: Structure and Change [Philadelphia, 1959], p. 199).

The tendency to expand endogamous boundaries has been visible among Kayasthas in Bombay for some time (see R. E. Enthoven's report on the "resumed" marriage connections between the Chandraseniya Kayastha Prabhus and the Darne Prabhus, in The Tribes and Castes of Bombay [Bombay, 1920], III, 236). The Iravas in Kerala were urged toward jati consolidation under the leadership of Sri Narayana Guru (see Daniel Thomas, Sree Narayana Guru [Christian Institute for the Study of Religion and Society; Bangalore, 1965]). Four previously endogamous castes of Kerala Iravas have broken down the barriers to intermarriage between them, according to the Travancore Census Report, 1931, I, 365 (cited in Michael St. John, "The Communist Party and Communal Politics in Kerala" [Senior honors thesis, Department of Social Relations, Harvard University, 1962], p. 44). The Ahir Kshatriya Sabha has also advocated intermarriage between hitherto separate endogamous units (M. S. A. Rao, "Caste and the Indian Army," Economic Weekly, August 29, 1964, p. 1440).

relatively endogamous collectivity—the three major faiths—than to dispense entirely with ascriptive endogamous groupings.

The likelihood that caste associations may reach toward more inclusive loyalties and structures is viewed with considerable uneasiness by such leading Indian social scientists as Irawati Karve and G. S. Ghurye.[14] The latter believes "it would lead to three or four large groups solidly organized for pushing the interests of each at the cost of others." On the contrary, it seems more plausible that the formation of three or four large groups on the Indian national scene, a remote contingency, or even in one state, a more likely one, would be attended by the same dilution of intense commitment and the same internal differentiation that make it difficult in America for large religious groupings to develop and pursue common goals effectively.

Another dimension to the growth of cultural homogeneity in India is the expansion downward of the twice-born Varnas' culture. The movement is reminiscent of the democratization of gentlemanly culture and standing in eighteenth-century England that preceded the shift from a society of relatively closed ranks and orders to one of relatively open classes. Daniel Defoe, as well as other pamphleteers of class and manner, by providing the English with popular literary instruction in the art of becoming and being a gentleman, and by celebrating that status, facilitated the expansion of the ideal to those previously excluded from its fold.[15] " 'En Angleterre, il y a beaucoup

[14] Karve, *Hindu Society*, p. 159; Ghurye, *Caste and Class in India* (Bombay, 1957), p. 222.

[15] See the works of Defoe for instruction in becoming a gentleman and celebration of the new gentleman. The works of Maximillian E. Novak, *Economics and the Fiction of Daniel Defoe* (Berkeley, Calif., 1962), and *Defoe and the Nature of Man* (London, 1963); and Ian Watt, *The Rise of the Novel: Studies in Defoe, Richardson and Fielding* (Berkeley, Calif., 1957), elaborate on this theme. Defoe's death register reads, "Mr. Defoe, Gentleman" (see John Robert Moore, *Daniel Defoe* [Chicago, 1958], p. 341). A. Goodwin (ed.), *The European Nobility in the Eighteenth Century,* covers the transition period in most European countries; see particularly the essays by H. J. Habakkuk on "England" and J. McManners on "France." For the shift from order to class as a principle of social stratification, see particularly Raymond Williams, *Culture and Society, 1780–1950* (New York, 1958). Williams dates the first use of class as a concept from about 1772 (p. xiii).

de messieurs qui s'appellent M. Esq.' It is a hoary French joke," the *Manchester Guardian Weekly* observed editorially,

> because the said M. Esq. is being Americanised out of existence by plain Mister. M. Esq. has been something of a chameleon in his long, richly traditional day, which will soon draw to a close. First a shield-bearer in the field of battle; captain or colonel or knight in arms and a number of Valiant things; later amended to a younger brother of a baronet, and extended to a justice of the peace, an Irish peer, an officer of the king's courts, a counsellor at law, and the head of a great landed family. Latterly he was anybody "bearing the port, carriage, and countenance of a gentleman": lastly he made the fatal step into commerce. Then he belonged to everybody who wished to claim him.[16]

"The tendency of the lower castes to imitate the higher," writes M. N. Srinivas, "has been a powerful factor in the spread of Sanskritic ritual and customs, and in the achievement of a certain amount of cultural uniformity not only throughout the caste scale, but over the entire length and breadth of India."[17] There has been a tendency to identify Sanskrit culture with Brahman. For our purpose here, the cultural similarities of the twice-born varnas that distinguish them from the non-twice-born, including the wearing of the sacred thread and the ability to command the services of Brahman priests and use Vedic rituals, are more important than the differences that distinguish Kshatriya, Vaishya, and Brahman cultures from each other. Srinivas himself preferred the more general term, Sanskrit-

[16] *Manchester Guardian Weekly,* August 26, 1965, p. 1. The "excesses" to which democratic manners may extend are apparent from this item bearing a London dateline, from the *New York Times* of August 12, 1964. "Luv, Ducks, Mate and other forms of casual endearment in Britain have now scattered through the conversational language like confetti. . . . When entering a restaurant, cafe, railway station, pub, shop and other places where people move in droves . . . the chances are one of these will be the term of address. . . . Luv, a corruption of love, is probably the most popular. . . . In London, a spokesman at the General Post Office said: "We don't have any specific instructions against using Luv and Dar but we do warn against friendliness becoming overfamiliarity. A spokesman for London Transport—which operates the buses and subways—said: 'We advise our staffs not to be familiar, but there's not much we can do about it.' "

[17] His concept of Sanskritization opened up the subject of internal culture change and integration.

ization, to the more particular one of Brahmanization because "certain Vedic rites are confined to Brahmans and the two other 'twice-born' castes."[18] He also emphasized that "in the study of Sanskritization it is important to know the kind of caste which dominates in a particular region."[19] Judging from the evidence of caste histories available to us, those bent on winning the Sanskritic equivalent of gentlemanly status claimed they were Kshatriyas more often than they claimed they were Brahmans, even though such elements of Brahmanical as opposed to Kshatriya culture as vegetarianism and teetotalism have sometimes characterized the emulation of higher castes by mobile ones.[20] Kshatriya as opposed to Brahman status and

[18] Srinivas, *Religion and Society among the Coorgs of South India* (London, 1952), p. 30.

[19] *Caste in Modern India and Other Essays* (Bombay, 1962), p. 62. Srinivas goes on, however, to link Sanskritization to Brahman culture when he observes that if the dominant caste is Brahman "then Sanskritization will probably be quicker and Brahmanical values will spread, whereas if the dominating caste is a local Kshatriya or Vaisya caste, Sanskritization will be slower, and the values will not be Brahmanical" (p. 62). He alters his view, stressing Brahman components less, in *Social Change in Modern India* (Berkeley, Calif., 1966).

[20] Srinivas refers to "the political fluidity of traditional India" and observes that the "varna-category of Kshatriya has often been assumed by peasant castes and even tribes which were able to capture political power" ("Mobility in Caste" [a paper presented at the Conference on Social Structure and Social Change, University of Chicago, June 3–6, 1965]). Elsewhere he observes that "the term Kshatriya . . . does not refer to a closed ruling group which has been there since the time of the Vedas. More often it refers to the position attained or claimed by a local group whose traditions and luck enable it to seize politico-economic power" (*Caste in Modern India*, p. 66). See Bernard S. Cohn's "Political Systems in Eighteenth Century India: The Banares Region," *Journal of the American Oriental Society*, LXXXII (July–September, 1962), 311–20, for the fluidity of power, within the ambit of "dominance," in a particular area and at a particular time. For the synthetic quality of Kshatriya status in Indian history generally, see K. M. Pannikar, *Hindu Society at the Crossroads* (Bombay, 1955), p. 8. Bernard Barber notes that the misapprehensions concerning the nature of the caste system—the overemphasis on its timeless unchangeability —may be related to methodological requirements, as in Weber's heuristic contrasts between Indian and Western social structures, and to self-justifying requirements, as in the case of British society and rule ("Social Mobility in Hindu India" [a paper prepared for the meeting of the Association for Asian Studies, Chicago, 1961], p. 15).

culture provided access to twice-born standing and respect without placing so severe a strain on historical credibility or characterological adaptability. That is, there is a greater likelihood historically that a caste was once made up of fighting men who dominated others than there is that it was made up of learned ones who cultivated or applied the sacred culture; and there may be a greater likelihood psychologically that the culturally patterned expressiveness of the Kshatriya—meat eating, drinking, fighting, hunting, broad humor —is more accessible than the culturally patterned asceticism of the Brahman.

The democratization of the Indian version of the gentleman through the spread of twice-born culture and status has been accompanied by the moral and social renaissance of varna, the four-fold classification of caste that constituted the sacred sociology of traditional Hindu texts: Brahman, Kshatriya, Vaishya, Sudra. Very influential in the resuscitation of this concept was Herbert Risley, commissioner for the census of 1901. So taken was he by the hierarchical motif of Hindu classic texts that he hoped to categorize all jatis, the thousands of groups that are the actual behavioral categories of the caste system, in terms of the varna order and to establish a warrant of precedence on a regional if not a national basis.[21] He

[21] Herbert Risley, *The People of India*, ed. W. Crooke (2d ed.; London, 1915). "In organizing the census of 1901 I suggested to my colleagues that an attempt should be made to arrange the various groups that had to be dealt with on some system which would command general acceptance, at any rate within the limits of the province to which it was applied. . . . The principle suggested as a basis was that of classification by social precedence as recognized by native public opinion at the present day, and manifesting itself in the fact that particular castes are supposed to be the modern representatives of one or other of the castes of the theoretical Hindu system . . ." (p. 111). Risley gave up the attempts of predecessors to create a national classification, believing the task to be "essentially a local one" (p. 114). But by local he meant provinces, units sufficiently large that they presumably raised similar problems to those of a national classification. At that time there was no such thing as a uniform province-wide social experience that could give rise to a homogeneous opinion; even today, a group that is considered high in one locality may be quite low in another. Risley was not the first to attempt such groupings. In 1891, classifications had already been established at the urging of Sir Denzil Ibbetson, which, for example, ranked the Khatris in "Group XV—Traders," "immediately after the Aroras of the Punjab, ten places lower than the Agarwals, and several places below the Kandus

believed that the hierarchy of Indian society essentially coincided with the teachings of the literary texts even though it might have become more complex as the centuries unfolded, and he meant to identify and place several hundred million Indians within it.

Paradoxically, his temerity loosed opposite impulses: on the one hand, the devaluation of varna as a scientific concept; on the other, its inflation as the social ideology of mobility movements. Social scientists reacted sharply, especially after Indian independence, against the assumption made by Sanskrit scholars and British ethnologists alike that the literary evidence of the classic texts provided valid and meaningful categories and evidence for understanding Indian society. They began to stress rather the indeterminancy of caste rank, particularly in the vast middle range between Brahman and untouchable, and the misleading implications of official and scientific attempts to discover and legitimize a varna social order. It became increasingly evident through census operations and anthropological fieldwork that villagers had some difficulty identifying their caste—was it their gotra, jati, or varna?—and even greater difficulty in identifying their varna; "caste" was obviously of little direct assistance in helping them objectively rank themselves or others.[22] It also became evident that the large diversity of local prestige systems resisted rankings beyond localities. Risley's work, as a scientific effort, seemed based on mistaken premises. Varna was not a behavioral concept.

---

and Kasarwanis of the United Provinces and Subaranabaniks of Bengal" (p. 113). (Risley reclassified the Khatris as Rajputs.)

[22] "One of the most striking features of the caste system as it actually exists is the lack of clarity in the hierarchy, especially in the middle regions. . . . Nebulousness as to position is the essence of the system in operation as distinct from the system in conception" (Srinivas, *Caste in Modern India,* p. 67). McKim Marriott has successfully confronted the complexities of establishing behaviorally valid rankings, but he confined his efforts to villages; see, for example, his "Caste Ranking and Food Transactions: A Matrix Analysis" (a paper presented at the Conference on Social Structure and Social Change, University of Chicago, June 3–6, 1965). He discusses differences between urban and rural ranking and mobility experiences, and also between village, regional, and civilizational systems, in "Multiple Reference in Indian Caste Systems," in Silverberg (ed.), "Social Mobility in Caste" (forthcoming).

In the area of social ideology, however, Risley's efforts at classification made varna more significant. His grand scheme played a major role in transforming the nature of social change in India from shifts in rank within a stationary system, which characterized pre-British India, to fundamental structural change in the over-all system, which occurred under British rule and afterward. The scheme loosed a storm from below, as hundreds of jatis used the occasion to convert their aspirations to high status into a scientific or historical truth.[23] By assuming an immanent reality and then giving it empirical expression, precisely at that moment when social movement and change were accelerating, Risley and others both aggravated rank consciousness and drew new attention to the reality-shaping possibilities of varna labels. Through identification with one of the twice-born varnas, mobile castes began to do to twice-born standing and culture what the democratization of the gentlemanly status did to "rank, order, and degree" in English society. In the pursuit of dignity and self-respect through new identities, mobile castes turned to varna for the history and symbols to furnish their transformed consciousness.

The fate of the varna concept suggests a general reciprocity between ideology and social reality. The social fiction employed by yesterday's parvenu—"I *am* a gentleman" or "I *am* a Kshatriya"—to better his self and social esteem may become tomorrow's operative social category. In fact, it seems evident from Indian history that today's "real" Kshatriyas are simply those who overcame their parvenu status at some earlier time.[24] Despite the objections of social

[23] William L. Rowe, on the basis of his survey of caste histories, writes that "undoubtedly to the Kayasthas and other castes attempting to change varnas at the turn of the [nineteenth] century, the villain for a long time was Mr. H. Risley. . . . Many of the caste publications are specifically addressed to Risley and other officials, ranging from district level census officers to the King Emperor himself" ("Mobility in the Caste System" [a paper delivered at the Conference on Social Structure and Social Change, University of Chicago, June 3–6, 1965], p. 2). See also our earlier discussions of Vanniyar and Nadar responses, pp. 29–64.

[24] See n. 20 above. A. M. Shah and R. G. Shroff have demonstrated how the traditional genealogists of Gujarat synthetically attached princes who had made themselves newly independent to the senior branch of their clan and how they attached castes of more modest origin—Patidars, Kunbis—to Rajput status

scientists, varna categories were always more than literary constructs even if they did not symbolize an immanent or empirical reality. As expressions of an overarching normative order and as elements of consciousness among strategically situated social groups, varna categories have always carried the potential for *shaping* reality.[25] It is to this end that they are now being employed, probably with increasing success. In the same Procrustean manner that Brahmanic categories and law were applied by British courts to the diverse customs of non-Brahman castes, producing a more uniform and manageable system,[26] varna categories have been and are being applied to simplify the vast diversity of the caste system, but with this great difference: the law was simplified and the result legitimized from above, whereas caste is experiencing a similar process from below. In both cases "mistaken" understandings of social reality are helping create new reality more suitable to modern circumstances. It seems reasonable to expect that over the next few generations the changes already evident among the proportions of twice-born (one-fifth), Sudra (three-fifths), and untouchable (one-fifth) Hindus will continue in the direction of upgrading a section of the Sudras and a much smaller proportion of the untouchables to twice-born standing. At the same

("The Vahivanca Barots of Gujarat: A Caste of Genealogists and Mythographers," in Singer [ed.], *Traditional India,* pp. 55, 62).

Martin Orans describes an early case of "Kshatriyization," in "A Tribe in Search of a Great Tradition: The Emulation-Solidarity Conflict," *Man in India,* XXXIX (1959), 108–14. A Munda tribal who had established himself as local raja attracted Brahmans to his court, who Sanskritized his rituals and manufactured a Rajput genealogy for him. For similar themes, see Surajit Sinha, "State Formation and Rajput Myth in Tribal Central India," *Man in India,* XLII (January–March, 1962), and Burton Stein, "Social Mobility in Medieval South Indian Hindu Sects," in James Silverberg (ed.), "Social Mobility in Caste" (forthcoming).

[25] "The *varna* scheme," Srinivas writes, "has certainly distorted the picture of caste but it has enabled ordinary men and women to grasp the caste system by providing them with a simple and clear scheme which is applicable to all parts of India. *Varna* has provided a common social language which holds good, or is thought to hold good for India as a whole. A sense of familiarity even when it does not rest on facts, is conducive to unity" (*Caste in Modern India,* p. 69).

[26] See Part III, p. 274.

time Westernization and secularization will continue to drain the sacred thread, symbol of twice-born status, of its affective load and social significance.

As the mobile castes, by joining the ranks of the twice-born, have become more alike culturally and more equal socially, their leading sections have begun, as the twice-born castes did earlier, to use the language (English) and adopt the occupations and cultural style of the West. Thus they are continuing the process in a new framework, even though, within it, they are soon divided by class, interest, and ideology. With the passage of time, it has become increasingly apparent that Westernization does not necessarily imply the assimilation of modern and secular values. An Indian who changes his dress, diet, and language does not so much demonstrate that he has become modern as that he is emulating the culture of a new dominant class; Indians were, after all, "Persianized" under Moghul rule. In so far as Western culture contains modern and secular elements and in so far as such elements take hold of the consciousness and behavior of those adopting Western models, it has resulted in modernity and secularism. This more modest view of Westernization does not take its modernizing and secularizing effects for granted but leaves them to empirical investigation.

The cultural and historical relation of Anglicized Indians, those who assimilated the cultural style or values of the West, to the traditional India remains problematic. Edward Shils points out that the Western-educated and English-speaking Indian intellectual often identifies his sense of separation from the people, whom he has been taught to regard as the source of wisdom and strength, with his use of a foreign language and his attachment to alien manners and habits. His alienation, Shils argues, lies less in his attachment to the forms and symbols of an alien culture and more in the survival of the caste system in his beliefs and behavior.[27] Similarly, M. N. Srinivas finds Westernized members of the upper classes, even though they have given up dietary restrictions and marry out of caste and region, have not escaped caste bonds and adhere to caste attitudes in surprising contexts.[28]

[27] Shils, *The Intellectual* . . . , p. 70.

[28] Srinivas, "The Indian Road to Equality," in *Caste in Modern India,* p. 88.

These are not the only implications for personal integrity and commitment of a simultaneous attachment to Indian and Western life styles, modes of thought, and social structures. Milton Singer, in a recent study of industrial leaders in Madras, found that they manage to lead meaningful and productive lives by compartmentalizing the "traditional" Indian and "modern" Western. He argues against a typological theory of society and culture change based on traditional and modern, however, believing that such a theory "tends to overstate the differences and to understate the similarities between the 'traditional' and the 'modern'" and to exaggerate "the degree of psychological conflict underlying their existence."[29]

Harold A. Gould, too, in his study of Lucknow rickshawallas, finds compartmentalization a pervasive mode of accommodating traditional and modern forces. He argues that "despite the disappearance of caste as an *occupational* factor in the urban division of labor, it cannot be simply asserted that caste had entirely disappeared from the life of either the migrant or urban-born rickshadriver." Work may be detached from its caste context without necessarily destroying or even altering the hold of caste on individual lives and social organization. Caste has become, "for the ordinary Hindu the basis of his self-hood and social identity. . . . These features of caste are rooted in and sustained by the kin group and the local community. . . ." None of Gould's sample married outside their endogamous groups or "showed [any] inclination to engage in fraternization outside the occupational context." All said they normally dined only with members of their own caste or ethnic group under domestic conditions despite the fact that during working hours they constantly violated the rule enjoining commensal exclusiveness. "Respondents," he continues, "saw no inconsistency in this; they held that their work is part of one domain with its specific necessities respecting social interaction while their domestic or non-work life is part of quite another. . . . Such compartmentalization of behavior," he concludes, "appears to be a major mechanism whereby the urban Hindu and Muslim both successfully balance the social requirements arising

[29] Singer, "On the Modernization of Cultural Traditions" (a paper presented at the Chicago Conference on Social Structure and Social Change, University of Chicago, June 3–6, 1965), p. 2.

from the opposing ascription and achievement oriented values which sustain the caste and class system respectively." Compartmentalization, Gould holds, is not confined to the menial worker; rather, it is "generally prevalent in varying degrees at all levels of Indian society."[30]

Compartmentalization not only physically separates the two spheres (primarily home and family from work place and colleagues) but also prevents the different norms of behavior and belief appropriate to modernity and tradition from colliding and causing conflict in the lives of those who live by both.[31] Put in another way, compartmentalization is a way for those who refuse both outright assimilation and cultural reaction to "Indianize" modernity.

Secularization, the fourth process favoring homogenization of culture, creates conditions under which all Indians, "Sanskritized" and "Westernized," modern and traditional, low and high, can find or create common norms and structures. It downgrades, neutralizes, or eliminates the beliefs, symbols, and barriers embedded in the ritual and sacred dimensions of society, substituting in their stead profane and mundane standards of wealth, power, and education. Unlike Westernization, secularization does not carry alien cultural baggage, baggage that may or may not be secular or modern. Like Westernization, secularization generates within itself criteria of and conditions for differentiation. Earlier generations opposed Sanskritic religion, culture, and social arrangements with Western values, life style, and language; secularization makes it possible to carry on the same confrontation in Indian terms. Like compartmentalization, it provides the possibility of Indianizing modernity.

Secularization has been "established" in constitutional and public law. The constitution describes India as a secular state, prohibits discrimination on the basis of caste, and takes the individual citizen as the basic unit of value and action by investing him with justiciable

[30] Gould, "Lucknow Rickshawallas: The Social Organization of an Occupational Category," *International Journal of Comparative Sociology*, VI (March, 1965), 30–31.

[31] Singer, "On the Modernization of Cultural Traditions," p. 95.

fundamental rights.[32] Ritual rank as a basis of social organization and access to power and wealth is further undermined by "progressive discrimination," which provides "privileges" to "backward classes" in the realms of political representation, government employment, and education.[33]

It has often been remarked, sometimes cynically, that public ideology and law favoring secular as against sacred standards of behavior have for generations been ahead of public opinion and even farther ahead of conduct. As they have gained in legitimacy, however, they have created the moral dilemmas out of which further movement in a secular direction has been generated. Although the nineteenth-century reformers who began to shape a secular ethic for India generated and spoke only to small publics and did not always adhere to their own doctrines, and although Gandhi's efforts on behalf of Harijans seemed to some educated untouchables patronizing and designed to serve the interests of the twice-born by "purifying" Hinduism, it is hazardous, from the perspective of better times, to underestimate the magnitude of their achievement. Without benefit of a secularized natural law tradition—indeed, in the face of religiously sanctioned inequality—the liberals and Gandhians created what is in effect an "Indian Dilemma."[34] Like the "American Dilemma," it confronts the nation with an unfinished agenda. The

[32] See *Constitution of India,* Art. 46, Directive Principles of State Policy; Arts. 15, 16, and 17, Fundamental Rights; and Arts. 330, 332, 335, 338, 340, and 341. The commissioner for scheduled castes and scheduled tribes, under the minister for home affairs, annually reports on progress, or lack of it, under these constitutional provisions in the *Report of the Commissioner for Scheduled Castes and Scheduled Tribes.* Donald Smith, in *India as a Secular State* (Princeton, N.J., 1963), reviews the secular state's relation to caste (pp. 292–329).

[33] The situation of "backward classes," a category that ordinarily comprises low castes above the "untouchables," is discussed in Government of India, *Report of the Backward Classes Commission* (Delhi, 1956), and in Government of India, Committee on Plan Projects, *Report of the Study Team on Social Welfare of Backward Classes* (Delhi, 1959). See also p. 144, n. 35.

[34] The allusion is to Gunnar Myrdal's *An American Dilemma* (New York, 1944). For a cogent discussion of the possibility that "public conformity" arising from legislation can produce equalitarian behavior, see Gerald Berreman, "Caste in Cross-Cultural Perspective" (a paper presented at the Conference on Social Change, University of Chicago, June 3–6, 1965), p. 77.

provisions and promises of constitutional and public law and of public ideology are important but modest instalments in the fulfilment of this agenda. And the past and present are not devoid of other evidence that the agenda is guiding social change.

Although reform movements have long pressed for intercaste marriages among caste Hindus, it is only recently that behavioral changes in this direction have become evident among urban, educated sections of the population.[35] Gandhi and others encouraged marriage between untouchables and caste Hindus;[36] and since independence, at least three Indian states have come to reward such marriages and provide benefits for children of them.[37] Other evidence of social

[35] Nirmal Kumar Bose suggests that radical changes have occurred among the urban and modern members of Bengal's twice-born castes: ". . . Just as caste has been changing undoubtedly in Bengal in the field of men's economic activity, there is an indication that, on the level of its cultural superstructure, there are forces at work which tend to weaken its hold on the mind of the urbanized, politically conscious people, eager for changes along the lines of the West. . . . What proportion of marriages," he wonders, "among politically active persons follow the traditional and reformed patterns. . . ." Is there, he asks, "any significant difference between parties belonging to different age groups?" ("Some Aspects of Caste in Bengal," in Singer [ed.], *Traditional India*, p. 202). Elsewhere he goes farther by observing that the "urbanized Hindu in Bengal has to all intents and purposes become like a Brahmo [a member of the Brahmo Samaj, which began to foster intercaste marriages and dedicated itself, among other objectives, to the elimination of caste differences]." And Ronald Inden confirms, after spending 1964 and part of 1965 in Bengal preparing a dissertation on Kayasthas, that intermarriage is becoming increasingly frequent among the urban sections of the Kayasthas, Brahmans, and Vaidyas, that is, among those Westernized and educated twice-born castes dominating the modern, better-paying, and more prestigious occupations of metropolitan Calcutta and constituting perhaps half of the city's population. C. T. Kannan has summarized some of the evidence on intermarriage in Chap. 1 of *Intercaste and Intercommunity Marriages in India* (Bombay, 1963). See also Maureen L. P. Patterson, "Intercaste Marriage in Maharashtra," *Economic Weekly Annual*, January, 1958. She suggests, as does Bose, that intercaste marriages are more apt to be upper caste phenomena.

[36] Gandhi writing in *Harijan*, July 7, 1946; see also M. K. Gandhi, *All Are Equal in the Eyes of God* (Delhi, 1964), pp. 68–69.

[37] Andhra, Kerala, and Maharashtra provide compensation for marriages between untouchables and non-untouchables. It is doubtful that these payments work as incentives. One observer of society among the untouchables believes

change is provided by radical doctrines calling for the destruction of the caste system and its replacement by a casteless society, which have affected upper caste intellectuals and lower caste illiterates alike. They are as old as the Bengal-based Brahmo Samaj, under Keshub Chander Sen, in the 1870's and Sree Narayana Guru's Sree Narayana Dharma Paripalna Yogam, which in the late nineteenth- and early twentieth-centuries, mobilized Kerala's largest caste community, the Iravas, under the slogan "One Caste, One Religion, One God."[38] More recently, in the generation preceding independence, such movements as E. V. Ramasami Naicker's Self-Respect Movement in Madras and those inspired by B. R. Ambedkar primarily but not exclusively among Mahars in Maharashtra attacked Brahmanical Hinduism and its social system in the name of atheism and anticlericalism, in the first instance, and in the name of the egalitarianism to be found in Buddhism and democratic political ideologies, in the second.

Caste associations, too, have exhibited marked tendencies toward secularization.[39] William L. Rowe, in reviewing the doctrinal orientations between 1873 and 1915 of *Kayastha Samacher,* later the *Hindustan Review,* of Allahabad, the journal of the All-India Kayastha Association, found a marked shift from a concern to upgrade the caste's ritual and social standing to a secular concern for national social reform and political integration. "By 1905," he writes, "the specifically 'caste' matters have been relegated to the rear section . . . with an increasing number of articles on national and political questions . . . (sometimes) by Parsi, Muslim and foreign writers."[40] An unsigned editorial entitled "Caste Conferences and National Progress," appearing in the June, 1901, number, argued that caste feeling hindered "true national feeling" and suggested that, instead of eight

---

they may take some of the burden off couples who would have contracted such marriages anyhow (personal communication from Eleanor Zelliott, April, 1966).

[38] The *Sree Narayana Dharma Paripalna Yogam* was said to have about 50,000 members in the late twenties of this century (see Thomas, *Sree Narayana Guru,* pp. 29, 39).

[39] As is to some extent evident from the account of the Nadars above.

[40] "Mobility in the Caste System," p. 6.

or ten annual province-wide caste meetings, "all caste conferences should be combined into the Indian Social Conference. . . ."[41] And in the March, 1902, number Alfred Nandy warned that the pursuit of ritual rank by caste associations is "antagonistic and destructive of national movements like the National Congress and the Social Conference."[42]

Changes in speech and dress mark the course of secularization even as they did those of Sanskritization and Westernization. Unlike the latter, however, which featured the attributes of ritual rank or cultural domination, secularized speech and dress patterns tend to express instrumental and egalitarian concerns. Aiyappan found that Kerala courts of law obliged all parties to employ the terms "Mr." and "Your Honor" in place of super- and sub-ordinate language forms.[43] A. K. Ramanujan relates differences in speech to the functions the dialects serve for each community. He points out that Brahman dialects in Madras are characterized by high levels of internal differentiation—for example, many words to distinguish a single concept such as water, and the preservation of unique features of Sanskrit and English terms—whereas non-Brahman dialects tend toward generalization—the assimilation of foreign words without preserving their uniqueness, and the utilization of one word in a variety of contexts. Among Brahmans, Ramanujan suggests, these differences are linguistic self-identification, intracaste communication, and the linguistic elaboration of the community's inward-looking and closed sacred world. For non-Brahmans, on the other hand, intercaste communication for mundane purposes is primary. The colloquial standard now developing all over Tamilnad, Ramanujan points out, is based on non-Brahman dialects.[44] This linguistic process parallels changes in patterns of dress described by Andre Beteille. Sect differences among Brahman women's dress are becoming less marked as they, along with low caste women, abandon their

[41] *Ibid.*, p. 7.

[42] *Ibid.*, p. 8.

[43] A. Aiyappan, *Iravas and Culture Change* (Madras, 1945), p. 32.

[44] A. K. Ramanujan, "The Structure of Variation: A Study in Caste-Dialects" (a paper presented at the Conference on Social Structure and Social Change, University of Chicago, June 3–6, 1965).

distinctive dress for the less differentiated standard of non-Brahman caste Hindus.[45]

Something of the complexity of the relationship among all of these factors—the expansion of ascriptive boundaries, the spread of twice-born culture and rank, Westernization and secularization—is captured in William L. Rowe's "The New Chauhans: A Caste Mobility Movement in North India."[46] His account suggests the sort of generational shifts in orientation to social mobility and its techniques that American ethnic studies also suggest. Large sections of the Noniyas, a Sudra caste found in Madhya Pradesh, Uttar Pradesh, and Bihar, have "become" over the past three generations Chauhan Rajputs, simultaneously expanding the scope of ascriptive solidarity and moving toward twice-born status. Starting with the formation in 1898 of the Sri Rajput Pacharni Sabha (Rajput Advancement Society) by the most advanced sections among the Noniyas, the Chauhan movement has spread eastward from Pratapgarh District, "making gains wherever a group of Noniyas existed whose wealth enabled them to attempt social emulation of the Rajput [Kshatriya varna] style of life.[47]

Donning the sacred thread, symbol of twice-born status for males of the Brahman, Kshatriya, and Vaishya varnas at the Vedic rite of *upanayana,* became the "symbolic justification" for Noniya claims to equivalent ritual rank. Twenty years after the Noniyas of Village Senapur, studied intensively by Rowe, had begun the process of becoming Chauhans at a historic meeting in 1936, "every child in the Noniya settlement . . . knew the story of their Rajput lineage and of their claim to recognition as Chauhans . . . ,"[48] and "Noniya rank in the hierarchy of the twenty-four castes which comprise Village Senapur [had] demonstrably risen. . . ."[49]

Among the leading sections of the Noniyas as well as among the poorer and less well-educated, there is now evidence of Westerniza-

[45] Andre Beteille, *Caste, Class and Power: Changing Patterns of Stratification in a Tanjore Village* (Berkeley, Calif., 1965).

[46] Rowe, "The New Chauhans: A Caste Mobility Movement in North India," in Silverberg (ed.), "Social Mobility in Caste" (forthcoming).

[47] *Ibid.,* p. 7.

[48] *Ibid.,* p. 8.　　　　　　　　　　[49] *Ibid.,* p. 4.

tion and secularization. These processes can be found in a kind of geological layering of generations. The sons and grandsons of those Noniyas who became wealthy by acting as labor, road, and bridge contractors for the British in the post-1857 period "are now successful lawyers, teachers and government officials."[50] It was the better-off and better-educated sections of this group that helped spread the Chauhan movement throughout northern India and to whom its twice-born symbols and rituals meant most. Yet the younger members of this regional elite, Rowe reports, are "becoming involved and committed to the newer (secular) message of political egalitarianism for modern India" by subscribing to the anticaste ideology of the predominantly untouchable Republican party. ". . . This young elite," Rowe believes, "will increasingly devote its attention to the 'modern' and directly political rather than the caste mobility activity characteristic of the last generation."[51] The generational geology of social change is also visible in Village Senapur: ". . . Most men of the very oldest Noniya generation do not wear the sacred thread, . . . a very considerable number of the middle generation do and . . . among the youngest generation there is a decreasing interest in this symbol of high ritual status. . . ."[52] At the same time, the dominant high castes who had earlier forcefully resisted, then sullenly acquiesced in, the Noniyas' wearing the sacred thread have come under secular influences and no longer care intensely about their doing so. Thus in the smaller society of the village as in the larger one of a region, secularization has raised the importance of education and income for social standing at the expense of ritual rank and has downgraded the village in favor of larger, more abstract, and more distant reference groups.[53] In the process, the *public* importance of Chauhan identity

[50] *Ibid.*, p. 11.

[51] *Ibid.*, p. 12.   [52] *Ibid.*, p. 11.

[53] Andre Beteille reports similar developments in a village in Tanjore District, Madras. "Even in the orthodox South," he writes, "Brahmin, non-Brahmin and Harijan children come together in school. In the villages of Tanjore district, for instance, it is a new experience for Harijan children to sit with the children of their Brahmin masters in the same room and study and play together. . . . The differences in attitude," he continues, "between the generations . . . were brought home to me vividly in the course of my field work. . . . In this village

to those who claimed it and to those who resisted the claim has begun to fade. Yet "caste endogamy remains unshaken ... ; there has been no generalized apostasy with regard to the New Chauhan movement."[54] The movement has, however turned inward to the more private world of marriage and the family, where its cultural patterns and moral norms early on help shape identity. Public activity is relatively secular, whereas aspects of private life retain a Sanskritic orientation.[55]

In tracing the growth of fellow feeling, we have examined ways in which Indians have come closer to political equality, cultural homogeneity, and structural unity. The relative saliency and weight of the processes involved—diffusion of political power, democratization of twice-born culture and status, expansion of ascriptive boundaries, Westernization, and secularization—have varied with time, place, and circumstance. Taking caste communities as the main focus of our analysis, we have found that their entry into extralocal social and political systems, their internal culture and structure, and their strategy have been affected by the declining hold of ritual rank on social standing as twice-born norms and symbols have become at once more accessible and less relevant; by the receding cultural influence of a once dominant and now distant Western imperial power; and by the growing influence on the definition and distribution of honor and authority and on the allocation of resources of wider

---

... the Brahmins live separately in their exclusive area of residence called the *agraharam*. The Harijans live apart, on the fringe of the village or a little away from it. Even today Harijan men almost never enter the *agraharam* ... ; the village school is situated in the *agraharam*, although at one end. The school is attended by a number of Harijan children whose movements within the *agraharam* are now hardly noticed. While children come and go, a Harijan elder still considers it an act of daring—perhaps a little impious—to enter the *agraharam* ("The Future of Backward Classes: The Competing Demands of Status and Power," *Perspectives,* Suppl. to the *Indian Journal of Public Administration,* XI [January–March, 1965], pp. 23, 24).

[54] Rowe, "The New Chauhans: A Caste Mobility Movement in North India," p. 15.

[55] *Ibid.*

access to political power, an emergent industrial and bureaucratic economy, and egalitarian and secular ideology and law.

If there are sequence and pattern here, they are as much dependent on available and influential ideas, leading personalities, important events, and particular historical circumstances as on objective conditions and forces. Nor are the sequences and patterns either necessary or irreversible. At the same time, the theory of cumulative causation suggests that the longer the institutions, beliefs, and habits associated with such sequences and patterns exist through time, the more likely they are to persist.

There remains the Indian dilemma, the contradiction between public ideology and private commitment. Private commitment to tradition, to ascriptive communities and their values, however, not only is compatible with continued modernization but also, as long as it remains private, facilitates it by providing adaptive institutions.[56] When preservation of family, caste, and religious community is translated from the realm of private commitment to that of public ideology, and when organized efforts are made to affect public opinion, law, and political institutions in terms of tradition, then contradiction and conflict may come to characterize the political relationship of tradition and modernity. Organized efforts to pursue power in the name of tradition were relatively unsuccessful until the fourth general election in 1967, when they made impressive gains. Two political parties that attempted to do so in the immediate postindependence period, the Ram Rajya Parishad and the Hindu Mahasabha, are moribund. Two others, however, the Jan Sangh and Swatantra parties, particularly the former, have succeeded in introducing traditional ideology into public dialogue and political competition. The Jan Sangh's concern to restore Hinduism to a dominant place in a more centralized and authoritarian Indian state—to strengthen Hinduism's hold on Indian culture and character—and its more latent and ambivalent concern to uphold the caste system constitute a potential challenge to the present public hegemony of modernity in India.[57] So too, may the Swatantra party under the leadership of

[56] Harold Gould, "The Adaptive Functions of Caste in Contemporary Indian Society," *Asian Survey*, III (September, 1963).

[57] There is no thorough study as yet of the Jan Sangh. Motilal A. Ghangiani's

C. Rajagopalachari.[58] Although he rejects the traditionalism of princely or "village" rule, he wants to combat the dislocations caused by industrialization and the "statism" of Congress party government with an individualism restrained and made responsible by a transformed version of traditional culture and by the co-operative-group self-help and social security of family, caste, and village. The future course of the Indian dilemma, which neither the Jan Sangh and Swatantra can escape, will be written in considerable measure in their future course and fate.

Jana Sangh and Swatantra: A Profile of the Rightest Parties in India (Bombay, 1967) makes a beginning. The Jan Sangh's ideas and policies can best be followed in the party journal, *The Organizer*. Myron Weiner traces the formation of the party and the failure of its efforts to merge with the Hindu Mahasabha in *Party Politics in India* (Princeton, N.J., 1957). Jean Curran, in *Militant Hinduism in Indian Politics* (New York, 1951), examines in some detail the Jan Sangh's militant sister organization, the Rashtriya Swayamsevak Sangh. The political ideas and programs of its leader, M. S. Gowalkar (Guruji) can be found in the pages of *The Organizer* and in occasional pamphlets issued by the RSS. An over-all view of Jan Sangh electoral and legislative strength through the third general election can be found in W. H. Morris-Jones, *The Government and Politics of India* (London, 1965). In the fourth general election, the Jan Sangh improved its position from 14 to 35 seats in Parliament. More detailed behavioral analysis is available in Paul Brass, *Factional Politics in an Indian State* (Berkeley, Calif., 1965), in which he examines the Jan Sangh's social base, ideological appeal, and voting strength in a number of districts in Uttar Pradesh, the state in which it has its greatest support.

[58] In the fourth general election, the Swatantra increased its share of the parliamentary seats from 18 (minus its Bihar associates of 1962) to 42. For an analysis that sees less value in tradition and continuity and greater political danger from their expression in public life, see Howard L. Erdman, "Chakravarty Rajagopalachari and Indian Conservatism," *Journal of Developing Areas,* I (October, 1966). Rajagopalachari's views contain "hidden conservatism in what appears to be flexible, expansive, moderate conservatism" (p. 18). Erdman examines the overt and latent economic and social forces that can be mobilized in support of tradition in "Conservative Politics in India," *Asian Survey,* VI (June, 1966), and analyzes the ways the Swatantra party has mobilized them in "India's Swatantra Party," *Pacific Affairs,* XXXVI (Winter, 1963–64). These and other themes are examined in greater depth and detail in his *The Swatantra Party and Indian Conservatism* (Cambridge, 1967).

Untouchability:
The Test of Fellow Feeling

Farthest beyond the reach of fellow feeling are India's sixty-five million untouchables. The pollution barrier that ritual rank and primary-group socialization interpose between them and the rest of Hindu society inhibits the capacity of caste Hindus to experience a sense of common humanity with them and tends in turn to alienate them from Hindu culture and society.[1] Integrating untouchables into Indian society and politics poses extraordinary problems.

Transcending untouchability may be easier for some castes than for others. The social history of castes like the Iravas of Kerala and the Nadars of Madras suggests that the distinction between "clean" and "unclean" castes is not so definitive as is often assumed. There is an indeterminacy in this distinction as in other symbolic and behavioral aspects of social distance. "Polluting castes" are not so much a separate category below a self-evident line as they are units on a continuum that extends between "clean castes," on the one hand, and those that deal with death, blood, feces, and other polluting substances, on the other. The first published ethnographies of the early nineteenth century located the Nadars (then Shanans) somewhere between the lowest clean castes and those thought to be unclean.[2] By

---

[1] For primary socialization to the pollution barrier, see Joseph Elder, "Growing up in Rajpur," in "Hinduism and Industrialism" (forthcoming). The difficulty caste Hindus have in accepting untouchables as fellow human beings was dramatically brought home to us by a senior upper caste officer of the Harijan Sevak Sangh. After describing a lifetime devoted to improving the social, moral, and technical lot of untouchables, particularly Bhangis, who do the bulk of urban latrine cleaning in north India, he observed sadly that "the dirt was under their skin."

[2] They were denied the right to carry umbrellas, wear shoes or gold ornaments, milk cows, or walk in certain streets. They resided in a separate *cheri* (hamlet) beyond the villages where they were a minority (Robert L. Hardgrave, Jr., "Organization and Change among the Nadars of Tamilnad" [Madurai, March, 1965; mimeographed], pp. 5, 6). Hardgrave cites Bishop Caldwell

132

such tests as temple exclusion, polluting occupations, and separate village locations, the Nadars were then untouchables. Today, even though some still tap the palmyra palm and distil toddy, they are not even classified as a backward class.[3] Similarly, the Iravas of Kerala were listed as a scheduled caste by the Travancore census of 1931 on the ground that they were required to remain beyond the walls of temple compounds.[4] More recently, several scholars have placed them among the middle castes of a three-rank division: "A" castes (Nambudri Brahmans, Nairs); "B" castes (Iravas and a number of artisan castes); and "C" castes (castes economically and ritually inferior to Iravas).[5] Today, the Iravas are no longer among the scheduled castes.[6]

The legal and administrative term "scheduled caste,"[7] used by the British raj to designate for purposes of special assistance those castes throughout India whose low ritual status, poverty, and lack of oppor-

---

as characterizing the Nadars in the mid-nineteenth century "as belonging to the highest division of the lowest classes or the lowest of the middle classes," a characterization less precise than one might desire (p. 5).

[3] Those that can establish that they are still engaged in toddy tapping and are "poor" are classified as backward, but the Nadar community as a whole, despite its best efforts, failed to be so classified (*ibid.*, p. 27).

[4] Lelah Dushkin, "The Backward Classes, III," *Economic Weekly,* November 18, 1961, p. 1729.

[5] A. Aiyappan, *Iravas and Culture Change* (Madras, 1945), p. 31; Kathleen Gough, "Village Politics in Kerala—I," *Economic Weekly,* February 20, 1965, p. 367. Gough does not use Aiyappan's alphabetic units, but her categories approximate them.

[6] Gough, "Village Politics in Kerala—I," p. 367.

[7] According to K. Santhanam, the term originated at the Second Round Table Conference. Dr. Ambedkar submitted a supplementary memorandum that stated that "the existing nomenclature of Depressed Classes is objected to by members of the Depressed Classes who have given thought to it and also by outsiders who take interest in them. It is degrading and contemptuous and advantage may be taken of this occasion for drafting the new constitution to alter for official purposes the existing nomenclature" (cited by Santhanam, in *Ambedkar's Attack* [New Delhi, 1946], pp. 4–5). It was in response to this request that the new term "scheduled castes" was inaugurated. See also Lelah Dushkin, "Scheduled Caste Policy in India" (a paper delivered at a meeting of the Association for Asian Studies, New York, April 4, 1966, p. 4).

tunities invested them with social and civil disabilities, lends the category "untouchable" a spurious social definitiveness and homogeneity.[8] The Mahars, located primarily in Maharashtra, with a literacy rate very near the Indian average[9] and with several generations separating its leading sections from the practice of polluting occupations, would seem to represent a quite different social reality than the Bhangis, located primarily in Uttar Pradesh, with few literates and with a relatively high proportion of the caste still engaged in the highly polluting occupation of cleaning latrines.[10] And with the spread of modern technology the problems confronted by mobile untouchable castes can no longer be identified as generically different from those of mobile clean castes. For example, in 1956 the Chamars of Rajasthan were eager to disassociate themselves from their customary trade of leather working. By 1963, however, because of generous government financial and technical support to an industry capable of earning desperately needed foreign exchange and because of the advent of appreciable technical upgrading in the work involved, Chamars were straining to exclude "opportunists" from invading their ancient monopoly.[11] Despite its intimate contact with blood and

[8] How "objective" the scheduling of castes and tribes is, is a question that has not been explored. It seems likely that political considerations can affect the decision. Scheduled castes range from 6 per cent of the population in Maharashtra to 21 per cent in Uttar Pradesh (Government of India, *Census of India,* 1962, Paper 1).

[9] "In fact, the literacy rate for Mahars is at present said to have reached 11 per cent, compared with 7 per cent for Marathas" (Maureen L. P. Patterson, "Caste and Political Leadership in Maharashtra," *Economic Weekly,* September 25, 1954). Eleanor Zelliot writes that the Buddhists of Maharashtra, who are mainly Mahars, are thought by themselves and by caste Hindus to be more interested in education than any other castes except the advanced ones (Brahmans, Kayasthas). But there are no statistics (personal communication, August 8, 1966).

[10] See N. R. Malkani, *Clean People in an Unclean Country* (Delhi, 1965), an autobiographical account by a high caste Hindu of a lifetime devoted to improving the moral, material, and technological lot of the Bhangis. "The Bhangi," Malkani writes, "is essentially a recent product of urban life . . . the latest and worst addition to the caste system" (p. 136).

[11] Interview with Amrit Lal Yadav, a former minister in the Rajasthan cabinet, Jaipur, 1963.

134

death modern medicine is not generally regarded as polluting. These examples merely suggest the transformations that modern technology can introduce in the symbolism of purity and pollution.

The pollution continuum varies not only with time and the particular occupations identified as polluting but also with region. Generally, the ritual structure of southern states, with Kerala leading the way, either placed larger proportions of their populations in the polluted category or, in behavioral terms, treated them more severely than the structure of northern states, or both. Because the pollution barrier is higher for some and lower for others and because, generally, the range varies by region, a variety of ways of coping with the problems of social and political integration has been used.

Like other castes, untouchables often attempted Sanskritization. But it seems likely that their exclusion and separation from the Brahmanic tradition made untouchables less hospitable to such processes from the beginning. Many who initially attempted it are finding the emulation of dominant Hindu cultural norms a less and less meaningful path to self and social esteem.[12] "The attempt to

[12] Untouchables have Sanskritized their cultural norms. Narayanaswami, the Guru of the Kerala Irava community who united its many jatis under the slogan, "One Caste, One Religion, One God," drew heavily on Hinduism in establishing the doctrines and symbols of his movement, although rejecting the caste system (see Daniel Thomas, *Sree Narayana Guru* [Christian Institute for the Study of Religion and Society; Bangalore, 1965], pp. 26–27, and Aiyappan, *Iravas and Culture Change,* p. 159). Those Shanans who became Nadars established that assimilation could, under some circumstances, enable a caste to cross over in their own and society's estimate. Bernard Cohn, in "The Changing Status of a Depressed Caste," in McKim Marriott (ed.), *Village India* (Chicago, 1955), pp. 53–77, and Cohn, "The Changing Traditions of a Low Caste," in Milton Singer (ed.), *Traditional India* (Philadelphia, 1959), pp. 207–15, provides us with an example of Sanskritization being practiced in North India by the Chamars. So, too, does Owen Lynch in "The Politics of Untouchability: A Case Study from Agra, India" (a paper presented at the Conference on Social Structure and Social Change, University of Chicago, June 3–6, 1965). Cohn and Lynch agree with the findings of several others that Sanskritization was a phase or stage later repudiated by most. See also Donald Rosenthal, "Caste Integration into Urban Politics" (unpublished MS); Andre Beteille, "The Future of the Backward Classes: The Competing Demands of Status and Power," *Perspectives,* Suppl. to the *Indian Journal of Public Administration,* XI (January–March, 1965); Robert J. Miller, "Button,

press for higher ritual status was almost elided as the Mahars discovered political activity early in their awakening," Eleanor Zelliot observes of this Maharashtrian scheduled caste.[13]

With the spread of social and political self-consciousness and educational and economic opportunity, some untouchables have rebelled by overtly becoming non-Hindus. This has meant embracing a "negative identity"[14] such as Islam, Christianity, or Buddhism.[15] The neo-Buddhist movement in particular, though limited in its influence to a small, highly self-conscious section of the scheduled castes, has

button . . . Great Tradition, Little Tradition, Whose Tradition" (mimeographed; University of Wisconsin, March 1, 1965).

[13] Eleanor Zelliot, "The Mahar Political Movement," in Rajni Kothari (ed.), "Caste and Politics in India" (forthcoming). Owen Lynch, however, suggests that the Agra Chamars, now Jatavs, strove unsuccessfully for several generations to cross the pollution barrier by assimilating twice-born culture and have only recently—in the forties—recognized that "Sanskritization is no longer as functional as political participation for achieving a change in style of life" (see his "Politics of Untouchability," p. 20). Before the Mahars turned to politics, they donned sacred threads in a conference at Ratnagiri in 1929, conducted weddings with Brahman rites, and attempted temple entry (Zelliot, "The Mahar Political Movement," pp. 10, 11).

[14] This is Erik H. Erikson's term. "We will call," he writes, . . . "self-images . . . which are diametrically opposed to the dominant values of an individual's upbringing, parts of a *negative identity*—meaning an identity which he has been warned *not* to become, which he can become only with a divided heart, but which he nevertheless finds himself compelled to become, protesting his wholeheartedness. . . . Such rebellion . . . when joined to a great collective trend of rebellion . . . can rejuvenate as it repudiates" (*Young Man Luther* [New York, 1958], p. 102). Harold Isaacs, in his *India's Ex-Untouchables* (New York, 1965), captures such experiences among educated untouchables.

[15] For a close examination of the background and circumstances of such a choice, see David Lindell, "Malas, Madigas and Mass Movements" (unpublished seminar paper, University of Chicago, Political Science 392, 1964), p. 12. The Malas and Madigas of Andhra converted to Christianity in large numbers between 1875 and 1925. The Christian drain on low castes was also notable in Uttar Pradesh between 1911 and 1931 (see Julie B. Defler, "A Study of the Types of This-Worldly Salvation Sought by the Chamars of Uttar Pradesh" [unpublished seminar paper, University of Chicago, Political Science 392, 1964]). The Christian community in Maharashtra, numbering some half million, has come in large part from the lower castes (Zelliot, "The Mahar Political Movement").

come to be a leading sector for the formation of scheduled-caste identity and public action. While other low castes are gradually moving away from Sanskritization as a mobility strategy because it is losing its relevance in a secularized society, the untouchables appear increasingly to be seeking dignity through a negative relationship with it. In symbolic terms, neo-Buddhism has something in common with the "Black Power" movement in America.[16]

B. R. Ambedkar, the talented untouchable lawyer who piloted India's constitution through the Constituent Assembly, led hundreds of thousands of his community, the Mahars of Maharashtra, into the Buddhist fold just before his death in 1956. This act and the subsequent growth of the Buddhist movement are of profound importance for the future of fellow feeling in India.[17] Neo-Buddhism could be a unifying or divisive force.

[16] Twenty years ago, K. Santhanam, answering Ambedkar's *What Congress and Gandhi Have Done to the Untouchables* (Bombay, 1946), in *Ambedkar's Attack,* anticipated the argument between Martin Luther King, leader of the Southern Christian Leadership Conference and an admirer of Gandhi, and Stokely Carmichael, who, after becoming chairman in May, 1966, of the Student Non-Violent Coordinating Committee, established, with Floyd McKissick, national director of the Congress of Racial Equality, a national platform for the slogan "Black Power." "Dr. Ambedkar," Santhanam wrote, "has drawn an analogy between the position of Negroes in the U.S.A. and Harijans in India. . . . He contends that having used them in the . . . Civil War, the Republican Party betrayed them, the position of the Negroes is worse than ever." Santhanam, answering Ambedkar, observes that it was the "white people of America [who] fought among themselves for the abolition of slavery. Continuous attempts have been made by American statesmen and political parties to remove the disabilities under which the Negroes suffer. If taking their cue from Dr. Ambedkar, the Negroes of the U.S.A. should attack and discredit all Americans as a people, question the motives of all reformers who are fighting for justice to the Negroes, what would they gain by it? Against a united American people, the Negroes have no chance whatever. Their hope lies in the fact that . . . the conscience and intelligence of large numbers of the American people will make the nation realize that their own human dignity requires the complete emancipation of the Negroes. Substantially, this is true in the case of Harijans in India. . . . It seems . . . evident . . . that the only way of emancipation for the scheduled castes is to line [sic] with the progressive forces among the Hindus and fight against the reactionary elements" (p. 75).

[17] Its numbers are hard to calculate in part because conversion to Buddhism

Ambedkar's rebellion was broadcast on fertile ground. Untouchable communities in a variety of linguistic-cultural regions have often been bearers of or adherents to India's cultural underground, those sectarian possibilities that were potential competitors of Brahmanic Hinduism.[18] They have adhered to the "little" traditions—pre-

---

has deprived the convert of eligibility for the privileges accorded members of the scheduled castes. The highest claim we have seen is 20,000,000 (Republican Party of India, *Charter of Demands,* October 1, 1964, p. 20). Eleanor Zelliot believes the census figure of 1961, 3,250,227, is minimal, because many Buddhist converts fail so to list themselves in order not to lose the privileges. The movement has been most important in Maharashtra, where the census reported 2,789,501, but it also has influence in Madhya Pradesh, Punjab, and Uttar Pradesh and a bit in Mysore and Gujarat ("The Social and Political Significance of the Buddhist Conversion" in Donald Smith [ed.], *Religion and Politics in South Asia* [Princeton, N.J., 1966], MS p. 1, n. 1).

[18] The 1931 census of Hyderabad reports a division among "untouchables" with respect to their orientation toward Hinduism: "While the caste Hindus maintained discreet silence, two opposing sections of Adi-Hindus entered the arena. The Adi-Dravida Educational League argued that, judged by the history, philosophy and civilization of the Adi-Dravidas, the real aborigines of the Deccan, the depressed classes are, as a community, entirely separate and distinct from the followers of Vedic religion, called Hinduism. The League's contention was that Hinduism is not the ancestral religion of the aborigines of Hindustan; that the non-Vedic communities of India object to being called 'Hindus' because of their inherited abhorrence of the doctrines of the adherents of Manu Smrithi and like scriptures, who have distinguished themselves as caste Hindus for centuries past; that the Vedic religion which the Aryans brought in the wake of their invasion was actively practised upon the non-Vedic aborigines and that the aborigines, coming under the influence of Hindus generally, gradually and half-consciously adopted Hindu ideas and prejudices. A section of Adi-Hindus emphatically repudiated the above arguments in a statement to the Press and deplored the tendency of the Adi-Dravidas Educational League to seek to impose an invidious distinction. The conception of God, the mode of worship, the system of rituals and code of customs, the manner of dress and way of life, of the socially depressed classes are identical with those of the caste Hindus and, therefore, they maintained that religiously Adi-Hindus are Hindus" (Government of India, *Census of India,* 1931, XXIII, "Hyderabad," p. 258). Lynch reports a similar vigorous debate within the Agra Chamars-Yadavs, who at an early stage expelled a spokesman for the Adi-Hindu ("original" Hindus) point of view but later, in their post-Sanskritizing phase, accepted Ambedkar's arguments, which resemble the arguments of

Aryan or non-Aryan village cults and deities—which the twice-born varnas, particularly the Brahmans, were at pains to reconcile and integrate with their "great" tradition.[19] And in recent times and perhaps in earlier eras, they have adhered to other, often anti-Sanskritic traditions such as Buddhism and the spiritually egalitarian bhakti cults.[20] These underground movements, especially the bhakti cults, have usually been ambivalent, at once rebellious and compliant, with respect to the dominant high culture definitions, damning ritual and social barriers but failing to convert critique into reform and remaining within the framework of Hinduism.[21]

Ambedkar's rebellion bears the marks of a careful choice, conditioned by strongly divided feelings toward Indian culture and religion. He did not choose either Islam or Christianity, both of which were embarrassed by their non-Indian connections, the former by its

---

the Adi-Dravida Educational League in important particulars ("The Politics of Untouchability," pp. 14, 27).

[19] See Milton Singer, "Indian Civilization," in *Traditional India*, for an analysis of the intellectual history of these concepts and their application to our present knowledge of the content and structure of Indian culture. For a close theoretical examination of the relation of the "great" and "little" traditions on their Indian community settings, see McKim Marriott, "Little Communities in an Indigenous Civilization," in *Village India*, 171–222.

[20] The Mahars, who form the core of the Buddhist cult, produced Chokhamela, a fifteenth-century devotee in the bhakti tradition whose songs have become part of the religious literature of both high and low caste pilgrims in Maharashtra (Zelliot, "Mahar Political Movement," p. 91). The U.P. Chamars enshrined Rai Das, a saint whose mythology has anti-Brahmanic overtones (Cohn, "The Changing Traditions of a Low Caste," pp. 214–15; see also his "The Changing Status of a Depressed Class," pp. 59, 75–76). In both citations, the ambivalence discussed in the text between "rebellion" and the "obedience" of assimilation to Sanskrit norms and practice are strikingly apparent. The most radical statement of the significance of alternate traditions is Miller's "Button, button . . . ," in which he argues that the Mahars from the middle of the nineteenth century and probably for centuries earlier, sometimes secretly, sometimes overtly, rebelled against Brahmanical culture in the name of contrary great traditions.

[21] For the work of bhakti poets, see the translations by Norman Zide, C. M. Naim, and A. K. Ramanujan in "Selected Materials in Indian Civilization" (syllabus, for Introduction to Indian Civilization, University of Chicago).

association with the established state religion of India's chief international rival, Pakistan, the latter by its association with an alien foreign culture and imperial subjection. To become a Buddhist was to reject Hinduism, to repudiate Brahmanism, but to remain closer to Hindu Indian traditions than either of the other faiths allowed.[22] He declared at a press conference at the time of his conversion

> that he had once told Mahatma Gandhi that though he differed from him on the issue of untouchability, when the time came, "I will choose only the least harmful way for the country. And that is the greatest benefit I am conferring on the country by embracing Buddhism; for Buddhism is a part and parcel of Bharatiya culture. I have taken care that my conversion will not harm the tradition of the culture and history of this land!"[23]

The emergence of democratic politics in India provided the structural opportunity for a separate political definition of untouchables. Untouchable politics are affected by the same ambivalence that characterized their choice of faith. Muslims in India had succeeded, as early as 1909, in establishing separate Muslim electorates that chose only Muslims to occupy specially reserved seats in the central and provincial legislatures. In the early thirties, on the occasion of negotiations surrounding the constitutional reforms of 1935, Ambedkar

[22] Ambedkar wrote, in *The Untouchables, Who Were They*, "Untouchability was born sometime about 400 A.D. . . . out of the struggle for supremacy between Buddhism and Brahminism which has so completely moulded the history of India . . ." (p. 155); cited in Miller, "Button, button. . . ," p. 7). Miller tells us that for the Mahars Buddhism is a call to "abandon designation as Mahar, cease worshipping Hindu images, and to 'opt out' of the Brahmanical Great Tradition and its social system. For Buddhism is seen as a distinct, separate system, and is considered so in origin by the New Buddhists. From the perspective of the more educated convert, Buddhism began as a new system, intended to supplant the Brahmanical system; it was taken over by Brahmins, who then proceeded to merge it into *their* Great Tradition as an 'unorthodox sect' but still allowable as a 'part' of the Great Tradition. To the New Buddhists, there is no difficulty in understanding the statement, literally, that they chose to leave one system and enter another—without leaving India, Maharashtra, or any specific locality" (*ibid.*, p. 13).

[23] Dhananjay Keer, *Dr. Ambedkar: Life and Mission* (Bombay, 1962), p. 495.

sought similar privileges for the untouchables.[24] The demand raised the question of the relationship of national identity to Hindu religion and society. Could untouchables be Indian nationalists under Congress leadership and at the same time establish their dignity and equality in Indian society?[25] In Gandhi's mind, the beliefs and practices of untouchability degraded caste Hindus and untouchables alike. The threat of a separate identity for untouchables pained him as a nationalist seeking a comprehensive definition of nationhood and as a Hindu reformer influenced by the spiritual egalitarianism of the bhakti cults and Christianity. Accordingly, he successfully dedicated himself to the task of converting the disparate protests of various untouchability reform movements into a public ideology, widely shared among nationalists, that condemned untouchability.

For many untouchables and notably Ambedkar, this effort was marked by the weakness of all reform from above: exclusion of the subject people from prime or even exclusive responsibility for their own fate.[26] Separate electorates and reserved seats, by giving them

[24] In 1919, before the Franchise Committee, Ambedkar favored separate electorates and reserved seats, but before the Simon Commission in 1928 he favored joint electorates; in 1930 at the Round Table Conference he returned to his old view (Zelliot, "Mahar Political Movement," pp. 19, 26).

[25] See Ambedkar, *What Congress and Gandhi Have Done to the Untouchables,* and Santhanam's counterattack, *Ambedkar's Attack.* For Gandhi's ideas and actions, see Mahadev H. Desai, *The Diary of Mahadev Desai,* trans. from the Gujarati and ed. V. G. Desai (Ahmedabad, 1953), Vol. I; and M. K. Gandhi, *All Are Equal in the Eyes of God* (Delhi, 1964). Gandhi changed his view of caste considerably between 1921, when he considered varna distinctions helpful to restraining striving and intemperate ambition (*Young India,* October 6, 1921), and 1932, when he declared his ashram would not help arrange marriages between members of the same subcaste. In 1946 he declared himself in favor of marriages between caste Hindus and untouchables and subsequently said he would attend only marriages of such a kind (*All Are Equal . . . ,* pp. 68–69; and M. K. Gandhi, *Ashram Observances in Action* [Ahmedabad, 1959], p. 57).

[26] Robert J. Miller argues that in the 1920's Mahatma Gandhi and the Indian National Congress, from the Mahar point of view, "stunted, blocked and diverted" the organization and development of a "system" expressing a tradition in "opposition to the Brahmanical system" ("Button, button . . . ," p. 10). He cites a statement by Mahar leaders in 1930 that makes quite clear the

the independence and freedom they needed to be masters of their own fate, would help them understand themselves and their future better. A conference even requested that scheduled caste villages be established away from caste Hindu villages.[27] Perhaps they were a nation within the nation. The majority of untouchables who supported Gandhi and Congress nationalism, and shared the belief that Hinduism is capable of internal transformation, were and are, from this perspective, at worst "Uncle Toms" and at best "Booker T. Washingtons."[28]

Caste differs from other ascriptive identities, particularly religion and tribe, in its symbiotic relation to other castes within the larger ambit of Hinduism.[29] Gandhi recognized that separate electorates and reserved seats for untouchables, established on analogy with those for Sikhs or Muslims, could result in their mobilization as a

---

opposition between the community and the nationalist movement under Gandhi: "In view of the fact that Mr. Gandhi, Dictator of the Indian National Congress has declared a civil disobedience movement before doing his utmost to secure temple entry for the 'depressed' classes and the complete removal of 'untouchability,' it has been decided to organize the Indian National Anti-Revolutionary Party. . . . The Party will regard British rule as absolutely necessary until the complete removal of untouchability and the overthrow of 'Chaturvarna'" (p. 11; extract from the *Bombay Chronicle,* April 2, 1930). Miller concludes that, for the Mahars, "the Congress' struggle for independence was merely an attempt on the part of 'modern Aryas' to maintain supremacy over 'modern Dasyus.'" In these terms, the conversion of Mahars to Buddhism in 1956, prepared for by B. R. Ambedkar from the 1940's on, was the last stage of a continuing escape "from a Tradition and its system which *could not, in their view, be changed*" (p. 11).

[27] Resolution of the Conference of the Depressed Classes Association, 1942; cited in Zelliot, "Mahar Political Movement."

[28] Congress massively swept the seats reserved for scheduled castes in 1952. Only a very few of these went to non-Congress candidates. In 1957 and 1962, however, other parties have cut deeply into these seats.

For a sympathetic account of Washington and his relevance to the American Negro, see Herbert J. Storing, "The School of Slavery: A Reconsideration of Booker T. Washington," in Robert A. Goldwin (ed.), *100 Years of Emancipation* (Chicago, 1964), pp. 47–79.

[29] See, "Politics of Caste," pp. 64–87 above.

separate political community,[30] and, in fact that this was likely to happen unless caste Hindus redefined themselves in ways which changed fundamentally their relations to untouchables. Gandhi compromised, as Ambedkar did later in embracing an Indian but non-Hindu religion, by agreeing to that reservation of legislative seats for untouchables which is still a feature of the Indian constitution, but he insisted that the constituencies from which the candidates were to be elected be "general" as opposed to separate.[31] In such electorates, untouchable candidates would be obliged to make cross-community appeals to caste Hindus as well as untouchables. The result was to help integrate untouchable voters into the national political community and to preserve the credibility of Hindu social reform.[32]

Fifteen years later Ambedkar, as law minister in Nehru's first government, played the leading role in devising a secular constitution that not only abolished untouchability[33] but also disestablished the sacral view of caste[34] and laid the basis for transferring privilege from caste Hindus to untouchables. Under this constitutional transfer of privileges, which built on British innovations, seats in legislatures, civil services, and educational institutions, as well as government subsidies, were made available to backward classes through a form of

[30] He said at the second Round Table Conference in November, 1931, "Sikhs may remain as such in perpetuity, so may Muslims, so may Europeans. Would 'untouchables' remain untouchables in perpetuity?" (cited in Dushkin, "Scheduled Caste Policy," p. 7).

[31] D. G. Tendulkar, *Mahatma: Life of Mohandas Karamchand Gandhi* (Delhi, 1961), VII, 150–54.

[32] A detailed study of how the joint electorate worked in double-member constituencies, and how the abolition of double-member constituencies in 1962 affected voting behavior, is an important and uncompleted research task.

[33] See Constitution of India, Pt. III, Art. 15, sec. 2, paras. (*a*) and (*b*) and Art. 17.

[34] By preventing the courts from recognizing its integrative principle and its vertical, hierarchic distinctions. This is the formulation of Marc Galanter; see his "Changing Legal Conceptions of Caste" (a paper delivered at the Conference on Social Structure and Social Change, University of Chicago, June 3–6, 1965), particularly p. 50.

progressive discrimination.[35] It would seem that Gandhi's recognition of some need for a special untouchable identity—in reserved seats—and Ambedkar's discovery that the constitutional framework was amenable to untouchable needs, represented compromises in their respective views of the untouchables' relation to the nation. Politically, as well as in matters of faith, untouchables maintained an identity that was both in tension with and yet part of a larger Indian system.

Both sides, the Indian state under the direction of the Congress party and those untouchables who followed Ambedkar, remained ambivalent about their mutual relations after independence and the adoption of the constitution. The Scheduled Castes Federation, founded by Ambedkar in 1942, contested the general elections in 1952 and 1957. It expressed in its name and policies a sense of communal separateness, and it pursued, for the most part, a strategy of horizontal rather than differential mobilization by appealing to and organizing Mahars. The more radical and ideological Republican party, which Ambedkar established after the second general election of 1957, attempted to move toward differential mobilization by combining appeals to the poor and dispossessed with efforts to broaden the party's community base.[36] This change of strategies may well

[35] Lelah Dushkin, "Scheduled Caste Policy in India," provides a summary of British policy, including scheduling for privileges. The transfer of privilege to backward classes is known as protective or progressive discrimination (see p. 146, n. 41). For a time, underprivileged caste Hindus were included on a caste basis in the transfer of privilege, but of late caste per se has been rejected by the courts as a criterion of backwardness. Now only the scheduled castes are entitled by law and policy to reservations and privileges on the basis of caste only. ". . . The higher castes," Marc Galanter writers, "have lost support legally for their claims for precedence and have lost some of the immunity once enjoyed by caste action in support of these claims. The lower castes have gained government intervention in favor of their claims for equality and preferential treatment in the distribution of benefits" ("Law and Caste in Modern India," *Asian Survey,* IV [November, 1963], 557). For protective discrimination, see his "Equality and 'Protective Discrimination' in India," *Rutgers Law Review,* XXI (Fall, 1961), and Lelah Dushkin, "The Backward Classes, I, II, and III," *Economic Weekly,* October 28, November 4 and 18, 1961.

[36] The move has brought other castes into the fold, but not as yet many who are not untouchables. The Agra Yatavs are the main supporters of the party in

represent the recognition that "opting out" by establishing an exclusive negative identity will profit untouchables less than creating a common front with other underprivileged groups.

In conjunction with the weakening of Congress, this strategy bore some fruit. Republican seats in the state legislative assemblies rose, between the 1962 and 1967 general elections, from eleven to twenty-four.[37] At the same time, 1967 saw Mahars and other untouchables who had been allied with the Republicans negotiating with Congress and other parties, notably the SSP, for tickets and alliances. Unlike the traditional, often passive connection of untouchables with Congress, these new connections were sought on the basis of strength by mobilized communities.

Eight years after Ambedkar's death the first demand of the Charter of Demands presented by the Republican party to Prime Minister Shastri in October, 1964, was that a "portrait of Baba Saheb Dr. B. R. Ambedkar 'The Father of the Indian Constitution' must be given a place in the Central Hall of Parliament" alongside the great national leaders and founding fathers now hung there.[38] The demand made clear that a critical section of politically conscious and organized untouchables were willing to recognize the nation's leaders if the nation would recognize their leader as one of them. Home Minister Chavan, formerly chief minister of Maharashtra, the Mahars' home state, and an engineer of the Maharashtra Congress' electoral approach to the Mahars, presided over a committee that raised a public subscription and in 1967 installed Ambedkar's statue in the courtyard of Parliament.[39]

Agra city. (Donald Rosenthal, "Bases of Conflict and Cooperation in Two Indian Cities," forthcoming in *Midwest Political Science Review*.)

[37] Government of India, Election Commission, *Report on the Third General Election in India, 1962* (Delhi, 1963), II (Statistical), 80–81; Government of India, Press Information Bureau, "Party Position, State Assembly" (New Delhi, 1967; mimeographed). In 1967 the Republican strongholds were Uttar Pradesh, 9 seats, and Maharashtra, 5 seats. In Maharashtra, their candidates won 12 per cent of the popular vote for the national Parliament.

[38] Republican Party of India, *Charter of Demands*.

[39] *Indian Express* (Madurai), April 3, 1967. "Dr. Ambedkar has been accorded a position of honour previously given only to Mr. Motilal Nehru whose

Another area where ambivalence and conflict have been apparent is access to the privileges accorded members of scheduled castes. The constitution forbids religious discrimination on the part of the state and guarantees freedom of religion. The courts have regularly invalidated laws which violate these provisions.[40] Yet the president's order designating the scheduled castes, chief beneficiaries of the privileges that flow from progressive discrimination, provided that "no person professing a religion different from Hinduism shall be deemed a member of a Scheduled Caste."[41] The courts have not only avoided reviewing the president's order[42] but have applied the

---

statue was installed some years ago a few yards away within the Parliament House Compound."

[40] Articles 16, 25, 26 and 30. For the place of religion in the Indian state, see Donald E. Smith, *India as a Secular State* (Princeton, N.J., 1963).

[41] We are indebted to Marc Galanter's paper "Changing Legal Conceptions of Caste," for the argument and facts here and below. Barbara Ravenell's unpublished seminar paper, "The Courts and Neo-Buddhist Claims to Scheduled Caste Privileges" has also been most useful. For the president's order, see Constitution (Scheduled Castes) Order, 1950, para. 3. Sikh members of four of the thirty-four scheduled castes listed for the Punjab were made an exception. Later, all Sikh members of scheduled castes were brought within the ambit of the order. See The Scheduled Castes and Scheduled Tribes Orders (Amendment) Act, 1956 (Act 63 of 1956), paper 3. The Constitution (Scheduled Tribes) Order contains no religious qualifications.

[42] The leading case here is S. Gurmukh Singh v. Union of India, All India Reporter, 1952 Punjab 143. The court found that the constitution vested in the president the entire power to determine which castes were to be designated as scheduled castes. It therefore refused to review his order including Hindu but not Sikh Bawarias, although its dicta made clear that it considered backwardness, not religion, the proper basis for inclusion. "The unreviewability of the Presidental order," Marc Galanter observes, "would seem open to question in the light of subsequent cases which have firmly established judicial power to review the standards used by government to designate the recipients of preferential treatment. *Balaji v. State of Mysore* A.I.R. 1963 Mys. 649. There is no indication in the Constitution that executive action, even in pursuance of expressly granted and exclusive Constitutional powers, is immune from judicial review for conformity with Constitutional guarantees of fundamental rights. See Art. 12. The position in the *Gurmukh Singh* case, must be seen as one of judicial restraint rather than judicial powerlessness" ("Changing Legal

"Hinduism test" to castes otherwise eligible for the benefits and privileges accorded the scheduled castes.[43] In doing so they have supported the view of caste as dependent on the sacral order of Hinduism, despite the fact that the existence of castes outside Hinduism (among Sikhs, Muslims, and Christians) "is well known and has long been recognized by the judiciary."[44] The president's and court's view became even less tenable in 1956 when Sikh but not Christian, Muslim, or Buddhist scheduled castes were recognized.[45] In the eyes of the courts, converts from Hinduism to religions that do not recognize caste, like Buddhism, automatically shed their caste identity, bonds and burdens (such as untouchability) even though accounts of behavior and attitudes, which have been recognized by the courts in other contexts where community membership was at issue, massively contradict such a finding.[46] The assumption that converted

Conceptions," p. 38, n. 121). It was executive action rather than the courts that brought the determination of which castes were scheduled into line with the Indian state's general commitment to secularism.

[43] See S. Gurmukh Singh v. Union of India, All India Reporter, 1952 Punjab 143; Michael v. Venkataswaran, All India Reporter, 1952 Madras 474, and In re Thomas, All India Reporter, 1953 Madras 21, all discussed by Galanter, "Changing Legal Conceptions of Caste," pp. 33–40. The commissioner for scheduled castes and tribes, following the presidential order, also ruled that "as Buddhism is different from the Hindu religion, any person belonging to a Scheduled Caste ceases to be so if he changes his religion. He is not, therefore, entitled to the facilities provided under the Constitution specifically for the Scheduled Castes" (*Report of the Commissioner for Scheduled Castes and Tribes,* 1957–58, I, 25, and II, 60).

[44] Galanter, "Changing Legal Conceptions of Caste," p. 39.

[45] See n. 41 above.

[46] In In re Thomas, All India Reporter, 1953 Madras 21, the Madras High Court held that converts, in this instance to Christianity, "ceased to belong to any caste because the Christian religion does not recognize a system of castes" (p. 88). And Marc Galanter reports a speech by Mr. B. N. Datar in the Rajya Sabha, August 26, 1957, in which he held that "Buddhism [does] not recognize castes" ("Changing Legal Conceptions of Caste," p. 39).
In tests of community membership, for example, in Chatturbhuj Vithaldas Jasami v. Moreshwar Pareshram, 1954 Supreme Court Reports 817, the Supreme Court held that a member of a scheduled caste who joined a Hindu sect (the

Hindus lose caste, Marc Galanter observes, "reflects the continued force of the sacral view of caste. . . . The 'caste' of which the court is speaking is not caste in the sense of a body of persons bound by social ties, but caste in the sense of a body which occupies a place in the ritual order of Hinduism."[47]

In the fall of 1964 after widespread demonstrations and satyagrahas, government responded positively to the seventh demand of the Republican party of India, which called for the "extension of all privileges guaranteed by the Constitution to such scheduled castes as embraced Buddhism."[48] In effect, Prime Minister Shastri, speaking

---

Mahanushava Panth) that repudiated the caste system remained a member of the scheduled caste if he identified himself and his caste accepted him as one. His conversion, the court held, "imports little beyond an intellectual acceptance of certain ideological tenets and does not alter the convert's caste status. . . . If the individual . . . [retains] his old social and political ties" the conversion does not affect his caste standing (p. 839).

The Madras Government did extend the school fee concession to scheduled caste members who had left Hinduism by conversion but did so as an "indulgence" rather than because it continued to recognize them as members of the scheduled castes (In re Thomas, All India Reporter, 1953 Madras 21 at 88). Converts to non-Hindu religions who reconvert to Hinduism and were born members of a scheduled caste are entitled to certain preferences, but those whose fathers converted and who were "born" of such converted fathers cannot regain scheduled caste standing by themselves embracing Hinduism (*Report of the Commissioner for Scheduled Castes and Scheduled Tribes,* 1953, p. 132).

[47] "Changing Legal Conceptions of Caste," p. 39.

[48] The mass satyagraha of the Republican party of India began on December 6, 1964, and was conducted at various times before Parliament in New Delhi, in Vidarbha and elsewhere in Maharashtra, and in Punjab (*Hindustan Times,* November 11 and December 7, 1964, January 3 and February 21, 1965; and *Times of India,* December 6, 7, 8, and 14, 1964, and January 4, 1965). The news reports suggest that participants in the various agitations ranged from 1,000 to 300,000 (*Times of India,* December 7 and 14, 1964) and persons arrested came to 530 in one instance (*Hindustan Times,* December 7, 1964). In the seventh demand (*Charter of Demands,* p. 20), the RPI there argued that "in spite of their conversion their economic and social conditions . . . remain unchanged. . . . The newly converted Buddhists are fully entitled to the benefits guaranteed to the Scheduled Castes under the constitution." See also interview with B. D. Khobragade, General Secretary of the RPI in Chicago, Illinois, October 20, 1965.

for the Congress government, agreed in principle to drop the "Hinduism test" for access to the "privileges" of backwardness. The government's subsequent statements and actions indicate that it means to do so by shifting over time from a caste to an economic criterion so that by the end of the sixth five-year plan in 1981 no caste (or tribe) will be scheduled.[49] Government has thus committed itself to removing a major obstacle to the integration of the political community on secular lines.[50]

[49] In the fall of 1965, government accepted in principle the recommendations of the Lokur Committee (Government of India, Department of Social Security, *The Report of the Advisory Committee on the Revision of the Lists of Scheduled Castes and Scheduled Tribes* [Delhi, 1965]). It held that "in the interests of national integration we feel that the time has come when the question of descheduling of relatively advanced communities should receive serious and urgent consideration" (p. 10). "To accelerate the pace of descheduling, a deadline may perhaps be fixed when the lists of Scheduled Castes and Tribes are totally dispensed with" (p. 24). Government subsequently suggested that the time limit for total elimination of schedules be fixed to coincide with the end of the sixth five year plan (1981). Government is now engaged in drawing up a phased program for descheduling advanced communities in consultation with the states on the basis of socioeconomic surveys. Members of Parliament from scheduled communities have been asked for information and comment (*Indian Recorder and Digest,* November, 1965, p. 10). Legislation "reclassifying" (i.e., descheduling) some castes was introduced but not acted upon in 1967 during the monsoon session of Parliament (*Tribune* [Ambala], June 9, 1967).

[50] The policy shift was not entirely unanticipated. A bill to treat Buddhists as members of the scheduled castes was introduced in the Lok Sabha in August, 1961 (*New York Times,* August 30, 1961, p. 2). The central government has pressed the state governments to extend the privileges available to the backward classes to Buddhist converts (*Report of the Commissioner of Scheduled Castes and Scheduled Tribes,* 1957–58, I, 25, and II, 60). Some states have extended such concessions to them, others have gone farther by treating them for some purposes as members of the scheduled castes, and still others have not extended any preferential treatment. Contributing to the shift has been the pressure of central government policies and Court decisions. Since 1961, the central government has pressed for the adoption of economic criteria in defining other backward classes, that is, other than the scheduled castes. Since 1963 its grants for scholarships to members of other backward classes have required the use of economic criteria for defining such classes. "By now," Andre Beteille reports that Home Secretary L. P. Singh informed him, "the majority of the States have adopted this criterion [economic] for defining back-

This policy shift does not, however, remove a critical contradiction built into the present constitutional and governmental efforts to eradicate the moral and practical consequences of untouchability. To obtain the privileges designed to elevate and transform the untouchable, he must affirm that he is one.[51] The price of discrimination in reverse has been a kind of blackmail in reverse; in return for access to opportunity and power the untouchable is asked to incriminate himself socially. This is not only profoundly disturbing but also an important source of alienation and rebellion.

However, government is moving away from requiring such declarations by establishing new and, it is hoped less demeaning ways to identify and help those who require it. The more secure untouchables believe they no longer need the crutch of progressive discrimination;[52] at the same time government and the courts increasingly seem inclined to substitute economic for caste criteria in their effort to make opportunities more equal.[53]

---

wardness for the award of scholarships to the Backward Classes other than Scheduled Castes and Scheduled Tribes" (". . . Backward Classes," p. 7). The leading cases involving the replacement of ritual standing with economic and educational criteria to assess the backwardness of a caste and, in so doing, to move toward standards of backwardness that are exclusively secular are Balaji v. State of Mysore, All India Reporter, 1963 Supreme Court 649, and Chitralekha v. State of Mysore, 43 Mysore Law Journal (Supreme Court Cases) 11 (1964).

[51] See Isaacs, *India's Ex-Untouchables,* Chap. 8, particularly p. 114: ". . . The individual who seeks help in getting rid of his identity must proclaim it." Beteille observes that "a Harijan must assert that he is a Harijan if he is to mobilize the support necessary for his political advancement. And it is here that the demands of power and status come into conflict. Whereas the Backward Classes are prompted to merge their identity with the higher castes to enhance their status, considerations of power and economic advantage lead them to define their identity in opposition to the advanced sections of society. This is the dilemma of backwardness" (". . . Backward Classes," p. 27).

[52] See *The Charter of Demands,* No. 10.

[53] To ascertain government's "direction" on this question is of course very difficult. State governments do not always see eye to eye with Delhi on this as on other matters. The interest of ministers at the center and in the states is to keep Congress in power. As long as reserved seats for scheduled castes help them to do so, it will be difficult to change policy and law on the reservation of seats in the legislatures. But Congress is losing its grip on such seats not only

Although negative self-definitions are available as alternatives to both the dominant Indian culture and the established political system, the leading sections among untouchables have not as yet used them to become a revolutionary class. In part, this may be merely a function of their still relatively depressed circumstances; revolution grows more out of knowledge and hope than out of ignorance and resignation. It may be that India's untouchables are not yet ready. But the evidence leads us to hazard a contrary view.

The neo-Buddhist movement and the Republican party represent the political response of a small but significant minority of advanced untouchables. Some would argue that both this advanced sector, and the majority of untouchables who continue to adhere to the Congress party, are not representative of the future. They would point out that untouchable landless laborers, who constitute a large part of the rural work force, might, under certain circumstances be mobilized for revolutionary political commitment or action. By acquiring a class consciousness that would unite a sense of economic exploitation with questions of dignity and status, untouchable landless laborers might, given effective and united leadership and organization and propitious circumstances, be welded into a revolutionary force. The available evidence suggests that this is most likely to happen when they are working under "factory-like" circumstances that unite physical contiguity with a shared sense of common grievances. Plantation workers in Kerala, for example, have been organized by the Communist and Revolutionary Socialist parties in support of not only trade union activities and demands and electoral efforts but also

---

to the Republican party but also to other opposition parties. The Chairman of the Backward Classes Commission, old-time Gandhian Kaka Kalelkar, emerged from the commission's work with the conviction "that backwardness could be tackled on a basis or a number of bases other than that of caste" (letter of transmittal in *Report of the Backward Classes Commission*). The *Report of the Study Team on the Social Welfare of Backward Classes* proposed the introduction of economic criteria in schemes of assistance to backward classes and scheduled castes (I, 329). And the central government has applauded the income-based educational policy of Maharashtra and Gujarat and suggested that other states follow suit (Dushkin, "The Backward Classes—III," p. 1732; see also nn. 49, 50 above).

direct action.[54] Even under the less propitious circumstances that prevail in Tanjore District in Madras State, where traditional patron-client relations have decayed and been replaced by what Marx would have called impersonal contractual relations, it has been possible for the Communist party to appeal to and organize untouchable landless laborers.[55] And in Naxalbari, West Bengal, bordering Pakistan, Nepal, and Assam and not far from China, local cadres of the left Communist party and a few dissident party veterans from Calcutta seemed to be reviving an Indian version of Mao's Yenan strategy when they successfully encouraged tribal agricultural laborers to rise against their landlords in a bow-and-arrow rebellion that radio Peking proclaimed as the beginning of peasant revolution in India.

Several other outcomes, however, seem more likely than local or state-wide much less national, radicalization and mobilization of untouchable (or tribal) landless laborers for revolutionary purposes. Most village untouchables remain subject to vertical mobilization by dominant castes upon whom they are economically dependent. Some local notables of such dominant castes have added force and fraud to

[54] Michael St. John's "The Communist Party and Communal Politics in Kerala" (Senior honors thesis, Department of Social Relations, Harvard University, 1962), and Dwight L. Mathes, "Kerala's Communist Regime: An Analysis and Interpretation" (M.A. thesis, Department of Political Science, University of Chicago, in draft), provide general contexts in which to judge the sources of Communist party strength in Kerala.

[55] Kathleen Gough reported joint organization of Pallans and Parayans, both untouchable castes, under Communist auspices in Tanjore to support each other in wage strikes against landlords ("The Social Structure of a Tanjore Village," in McKim Marriott, *Village India*, p. 51). She also found some one hundred tenant farmers in a Kerala village belonging to a peasant union ("Village Politics in Kerala—I, *Economic Weekly,* February 20, 1965, p. 371).

Dagfinn Sivertsen discussed the formation, also under Communist auspices in Tanjore, of the Poor Cultivator's Association to bargain for wages and otherwise protect tenants (*When Caste Barriers Fall* [Oslo, 1963], p. 121). Both Sivertsen (p. 85) and Edward Harper, "Social Consequences of an 'Unsuccessful' Low Caste Movement," in James Silverberg (ed.), "Social Mobility in Caste" (forthcoming), report the decay of the traditional patron-client relations, which presumably leaves untouchables more accessible to horizontal mobilization. See also Andre Beteille, who depicts a rather irregular and individualist relation between casual labor and *mirasdars* (in Tanjore) (*Caste, Class and Power* [Berkeley, Calif., 1965], pp. 123–24).

traditional social discipline to maintain their ascendancy in new electoral contexts. But many others have responded to the untouchables' burgeoning political power, conferred by the secret ballot, and their independence, made possible by education and extravillage economic opportunities, by recognizing their interests in the conduct of elections and of government. Vertical mobilization in one form or another helps to explain the success among scheduled caste voters of the conservative Swatantra and the right radical Jan Sangh parties in Rajasthan and of Andhra Reddi notables both within and without the Congress party.

More advanced castes, such as the Nadars, Iravas, and Yadavs (advanced Chamars), are, in great measure, no longer accessible to vertical mobilization by dominant castes. Such caste communities have been characterized by "elongation," a stringing out of their members on a socioeconomic continuum, with the more advanced mobilizing and dominating a caste association. For a time at least, such associations, by fostering social mobility through Sanskritized or secular means, promote social and political integration, not revolution. Later, as they become more elongated, their capacity to represent the now more narrowly defined common interests of the caste community and to affect electoral behavior by evoking caste identity strengthens pluralism rather than the growth of revolutionary consciousness and class organizations.[56] They are of course, subject to penetration from without by a variety of appeals and structures, including revolutionary ones, but the give and take which characterizes the relationships of parties and caste communities has led more often to differential mobilization in which class and community both play a part than to horizontal mobilization in class terms only.[57]

[56] For example, the SNDP, Sri Narayana's movement in Kerala, acts politically, recommending Irava candidates to Irava voters (Gough, "Village Politics in Kerala—I," p. 367). The Jatav Vir Mahasabha and Jatav Pracharak Mandal, associations of the Agra Chamars, successfully pressed for political representation in the state Legislative Council of U.P. in 1920; in the thirties they attempted to establish a solid voting front of Chamars, regardless of party, on community issues (Lynch, "The Politics of Untouchability," p. 18). For Vanniyar and Nadar political mobilization and representation, see pp. 40–54 above.

[57] Kathleen Gough interprets the admitted congruence between party and caste in Kerala by relating it to the close relationship of caste and class. In sup-

Vertical mobilization by dominant castes, horizontal mobilization by caste communities and differential mobilization by parties, even those with revolutionary ideologies, will not easily produce revolutionary consequences among India's untouchables. Lenin is more likely to be right than Marx; revolutions are made more by professional revolutionaries than by revolutionary classes. India's untouchables have not yet made themselves easily accessible to such leadership.[58]

---

port of her contention that class will pull ahead, she marshals two tables, one showing caste-party and one class-party correlations in her two villages. The tables reveal a slightly higher congruence between class and party than between caste and party ("Village Politics in Kerala—II," *Economic Weekly,* February 27, 1965, pp. 415–16).

[58] See, for example, Isaacs, *India's Ex-Untouchables,* for the degree to which educated, mobile, urban ex-untouchables cut themselves off from their community as far as political leadership is concerned and identify with ideological positions appropriate to their white-collar or professional social standing.

PART TWO

The Traditional Roots
of Charisma: Gandhi

In an era that takes matters of religious faith lightly, it is difficult to consider a man who is suspected of saintliness. The task is particularly vexing for Americans whose origins in flight from Europe and its feudal legacies mute their memories of a time when saints were important people. Was Gandhi's political shrewdness compatible with the essential innocence of heart that one asks of saints? A generation of ambivalent skeptics in one breath denies that saints exist and in the next avers that Gandhi could not have been one because he did not meet such and such criterion of saintliness. For us, Gandhi's meaning and contribution can best be explored outside the framework of saintliness.

Whether Gandhi did or did not speed Britain's exit from India provides another distraction. It can plausibly be argued that Britain would have departed from the subcontinent in or about 1947 whether or not Gandhi occupied the historical stage. A review of Gandhi's role in gaining the political objective of Indian independence fails to touch what may prove to be his most important contribution, what he did for Indian character and capacities. Gandhi's leadership, regardless of its objective success or failure, had important subjective consequences, repairing wounds in self-esteem inflicted by generations of imperial subjection, restoring courage and potency, recruiting and mobilizing new constituencies and leaders, helping India to acquire national coherence.

That Gandhi should have been one of the most conspicuous modernizers of Indian politics suggests that some elements of tradition can serve modern functions. Indian history exhibits great variety in the realm of non-Kshatriya leadership, from the Brahmanic teacher addressing himself to a limited elite in an esoteric medium (Sanskrit) to the bhakti (devotional) teacher communicating with popular audiences through familiar symbols and local languages. If the

Sanskritic and textual bias of Indology placed the first mode in the foreground of scholarly and world perspectives of India, the second is today becoming more visible as a result of a new Indology that looks beyond Sanskrit texts and of the replacement in Indian historiography of an elite by a democratic bias. Gandhi came from an area and family strongly influenced by bhakti. His identification with it shaped his political style and helped him, in the face of the limitations imposed by illiteracy and the dearth of mass communications, to do what great bhakti teachers for centuries past had done, to reach mass audiences by peripatetic teaching throughout the subcontinent.

Gandhi's commitment to non-violence and truth (satyagraha, or "truth force"), too, suggests how traditional ideals can be transformed for modern purposes. He self-consciously rejected the fatalistic, otherworldly, and ritualistic orientation that some Jain and Hindu practioners had lent them. His private struggle for competence and potency taught him to evoke their humanistic, evangelical, and world-mastering implications. If his commitments to non-violence and satyagraha had instrumental dimensions, fitting the requirements of an unarmed nation confronting an imperial conscience capable of responding to moral appeals, he infused their practice with meanings that transcend utility and national boundaries.

Gandhi's concern to rationalize and extend the organizational bases of Indian political life and his capacity to use efficiently himself, time, and resources were rooted in a Hindu expression of this-worldly asceticism. Here again a component of tradition functioned in a modern manner, helping Gandhi to master or manufacture his political environment. Like his political style and commitments to truth and non-violence, Gandhi's this-worldly asceticism arose out of the interaction between the religious and secular culture of family, community, and region and the psychological circumstances of a particular life. Like the religious asceticism required for virtue and potency, it found expression in his sense of vocation: "For me there is no distinction between politics and religion."[1] ". . . When I say that I prize my own salvation above everything else," he wrote, ". . . it does not mean that my personal salvation requires a sacrifice of

[1] "Interview to the 'Bombay Chronicle,' *The Bombay Chronicle*, February 18, 1922," in *Collected Works of Mahatma Gandhi* (Delhi, 1958——), XXII, 404.

India's political . . . salvation. But it implies that the two go together."[2]

Gandhi contributed to Indian political modernization too by asserting in example and precept a public ethic against the standards of private obligation to friends and family. In doing so, he translated into indigenous terms the civility that British law and administration brought to India by imbuing it with the moral remorselessness associated with the traditional practice of virtue and by applying it in traditional contexts.

Gandhi's leadership helps to illuminate the dynamics and particulars of charismatic leadership. Because signs of grace feature as an essential but transcendent aspect of charisma its human meaning is hard to fathom. Gandhi's doubts about his worthiness arose from the idiosyncratic circumstances of his psychological development. His uncertainty helped generate the energy and ideas that he invested in a personal quest for competence, meaning, and integrity. Drawing upon the social and historical resources that surrounded his life path, he fashioned an identity and a message that spoke to the experiences and problems of Indians living under foreign imperial subjection. The saliency and resonance of these personal solutions enabled them to be translated into public and historical ones. If he remained uncertain until the end about his worthiness, he yet perceived a relationship between his attempts at perfection, on the one hand, and the course of history and his public reception, on the other.

Gandhi's charisma had a cultural referent. His effectiveness as a peripatetic teacher was related less to his oratorical or theatrical skills —he never became a great speaker—than to the reputation that preceded him and the ideal that he embodied. The authenticity with which he sought virtue and the highest religious goals through self-control, truth, and non-violence re-enacted a familiar but rarely realized cultural model, that of the saintly man. By communicating in a fresh and historically relevant manner the idea that those who could master themselves could achieve serenity, religious merit, and mastery of their environment, he evoked a response that his authority as a consummate and skilled politician could not alone have commanded.

[2] "No End to My Sorrows," *Young India,* February 23, 1922, in *ibid.,* p. 462.

The ideological need to relate national identity and self-esteem to indigenous cultural traditions has lost urgency with the demise of the imperial power. As Gandhi's ideals and methods have faded among Indian generations more interested in economic development, social mobility, and national security, they have traveled abroad. Freed from their particular cultural and national setting, they can be found particularly in the United States where Martin Luther King has translated them for use in the struggle by American Negroes for equal rights and opportunities. Their continuing relevance in these and other circumstances suggests in yet another way how the opposition of modernity and tradition may obscure more than it clarifies processes of social change and political development.

The Fear of Cowardice

Like many thinkers and actors in the Indian tradition, Gandhi cared more for man's inner environment than his outer and was highly self-conscious about his effect on how Indians felt about themselves. The young Nehru, who often questioned the Mahatma's political strategy and tactics, concedes again and again his effect on the nationalist generation:

> Much that he said we only partially accepted or sometimes did not accept at all. But all this was secondary. The essence of his teaching was fearlessness and truth and action allied to these. . . . So, suddenly as it were, that black pall of fear was lifted from the people's shoulders, not wholly, of course, but to an amazing degree. . . . It was a psychological change, almost as if an expert in psychoanalytic method had probed deep into the patient's past, found out the origins of his complexes, exposed them to his view, and thus rid him of that burden.[1]

[1] Jawaharlal Nehru, *The Discovery of India* (New York, 1946), pp. 361–62.

160

The portrait of Gandhi probing the nation's historical subconscious is a telling one. Gandhi had a unique sensibility both for the nightmare terrors of the Indian psyche and for its commonplace daytime self-doubts. He understood both the fundamental fear of Indians that those Britons who judged them as lacking in basic components of moral worth—like courage—might be right and the more superficial doubts about their technical ability to do anything about removing the raj. The nightmare fears he understood in part by analogy with his own personal terrors, terrors involving especially the issue of courage. The shape that he gave to the national movement, above all the technique of satyagraha, had much more than strategic significance; it provided a path for action that "solved" some problems of Indian self-esteem arising from acceptance of the negative judgments of Englishmen.

One result of British rule had been to strengthen the appearance and reality of non-violent cultural norms. By the middle of the nineteenth century the last vestiges of organized Indian military power had sunk from view. Kshatriya rule and culture, particularly after 1858, lost their violent capabilities and concerns. Under the sheltering umbrella of British guarantees, ceremony and conspicuous consumption atrophied the will and diverted the resources of India's fighting classes. Even while British rule was making clear that Indians lacked power, it strengthened the non-violent dimensions of Indian culture by providing educational and related service opportunities that required the skills and temperament of the office rather than the scepter and sword. Adherence to non-violence, while conspicuous among the qualifications for reaching the eschatological goals of Sanskritic Hinduism, is only one of the social ideologies found in traditional thought. Violence, too, has occupied an important place in thought and history and has its share of legitimizing religious and secular norms. But as the psychological and moral effects of Britain's conquest and subjection of India spread and deepened, and Indians adapted to the roles the empire required, both Britons and Indians began to believe that non-violence and the corollaries the British attributed to it—passivity, weakness, and cowardice—were the norms of Indian culture and character. The belief led many Britons to think that the superiority of British power and culture was an inherent rather than a historical phenomenon. India's military heritage, the heroes and social ideology that legitimized the use of violence and the character and rule of those who practiced it were, if not forgotten, at least moved into the background. Within the literary heritage of Indian civilization the texts sanctioning the authority and sanctifying the norms of the non-martial twice-born received the lion's share of scholarly and official attention. This image of India survived the sufficiently violent if disorganized and politically unproductive events of the 1857 Rebellion and the partition agitation of 1905. It was out of such circumstances and materials that the British constructed the unsystematic theory of imperialism that legitimized and explained British domination and Indian subjection.

The things that Britons had to say about India varied so widely that any attempt to distil their judgments seems presumptuous. And yet, in the second half of the nineteenth century and at the turning of the twentieth, even as the nationalist movement was gathering strength and even as new policy decisions by Britons carried India farther toward self-government, distinctive themes in British judgments of India emerged. These judgments distinguished between certain categories of Indians, especially between "masculine" and "feminine" races, between the "natural" Indian leaders and the unrepresentative babus ("clerks") "posing" as leaders, and between the "real" Indians and the assimilated ones. In each case, the categories carried within themselves implications as to who was and was not with the angels. These themes are to be found more in the pronouncements of men like Lytton, Fitzjames Stephen, John Strachey, and Curzon, who were hostile to Indian self-rule, than Ripon or Allen Octavian Hume, who were sanguine on the same topic.

The distinction between masculine and feminine races is an especially pervasive theme in this unsystematic imperialist theory and appeared most frequently in connection with the Bengalis, whom most Englishmen knew best and who had most swiftly responded to English culture. The late Joseph Schumpeter remarked in his account of imperialism that many imperialists were feudal atavisms, men whose hunger for the chivalric life could not be accommodated by the middle-class civilization of nineteenth-century Europe and who turned to the new frontiers of the colonies for the challenge they could not find at home.[2] The picture one has of the precompetition wallahs, the early nineteenth-century English in India, clodhopping Collectors, trusty rifles slung over their shoulders, boar spears in their left hands, confirms this view.[3] Such men felt impatience with the allegedly unathletic Bengalis, and admiration for the muscular and venturesome tribal people of the Northwest. Although many came for reasons less romantic than feudal nostalgia, because of family traditions or interest in a remunerative and respectable career, and although many pursued timid Victorian and bureaucratic life styles rather than feudal virtues, practitioners of the swashbuckling style shaped the dominant image of Englishmen in India and, by contrast, the mirror image of Indians.

When Kipling, sedentary ideologue of the swashbuckling style, rhymed his verse and found that "East is East and West is West, and never the twain shall meet," he added that there was, however, *one* equalizer of national difference: courage. The frontier Pathan and the English soldier of his ballad could understand one another as warriors: "But there is neither East nor West, Border, nor Breed, nor Birth/When two strong men stand face to face, though they come from the ends of the earth."[4] Englishmen fancied, though, that this leveling element was available only among a limited number of Indians.

By the second half of the century, venturesome Englishmen went to Africa as often as to India; and if men of Strachey's and Curzon's era speak with contempt of Bengali "feminism," it is as much with the ambivalent masculinity produced by *fin de siècle* British public school training as with the knowledge gained from experience with Bengali character. There is an empirical basis for their perception. Much of Indian society, particularly that part made up of the nonmartial twice-born castes, does seem to tolerate a larger component

[2] Joseph Schumpeter, "The Sociology of Imperialism," in *Social Classes and Imperialism,* trans. Heinz Norden and Paul Sweezy (New York, 1951), pp. 65–98.

[3] Philip Woodruff's two volume work, *The Men Who Ruled India* (London, 1953–54), admirably develops this picture.

[4] Rudyard Kipling, "The Ballad of East and West," in *Rudyard Kipling's Verse* (New York, 1940), p. 233.

of feminine qualities in its men than most Western societies do, even while homosexuality appears to be a less significant issue in India than in more "masculine" countries.[5] The differences in cultural patterning were sharpened by the compulsions of roles. Occupying inferior bureaucratic positions in the context of their conquest, Indians were obliged to nurse compliance, with its female implications, as a condition of success. In any case, a substantial number of the English felt ill at ease, or thought they ought to, among Indians who demonstrated a notable lack of interest in proving their manhood by overt signs of martial, leather-faced masculinity. They much preferred the "races"—such as the Sikhs and Mohammedans and Rajputs and Pathans—that exhibited a more familiar aggressive spirit.

For a passage that exhibits this particular theme, one may turn to John Strachey's book *India*, a standard training assignment for Indian Civil Service probationers just before the turn of the century. Describing the diverse races of India, it begins with a quote from Macaulay characterizing the Bengalis:

> The physical organization of the Bengali is feeble even to effeminacy. He lives in a constant vapor bath. His pursuits are sedentary, his limbs delicate, his movements languid. During many ages he has been trampled upon by men of bolder and more hardy breeds. . . . His mind bears a singular analogy to his

[5] Percival Spear's *The Nabobs* (London, 1932), pp. 198–99, lists twenty-six quotations expressing European sentiments about Indians in the eighteenth century. Of these, ten include such allusion to weakness or feminine qualities as the following: "Indians are a very sober people and effeminate . . ." (Sieur Luillier, *A Voyage to the East Indies* [1702], p. 285), or the more perceptive, "Tis a mistake to conclude that the natives of Hindustan want courage. . . . With respect to passive courage the inhabitants of these countries are perhaps possessed of a much larger share of it than those of our own" (Major Rennell, Diary, Home Miscellaneous Series, No. 765, p. 182 [20 January 1768]). A. L. Basham has pointed out in *The Wonder That Was India* (London, 1954), p. 172, that homosexuality was rare in ancient India and certainly never became as widespread or legitimate as in Greece or Rome. What precisely the nature of contemporary behavior is would have to be a matter of inquiry, but it is rarely mentioned in nineteenth- or twentieth-century accounts. Morris Carstairs suggests that it occurred in his village among children, was perhaps practiced on occasion among adults, and played a role in phantasy (*The Twice Born: A Study of a Community of High-Caste Hindus* [London, 1957], p. 167).

body. It is weak even to helplessness for purposes of manly resistance; but its suppleness and tact move the children of sterner
climates to admiration not unmingled with contempt. . . .[6]

Strachey himself proceeded to distinguish the more vigorous Mohammedans from the feeble (Hindu) Bengalis, only to be drawn
back in a kind of horrified fascination to his previous subject:

> The Mohammedan peasantry of the eastern portion of the prov-
> ince are men of far robuster character. . . . It has often been said,
> and it is probably true, that Bengal is the only country in the
> world where you can find a great population among whom
> personal cowardice is looked upon as in no way disgraceful.
> This is no invention of their enemies: the Bengalis have them-
> selves no shame or scruple in declaring it to be a fact. . . . This
> for such reasons that Englishmen who know Bengal, and the
> extraordinary effeminacy of its people, find it difficult to treat
> seriously many of the political declamations in which English-
> speaking Bengalis are often fond of indulging.[7]

The contrast to the supple, vapor-bathed creatures was to be found
among the "martial" races, the Sikhs, Pathans, Rajputs, and Muslims, peoples who either by caste ethic, religion, or geographic circumstance adhered to a more overtly aggressive world view.

The distinction between the martial and non-martial was no in-
vention of the English. It had accumulated ethical and historical
meaning in Hindu caste structure and culture, which inculcated a
non-violent perspective in some castes and an aggressive one in
others. But in English minds at the end of the century, the distinction was stressed as much for its instrumental utility in the imperialist theory as for its academic interest as a description of caste or
regional character. The "martial" races for the most part adhered
to the British raj, not because they were martial—the unlikely collab-
oration of the Pathans with Gandhi must have come as a fearful
shock to many Britons—but for political considerations, the Rajputs
because they were the princes of states whose autonomy was threat-

[6] John Strachey, *India, Its Administration and Progress* (London, 1888), pp.
411–12.

[7] *Ibid.*, pp. 412–13.

ened by a self-governed India, the Muslims because they feared a Hindu majority in an independent India.

Those described as the non-martial races produced nationalism. The allegedly non-violent Brahmans, Vaishyas, and Kayasths provided the shock troops of the pen, office, and pocketbook to publicize, organize, and finance the message of national freedom and regeneration. They launched nationalist polemics in dailies and pamphlets and provided the speakers in official and unofficial public forums to attack government with the Mill and Mazzini inculcated in Anglicized university classes. The Indians whom Englishmen most frequently encountered, once they had established themselves on the subcontinent and the memory of armed resistance had faded, were those recruited to fill bureaucratic roles. By virtue of their tasks, they represented a deceptively one-sided picture of the traditions of the castes from which they were drawn. Beyond this, Englishmen seem to have excluded from their conscious and articulated perceptions evidence conducing to a different picture. Bengali Kayasths have been local notables with fighting traditions as predators and protectors as well as bureaucrats for Moghul and British rulers.[8] Other Bengali castes who served the British also possessed differentiated traditions. But because the imperial capital, Calcutta, was in Bengal it was not unnatural for many secretariat-centered Britons to form their impressions about Indians on the basis of their relations with some Bengalis, generalizing from their civil servants to castes as a whole, and from their regional impressions to India. Such obvious anomalies as, for example, applying non-martial epithets to nationalist Chitpavan Brahmans who spoke for a Maharashtra that had given Britain much pain on the field of battle were easily and often overlooked.

The masculine-feminine distinction overlapped those between "natural" leader and "unnatural" *babu* and between the "real" Indian and the assimilated Indian. What could be more "natural" in a leadership position than a sturdy Rajput whose fighting arm maintained his dominion over the land won by his forefathers and who stood in paternal and autocratic relationship to traditional followers?

[8] For the traditions of the Bengali Kayasthas, see Ronald Inden, "The Kayasthas of Bengal: A Social History of Four Castes" (Ph.D. thesis, Department of History, University of Chicago, 1967).

What less "natural" than the socially mobile men seeking to add political power to traditional priestly, commercial, and literary power, the non-martial Brahmans, Vaishyas, and Kayasths whose new status was often a product of English-created opportunities and who claimed they could lead a parochial and traditional rural India in which they had no long inherited leadership ties? These *nouveau arrivé* politicians and thinkers were not even "real" Indians. They had cut themselves off from India by successfully embracing Western, or more particularly English, ideas and manners. Britons greeted their success in doing so with the special brutality reserved by established classes for new men: if they failed to emulate, they showed their incapacity to appreciate and strive for higher ideals; if they emulated badly, they were easy targets for ridicule; and if they successfully modeled themselves on their masters, they lost their integrity by trying to be something they "really" were not.

What is most significant about these distinctions, and what makes them relevant to the consideration of Gandhi, is that nationalist Indians half-accepted them. No ideology legitimizing superior-inferior relations is worth its salt unless it wins at least a grudging assent in the minds of the dominated. By this measure the unsystematic theory of imperialism was a notable success. Within twenty years of the deliberate exclusion of United Province Brahmans from the Bengal Army because of their leading role in the rebellion of 1857, the idea that Brahmans lacked fighting qualities had become prevailing opinion. Reading recent history back into an undifferentiated past, Indians came to believe that they lacked valor and moral worth. As the young Gandhi put it, "It must be at the outset admitted that the Hindus as a rule are notoriously weak."[9] Why inferiority in arms, technology, and organization, circumstances related to particular historical contexts that may be reversed, has led colonial peoples to more essentialist conclusions about themselves is not entirely clear. The fact that they frequently did come to such conclusions was one of the most degrading consequences of colonialism. This state of mind—a sense of impotence combined with the fear of moral unworthiness arising from impotence—was not unique to India. It provided a central theme in other nationalist movements

[9] *The Vegetarian,* February 28, 1891, in *The Collected Works of Mahatma Gandhi* (Delhi, 1958———), I, 30.

167

and led to attempts—to use the Chinese nationalist phrase—at self-strengthening.

The Indian fear that their weakness was innate was fed by the scientism of late nineteenth-century post-Darwinian race theory. Ethnologists, particularly ethnologists of India, were fond of imputing a biological fixity to culturally transmitted traits. Further, men of the nationalist generation were by no means sure that they were "natural" leaders or that they were still Indians. A good bit of the Hindu fundamentalism that suddenly gripped men like Sri Aurobindo, raised in an emphatic Western tradition, may be related to this quest to be "really" Indian.

One of the first items on the agenda of nationalism once it stepped beyond the loyal, reasonable, but ineffectual parliamentarism of the early nationalists and began to grapple with the moral and emotional issues of Indian self-definition was the creation of an answer to the charge of national impotence. A variety of answers were formulated —among them the calisthenic muscle-building and aggressive Hindu spirit-building launched by the gymnastic societies of militant Mahrattas at Poona, and Dayanand's Arya Samaj path. "Our young men must be strong," Swami Vivekananda urged a generation. "Religion will come afterwards. . . . You will be nearer to Heaven through football than through the study of the Gita."[10] There was the ascetic soldiery of the novel *Anada Math,* training in a forest Ashram, brave, celibate, sturdy, disciplined, which provided a model for future Hindu fundamentalist parties and the blood deeds of a terrorist generation in Bengal and the Punjab.

There seems to be some perverse historical dialectic in violent Bengali nationalism, as though the young men of Calcutta were saying no to Macauley's and Strachey's assertions of their physical ineffectualness. But their noes failed to convince. Britain could in good conscience manage young men who threw bombs, especially if they threw them at ladies on a Sunday afternoon. Violence did not in fact turn out to be an effective basis for rallying a mass Indian nationalism. These proofs of courage helped, but they did not help most people, and they did not suffice in the long run to build a sense

[10] Swami Vivekananda, "Lectures from Colombo to Almora," in *The Complete Works of Swami Vivekananda* (3d ed.; Almora, 1922), III, 242.

of national self-esteem. Gandhi's formulation proved a better statement of the issue of courage, and spoke to the issues of potency and integrity as well, even if it did not speak to or for the entire country. Large sections of opinion in Bengal, Punjab, and Maharashtra continued to subscribe to violent methods. Some classes, like middleclass Muslims or non-Brahmans in Madras and elsewhere found his style or his followers too Hindu or Sanskritic; some intellectuals found his religious style and symbolism repugnant to their secular and rationalist values. Still others rejected civil disobedience in the name of establishmentarian or reformist loyalism. Yet Gandhi's approach succeeded in capturing control of nationalist ideology.

Two issues of self-esteem that afflicted Indian nationalism, strength and weakness and cultural integrity, "afflicted" Gandhi in his own life. He confronted them over a period of some thirty-five years before they were fully mastered; his "solution" helped the generations who knew him to deal with them as well. For him the issues of courage and integrity were connected, and he resolved them together. Much of his early life was spent deciding whether he could best master himself and his environment by embracing in greater or lesser measure a British life path or by committing himself to a certain kind of Indian way. The dilemmas of the young Gandhi did in many ways approximate those of the surrounding generations. They can be found in his autobiography, a document that makes clear that Gandhi meant to be simultaneously judged as a private and a public person.

The book he called *The Story of My Experiments with Truth* poses a puzzle for his Western readers. They think they are to read the autobiography of a political leader. Instead they find something so heavily concerned with the Mahatma's "private" activities that it might better have been entitled "Confessions." Confessions are acceptable in saints, like Augustine, or in professional sensualists, like De Sade, or understandable in a tortured exhibitionist, like Rousseau. But in a political man? The relative privacy and reserve of Nehru's autobiography seem more appropriate, not merely as a matter of taste, but as a matter of the life emphasis suitable for a public man. The Western reader is apt to conclude that *My Experiments with Truth* are evidence that the saintly man mattered more than the

169

politician and that Gandhi cared more for his private virtue than his public efforts. But that conclusion rests on the belief, quite pervasive in Western estimates of Gandhi, that saintly striving and political effectiveness must conflict, cannot be merged, and that anyone who seeks to do both must be a fraud either in his pretensions to be a politician or in his pretensions to be a saintly man.

My Experiments with Truth may provide evidence to support different conclusions.[11] In the Indian context it is very much a *political* document, central to Gandhi's political concerns in a double sense, the function it served for him and that which it served for his public. It is from his "experiments in the spiritual field" that he believed he had "derived such power as I possess for working in the political field."[12] And it was not only he who believed this. Many of his immediate and distant followers attributed his political effectiveness to his personal virtue. When thousands assembled to hear him in remote, rural areas, they did so because he was preceded by his reputation for saintliness. When he wrote the autobiography as weekly instalments for his Gujarati journal *Navajivan,* with translations in his English journal *Young India,* he gave wider currency to his attempts at self-perfection.[13] The Gujarati original sold nearly fifty thousand copies by 1940, and the English twenty-six thousand by 1948, making it a best seller in the context of India's literacy and income levels.[14] The installments provided reassurance that the conditions of his political strength had been long preparing and severely tested, even while they conveyed moral aphorisms to young men who would be virtuous. The autobiography, then, must be read with

[11] Erik H. Erikson has suggested the ways in which the autobiography acts not merely as a recollection of the past but as a cautionary tale meant to advise and guide young men, "for the purpose of recreating oneself in the image of one's own method; and . . . to make that image convincing" ("Gandhi's Autobiography: The Leader as a Child," *American Scholar,* XXXV (Autumn, 1966), 636).

[12] *Gandhi's Autobiography, or, The Story of My Experiments with Truth,* trans. from the Gujarati by Mahadev Desai (Washington, D.C., 1948), p. 4.

[13] *Ibid.,* p. 3.

[14] This is in addition to the eight thousand copies the *Navajivan* and *Young India* serializations were selling when Gandhi wrote the autobiography (*ibid.,* pp. ii, iii, and 581).

a particularly sensitive ear, one that hears what he has to say concerning his diet, or his relations to his wife, and considers what it might mean for his political style and for how that style was received. To relegate these remarks to the category of personal frills and curiosities that constitute the gossip rather than the serious significance of a great man is to miss what was central to his leadership.

The small princely state of Porbander, in Kathiawad, where he was born in 1869, lies on the Arabian Sea, in the center of an area that has always been open to the trade of Persia, Arabia, and Africa, on the one hand, and the interior of India, on the other. He was born a Vaishya, a member of the Modh Baniya caste, one of many trading castes that have flourished in that region because of the hospitable conditions for commerce. His grandfather, whose memory had taken on mythical grandeur for the family by the time Gandhi was a child, served, as members of Vaishya castes often did in western India and the Rajput states, as prime minister of a princely state.[15] Gandhi's father did the same, though with less distinction.

Gujarat resembled the "burned-over" district of western New York in its religious eclecticism and susceptibility to intense religious experience and leadership; it is from its soil that both Swami Dayanand and Mahatma Gandhi sprang. Strains of Hindu, Jain, and Muslim belief found expression in a variety of sects that sought to transcend the clash of faiths through synthesis or syncretism.[16] The religious culture of Gandhi's family reflected many of these ideological forces and syncretic tendencies. Followers of Vaishnavism, a bhakti (devotional) path, they nevertheless adhered strictly to the social and ritual requirements of Brahmanic Hinduism. Jain ideas and practice powerfully influenced Gandhi, too, particularly through his mother: asceticism in religious and secular life; the importance of vows for religious merit and worldly discipline; and *syadvad,* the doctrine that all views of truth are partial, a doctrine that lies at the root of satyagraha. Putali Ba (Gandhi's mother) descended from the Pranami, or Satpranami, sect, whose eighteenth-century founder, Prannath,

[15] Prabhudas Gandhi, *My Childhood with Gandhi* (Ahmedabad, 1957), Chap. 2.

[16] Pyarelal [Nair], *Mahatma Gandhi: The Early Phase* (Ahmedabad, 1965), I, 173.

attempted to unify Islam and Hinduism in a Supreme God. Gandhi remembers, in his only visit to the sect's temple, the absence of images and the Koranic-like writing on the walls. Followers of Prannath were forbidden addictive drugs, tobacco, wine, meat, and extramarital relations.[17]

Of the many strands in Gujarat's eclectic and often competing religious cultures, the most powerful in shaping Gandhi's outlook and style was bhakti, the devotional path to religious experience and salvation. "The culture of Kathiawar," Pyarelal writes, "is saturated with the Krishna legend."[18] Ota Bapa, Gandhi's grandfather, was a follower of the Vallabhacharya sect of Vaishnavism whose Krishna-Bhakti doctrine of love of and surrender to God, personified by Lord Krishna, makes Him accessible to all regardless of social standing or cultural background. Both he and Gandhi's father habitually read *Tulasi Ramayana,* a text that became Gandhi's favorite too.[19] It told of Rama's love for his devotees, his graciousness, his compassion for the humble, and his care for the poor. These qualities of bhakti have enabled it to appeal to democratic constituencies and to become the carrier of implicit social criticism of the hierarchy, social distance, and exclusivity of Brahmanic Hinduism.[20] Its contempt for classical Hindu social categories was expressed in the low caste social background of many of those attracted to it, both leaders and followers, and in the substance of bhakti songs, its main means of communication. If bhakti, like chiliastic Christianity but unlike Gandhi's political strategy and methods, sublimated social discontent rather than channeling it in a rebellious or revolutionary direction, the mature Gandhi yet found in the bhakti tradition an orientation and a style that suited him and those to whom he spoke.

Gandhi's mother painstakingly observed the more rigorous demands of her faith. Her strong ascetic demands on herself—"self-

---

[17] *Ibid.,* p. 214.   [18] *Ibid.,* p. 117.

[19] Gandhi's grandfather Uttamchand was a follower of Khaki Bapa, of the order of Ramanand, a bhakta devoted to Rama; both Uttamchand and Gandhi's father, Kaba Gandhi, devoted their later years to reading the *Ramayana (ibid.,* I, 179).

[20] The opposition between the bhakti cults and Brahmanic Hinduism is modified by the fact that orthodoxy, too, accepted bhakti as a path to God. See especially the *Bhagavad-Gita.*

suffering," as Gandhi was to call it when he made it part of his political method—seem to have been a central virtue in the Gandhi home. Mrs. Gandhi fasted frequently and practiced other austerities. "During the four months of *chaturmas* Putlibai lived on one meal a day and fasted on every alternate day."[21] The concern for non-violence also received impetus from her: Jain monks, with their emphasis on the sanctity of all life, frequented the house.[22]

"Self-suffering" was important in other ways to the family. If one member of the household was angry with another, he would punish him by imposing some penalty on himself. Thus young Gandhi, angry because his family failed to summon to dinner a friend whom Gandhi wished to invite—it may have been a Muslim friend, with whom the family could not dine without transgressing the caste ethic—ceased to eat mangoes for the season, though they were his favorite fruit. The family was duly distressed.[23] On another occasion, Gandhi, finding difficulty in confessing a minor theft to his father, wrote him a note. "In this note not only did I confess my guilt, but I asked adequate punishment for it, and closed with a request to him not to punish himself for my offense."[24] It was the father's self-suffering, not punishment, that he claims to have feared most, although it is possible that he may in fact have feared being beaten. Gandhi's father, in turn, had used the threat of self-punishment in his relations with the ruler he served by announcing he would go without food and drink until arrangements were made for his transport out of the state when his master was reluctant to accept his resignation.[25] And above all, self-suffering in the sense of self-sacrifice was a dominant theme in the life of a boy who, for some three years, daily spent most of his after school hours nursing a sick father—a theme to which we shall return.

[21] D. G. Tendulkar, *Mahatma: Life of Mohandas Karamchand Gandhi* (Bombay, 1951——), I, 28.

[22] Pyarelal, *Mahatma Gandhi: The Early Phase,* I, 214.

[23] Tendulkar, *Mahatma,* I, 31.

[24] *Gandhi's Autobiography,* p. 41. Gandhi's sister Raliatbehn, on the other hand, recalls that Gandhi was quite nervous about the prospect of a beating for this offense (P. Gandhi, *My Childhood with Gandhi,* p. 22).

[25] P. Gandhi, *My Childhood with Gandhi,* p. 22.

Gandhi pictures himself as a shy, fearful, and pathetic child. "I was a coward. I used to be haunted by the fear of thieves, ghosts and serpents. I did not dare stir out of doors at night. Darkness was a terror to me."[26] He feared school and his schoolfellows: "I used to be very shy and avoided all company. My books and my lessons were my sole companions. To be at school at the stroke of the hour and to run back home as soon as school closed—that was my daily habit. I literally ran back, because I could not bear to talk to anybody. I was even afraid lest anyone should poke fun at me."[27] He shunned the actively virile and competitive sports, possibly, as we will presently see, because he was obliged to shun them. He participated in neither cricket nor gymnastics, which a headmaster made compulsory in line with English public school models. Gandhi's father, entertaining a rather different idea of what was good for the character of a young man, had him exempted from sports so the boy might come home and nurse him.[28] It was uncompetitive, unassertive walking that the young man learned to like, and gardening.[29]

His wife Kasturbai, whom he married at the age of thirteen, was no help in enhancing the self-esteem of a fearful child. She was wilful and self-assertive, did not reciprocate his passion, and resolutely refused to be the deferential Hindu wife he had hoped for, adding to his sense that he could not command where others had traditionally done so.[30] His self-description pictures him as a boy of

[26] *Gandhi's Autobiography*, p. 33.

[27] *Ibid.*, p. 15. Gandhi's relations with his age companions may have been affected by the fact that he would not fall in with the usual rough and tumble of youthful life. He could not be relied upon to tell white lies to cover up group pranks and would not strike back in any encounter. Whatever moral precocity was involved in these deviations received some positive recognition by his schoolmates, who used him regularly as a referee in games. These recollections spring from Gandhi's sister's memories (P. Gandhi, *My Childhood with Gandhi*, pp. 27–28). The memories are retrospective, recalled after Gandhi became "Mahatma," and may deserve a little caution.

[28] *Gandhi's Autobiography*, p. 28.

[29] Pyarelal, *Mahatma Gandhi: The Early Phase*, I, 197.

[30] "She could not go anywhere without my permission . . . and Kasturbai was not the girl to brook any such thing. She made it a point to go out whenever and wherever she liked. More restraint on my part resulted in more liberty being taken by her . . ." (*ibid.*, p. 22).

thirteen or fourteen who had failed to develop a sense of personal competence.

The Mahatma's description of the boy he was probably over-stresses his timid nature. All accounts of his youth speak of his enormous energy, as well as his considerable independence.[31] He was the favored child of both mother and father.[32] Capable of a self-confident naughtiness, he ran away from those sent to find him, scattered the utensils of the home shrine, including the image of the deity, scrawled on the floor, and committed other spirited pranks.[33]

Yet to judge from his subsequent actions one must conclude that he found inadequate support in his immediate environment for solving the issue of personal competence. He felt himself insufficiently strong and courageous and longed to be brave and masterful. The caste ethic of the Modh Baniyas as well as the family's faith closed many paths of assertive self-expression that might seem obvious to a boy beginning to become a man. Sexual expression, although formally sanctioned in marriage, was frowned upon. What one might call culinary masculinity, the eating of meat, was equally discouraged in a society that was vegetarian. The caste ethic, to say nothing of the local Jain influence stressing absolute non-violence, de-emphasized physical aggressiveness, which was in any case against young Mohandas' nature.[34] Not that Gandhi's environment provided no opportunities for self-assertion. The merchant castes of west India have found sufficient scope for assertiveness, even aggressiveness, within the bounds of commercial or bureaucratic caste roles. Members of Gandhi's family, despite the rhetoric of non-violence, allowed them-

[31] "The first three children of Kaba Kaka and Putliba gave them little trouble, but young Mohan was a bit of a problem. Not that he was mischievous or one to annoy his elders. He was not a difficult child but he was exceedingly active and energetic. He was never at one place for long. As soon as he was able to walk about, it became difficult to keep track of him" (P. Gandhi, *My Childhood with Gandhi,* p. 25).

[32] "I was my mother's pet child, first because I was the smallest of her children . . ." (Gandhi as cited by Pyarelal, *Mahatma Gandhi: The Early Phase,* I, 193). Kaba Gandhi believed Mohandas would take his place: "Manu will be the pride of our family; he will bring lustre to my name" (*ibid.,* I, 202).

[33] *Ibid.,* p. 195.

[34] Young Mohandas did not like to fight or hit back (*ibid.,* p. 195).

selves aggressive behavior, including his mother's willingness to see her boys defend themselves and Kaba Gandhi's willingness to beat an offender. But what the opportunities were is less important than how they appeared to Mohandas; he thought himself restricted.

Gandhi staged a massive revolt against his family, caste, and religious ethic in an effort to gain a more helpful perspective. Between the ages of thirteen and sixteen, he undertook a resolute program of transgressing every article of the codes that mattered to those around him. The counselor in revolt was Sheikh Mehtab, a Muslim, significantly enough, representing an ethic quite different from his own, the ethic of one of the "martial races." The friendship was the most significant and enduring of Gandhi's youth, lasting well into his South African years. He sent Mehtab money from England[35] and brought him to South Africa. Mehtab came to live with him there until Gandhi, discovering his friend was bringing home prostitutes, threw him out.[36]

It is usual among Gandhi biographers to endorse the Mahatma's description of the relationship, that he took up Mehtab in order to reform him.[37] It is true in that Gandhi all his life tried to overcome men like Mehtab by "reforming" them. But there was more to the relationship. On the evidence of Gandhi's own words, Mehtab was a model, and a model from whom he only gradually liberated himself. Mehtab was everything Gandhi was not—strong, athletic, self-confident, lusty, bold. As Gandhi writes, he was "hardier, physically stronger, and more daring. . . . He could run long distances and extraordinarily fast. He was an adept in high and long jumping. He could put up with any amount of corporeal punishment. He would often display his exploits to me and, as one is always dazzled when he sees in others the qualities he lacks himself, I was dazzled. . . ."[38]

Mehtab encouraged Gandhi to eat meat, saying that it would have a physiological effect in lending him new strength. "You know how hardy I am, and how great a runner too. It is because I am a meat-eater."[39] But there was a larger social context to the meat-eating

---

[35] *Ibid.*, p. 211.

[36] Louis Fischer, *The Life of Mahatma Gandhi* (London, 1951), p. 75.

[37] *Gandhi's Autobiography,* p. 31.

[38] *Ibid.*, pp. 32–33.   [39] *Ibid.*, p. 32.

issue. It had become attached to the problem of cultural virility for people other than Gandhi. Many people in Kathiawad, according to Gandhi, thought meat-eating was, so to speak, responsible for British imperialism, being the essence that made the Englishman strong. "Behold the mighty Englishman; He rules the Indian small; Because being a meat eater; He is five cubits tall . . ." went the ditty of Gandhi's school days. "I wished to be strong and daring and wanted my countrymen also to be such, so that we might defeat the English and make India free."[40] Actually, Gandhi did not have to look to British culture to discover that meat-eating "produced" courage. The fighting castes of India, particularly the Kshatriyas, have always eaten meat, and it has always been thought to contribute to their strength. But meat-eating was not the only kind of demonstration of strength in which Mehtab supported Gandhi. There was also a brothel episode, presumably meant to lead Gandhi to a more zestful lustiness than the guilty pleasures of his legitimate bed. But Gandhi suffered a Holden Caulfieldesque experience of tentative approach and horrified retreat.[41]

This rebellion was a search for courage and competence, an attempt to overcome fearfulness and shyness through following an ethic other than the one to which Gandhi had been born, an ethic practiced by Englishmen and the "martial races." But it should be pointed out that the search for courage itself exacted a courage of another kind that the ultimately dependent Mehtab did not have. To revolt in secret against strongly held family prejudices over a period of three years required considerable inner strength, strength of the kind the mature Gandhi would have approved, though in the service of other objectives.[42] He demonstrated the same kind of courage, although he described himself as still a coward, when at the age of nineteen, after his father's death, he decided to go to England for an education. He was obliged to confront the opposition of the caste council at Bombay. In an open meeting where he appears to have been afflicted by little of the shyness he always attributed to himself, he faced the elders who forbade his English trip and who

[40] *Ibid.*, p. 34.   [41] *Ibid.*, p. 37.

[42] "The opposition to and abhorrence of meat-eating that existed in Gujarat among the Jains and Vaishnavas were to be seen nowhere else in India or outside in such strength" (*ibid.*, p. 34).

threatened all the sanctions of outcasting if he defied their verdict. "I am helpless," he told them.[43]

In some respects, the English experience, during which Gandhi studied for the matriculation exam and was eventually admitted to the bar, represented an attempt to solve the issue of competence and self-esteem by acquiring a new cultural style and by escaping cultural ties that he still deemed in some way responsible for his incompetence and weakness. For three months after his arrival, he dedicated himself to a systematic effort to become an English gentleman, ordering clothing of the correct cut and a top hat in the Army and Navy Stores and evening clothes in Bond Street, worrying about his unruly hair, which defied the civilizing brush, acquiring from his brother a gold double watch chain, spending time before the mirror in the morning tying his cravat, and taking dancing lessons so that he might be fit for elegant social intercourse and violin lessons to cultivate an ear for Western music so that he might hear the rhythm that escaped him when dancing. In the hope of overcoming his incapacity to communicate effectively, he took elocution lessons only to find that they helped him in neither public nor private speaking.[44]

Some of this systematic attempt to approximate urbane English manners stuck for a long time: the pictures of the young Gandhi, as a thirty-thousand-dollar-a-year lawyer in the South Africa of 1900[45]—one is apt to forget that he was capable of that kind of

[43] *Ibid.*, p. 58. The account that he gave to an interviewer from *The Vegetarian*, June 20, 1891, is slightly different. There he says he told the senior patel, who told him crossing the waters was against caste rules: ". . . If our brethren can go as far as Aden, why could not I go to England?" (*The Collected Works of Mahatma Gandhi*, I, 59).

[44] *Gandhi's Autobiography*, pp. 70–71. Gandhi in London "was wearing a high silk top hat burnished bright, a Gladstonian collar, stiff and starched; a rather flashy tie displaying almost all the colors of the rainbow under which there was a fine striped silk shirt. He wore as his outer clothes a morning coat, a double breasted vest, and dark striped trousers to match. And not only patent leather boots but spats over them. He carried leather gloves and a silver mounted stick, but wore no spectacles. He was, to use the contemporary slang, a nut, a masher, a blood, a student more interested in fashion and frivolity than in his studies" (quoted in B. R. Nanda, *Mahatma Gandhi: A Biography* [London, 1958], p. 28).

[45] Fischer, in *The Life of Mahatma Gandhi*, says Gandhi earned five to six thousand pounds a year (p. 74).

worldly success—which present a punctilious late-Edwardian appearance, bear witness to the experience. So did his English, which, after three years in South Africa, bore the marks of relatively cool English understatement. The writings of his early maturity strike quite a different note from the un-English moralizing of the autobiography, written after he had become the Mahatma and had returned to more Indian modes in all respects.[46] His family's clothing and the accouterments of his house were Anglicized on his return to India. Less superficial aspects of English culture left a permanent mark. Throughout his life he remained a barrister, deeply influenced by ideas imbedded within British law, administration, and political values, including respect for correct procedure, evidence, and rights, and for the distinctions and conflicts between private and public obligations.

But the attempts at Anglicization failed to satisfy Gandhi, partly because he could not make a go of it, partly because it didn't "feel" right to him when he could. Besides, the England he met was not the England of public schools and playing fields, of clubs and sporting society, but an England closer to Kathiawad, an England of vegetarian Evangelicals and Theosophical reformers, an England suffering like Kathiawad from the effects of industrialization and protesting against them.[47] After three months he "gave up" much of the Anglicization effort, although less than he suggests in the autobiography, and began a very gradual return to a personal style of life more in keeping with the ascetic, self-denying, and non-violent ethic that he had left behind when he began his rebellion at home almost seven years before.

He started to live very thriftily, partly through economic necessity, partly because the change "harmonized my inward and outward life."[48] Earlier, he had restricted himself to vegetarian restaurants because of a vow to his mother but had remained committed to meat-eating in the interest of reforming the Indian character.[49] Now he

[46] See, for example, "The Grievances of the British Indians in South Africa—The Green Pamphlet," written in 1896, in *The Collected Works of Mahatma Gandhi*, II, 1–53.

[47] We are indebted for this point to Dr. Chandran Devanesan's manuscript of a forthcoming work on Gandhi.

[48] *Gandhi's Autobiography*, p. 75.   [49] *Ibid.*, p. 67.

embraced vegetarianism by choice, in a spirit that stressed a different kind of strength than that promised by meat. He began to rejoice in the effort of denying himself, in the strength of mastering his pleasures. He walked rather than rode to his studies[50] and took up moral and philosophic writings seriously for the first time, although more in the spirit of one seeking confirmation than of one seeking. He was moved by the biblical exhortation "that ye resist not evil" and by passages urging self-suffering as a mode of conversion. Carlyle's hero impressed him as much by his austere living as by his bravery and greatness. He noted passages in the Gita condemning the senses and concluded "that renunciation was the highest form of religion."[51]

In this time lay the beginnings—it took another two decades to complete the process—of a rejection of any solutions to his personal dilemmas that were radically foreign to his early experiences in the Gujarat cultural setting of family, caste, and religion. Solutions drawn from England or from features of Indian culture closer to English culture began to recede. In this period lay the beginning, too, of his construction of an Indian definition for himself, a definition expressed in the Gandhi who in 1906 began political action in South Africa and in 1920 took charge of the Indian nationalist movement. In the long run, these new experiments lead to the development of a personal style consistent with a traditional Indian model rather than with the model of a London-touched barrister, which other Indian nationalists found congenial. The early experiments in vegetarian restaurants and the considered return to an un-English asceticism were not unrelated to those later appeals and techniques of agitation that touched traditional Indian sensibilities and perceptions.

By the end of the English experience, Gandhi had begun to learn that the English solution was not the one to resolve those personal dilemmas that had accompanied him to England. The man who returned to India, and spent several years in practice there, felt himself still a failure. "But notwithstanding my study, there was no end to my helplessness and fear."[52] Though he was a barrister-at-law, more highly qualified than a great many of the traditional vakils

[50] *Ibid.,* p. 73.   [51] *Ibid.,* p. 92.   [52] *Ibid.,* p. 105.

who had no such elevated training, he knew little Indian law and could not even master the fundamental skill of the courtroom lawyer—public speaking. In England, he had made several attempts to give public speeches, generally at vegetarian societies. Each time he failed.[53] On one occasion, to encourage himself, he decided to recite the anecdote of Addison, as diffident as Gandhi, who rose on the floor of Commons and tried to open his speech by saying, "I conceive." Three times the unfortunate man tried to open with the same phrase but could get no further. A wag rose and said: "The gentleman conceived thrice but brought forth nothing." Gandhi thought the story amusing; unfortunately, in his recitation of the anecdote he, too, got stuck and had to sit down abruptly.[54]

His first court case in India was a disaster; obliged to cross-examine plaintiff's witness in a petty case, he was unable to bring himself to open his mouth. "My head was reeling and I felt as though the whole court was doing likewise. I could think of no question to ask. The judge must have laughed, and the *vakils* no doubt enjoyed the spectacle."[55] His model in the law had something in common with the bold Sheikh Mehtab: Pherozeshah Mehta, a strong and effective barrister, who dominated the Bombay bar with his vigorous courtroom style. Gandhi had heard that he roared like a lion in court. But the model seemed increasingly out of reach. He retreated from court work altogether to return, more or less defeated, to the backwaters of provincial Kathiawad, where he took up briefing cases for other lawyers, earning a respectable three hundred rupees per month but feeling that he was getting nowhere.[56] Yet a twenty-three-year-old Indian in 1892 who considered himself a failure at three hundred rupees per month had high standards. At twenty-four a personal tiff with the political agent—an Englishman—at Porbandar convinced him that he had no future there.[57] He determined to retreat from the Indian situation. "I wanted somehow to leave India."[58] The flight seems to have come at the lowest moment of his life.

The low point was also the turning point. His first experiences in South Africa, where he went as a barrister for a Muslim firm, persuaded him that the humiliation and oppression of Indians in South

[53] *Ibid.*, p. 83.
[54] *Ibid.*, p. 84.
[55] *Ibid.*, p. 120.
[56] *Ibid.*, p. 123.
[57] *Ibid.*, p. 125.
[58] *Ibid.*, p. 129.

Africa were worse than in India. He was discriminated against on trains and beaten by a white coachman who laughed at his legalistic insistence upon his rights.[59] Discussing his experience with other Indians, he discovered that the South African Indian community had suffered such humiliations for many years, pocketing insults as part of the conditions of trade. The discovery had a curious effect on his outlook. He recognized, rather suddenly it seems from the autobiography, that the skills that he had acquired in recent years, particularly a facile use of English, a familiarity with law codes and legal processes, and a belief that English justice must be enforced, were desperately needed and lacking among the Indian community. The South African Indians consisted of a merchant community and a much larger group of Tamil indentured laborers. Both lacked political consciousness and skills and were ineffectual at dealing with any part of the environment that transcended their economic tasks.[60] In this setting Gandhi, as the only Indian barrister, found himself to be the entire Indian professional middle classes.

Skills that in India had seemed ordinary here seemed extraordinary and enhanced Gandhi's self-estimate with an apocalyptic abruptness. Within three weeks of his arrival in South Africa, the shy boy of twenty-four suddenly called a public meeting of all Indians in Pretoria for the common discussion of their wrongs and oppressions in the Transvaal.[61] With a new-found authority, the man who had been unable to speak in public rose to sum up the problems of the community and propose an agenda for its amelioration. One has the sense that the overwhelming humiliations of the community around him suddenly carried him beyond the self-consciousness of his own failings, in a manner reminiscent of the "cured" stutterer in Nikos Kazantzakis' *The Greek Passion* ("He Who Must Die"). While speaking in court was an exercise that would show whether he measured up to the standard set by famous barristers like Pheroze-

[59] *Ibid.*, pp. 140–41, 143–44.

[60] Gandhi's first South African client told him: "What can we understand in these matters? We can only understand things that affect our trade. . . . We are after all lame men, being unlettered. We generally take in newspapers simply to ascertain the daily market rates, etc. What can we know of legislation? Our eyes and ears are the European attorneys here" (*ibid.*, p. 173).

[61] *Ibid.*, p. 157.

shah Mehta, a performance profoundly disturbing to a precarious ego, this speech had, ostensibly, nothing to do with his own standing. The new context, service, seems to have made it possible for the young man to do what he could not do when his own reputation was at stake. That service could lend him the effectiveness and potency he otherwise lacked must have had much to do with the life path he chose.[62] Away from home and the omnipresent memorials of early failure and performing a new task, he writes, "I acquired some measure of my capacity."

The South African experience helped him recognize that his salvation lay in devoting himself to the problems of those more helpless than he. As he did so, his capacity to act effectively and courageously grew. The techniques that expressed his new sense of competence rallied Indians to refute English charges of cowardice without, however, repairing to the English standard of courage. His style of leadership confounded the English charge that the new Indian middle classes had lost touch with their own people without, however, alienating those classes.

Gandhi and the New Courage

Indian nationalism had tried the paths of loyal constitutionalism and terrorist violence and found them wanting. Gandhi's answer was satyagraha ("truth force"), expressed through non-violent but non-constitutional direct action.[1] Satyagraha compels adherence to its

[62] A contributing factor in the success of the first speech may have been that Gandhi spoke in Gujarati. His audience consisted mainly of Memon Muslims, and "very few amongst his audience knew English" (Tendulkar, *Mahatma*, I, 46; see also *Gandhi's Autobiography*, p. 158). It is interesting that when Gandhi returned to India in 1896, with three years of South African successes behind him, he failed once again to manage a public speech before a large Bombay audience (*Gandhi's Autobiography*, p. 216).

[1] For a full-length and sympathetic treatment of Gandhi's philosophic and

cause not by mobilizing superior numbers or force but by mobilizing a general recognition of the justice of its cause. Civil disobedience under certain circumstances compels those who rule to confront the choice of enforcing what they themselves may suspect is injustice or altering policy and practice; for Gandhi, satyagraha was a means to awaken the best in an opponent. To resist, to retaliate or strike back if beaten, jailed, or killed, was at once to lack courage and to abandon the means to the common realization of justice. Satyagraha, Gandhi said, was "the vindication of truth not by infliction of suffering on the opponent but on oneself." Non-violent resistance to injustice is not unique to the East, much less to India, but it had an extraordinary appeal there during the three decades preceding Indian independence in 1947. Neither constitutional petition and protest nor violent acts of resistance and terrorism had been able to command popular support or unite nationalist leaders. Satyagraha did both, in part because Gandhi used it in relation to issues—urban labor grievances, rural tax relief, protests against untouchability—that mobilized new groups for nationalism, and in part because it expressed deeply embedded cultural values in an understandable and dramatic form. Central to these values were a definition of courage and a view of conflict resolution.

The prevailing Western definitions of courage, as well as definitions embraced by those Indians Englishmen called "the martial races," have generally stressed masterly aggressiveness, taking as their model the soldier willing and eager to charge with fixed bayonet the numerically superior enemy in a heroic act of self-assertion. The military analogy is merely the most extreme symbolic expression of a whole set of cultural attitudes—an aggressive, "meat-eating," masterful personal style, overt self-expressiveness, self-confident lustiness —that go well beyond military action. The opposite cultural attitude, cultivated by sections of the explicitly and self-consciously nonmartial castes and communities of Indian society, draws on self-control rather than self-expression, on self-suffering, and calls for restraint of the impulse to retaliate. It is misleading to see this willingness to suffer as a failure of will or surrender to fatalism, although it

---

tactical contributions, see Joan V. Bondurant, *The Conquest of Violence; Gandhi's Philosophy of Conflict* (Princeton, N.J., 1958).

may have that meaning as well. Self-restraint may be and has been another way of mastering the environment, including the human environment. The Hindu who sat *dharna* (a protest through fasting) at the house of an alleged oppressor, starving himself, was doing the very reverse of submitting. His courage was in some ways like that which Gandhi stressed. Not to retreat, to suffer pain without retaliation, to stay and suffer more in order to master a hostile or stubborn human reality—these expressions captured important elements of what Gandhi asked of India. Such courage relies for its effectiveness on the moral sensibilities, or at least capacity for guilt, of the more powerful perpetrator of injustice, using his conscience to reach and win him. Gandhi turned the moral tables on the English definition of courage by suggesting that aggression was the path to mastery of those without self-control, non-violent resistance the path of those with control.[2]

This kind of courage tends to go with other cultural practices and attitudes—vegetarianism, asceticism—found especially among the non-fighting twice-born castes, Brahmans, Vaishyas, and Kayasths, who provided the core of nationalist leadership.[3] The traditions of

[2] When with an old man's despair Gandhi watched the violence of partition, he questioned whether Indians had ever understood *his* non-violence. "Gandhi then proceeded to say that it was indeed true that many English friends had warned him that the so-called non-violence of India was no more than the passivity of the weak, it was not the non-violence of the stout in heart who disdained to surrender their sense of human unity even in the midst of a conflict of interests but continued their effort to convert the opponent instead of coercing him into submission" (N. K. Bose, *My Days with Gandhi* [Calcutta, 1953], p. 271).

[3] In Bihar, Kayasths, who constituted 1.18 per cent of the population of the state, constituted 54 per cent of the Bihar Pradesh Congress Executive Committee in 1934. Their disproportionate role in Indian nationalism, like that of other non-martial twice-born castes, was in the first instance due to the fact that they were the first to have Western education (see Rameshray Roy, "Congress in Bihar" [Ph.D. thesis, Department of Political Science, University of California, 1965]).

For the nature of Gandhi's appeal to these men, see Rajendra Prasad, *Satyagraha in Champaran* (Madras, 1928), and *At the Feet of Mahatma Gandhi* (New York, 1961). The Madras Congress until the 1940's was mainly Brahman. For the dominance of Congress politics by Brahmans, and especially the effect this had in limiting its appeal, see Eugene Irschick, "Politics and Social Conflict in South India: A Study of Tamil Separation and the non-Brahman Move-

these castes were not, of course, uniform. The Brahmans of Maharashtra have often supported violent nationalism, as did the merchant castes of Punjab or the Kayasths and Vaidyas of Bengal. Tilak, Lala Lajpat Rai, and Subhas Bose mobilized different potentials in the same social groups, but with less effect. The Gandhian definition was more resonant with their style and capabilities. The more aggressive kind of courage is, of course, no monopoly of the West but has its counterpart in the ethic of certain Indian castes and communities, just as self-suffering courage has its Western equivalents. The Christian injunction to turn the other cheek, which so impressed Gandhi, is a compelling version of self-suffering—although it is perhaps more closely related to the tender ideals of meekness and love than the acerbic one of self-control.

Self-suffering courage is susceptible of two rather different moral emphases, one that is quite as aggressive in spirit, if not in form, as violence, and one without such overtones. As the traditional weapon of the Brahman, whose protest against oppressive rule was often fasting, self-injury, or even suicide, which would draw upon the oppressor the supernatural sanctions of having caused the death of a Brahman, it substituted spiritual violence for physical.[4] As used in many Indian homes, not merely Gandhi's, where family members sometimes expressed protest by abstaining from meals, it may substitute psychological violence for physical. For Gandhi, such satyagraha was nothing more than the passive resistance of the weak.[5] Satyagraha in his sense was to be purged of these connotations and infused with a positive moral task. Satyagrahis (those who practice

---

ment" (Ph.D. thesis, Department of History, University of Chicago, 1964). The Praja Mandals, Lok Parishads, and Harijan Sevak Sanghs (Congress-connected political and social service organizations in Rajasthan) were, through the nineteen-forties, dominated by Brahmans, Vaishyas, and Kayasths (see Rudolph and Rudolph, "From Princes to Politicians in Rajasthan: The Political in Social Change" [Cambridge, Mass.: Harvard University Press (forthcoming)], Chap. 2).

[4] For a discussion of the moral and psychological subtleties of non-violence, see Joan Bondurant, "Satyagraha versus Duragraha: The Limits of Symbolic Violence," in *Gandhi: His Relevance for Our Times,* ed. G. Ramachandran and T. K. Mahadevan (Bombay, 1964), pp. 67–81.

[5] N. K. Bose, *My Days with Gandhi* (Calcutta, 1953), p. 270.

satyagraha) were to act so as to elicit the better element in an opponent, rather than the worst, as violence would do. Ill will was the enemy of this effort and hence of satyagraha. To purge oneself of ill will was a task requiring strengths most men found hard to command. Gandhi demanded no less of himself and his followers, although he was under no illusion that either he or they always, or even usually, succeeded.

But beyond the distinction between English and Indian definitions of courage lie other cultural differences concerning the honorable and "moral" way to manage conflict in general.[6] The belief that conflicts are best resolved through the frank confrontation of alternatives, the clear articulation of opposites, their clash and the victory of one alternative over the other, is embodied, at least in theory, in much of the adversary legal tradition of the West and in its political life. Traditional Indian ideas of conflict management in both politics and law, as we suggest in Part III, tend to stress arbitration, compromise, and the de-emphasis of overt clashes, of victories and defeats. The rhetoric, if not always the practice, of Indian foreign policy, the continued striving to "restore" consensus processes in village affairs, and opposition to the "evil" of partisanship are receding but still significant expressions of these traditional norms. Their desirability is related to the psychological attraction of self-control and harmlessness over aggressive self-assertion.

Resistance to the notion of conflict arises partly from the romance and reality that surround the image of the village in the minds of many Indians. When the council of five, the panchayat, spoke as one, it was said to be the voice of God; it gave expression to the consensus of the traditional moral order. If the consensus was often merely a rhetorical one that obscured real divisions, it was nonetheless valued.

---

[6] For an extended discussion, on which these pages draw, of Indian approaches to conflict management, see Susanne Hoeber Rudolph, "Conflict and Consensus in Indian Politics," *World Politics,* XIII (April, 1961). Hugh Tinker suggests other threads of the conciliation ethic in his article "Magnificent Failure? The Gandhian Ideal in India after Sixteen Years," *International Affairs,* XL (April, 1964), 262–76. Vallabhai Patel had yet another interpretation of Gandhi's consensualism: "You can work in harmony with everybody. It does not cost you any effort. Vaniks (merchants) do not mind humbling themselves" (cited in *The Diary of Mahadev Desai,* trans. from the Gujarati and ed. V. G. Desai [Ahmedabad, 1953], I, 53).

The apotheosized village republic, representative, deliberative, and harmonious, rested on the moral basis of *dharma,* of sanctified custom in which rank and distance, privilege and obligation, rights and duties, were acquired at birth and legitimized by religion.

Studies of village government document the resistance to adversary processes.[7] The consensual process, unlike the adversary, assumes that law will be found (not made) and decisions arrived at by some traditionally recruited body, such as the general panchayat dealing with village affairs or the caste panchayat dealing with the affairs of a single jati (subcaste). All who should be heard will be, and discussion will reveal what most, if not all, agree is the proper disposition of the problem. Discussion, according to one village study, continued until a satisfactory consensus could be arrived at or, in the event of a standoff between two powerful elements, until it was obvious that no agreement was possible.[8] In the meeting's ideal form there remains no opposition, for all have been convinced of the wisdom and necessity of the particular decision.[9] Support is determined not by a show of hands but by judging the participants' sense of moral fitness. Evidence, "witness," and deliberation are important in establishing consensus, but without a common and intimate moral universe that legitimized the domination of some and the subjection of others, traditional consensus would be hard to realize.

Partisanship expressed through the adversary process in politics, government, and law proceeds on the quite different assumption that there are a variety of "interested" answers and that the best one will emerge from the conflict of alternatives. The better each side mo-

[7] See also Part III, pp. 251–292, for a discussion of a preference for consensus in the law. Ideas about political consensualism as opposed to adversary modes and partisanship have been most strikingly developed in the postindependence period by Jayaprakash Narayan, who argues for a neo-Rousseauist politics in the context of a radical decentralization of life lived in small-scale communities. See especially his "Reconstruction of Indian Polity," in Bimla Prasad (ed.), *Socialism, Sarvodaya and Democracy* (London, 1964). A vigorous critique and defense of the essay may be found in W. H. Morris-Jones, "The Unhappy Utopia: J. P. in Wonderland," *Economic Weekly,* June 25, 1960; and William Carpenter, "Reconstruction of Indian Polity: Defense of J.P.," *Economic Weekly,* February 4, 1961.

[8] Ralph Retzlaff, *Village Government in India* (Bombay, 1962), p. 24.

[9] *Ibid.,* p. 25.

bilizes its arguments and resources and support, the better the victorious solution will be. The psychological quality of adversary relationships is self-interested and contentious; in a legislature, election, or court, one side wins and the other side loses. The relationship between opponents, at a certain level, is meant to be critical and combative, not conciliatory and accommodating; the arm's length relationship is an aspect of the adversary mode. Compromise, although it is often resorted to, is not the overt objective. There is a final accounting, a choosing between alternatives, and disagreement is exposed and emphasized by quantification through a vote.

To many Indians of Gandhi's time and since, establishing a consensus appeared to sustain and foster community solidarity and mutual accommodation, whereas adversary proceedings in politics and law appeared to sacrifice them by legitimizing partial statements of community purpose and interest. But this is too extreme a juxtaposition: to be viable, adversary proceedings must rest upon substantial if sometimes latent community agreement on values and procedure, and the process of consensual agreement often involves latent partiality and coercion. In the Indian village context especially, consensus was frequently acquiescence in the self-interested rule of a "dominant caste."[10] But the matter of appearance is important; many Indians view the "traditional" consensual way as moral and the "modern" adversary way as evil.

The suspicion of overt hostility seems to be as significant for the nation as the village and for the unconscious as the conscious. In his psychoanalytic study of the twice-born castes in a Rajasthan village, Morris Carstairs found two basic and interdependent patterns—one of mistrust and hostility, which destroyed mutual confidence and often erupted into violence, the other of self-restraint, which characteristically depended on a third person to intervene and bring the

[10] The dominance of higher landowning castes and their special role in determining the nature of the "consensus" are well documented. See, for example, M. N. Srinivas' discussion of the numerically and economically superior Okkaligas in "The Social System of a Mysore Village," and Kathleen Gough's discussion of the Tanjore Brahmans in "The Social Structure of a Tanjore Village," both in McKim Marriott (ed.), *Village India* (Chicago, 1955). These two studies make a useful contrast in that Srinivas indicates that economic power and numerical strength are as important as ritual superiority in determining dominant caste status with respect to village affairs.

antagonists back to their senses. Here human conflict was evidently feared because of its propensity to release uncontrollable passions. "When feelings of ill-will did find open expression . . . the utter collapse of self-control [was] all the more remarkable for its contrast with the formality of normal exchanges." The participants "abandoned themselves to anger with a completeness which previously had been familiar to me only in the temper tantrums of young children. I was able to understand for the first time the epidemic of massacre and counter-massacre which had swept over this 'nonviolent' country only a few years ago."[11] The severe emphasis on self-restraint, on formality and harmlessness, may well be allied to the omnipresent fear of loss of control. In Carstairs' account, it was the peacemaker who restored restraint by intervening "between the disputants, reminding them how wrong it was to give way to anger, urging self-control and compromise." He found the third-party role of mediator to be so regular a feature of conflict in the village that it recurred in dreams. It was considered better to be the "third party" to a dispute than the victor; "in time, the verb *samjhana* (to impart instruction) became recognizable as an element in everyone's experience, providing a counterpoint to the prevailing distrust. The role of moral adviser, counselling moderation and control of one's passions, is one which compels an impulse to obey, and at the same time, a surrender, however temporary, of one's customary suspiciousness."[12]

Gandhi began to embody these cultural themes concerning courage and conflict resolution in techniques of action relevant to his countrymen's problems in South Africa. Concluding his first big case, the one that had called him there, he believed he had found the path to his future work. Not only had the case been settled by arbitration out of court, but Gandhi had persuaded his client to take payment from the loser in instalments so as not to ruin him. Both actions could have been justified on the mundane ground of ordinary legal or business prudence, but Gandhi did not choose to view the settlement in that light: "My joy was boundless. I had learnt the true practice of law. I had learnt to find out the better side of human nature and to enter

[11] Morris Carstairs, *The Twice Born: A Study of a Community of High-Caste Hindus* (London, 1957), p. 46.

[12] *Ibid.*, p. 47.

190

men's hearts. I realized that the true function of a lawyer was to unite parties driven asunder."[13] The principle of adversary proceedings, that out of the conflict of two parties, each of whom tries to win by scoring off his opponent, justice will emerge, seemed to him a doubtful doctrine. "The counsel on both sides were bound to rake up points of law in support of their own clients,"[14] he complained. Solutions based on compromise seemed better because they rested on mutual confidence rather than institutionalized conflict.

A more mature Gandhi would formulate the approach in terms of *ahimsa,* the doctrine of harmlessness or non-violence translated into opposition to destructive conflict in general, not merely to physical violence. Had Gandhi developed a different, more aggressive personal style, had he been less diffident, bolder in court and public, he might have taken a different view of the issue of courage and the adversary mode and found himself with or at the head of Indians of quite a different sort. As it was, he turned what he once considered a failing in himself, an incapacity for aggressiveness, into a virtue and an effective political technique. His solutions were of a piece with the renewed concern for the harmlessness ethic of his youth and opposed to the path of aggressive self-assertion that he had tried and rejected.

What Gandhi concluded about the law, he applied thereafter to all other situations of conflict, including his struggles in South Africa and in India. The thread of compromise, of avoiding conflict to find areas of agreement that could produce settlement, remained central to his technique, sometimes to the despair of his followers, some of whom wanted to confront the issue and the enemy by taking a clear stand. To this technique, he added the "witness" of self-suffering. A coercive technique and a means of psychic survival in his home, it was reminiscent of the traditional means that the non-martial classes used to cope with opposition and hostility. When Gandhi fasted or his followers suffered themselves to be beaten, he and they demonstrated the courage required for self-control rather than self-assertion. For those who described such behavior as "unmanly," Gandhi reformulated the imputation. Such non-violence expressed not the im-

[13] *Gandhi's Autobiography,* trans. from the Gujarati by Mahadev Desai (Washington, D.C., 1948), p. 168.

[14] *Ibid.,* p. 63.

potence of man but the potency of woman: "Has she not greater intuition, is she not more self-sacrificing, has she not greater powers of endurance, has she not greater courage?"[15] And the courage of non-violence was, moreover, apt. "Self-suffering" touched the conscience of Englishmen as it might not that of some other imperial rulers.

Self-Control and Political Potency

The distinction between "real" and assimilated Indians, like that between the masculine and feminine races, left a psychic wound. Those Indians who became like Englishmen after being educated in Anglicized schools could no longer be respected nor respect themselves—so went the British imputation—because they no longer recognized their Indian birthright. The "real" India of princes and peasants and martial races retained its integrity; the assimilated India of babus did not. How could the babus expect to lead, much less rule, India? The charge was a telling one, especially in the decades before the turn of the century when nationalism and its leaders were strongly influenced by liberal England and its parliamentary life. However "Indian" the private lives of Ranade, Gokhale, Srinivas Iyengar, and Surendranath Banerjee may have been, their public ideas, idiom, and often dress were those of cultivated English gentlemen. Their nationalism and political principles seemed not to speak to those who lacked their rather special intellectual and cultural experiences. It was convenient for Englishmen to characterize those experiences as somehow fraudulent. Their friends the "real" Indians—peasants untouched by middle class intellectuality, traditional ruling classes—were generally indifferent to nationalist appeals and demands for responsible government, exhibiting instead a gratifying satisfaction with an administrative state managed by British civil servants.

[15] M. K. Gandhi, *Woman's Role in Society,* comp. R. K. Prabhu (Ahmedabad, 1959), p. 8.

The leadership of the political generation preceding Gandhi's, Tilak, Sri Aurobindo, Lala Lajpat Rai, and B. C. Pal, searched for a way to master the moral and strategic consequences of the distinction —and division—between "real" and assimilated Indians. The issue was one of identity, of a national self-definition that could renew a sense of Indian distinctiveness while incorporating ideas suitable for a changing world. It was also one of political effectiveness, of reaching wider constituencies and broadening the base of nationalism. Both dimensions of the challenge pointed toward more traditional symbolism. Many of these leaders embraced traditional symbolism, often supporting, in consequence, conservative Hindu practices, exacerbating Hindu-Muslim relations, and countenancing violence.

Gandhi's response was shaped by such recent national experiences as the evocation of a hero (Shivaji) and religious symbolism by Tilak in Maharashtra, the appeal of sentiment in the politics and literature of the anti-partition movement in Bengal, and the reforming zeal with which the Arya Samaj was able to modify Hinduism in the Punjab and Uttar Pradesh. But unlike his predecessors Gandhi leavened traditional symbolism with reformist ideas, tried to find symbols and issues that would avoid Hindu-Muslim confrontations, and pursued a non-violent strategy. Even if he did not fully succeed, he did distinguish himself from his predecessors by infusing these inherited elements with the exceptionally compelling remorseless moral vision of a "religious." Most striking symbolically was his resuscitation on a national plane of the style of a *sanyasin,* the ascetic seeking enlightenment and virtue. As in his reformulation of the issue of courage, he again responded dramatically to a telling British critique; he was a nationalist leader not cut off from his own people by assimilation.

There is no country whose people do not in some way worry about the private morality of their public leaders. Gossip about the highly placed is never merely gossip; to some extent it reflects the assumption that there may be some continuity between a man's personal self-indulgence or self-constraint and his capacity to act disinterestedly in matters of state and the general welfare. But in modern times we have come to assume that the processes of differentiation that characterize our lives and that touch all our affairs have made private morals less relevant for public action. In the United States, it is assumed that if a senator or perhaps even a president pays attention to ladies other than his wife, doing so will not affect his capacity to manage affairs of state—provided he conducts himself with some circumspection and gives no cause for scandal. It is the differentiation of realms of conduct that suggests to us that conduct in one realm need not be affected by conduct in others.

Certain constitutional assumptions also lie behind the belief that private behavior is to a point irrelevant to public, in a public man. The Western political tradition has been disposed to rely upon external rather than internal restraints, on institutional rather than ethical limits, to control those who wield power. The emphasis on institutional limitations—the balancing of branches of government or of class interests or of church and state—is already found in Greek and Roman thought and remains evident even during the more ethically-oriented periods of medieval polity. Institutional limits have not, to be sure, been the exclusive means of restraining the arbitrary exercise of power. Political theorists in the West have emphasized the virtues kings must have and practice and have found in ethical restraints and their acceptance by kings the means to curb arbitrary action. But in the main, there has been a greater emphasis on institutional rather than on ethical means of ensuring that those who rule use their power for good rather than ill.

It is from "experiments in the spiritual field," Gandhi wrote, "that I derived such power as I possess for working in the political field."[1] His belief that private morality had public consequences reflects the emphasis in traditional Hindu thought on ethical as against institutional restraints. Traditional Hindu political thought, the *dharmasastras* and the epics, stressed the importance of inner over external restraints on rulers, relying not upon countervailing institutions but upon ethical commands to guarantee the public spirit of traditional kings. In practice, of course, countervailing institutions did act as irregular restraints.[2]

[1] See p. 197, n. 10.

[2] In Rajputana, the nobility acted as a restraint upon the activities of Maharajas, as did, in lesser ways, the Brahmans. But these restraints were irregular. See Lloyd I. Rudolph and Susanne Hoeber Rudolph, "From Princes to Politicians in Rajasthan" (Cambridge, Mass.: Harvard University Press [forthcoming]), Chap. I. Brahman councilors are often mentioned as restraining influences in classic writings.

Ethical commands had a private and a public variant. A king was commanded in private life to restrain his lust, control and master his passions, live simply, and rule his subjects justly. The *Manusmriti* declares "that king [is] a just inflicter of punishment, who is truthful, who acts after due consideration, who is wise, and who knows the respective value of virtue, pleasure and wealth."[3] "For a king who is attached to the vices springing from love of pleasure, loses his wealth and his virtue, but he who is given to those arising from anger, loses even his life. Hunting, gambling, sleeping by day, censoriousness, excess with women, drunkenness, an inordinate love for dancing, singing, and music, and useless travel are the tenfold set of vices springing from love of pleasure."[4] The king who overcomes attachment, who reigns with mind serene, who achieves that expunging of self-interest, can judge clearly and fairly the interest of others. (A problematic assumption, to be sure. There is no reason to believe that such virtue may not itself become a vested interest, seeking to propagate itself among subjects who would live more "attached" lives or giving rise to that *hubris* of the disinterested, that their virtue gives them the right to prescribe for others. A prescription may not be loved any better for being imposed by one who has no "interest" except in virtue.) The public variant of the ethic of restraint was the *rajadharma,* the commands that prescribed for kings what they must or must not do in their public function. There was an implicit assumption that a man who mastered himself could be relied upon to follow *rajadharma.*[5]

We are not concerned with whether these ethical hopes ever became operational restraints for most kings in distant or recent Indian history. The reputation of Indian princes in the last two hundred years would lead one to suppose that an ethic of self-restraint was honored as much in the breach as in the realization. A reputation for

[3] Georg Bühler, *The Laws of Manu—Translated with Extracts from Seven Commentaries,* Vol. XXV of *The Sacred Books of the East,* ed. Max Müller (Oxford, 1886), Chap. VII, vs. 26, p. 220.

[4] *Ibid.,* vss. 46 and 47, p. 223.

[5] "A king . . . who is voluptuous, partial, and deceitful will be destroyed, even through the unjust punishment which he inflicts. . . . Punishment cannot be inflicted justly by one . . . addicted to sensual pleasures" (*ibid.,* vss. 27 and 30, p. 220).

a lively libidinal life may even have enhanced the status of princes and nobles by affording commoners a vicarious opportunity to consume and participate in those pleasures that did not usually come their way.

Yet ethical standards that are steadily breached need not lose their meaning. They remain an ideal, and if someone appears who can enact the ideal, he may fall heir to all the pent up hopes that have survived the experience of repeated disillusion; he may, indeed, command the more respect, inspire the more reverence, because the standard has remained unrealized. It is in this light that the public impact of Gandhi's asceticism must be understood. If Gandhi lived his private life in public, it was because both he and those who observed him believed that a man's claim to be just, to command others, to attain wisdom, was proportional to his capacity for self-rule.

Asceticism was thought to have a power-enhancing function, too. The practitioner of *tapasya* ("austerities") accumulated special powers. This belief rests on what might be called a theory of sexual and moral hydrostatics: the classics suggest, and many Hindus believe, that men are endowed with a certain amount of "life force," which, if used up in passionate or lustful or self-seeking endeavors, will no longer be available for other and higher purposes. Freud, too, found the capacity for sublimation proportional to the diversion from more direct expression of libidinal energies. For him, the discontents arising from self-restraint were the prerequisite, the motor force, of civilization.[6] The *Manusmriti* states the same theory very graphically: "But when one among all the organs slips away from control, thereby a man's wisdom slips away from him, even as the water flows through the one open foot of a water-carrier's skin."[7]

The theory is no rarefied philosophic construct but enjoys popular acceptance. Morris Carstairs, in his study of the twice-born castes of a traditional Rajasthan village, and Joseph Elder, in his study of an Uttar Pradesh village, found much preoccupation with this life force.

[6] See Sigmund Freud, *Civilization and Its Discontents*. The idea of a sexual hydrostatics is developed in David Riesman, "The Themes of Heroism and Weakness in the Structure of Freud's Thought," in *Individualism Reconsidered* (Glencoe, Ill., 1954). The Freud comparison has a limit: for him, an excess of restraint produced pathology.

[7] Bühler, *The Laws of Manu,* Chap. II, vs. 99, p. 48.

Carstairs' villagers conceptualized it in a prescientific medical theory as a thick viscous fluid stored in the head; a plentiful quantity of it was thought necessary for fitness and strength. It could be preserved by the practice of celibacy and the careful observance of ritual restraints and commandments and was diminished by ritual carelessness and sexual self-expression. It could also be enhanced by the consumption of certain foods. Unworldly devotees, by their austerity, accumulated such substantial quantities of this life force that they were believed to have special powers, believed to be capable, as ordinary men could not hope to be, of compelling the environment.[8]

Gandhi fully accepted the essentials of this theory: "All power," he said, "comes from the preservation and sublimation of the vitality that is responsible for the creation of life. . . . Perfectly controlled thought is itself power of the highest potency and becomes self-acting. . . . Such power is impossible in one who dissipates his energy in any way whatsoever."[9] If he was able to compel the environment, it was because he practiced *brahmacharya,* celibacy and more general self-restraint; if he was unable to do so, it was because of failures in control. "It is my full conviction, that if only I had lived a life of unbroken *brahmacharya* all through, my energy and enthusiasm would have been a thousand fold greater and I should have been able to devote them all to the furtherance of my country's cause as my own."[10]

In the late 1930's, when the nationalist movement was experiencing severe difficulties, Gandhi characteristically looked for the source of trouble not in society and history but in himself. "A Congress leader said to me the other day, . . . 'how is it that in quality, the Congress is not what it used to be in 1920–25? It has deteriorated'. . . ." Special historical forces were part of the answer, but only a part:

[8] Morris Carstairs, *The Twice Born: A Study of a Community of High-Caste Hindus* (London, 1957), p. 86. Conversely, Joseph Elder found that in "Rajpur" all castes shared the view that intercourse deprived a man of some of his soul stuff and thereby shortened his life ("Growing up in Rajpur," chapter of forthcoming book entitled "Industrialism and Hinduism").

[9] Quoted in Pyarelal [Nair], *Mahatma Gandhi: The Last Phase* (Ahmedabad, 1956), I, 573.

[10] M. K. Gandhi, *Self-Restraint v. Self-Indulgence* (Ahmedabad, 1958), p. 56.

". . . There must be power in the word of a *satyagraha* general—not the power that possession of limitless arms gives, but the power that purity of life, strict vigilance and ceaseless application produce. This is impossible without the observance of *brahmacharya* . . . ; *brahmacharya* here does not mean merely physical self-control. It means much more. It means complete control over all the senses. Thus an impure thought is a breach of *brahmacharya,* so is anger." He had not achieved such complete control—a terrible self demand; had he succeeded, the movement, he thought, would not be encountering difficulties. "I have not acquired that control over my thoughts that I need for my researches in non-violence. If my non-violence is to be contagious and infectious, I must acquire greater control over my thoughts. There is perhaps a flaw somewhere which accounts for the apparent failure of leadership adverted to in the opening sentence of this writing."[11]

The ideal of self-restraint has not been confined to Indian public men; it seems to be broadly shared by Hindu Indians even though the intensity with which it is held varies by caste and locality. Its salience is greater among the higher than among the lower castes.[12] Among higher castes, those who share the more self-expressive Kshatriya (warrior-ruler) culture seem less responsive to the ideal of self-restraint than do the Brahmans, Vaishyas, and Kayasths, who formed so conspicuous a part of Gandhi's devoted lieutenants and followers.

Here, as in other areas of Indian life, the ideal asks more of men than most are able to manage. Not only are students, those who have withdrawn from society or those who live as recluses in distant places, asked to observe it, but so, too, to a lesser extent, are married householders. The result is that the ideal is not often fulfilled.[13] The felt disparity between the moral imperative and the capacity to real-

[11] *Harijan,* July 23, 1938, reprinted in *ibid.,* pp. 150–51.

[12] "My general impression was that conjugal intercourse occurred more frequently and was enjoyed more uninhibitedly among the lower castes than the higher castes" (Elder, "Industrialism and Hinduism," p. 218).

[13] Carstairs suggests that the disparity between the ideal and its fulfilment produces "the commonest expression of anxiety neurosis among the Hindu communities of Rajasthan, and perhaps elsewhere as well" (*The Twice Born,* p. 87).

ize it in daily life—a disparity that suggests that Indians are more prone than others to formulate ideals beyond the capacity of ordinary men, not that they are more erotic—also helps explain the impact of Gandhi's experiments: his achievement of a goal that many Indians recognize but do not realize became a form of vicarious fulfillment of an ego ideal.

The political effectiveness of Gandhian asceticism, then, lay partly in its expression of the traditional view of how rulers are restrained, partly in its coincidence with ideas about how a man's control over his environment might be enhanced, and partly in the fact that it vicariously achieved a personal moral ideal of many Indians. But there is yet another dimension. A great leader's capacity to compel his environment is related to his belief that he can do so. Such self-confidence creates the phenomenon social science calls "charisma." It involves, on the part of him who possesses it, a belief that he can perform, if not precisely superhuman, then at least extraordinary, deeds. Among those who perceive such self-confidence—the army calls it command presence—it produces a faith that he can indeed do what most men cannot.

In a curious way, the psychological chemistry of the relationship between the public man and his constituents is such that—if everything else is reasonably favorable—the belief produces its own justification. In response to such a leader, followers can sometimes mobilize resources within themselves that they do not ordinarily command, thus corroborating the faith that caused them to respond. The psychological logic of this is the reverse of that envisioned by Freud in his writings on leadership and mob psychology: that in a mass response to an apocalyptic call controls break down and libidinal energies are released in actions that express the lowest common moral denominator.[14] Rather, a great leader may mobilize in his followers un-

[14] From Sigmund Freud, "Group Psychology and the Analysis of the Ego." The following quotations are from *General Selections from the Work of Sigmund Freud,* ed. John Rickman (Anchor ed., 1957). "What it [the group] demands of its heroes is strength, or even violence. It wants to be ruled and oppressed and to fear its masters. . . . All their individual inhibitions fall away and all the cruel, brutal, and destructive instincts are stirred." The burden of Freud's argument lies in this direction, although he concedes that "groups are also capable of high achievements in the shape of abnegation, unselfishness, and devotion to an ideal . . ." (p. 173).

suspected strengths and virtues, superego strivings not previously lived up to, which are made active by his moral challenge. The psychology of leadership has tended to neglect this dimension in its pursuit of the causes and consequences of the demagogue and his mass followers. The fear of mass response should not obscure the creative possibilities of charismatic leadership. Gandhi evoked in himself and those who "heard" him responses that transcended the routine of ordinary life, producing extraordinary events and effects on character, which, metaphorically, can be described as "magical."

We are concerned not only with the abstract dimensions of the theory of asceticism but also with how Gandhi came to believe that through its practice he might compel the environment and how the cultural ideal of asceticism came to mean so much to the private man.

It seems fairly evident that Gandhi's extreme fearfulness and self-contempt as a child had much to do with his relations to an ailing father. Gandhi's marriage at the age of thirteen coincided with a stagecoach accident in which his father was seriously injured, never to recover fully.[15] The event itself was sufficiently symbolic and seemed so to the mature Gandhi, suggesting an inauspicious connection between the son's becoming a man and the beginning of the father's decline. Between the ages of thirteen and sixteen, Gandhi spent a substantial part of his free time nursing and ministering to his father's needs. "Every night I massaged his legs and retired only when he asked me to do so or after he had fallen asleep. . . . I would only go out for an evening walk either when he permitted me or when he was feeling well."[16] The father, at least in these years, appears to have discouraged the more venturesome and independent side of his son's activities and favored those of service and nursing, which the young Gandhi shared with his mother. If Gandhi disliked active sports and ran home anxiously after school, the antipathy was

[15] *Gandhi's Autobiography,* trans. from the Gujarati by Mahadev Desai (Washington, D.C., 1948), p. 20. He eventually died of a malignant growth, pp. 43, 44.

[16] *Ibid.,* p. 43; and D. G. Tendulkar, *Mahatma: Life of Mohandas Karamchand Gandhi* (Bombay, 1951———), I, 27–28. Tendulkar says that Gandhi nursed his father for five years, which would carry the ailment back before the stagecoach accident.

probably partly inculcated. ". . . The reason of my dislike for gymnastics was my keen desire to serve as a nurse to my father. As soon as the school closed, I would hurry home and begin serving him. Compulsory exercise came directly in the way. . . ." And in case Gandhi's "keen desire" should ever be overweighed by an interest in sports, "my father wrote himself to the headmaster saying he wanted me at home after school. . . ."[17]

These restrictions on behalf of nursing, which among other things produced in Gandhi a lifelong love of nursing and medical ministrations—we learn to want to do what we have to do—may not have been easy to accept. What physical or temperamental endowments children bring with them seem in Gandhi's case to have been weighted to the energetic side. His older sister described him as a sprightly boy, active and adventuresome, a boy who liked to get away from home and climb trees and lead his own life. He was, says his sister, "a bit of a problem . . . exceedingly active and energetic. He was never at one place for long. As soon as he was able to walk about, it became difficult to keep track of him. . . ."[18] He was not, in short, the sort of boy to whom the home-bound tasks of regularly nursing a sick father are likely to have come easily and naturally.

The mature Gandhi looked back on this experience with a recollection that suggests he took bitter medicine: "When I was younger than you are today," he wrote his son in 1901, "I used to find real enjoyment in looking after my father. I have known no fun or pleasure since I was twelve"—a passage that seems to be saying two things at once.[19] The father was demanding and probably inspired fear and anger. "I did not talk with him much. I was afraid to speak."[20] Gandhi recalls that he found him short-tempered and remembers an occasion when the father responded with forgiveness rather than fury as one of the most striking and surprising of his youth.[21] A sense of unfreedom pervades the mature man's accounts

[17] *Gandhi's Autobiography,* p. 28.

[18] Prabhudas Gandhi, *My Childhood with Gandhi* (Ahmedabad, 1957), p. 25.

[19] *Ibid.,* p. 31.

[20] Pyarelal [Nair], *Mahatma Gandhi: The Early Phase* (Ahmedabad, 1965), I, 202.

[21] *Gandhi's Autobiography,* p. 12, and the incident of the stolen arm bracelet.

of his youth: "When they [the parents] are no more and I have found my freedom . . ."; "all happiness and pleasure should be sacrificed in devoted service to my parents."[22]

That the story of Maharaja Harishchandra, a well-known classic tale acted by a passing traveling troupe, "haunted" Gandhi as a boy may tell something about Gandhi's feeling for the relationship between father and son. He re-enacted it "times without number"; his ideal was "to go through all the ordeals Harishchandra went through." The maharaja's endless misery and suffering, unlikely to speak to the mind and heart of a Western youth, apparently seemed to the young Gandhi a paradigm of existence and a moral guide. "I literally believed in the story of Harishchandra."[23] The story tells of the king's dreadful degradation as he seeks to satisfy the merciless and relentless demands of a saintly Brahman to whom he owes a debt. The Brahman's insistence on payment, that a promise must be honored, is utterly untempered by common sense or charity. To those accustomed to an ethic of consequences related to human capacities, the Brahman's absolute ethic seems incomprehensible. Maharaja Harishchandra is driven from horror to horror in a descent for which Dante might have found words. His kingdom, wealth, wife, and child gone, he is to serve, as a final degradation, as an untouchable menial among fetid corpses in a cremation ground. Harishchandra's submission is total; he laments but accepts his fate. Self-suffering in the name of honoring duty and of pursuing truth, which Gandhi identified with each other, has its reward.[24] The gods themselves come to his side, rewarding his self-control, fortitude, and respect for truth with heaven itself.

The theme of a severe older man who imposes painful demands that must not be resisted recurs in the story of the boy Prahlad,

[22] *Ibid.*, pp. 20, 36.

[23] *Ibid.*, pp. 16–17. The story of Maharaja Harishchandra occurs in many versions. We have drawn on a translation of a Bengali version by Edward C. Dimock in *The Thief of Love* (Chicago, 1963).

[24] " 'Why should not all be truthful like Harishchandra?' was the question I asked myself day and night," Gandhi writes in his autobiography. "To follow truth and go through all the ordeals Harishchandra went through was the one ideal it [the play] inspired in me" (*Gandhi's Autobiography*, p. 17).

whom Gandhi invoked repeatedly as a model of non-violence.[25] Prahlad, who loves God, is commanded by his father to deny him. When Prahlad refuses, the father has him trampled by elephants, and when he survives, he forces him to embrace a red-hot iron pillar. God springs from the pillar to save the boy and slay the father.

The parent who constrained may not have been easy to love or to respect with a full heart. Not only was he short tempered but also "to a certain extent . . . given to carnal pleasures. For he married for the fourth time when he was over forty."[26] This passage from the autobiography seems mild enough until we recollect Gandhi's harsh view of the carnal life and note that Gandhi ignores an important consideration in his father's decision, the fact that he produced no male heir in his previous marriages and was without hope of having one unless he married again.[27] "If you notice any purity in me," he

---

[25] Tendulkar, *Mahatma,* I, 77, 169; II, 4, 247, 378. The nearest equivalent in the Judaeo-Christian tradition to the virtues of Prahlad and Harishchandra is probably the virtue of Job—but he does not suffer at the hands of humans. We have stressed for the purpose of this account a particular set of relations in the two stories. But the tales speak for the psychology of the bhakti (devotional) cults more generally.

[26] *Gandhi's Autobiography,* p. 12.

[27] "The first marriage," Pyarelal writes, "took place when he was fourteen; the second at the age of twenty-five, after the death of his first wife. From his first and second marriages he had two daughters; the third marriage proved issueless, and his wife was stricken with an incurable ailment which made her an invalid for life. Already then fortyish, without male issue or hope of having any, he yielded," according to Pyarelal's version of these events, "to the importunity of his elders and decided to remarry" (*Mahatma Gandhi: The Early Phase,* I, 186). P. Gandhi, a relative, tells us, however, that "the elders in the family in Porbandar have no knowledge of the third marriage" (*My Childhood with Gandhi,* p. 18). Pyarelal, too, in the quotation above, does not make clear what happened to Gandhi's second wife. Gandhi's allegation of carnality rests not only on the fact of four marriages but also on his father's advanced age ("over forty") at the time of the fourth marriage. Here again Gandhi's feelings may have colored his interpretation of the facts. Pyarelal describes Kaba Gandhi as "fortyish" when he married Putali Ba, Gandhi's mother. Yet when Gandhi was born his father was forty-seven and had had three previous children, two boys and a girl, by Putali Ba. The second of these children, Raliat, was "Gandhiji's senior by seven years," a fact that suggests that Gandhi's father may have been thirty-eight or nine at the time of the fourth marriage. See Pyarelal, *Mahatma Gandhi: The Early Phase,* I, 186–87, for the details of Kaba Gandhi's marriages and children.

said to a friend in 1932, "I have inherited it from my mother, and not from my father."[28]

Gandhi dealt with the constraint that he felt surrounded him by acceptance and rebellion, exploring both paths more or less simultaneously. He found a guide in his mother's qualities. She, too, sacrificed herself to an invalid requiring much care. It was her suffering and self-suffering and self-control, particularly the last, that he hoped to emulate.[29] But even while he was forcing himself to exhaust the depths of filial devotion, Gandhi set out on the previously discussed secret rebellion under the guidance of Sheikh Mehtab. He appeared for the nursing work and dutifully ministered each day. But he led a double life. In one, he experimented with everything that was forbidden in the other. Gandhi in his inner being and in his "other" life was quite the reverse of the filial model pictured in the autobiography. His venturesomeness and independence survived the parental restraints—in secret and at a high cost to his conscience.

The demands made on Gandhi's filial devotion were not unique. The relationship between this particular Hindu son and his father gives expression to a more general pattern: service to an aging father who remains in charge of a joint family home after his sons have reached maturity and demands at least formal self-effacement of their masculinity and a commitment to devoted service. The pleasure of filial service is real. Like many cultural demands that initially require sacrifice and discipline, it becomes itself a satisfaction. Yet there may be limits to the kind or degree of self-effacement that can be expected. By the side of the satisfactions, and depending perhaps on the degree of devotion demanded, reside the more or less suppressed discontents of the effacement. The demands of the Hindu joint family, especially as they are expressed in the more ascetic sects and castes like Gandhi's, can require "too much" of some sons. The circumstances of his father's illness, Gandhi's great sensitivity to the moral demands of the culture, and his innate vigor seem to have at once heightened the compulsions of filial devotion and the inner resistance to them. The conflict between duty and an insufficiently

[28] *The Diary of Mahadev Desai,* trans. from the Gujarati and ed. V. G. Desai (Ahmedabad, 1953), I, p. 52.

[29] *Gandhi's Autobiography,* pp. 12, 13.

effaced self was exacerbated. That these events occurred during what a nineteenth-century novel would have called "impressionable years" places them centrally in his development.

Gandhi speaks of the circumstances surrounding his father's death as a crisis that revealed to him his shameful moral insufficiency. The crisis represents a crucial turning point in his gradual commitment to asceticism. Its background included a father who commanded the personal ministrations of his son, superseding the claims of the young man's venturesomeness, and a son who had acquired the self-discipline to meet these demands with apparent equanimity and yet who, at great cost to his conscience, launched a secret massive rebellion. The circumstances themselves are quickly related. Gandhi, who had spent the afternoon as usual massaging his ailing and sinking father, left him to join his wife in their bedroom. She was pregnant and hence ritually impure and sexually forbidden. A short time later, he was summoned to his father's room by an uncle to find him dead. If "animal passion had not blinded me, I should have been spared the torture of separation from my father during his last moments." And, "this shame of my carnal desire even at a critical hour of my father's death . . . is a blot I have never been able to efface or forget, and I have always thought that although my devotion to my parents knew no bounds and I would have given up anything for it, yet it was weighed and found unpardonably wanting because my mind was at the same moment in the grip of lust."[30] The child born after these events died.

The event confirmed Gandhi's readiness to believe that his venturesomeness, especially sexually, was in conflict with his duty to nurse and minister. He generalized this belief over time into the view that a life governed by desire conflicts wtih one governed by duty. Ministering to those who came to depend upon him as a public man was incompatible with anger and passion. His readiness to interpret his father's death in such terms had the weightiest cultural sanction: Those who acted in the grip of lust could not be guided by duty, whereas those who were capable of restraint could. The caste and sect from which Gandhi came perceived the expressive life in ways that could not balance this interpretation by providing a humane or sentimental view of sexuality. For Gandhi as for many others with

[30] *Ibid.*, pp. 45–46.

similar backgrounds, sexuality was virtually an excretory function, not a vehicle for intimacy. If he slept with his wife, it was because he was weak and could not control his impurity, not because the experience provided a context to express their love. The fact that Gandhi's relationship with Kasturbai and hers with him was based on duty and habit meant that the experiences of his own marriage could do little to dissuade him of this view. "The husband," Gandhi later wrote, "should avoid privacy with his wife. Little reflection is needed to show that the only possible motive for privacy between husband and wife is the desire for sexual enjoyment."[31] Such a view of sexuality finds support in the culture and circumstances of the traditional arranged marriage and joint family household. Boys and girls were not taught nor did they have opportunities to learn the manners and mores appropriate for relations with those of similar age but opposite sex before their marriage was arranged to a stranger from within the caste fold. Respect for the older members of the joint family obliged the couple to avoid each other in the daytime and to deny if it should exist any overt expressions of the meaningfulness of their relationship. Before and after marriage there were often few opportunities for the creation of affection, under-standing, and reciprocity, of the larger human context of sexuality, and thus it had no chance to stand for anything but itself.

His father's death not only spoke to Gandhi of the horrors of sensuality but also reached deeper into the recesses of his being. Its background, the imperfect realization of filial devotion through self-control and the "descent" into self-expression, suggested to him that a culturally impermissible sentiment, lust, had been brought together with a psychologically and culturally impermissible sentiment, anger, and had produced an unthinkable result. "Lust" had "killed"; in some so far unconfronted recess of himself he had "wanted" it to do so.

The circumstances surrounding his father's death moved Gandhi toward celibacy and the consensual mode. Their appeal and morality reach well beyond any particular life into Indian philosophic and historical thought and experience. To become a *brahmachariya,* to become not only a celibate but also one whose self-control extends

[31] Gandhi, *Self-Restraint v. Self-Indulgence,* p. 56.

to anger and aggression, was written large there. Such preoccupa-
tions "incapacitated" him for a life of self-expression and aggressive
self-assertion. That side of him that had experimented with the
cultural style suggested by Sheikh Mehtab—meat-eating, sensualism,
conflict and partisanship in law and politics, violent nationalism—
fell into the shadow. They were the paradigms of the assertiveness
from which he had been systematically and authoritatively deterred
during the nursing years. Vegetarianism, *brahmachariya,* consensual
modes in law and politics, non-violent nationalism, became the channels of venturesomeness and the means to affect and master the
environment. They did not raise the spectre of forbidden conduct or
the anger and fatal consequence that it "produced." It was among
the Indians at Pretoria that Gandhi was able for the first time to
speak in public. He could serve them, minister to their needs, ease
their suffering, right their wrongs, modes of action that combined
venturesomeness with duty.

When the mature Gandhi spoke of self-control, he had in mind
not merely the control of the "carnal self," although that was how he
often put it. It was hatred and anger as much as sexual self-expression
that he sought to pacify and control. Such emotions did not die easily
in him. His capacity for fury at his wife and sons, in whom he could
not bear to see the human frailties he would not tolerate in himself,
remained long into his South African sojourn. It re-emerged to
trouble him in his last years. Yet the energy that lay behind fury
and his sexual desire was to be transformed into something con-
structive. A variety of observers commented over many years on the
serenity to be found in Gandhi's presence.[32] But accounts of him
by close disciples in his ashram suggest a man who gave them anything but peace; his serenity in great moments and in public life
seems to have coexisted with great restlessness and testiness over the
details of life. The serenity was, we must assume, most painfully
constructed in part out of the necessity of mastering its opposite, internal war. Gandhi's techniques of public action in the nation sought
to exclude anger. His private horror of private anger remained.
Gandhi turned to the Gita, taking from it an ethic that could serve

[32] "One cannot talk to Gandhi or listen to him or even see him from a distance
without becoming aware both of the peace that is in him and of the energy he
radiates" (Edmond Taylor, *Richer by Asia* [Boston, 1947], p. 412).

his private and public self: to become he "who gives no trouble to the world, to whom the world causes no trouble, who is free from exultation, resentment, fear and vexation."[33] To live it meant peace from the inner strife between filial duty and self-expression and enabled the public man to inspire the confidence and possess the authority that detachment brings.

There have been simpler explanations of Gandhi's serenity. Ritchie Calder, in *Medicine and Man,* writes: "Whenever Mahatma Gandhi was under the stress of the modern world Rauwolfia would restore his philosophic detachment."[34] This explanation seems to have gained a certain currency despite lack of supporting evidence. In view of Gandhi's profound suspicion of all stimulants or tranquilizers (from coffee through opium) because they distracted a moral man from his essential task of self-control[35] and in view of his belief that avoidance of temptation, by withdrawal from society as a wandering ascetic or as a forest recluse, was a less worthy means to gain self-control, such an explanation seems implausible. The same moral considerations that would have deflected him from becoming a eunuch to control his "lust" would have deflected him from using a tranquilizer to produce serenity. At the level of ethics, serenity assumed for Gandhi the nature of a moral transcendence, not merely freedom from a case of nerves, and its moral significance would have been diminished by the employment of a chemical short cut. At the level of psychology, Gandhi valued self-control too highly, and feared its loss too much, to risk it for gains in what he would have regarded a specious serenity, specious because it involved a dulling of perception and the loss of control. The additional difficulty with the allegation is that none of the Gandhi literature provides evidence for it; one suspects that an era unfamiliar with the moral remorse-

[33] Mahadev Desai (trans. and ed.), *The Gita according to Gandhi* (Ahmedabad, 1946), Chap. XII, vs. 15, p. 312.

[34] Calder, *Medicine and Man* (New York, 1958), p. 50. Calder offers no source for the statement.

[35] See his *Drinks, Drugs and Gambling,* ed. Bharatan Kumarappa (Ahmedabad, 1952). He believed smoking stupefied and liked to cite the case of the hero in Tolstoy's *Kreuzer Sonata,* who kills once a cigarette has numbed his feelings (Pyarelal, *Mahatma Gandhi: The Early Phase,* I, 208).

lessness of a "religious" is too readily hospitable to a biochemical explanation.[36]

Gandhi ultimately took the vow of *brahmacharya,* of celibacy, at the age of thirty-seven.[37] His determination to do so was strengthened during the Zulu rebellion, when, as in the earlier Boer War, he undertook nursing service by forming an ambulance corps. "... The work," he wrote, "set me furiously thinking in the direction of self-control," the self-control that so conspicuously failed him when he last nursed his father.[38] The *brahmacharya* vow culminated a gradual but growing commitment to asceticism. It began before Gandhi left for London as a young man of nineteen when he vowed to his mother that he would not touch meat, wine, or women.[39] It continued there with his principled return to vegetarianism and a growing awareness of and concern for ascetic living. His marriage, because it failed to provide a meaningful alternative to asceticism, strengthened rather than deflected him from the life course leading toward self-control. He gave institutional expression to the simple, unadorned life of limited wants in the Phoenix settlement, the utopian colony he established in South Africa and named after the bird who has no mate but renews life by a somewhat different procedure.[40] Those who lived there followed a Benedictine sort of discipline, each man serving according to his aptitude and calling and at the same time pursuing the Ruskinian virtues of dignity in labor and simplicity of wants.[41]

Phoenix and the *brahmacharya* vow were indispensable preconditions for his first great non-violent resistance campaign. "Without Brahmacharya, the Satyagrahi will have no lustre, no inner strength to stand unarmed against the whole world ... ; his strength will

[36] The one bit of evidence that could prove compatible with everything else we know about Gandhi is an account that he, among the many natural remedies he used in the course of his life, especially for constipation, may have incidentally taken rauwolfia. Such evidence would carry this line of explanation no farther than the discovery of paragoric in a family's medicine chest would establish the existence of an opium habit.

[37] *Gandhi's Autobiography,* p. 254.   [38] *Ibid.*   [39] *Ibid.,* p. 56.

[40] A fact that helped recommend the name to him (P. Gandhi, *My Childhood with Gandhi,* p. 37).

[41] *Ibid.,* pp. 45–46.

fail him at the right moment."[42] He assumed that his capacity to compel the environment depended upon the degree of his self-perfection, the degree to which he had purged himself of lust, self-interest, and anger, and he prepared himself by self-imposed discipline. When things went wrong around him, when he felt helpless to shape events, he would conclude invariably that his impotence to do so was the consequence of a lapse into lustfulness or anger. In such moments, he would retreat to fast and observe other austerities, to renew that inner purity that could give him the strength to affect external events.

The relationship between Gandhi's asceticism and his belief that through it he might compel the environment is arrestingly illustrated by a series of events in his last years. He precipitated a scandal by asking at different times, several young women co-workers to share his bed.[43] The incidents tend to evoke either a kind of lascivious *schadenfreude* or a protective silence.[44] More plausible is the view that they were almost desperate attempts by Gandhi to master tragic and overwhelming events by using an extreme version of an old remedy while relying on the reduced resources of an old man. The events coincide with the frightful period between 1946 and 1948, when, in the midst of the partition bloodshed, Gandhi at seventy-seven brought something like peace to Bengal by becoming what Lord Mountbatten called a One Man Boundary Force.[45]

[42] *Harijan,* October 13, 1940, p. 319; cited in Pyarelal [Nair], *Mahatma Gandhi: The Last Phase* (Ahmedabad, 1956), I, 570.

[43] "He did for her everything that a mother usually does for her daughter. He supervised her education, her food, dress, rest, and sleep. For closer supervision and guidance he made her share the same bed with him" (Pyarelal, *Mahatma Gandhi: The Last Phase,* I, 576). "Gandhiji said that it was indeed true that he permitted women workers to use his bed ..." (N. K. Bose, *My Days with Gandhi* [Calcutta, 1953], p. 134).

[44] Arthur Koestler overstated the case when he wrote that "the Gandhians ... were so thorough in effacing every trace of the scandal that [Nirmal Kumar] Bose's book is unobtainable in India" (*The Lotus and the Robot* [New York, 1961], p. 150 n.). We obtained it by writing to a well-known Indian bookseller, and so did several colleagues. Pyarelal's book, a standard work that is everywhere available, discusses the matter in detail.

[45] Pyarelal [Nair], *Mahatma Gandhi: The Last Phase* (Ahmedabad, 1958), II, 382.

He began in the Muslim majority area of Noakhali, where Hindus were being slaughtered, and continued in Bihar, where Hindus were doing the same to Muslims. The work was desperately taxing. His walks took him through riot devastated villages, over difficult countryside, and among people who had lost those nearest to them through ghastly brutalities practiced by neighbors on neighbors. Noakhali deeply shook his serenity: "I find that I have not the patience and technique needed in these tragic circumstances; suffering and evil often overwhelm me and I stew in my own juice";[46] and again, "the happenings in Noakhali succeeded in upsetting me; for there are moments when my heart gives way to anxiety and anger."[47] Nirmal Bose, who worked with him in those days, speaks of him as preoccupied with a way to cope with these events—evidently as much the inner events, the wavering of serenity, the rise of anger, as the external events, the bloodshed all around. His capacity to affect the external, he was confident, rested on his capacity to control the internal. Desperate events required desperate remedies. He warned his friends that he was thinking of a bold and original experiment, "whose heat will be great."[48]

He asked Manu Gandhi, his nineteen-year-old grandniece, to share his bed. He appears to have regarded the matter at one and the same time as a test of his "lust control," whether as a man he could withstand temptation, and of his success in creating in himself the feelings and perceptions of a mother, kin to woman, a test that suggests a certain ambiguity of self-definition. "Manu Gandhi, my grandniece, shares the bed with me, strictly as my very blood . . . as part of what might be my last *Yajna* [sacrifice]," he wrote Acharya Kripalani.[49]

[46] Bose, *My Days with Gandhi*, p. 96.   [47] *Ibid.*, p. 107.

[48] "Referring to Manu, he said, that he had been telling her how he personally felt that he had reached the end of one chapter in his old life and a new one was about to begin. He was thinking of a bold and original experiment, whose 'heat will be great.' And only those who realize this and were prepared to remain at their posts, should be with him" (*My Days with Gandhi*, p. 116).

[49] Pyarelal, *Mahatma Gandhi: The Last Phase*, I, 581. Kripalani responded that he trusted Gandhi and that he was sure Gandhi had considered the danger that he might "be employing human beings as means rather than as ends in themselves" (p. 582). One of his skeptical friends was reassured by the sight of

Gandhi had always held, in sharp contrast to some more orthodox views, that self-control was worthless if it was achieved by withdrawal from society and thus from temptation. Only self-control in the midst of temptation was worthy. Now he evidently increased temptation to test and thus strengthen himself. His activities were no secret, although many of his warmest adherents wished they were. He discussed the matter in two prayer meetings in February, 1947, telling his audience—Muslims among whom he was working for peace—that his granddaughter (-niece) shared his bed, that the prophet had discounted eunuchs who became such by an operation but welcomed those who became it by prayer.[50] The scandal seems to have made his task in Noakhali more difficult, and a number of his co-workers left him. These events, if anything, confirmed him in his belief that he had to persist. If he did not have the serenity to bear such disapproval, surely he was not yet master of himself. Bose heard him say to a visitor that "the courage which made a man risk public disapproval when he felt he was right was undoubtedly of a superior order. . . . I get impatient and worried when I am confronted with silly arguments. . . . I sometimes flare up in anger. This should not be so. I am afraid I am yet far from the state of *sthita prajna* (self-mastery)."[51]

These events are not characteristic of Gandhi at the height of his powers. Then, his experiments in self-mastery, while often unconventional, remorseless, and directed at the inner environment, were mingled with great common sense concerning their effect on the world around him. And he was often more sensitive to the proper use of human beings. But the logic of these events, even though executed with the declining moral and psychological capacities of an old man, illuminate the ascetic dimension of his character: to control his outer environment he must control the inner, testing it to the utmost limits.

Gandhi and Manu peacefully asleep. It is relevant for the meaning of these events that Gandhi's bedroom was not private and unaccessible but virtually a public room.

[50] Bose, *My Days with Gandhi*, p. 154. Bose, who acted as Gandhi's Bengali translator, chose not to translate these remarks, a procedure that greatly displeased Gandhi.

[51] *Ibid.*, p. 159.

Gandhi's meticulous concern for diet was related to his quest for sexual asceticism. He had a horror of drink because it threatened to undermine self-control. Moderate in his criticism of many things he found objectionable, he was wholly immoderate in his concern to realize temperance: "Drugs and drink are the two arms of the devil with which he strikes his helpless slave into stupefaction and intoxication."[52] This is not an unfamiliar point of view in men who place a high value on self-restraint. What is a little less obvious is the significance of his concern with food. The cultural context of the concern is the close connection classical Hinduism makes between ritual status and what goes on at either end of the alimentary canal. An extremely fastidious management of both input and output marks the practice of the higher castes. It is possible—although we have not been able independently to verify it—that Gandhi's mother carried this general cultural preoccupation with pollution to extraordinary extremes, deploring that she could not be like the honey bee, who converted all input into the purest output.[53] In her case, the preoccupation was associated with chronic constipation, as it was with Gandhi.

In the Indian cultural setting, the human processing of food has implications that go beyond ritual pollution and ritual rank. Food is also violent or non-violent, as Gandhi explicitly recognized in his early, tentative meat-eating experiments. Vegetarianism has a moral as well as a physiological and cultural dimension. Certain food doctrines concern the man of self-restraint.[54] It is generally believed that some foods, "cool" foods, promote a cool disposition, one that is calm, undisturbed, unaggressive, resistant to lust,[55] whereas others

[52] Reprinted from *Harijan*, May 10, 1942, in Gandhi, *Drink, Drugs and Gambling*, p. 130.

[53] Ranjee (Gurdu Singh) Shahani, *Mr. Gandhi* (New York, 1961), p. 5. Shahani offers no citations.

[54] Many texts stress the connection between food and character, notably the Bhagavad-Gita, which associates types of food with levels in the hierarchy of worshippers; see Gandhi's version, *The Gita according to Gandhi,* Chap. XVII, vss. 4–11, pp. 356–57. The categories of "masculine" or "lusty" foods are similar in other cultures: "We Amhara are tough people. We love to eat hot pepper. We love to drink hard alcohol. We don't like smooth foods" (Donald N. Levine, "The Concept of Masculinity in Ethiopian Culture" [paper delivered at the Fourteenth Annual Symposium of the Committee on Human Development]).

[55] Elder, "Industrialism and Hinduism," p. 217; Carstairs, *The Twice Born,* pp. 83, 84.

produce a "hot" disposition, aggressive and lusty. The cool foods are thought to augment that part of life force conducive to saintly power, the hot that part of life force given to lust. "Ghi (clarified butter) gave one a controlled strength, a power of mind and body that could enable one to perform acts bordering on the divine."[56] Although opinion on which foods precisely are hot and cool is not fully consistent, the cool are mainly milk, clarified butter (*ghi*), curds, vegetables, and fruits.[57] Meat and strong spices figure prominently among the hot. The cool list was largely embodied in that developed by Gandhi and his followers in the twenties and also in the menu adopted at Phoenix settlement in South Africa at the beginning of the century.[58] The list of the twenties included sprouted wheat, sprouted gram, coconut, raisins, lemon, milk, fresh fruit, *ghi,* and honey. Gandhi even had doubts about milk, sharing the fear expressed in certain classical Hindu texts that milk is a stimulant.[59]

"Control of the palate," wrote Gandhi, "is the first essential in the observance of the vow (of celibacy)," and "*brahmacharya* needed no effort on my part when I lived on fruits and nuts alone."[60] This apparently unpolitical subject, too, then, had political relevance: what appeared to some as sheer food faddery was understood by many Indians who read or heard about it as an integral part of Gandhi's efforts at self-mastery and an index of his progress.

Gandhi's efforts to control his sexuality, to achieve, as it were, the serenity of neutrality, were reinforced by his very explicit feminine identification. He found his mother a more appealing figure than his father and tried to be like her rather than him.[61] "But the manner in which my *brahmacharya* came to me irresistibly drew me to woman as the mother of man . . . ; every woman at once became sister or daughter to me."[62] His love of nursing was the most prom-

[56] Elder, "Industrialism and Hinduism," p. 186.

[57] *Ibid.*, p. 217; Carstairs, *The Twice Born,* p. 84.

[58] P. Gandhi, *My Childhood with Gandhi,* pp. 36, 50.

[59] Reprinted from *Young India,* July 18, 1927, in *Diet and Diet Reform* (Ahmedabad, 1949), p. 13.

[60] *Ibid.*

[61] See *Gandhi's Autobiography,* Chap. 1, "Birth and Parentage."

[62] Bose, *My Days with Gandhi,* p. 199. Bose throughout offers a psychologically sophisticated account, in which he reveals himself as equally a social scientist and a sympathetic friend of Gandhi.

inent aspect of his maternal capacity: he welcomed all opportunities to practice this skill, acting as midwife at the birth of his fourth son, taking care of his wife and babies when they were ill. In his old age, he liked to think of himself as a mother to his grandniece, Manu, the girl who shared his bed as a daughter might her mother's and who had lost a mother. She has written a book entitled *Bapu— My Mother*.[63] He admired, first in his mother, then in women generally, their capacity for self-suffering. The admiration inspired confidence in women co-workers. When he converted self-suffering into a potent political weapon through non-violent resistance, its implication that it would be necessary to suffer violence without retaliation led him immediately to conclude that women would be most apt at it. "Woman is the incarnation of *ahimsa* (non-violence). *Ahimsa* means infinite love, which again means infinite capacity for suffering."[64] (Again, perhaps a curious definition of love.) His belief had enormous consequences for the politicization of Indian women, many of whom took part in public life for the first time during his non-violent resistance campaigns.

Gandhi built a life on rejecting the aggressive, "masculine" aspect of the human potential, accepting instead the peaceful, communitarian, adaptive aspect associated—in the West—with the culture of women.[65] But if, in law, he adopted conciliation rather than the adversary mode or, in politics, he opposed partisanship and praised consensus, he did so to alter the environment, not in order to yield to it. If we stress Gandhi's feminine identification, it is not, as a friend of the rector of Justin remarks, to invite readers to jump over a Freudian moon. Indian culture appears to distribute somewhat differently among men and women those qualities that the West associates with male and female. Effective masculinity seems to be compatible with a broader range of human qualities than many Americans are inclined to accept. "Male" and "female" are not clear and self-evident, much less dichotomous, categories but open to great variations in cultural patterning. To insist that courage or assertive-

[63] Manubehn Gandhi, *Bapu—My Mother* (Ahmedabad, 1955). She reports him as saying to her, "Have I not become your mother? I have been father to many, but only to you I am a mother" (p. 3).

[64] *Harijan,* February 24, 1940.

[65] David Bakan, "Agency and Communion in Human Sexuality," *The Duality of Human Existence* (Chicago, 1966).

ness must be expressed in familiar patterns and idioms is to miss how others may express them. Gandhi's communitarian and peace-seeking ethic and method, "in the manner of women," evoked a broad and deep response in India.[66]

This-Worldly Asceticism and Political Modernization

Many of those who were Gandhi's followers in the nationalist movement accepted his political leadership even while rejecting or not hearing his message of religious commitment and social reform. With each passing generation his image and ideas have declined in public understanding and acceptance. One era's inspiration has become the next era's cliché. Postindependence Indians have little regard for Gandhi's vision of India as a nation with a special "spiritual" vocation and with the will and means to live simply in self-sufficient villages. One hears less and less in political discourse of the Vedas, Upanishads, and Gita or of the public relevance of the quest for union with the eternal. The conception of India as a spiritual nation formulated in the nineteenth and early twentieth century by Dayanand, Vivekananda, Tagore, Aurobindo, and Gandhi himself played a significant part in shaping India's national identity and helping her to make a name and place for herself in the world. With the coming of independence and democratic self-government, new age groups have emerged for whom the nationalist struggle, in which Gandhi played so central a part, has become a history book happening or the memory of old men's youth. Castes and classes have come to power whose cultural backgrounds, political experiences, and moral concerns are less rooted in the Sanskritic tradition and its ideological norms. They pursue goals that are increasingly instrumental. Self-sufficient villages stand in the way of their quest for a release from poverty and dependence. The otherworldly concerns of Gandhian followers detract from the moral and material tasks of economic development and social mobility.

[66] Again it can be argued that these qualities are particularly appealing to the non-violent twice-born castes.

The men of power in India today also have little patience with Gandhi's postindustrial critique of industrial civilization and the alternatives he advocated. Living in an era when industrialized civilization was already well established in the West, Gandhi was of a nation that was just beginning to industrialize. He could still hear and sympathize with the critics of early industrialism, Ruskin, Thoreau, and the European and American utopian socialists, who found that it brutalized men, alienating them from self and society and depriving them of the capacity to govern themselves. Like those who founded utopian colonies, he hoped to revitalize the village community economically and morally, transforming it into a viable and attractive alternative to urban and machine civilization. By freeing men from the dehumanizing tyranny of artificial wants and the production required to satisfy them, the Gandhian village would enable them to live simple, worth-while lives in meaningful communities. These conceptions have influenced postindependence policies, by providing some of the rationale and legitimation for political and economic decentralization.[1] But they are suspect as an unrealistic village romance that fails to appreciate how rapid industrial development can replace poverty with abundance and national weakness with national power. For many among India's intellectual and professional classes, the village is backward and conservative, a place where higher castes and classes dominate lower and new ideas and technology advance at a snail's pace, the place least rather than most likely to provide the inspiration and the means for tomorrow's utopia.

Both at home and abroad Gandhi's philosophy of non-violence has been more sympathetically and broadly received than has his apotheosis of village life. It helped to explain and legitimize, even if it was not the basis of, Nehru's non-aligned foreign policy, and it continues to influence the political tactics of organized political forces. Abroad, its most conspicuous influence has been on the ideas, strategy, and tactics of Martin Luther King in his struggle to win equal rights

[1] Balwantray Mehta, chairman of the team established to consider the possibilities of decentralizing political decision-making, was an old Gandhian worker from Gujarat. The team proposed schemes which served as the pattern for subsequent legislation establishing *panchayati raj* (local political authorities) at the district, development block, and village levels (Government of India, Planning Commission, Committee on Plan Projects, *Report of the Team for the Study of Community Projects and National Extension Service* [New Delhi, 1957]).

217

and opportunities for American Negroes. Yet it, too, has been a casualty of historical events and forces. Gandhi was gunned down by a fundamentalist Hindu who thought he was too soft toward Muslims and Pakistan. Although just prior to his assassination Gandhi had been able to restore sanity and order in parts of Bengal and in Delhi, he had not been able to do so generally; the partition of India released the furies of communal hatred and vengeance, shattering the civilizing controls of respect for non-violence and for public force. In December, 1961, Jawaharlal Nehru took the decision that he had been resisting for fourteen years, to use military force against the Portuguese colonial presence in Goa. In October, 1962, the Chinese penetrated India's Himalayan frontiers, driving India's badly equipped and trained mountain forces to the plains of Assam. In September, 1965, full-scale hostilities broke out between India and Pakistan. These encounters dramatically illustrated the limits of non-violence in international politics, weakened its hold on the Indian public mind, and undermined its place in official ideology. It still is invoked to help justify India's decision not to build nuclear weapons, but with each passing Chinese weapons test the decision seems less relevant and less politically effective. The last ten years have witnessed the emergence of a vigorous new nationalism; it is more chauvinistic and parochial than that of Nehru, less tolerant and more intemperate than that of Gandhi. It speaks especially to the urbanized young men who have benefitted from expanding if deficient collegiate education. They and others more senior and influential would like India to have more muscle, larger armed forces and nuclear weapons to lick China, Pakistan, or whoever else might be looking for a fight.

On all these counts, spirituality, the self-sufficient village, and non-violence, Gandhi no longer speaks to the needs of the politically active classes of the sixties. For them Gandhi is a virtuous old gentleman, good in his time. His memory is being ritualized and devalued by proliferation of district town statues and stereotyped praise. But there is an aspect of Gandhi's character and work that is relevant to the political modernizer.

Gandhi's greatest contribution to political modernization was the one we have already discussed, helping India to acquire national coherence and identity, to become a nation, by showing Indians a way to courage, self-respect, and political potency. But because these contributions were rooted in the experience of imperial domination and colored by Gandhi's transcendental morality and appeal to traditional ideas, they have become less meaningful to postindependence generations. It is those aspects of Gandhi's leadership that relate to middle-level norms of conduct and to instrumental rather than ideological effectiveness that remain relevant. Obscured by the grand legacies of saintliness and independence, they require analysis and understanding not only because of their continuing significance but also because they were necessary conditions for Gandhi's greatness.

Gandhi's more mundane contributions to political modernization include introducing in the conduct of politics a work ethic and economizing behavior with respect to time and resources, and making India's political structures more rational, democratic, and professional. A man with Gandhi's spiritual concerns might be supposed to show little interest in the more routine tasks of modern politics. Yet far from being incapacitated for mundane political entrepreneurship by his religious heritage, Gandhi drew from it a this-worldly asceticism. His efforts to build effective political organizations were associated with a psychological disposition toward work and efficiency that mobilized like propensities among those whose lives were affected by his example and teaching.

Gandhi approached his public work with the frame of mind of those modernizing men who confront all tasks with the calculation of the metronome and the balance sheet. While Weber and contemporary social psychologists associate industriousness and the economizing of time and resources with achievement drives rooted in "Protestant" character, Gandhi came to them through familial and religious socialization in the Vaishnavite and Jain traditions of Gujarat. His life course does not support Weber's belief that "it could not have occurred to a Hindu to prize the rational transformation of the world in accordance with matter-of-fact considerations and to undertake such transformation as an act of obedience to a divine will."[2] The disposition to work, save, and rationally allocate

[2] Max Weber, *The Religion of India: The Sociology of Hinduism and Buddhism,* trans. and ed. H. H. Gerth and D. Martindale (Glencoe, Ill., 1958), p. 326. In his classic but much disputed *The Protestant Ethic and the Spirit of Capitalism,* trans. Talcott Parsons (New York, 1958), he argued that the modernization that flowed from industrial capitalism in the West was rooted

time and resources in order to realize given goals is not necessarily modern. It appears, for example, among religious orders, both East and West, where self-control and asceticism in the service of spiritual ends find expression, as they did for Gandhi, in strict observance of schedules, hard work at physical, intellectual, or spiritual tasks, and the practice of thrift. Traditional merchant castes, too, such as Gandhi's, the Modh Baniyas, exhibit such psychological dispositions and habits. But it is also true that the elevation of these characteristics to universal virtues is particularly associated with the emergence of modern entrepreneurship and scientific technology and the expectations they raised that men could master their material and human environment. In the West, the preaching of these characteristics as virtues and attempts systematically to inculcate them into

---

in Protestant "this-worldly asceticism," the sanctification of the asceticism and acquisitiveness that made for business success. Weber found in Hinduism the mirror image of Protestant Christianity. Despite his awareness and appreciation of elements of Indian culture and society that were conducive to sanctified asceticism and acquisitiveness, he concluded that "it could not have occurred to a Hindu to see the economic success he had attained in his calling as a sign of his salvation" (*The Religion of India,* p. 326). Milton Singer observes that "on *prima facie* grounds one could make a pretty plausible case for the thesis that Hindu metaphysics should produce just those kinds of 'character' and 'character traits' which Weber regarded as necessary for modern industrial society. . . . But I do not think that such a *prima facie* argument is any more conclusive than the opposite argument, which holds that Hindu metaphysics cannot produce a 'capitalist spirit' in a good Hindu" ("Religion and Social Change in India: The Max Weber Thesis, Phase Three," *Economic Development and Cultural Change,* July, 1966, p. 501). See also his important review article of Weber's *The Religion of India,* in *American Anthropologist,* LXIII (February, 1961), and Amar Kumar Singh's very able criticism of the Weber thesis in an Indian context, "Hindu Culture and Economic Development in India," *Conspectus,* III, No. 1 (1967).

David McClelland's *The Achieving Society* (Princeton, N.J., 1961) is probably the leading example of the use of the Weber thesis by social psychologists. He finds that "Hinduism explictly teaches that concern with earthly achievements is a snare and a delusion. . . . It is hard to see how they [Hindu parents] would set high standards of excellence for their son's performance, or show great pleasure over his achievements or displeasure at his failures" (p. 357). McClelland's exemption of Jains and Vaishnavas, who provide some of India's most successful businessmen, is difficult to appreciate since it is not at all clear that their metaphysics, practice, and socialization differ from those of Brahmans in respects critical for McClelland's theory of the need for achievement.

emerging generations through sermons, aphorisms, penny pamphlets, and public education began in the eighteenth century and peaked in the nineteenth.[3]

Much in the petty details of Gandhi's life corresponds to the practice of those eighteenth- and nineteenth-century figures in Britain and America whose lives and teaching popularized the Protestant ethic and applied technology. Pre-eminent among them in America was Benjamin Franklin. In *Poor Richard's Almanac* the inventor, people's philosopher, and statesman offered practical advice to the modernizing and mobile youth of a bustling, ambitious new nation. Some might boggle at the attempt to bracket Franklin and Gandhi, one a herald, the other a critic, of industrial civilization. At certain fundamental points, indeed, the two men undoubtedly were poles apart. Gandhi would not have enjoyed Parisian life, as did Franklin. And Franklin's attitude was highly instrumental toward the practice of virtue. Gandhi would never have congratulated himself, as Franklin did, by saying: "I cannot boast much success in acquiring the reality of [pridelessness] but I had a good deal with regard to the appearance of it."[4] And Gandhi would have been scandalized by a similar Franklinism: "Nothing [is] so likely to make a man's fortune as virtue."[5] For Franklin, a practical man, moderation—in food, drink, and venery—was a virtue. For Gandhi, a religious who refused to separate means and ends, and found the passions a permanent threat, moderation in these areas of life was a shortfall from virtue. Food should be taken like medicine, privately and sparingly, not for pleasure but to sustain life.[6] Celibacy was too serious to be treated

[3] See, for example, *Reinhard Bendix, Work and Authority in Industry* (New York, 1956), and Robert Kiefer Webb, *The British Working Class Reader, 1790–1848* (London, 1955).

[4] Leonard Labaree (ed.) *The Autobiography of Benjamin Franklin* (New Haven, Conn., 1964), p. 159.

[5] Charles L. Sanford, *Benjamin Franklin and the American Character* (Boston, 1955), p. 18.

[6] "His diet," Pyarelal writes, "consisted of goat's milk, raisins and fruit and was weighed out and measured with a druggist's exactness and care. The menu for each meal was adjusted carefully according to how the system had responded to the previous meal, the amount of sleep he had or expected to have, and the physical or mental strain already undergone or in prospect"; *Mahatma Gandhi: The Early Phase* (Ahmedabad, 1965), I, 12.

with "moderation." For Franklin, virtue was useful; for Gandhi, it was self-justifying.

These are important differences but they should not be allowed to obscure what the two men held in common; by exploring the points of congruence, Gandhi's contribution to Indian modernity can be better understood. Gandhi and Franklin subjected their environment to rigorous calculations that linked psychic and material expenditures to their returns. And, despite Franklin's contingent view of virtue, they shared a propensity to invest with moral, not merely utilitarian, implications the observance of certain "Protestant" habits. Silence, order, resolution, frugality, industry, cleanliness, and chastity are seven of Franklin's virtues about which Gandhi would have been enthusiastic. However differently they viewed their ultimate fate, neither man proposed to let the control and mastery of his worldly environment escape him.

It is no accident that a large watch was among the few effects Gandhi valued in his lifetime and left behind at his death.[7] Gandhi was extremely meticulous about time, as it was measured by the clock, the more so as he found a good many of those about him indifferent to its compulsions. He employed his watch as a species of tyrant to regulate his own affairs and the lives of those associated with him. Arrivals and departures frequently were crises; Gandhi considered the normal practice of great public figures, to keep their audiences waiting, a transgression. Many were the arrangement committees and colleagues whom he upbraided for failures on this score. Introducing the venerable B. G. Tilak, who was late, to a conference in 1917, Gandhi remarked: "I am not responsible for his being late. We demand *swaraj*. If one does not mind arriving late by three-quarters of an hour at a conference summoned for the purpose, one should not mind if *swaraj* too comes correspondingly late."[8] Once, in his earlier work in 1917 among indigo workers in Bihar, when it became apparent that a decision to move himself and his co-workers

[7] Nirmal Kumar Bose, Gandhi's able—and skeptical—secretary in Bengal in the mid-forties has developed the theme of Gandhi's preoccupation with time and with the watch (in a lecture, South Asia Seminar, University of Chicago, Spring, 1965).

[8] "Speech at Gujarat Political Conference," in *The Collected Works of Mahatma Gandhi* (Delhi, 1958——), XIV, 48.

would not be carried out by the end of the appointed day, he picked up his bedroll at ten o'clock at night and began to move his effects. His associates, for the most part from the upper castes and classes and accustomed to be waited on by servants and to adjust to their inefficiencies, were obliged willy-nilly to move themselves also.[9]

The timetable he blocked out for his first Indian ashram is faithful to his own schedule and recalls a similar affection for orderly schedules in Franklin. Their respective schedules read as follows:[10]

Gandhi			*Franklin*
4	A.M.	Rising from bed	5 Rise, wash and address *Powerful*
4:15 to 4:45		Morning prayer	6 *Goodness!* Contrive day's business,
5 to 6:10		Bath, exercise, study	7 and take the resolution of the day; prosecute the present study, and
6:10 to 6:30		Breakfast	breakfast
6:30 to 7		Women's prayer class	8 Work
			9
7 to 10:30		Body labour, education, and sanitation	10
			11
			12 Read, or overlook my accounts,
10:45 to 11:15		Dinner	1 and dine.
12 to 4:30 P.M.		Body labour, including classes	2 Work
			3
4:30 to 5:30		Recreation	4
5:30 to 6		Supper	5
6 to 7		Recreation	6 Put things in their places. Supper. Music or diversion, or
7 to 7:30		Common worship	7 per. Music or diversion, or
7:30 to 9		Recreation	8 conversation. Examination of the
9		Retiring bell	9 day.
			10 Sleep
Note: These hours are subject to change whenever necessary			11
			12
			1
			2
			3
			4

[9] Rajendra Prasad, "Gandhi in Bihar," in Homer A. Jack (ed.), *The Gandhi Reader* (Bloomington, Ind., 1956), pp. 149–50.

[10] M. K. Gandhi, *Ashram Observances in Action* (Ahmedabad, 1955), pp. 123–24, and Sanford, *Benjamin Franklin and the American Character,* p. 16. Gandhi did, however adjust his schedule when he was on tour or in action politically.

Franklin's timetable differs from Gandhi's mainly in its less picayune calibrations and in allowing more time for dining.

Gandhi took the timetable most seriously: "All members," runs the first rule of the ashram, "whether permanent or otherwise will turn every minute of their time to good account."[11] A few days after Kasturbai died in jail in 1944, his morning meal was served at 11:45 rather than at 11:30; those responsible for the meal were lectured: "You know she never sent me food late, even by one minute."[12] Any item included in his schedule was ruthlessly attended to. In late 1946, when Hindu-Muslim disturbances had broken out in Bengal and Gandhi at seventy-seven went to Noakhali district to try to restore peace, he began his day at 2:30 and took up Bengali.[13] Manu Gandhi's diary records: "After taking fruit juice, he began to pore over his Bengali primer. While doing so, he dozed off for about ten minutes. . . . At 7:25 we started on our day's march, reaching . . . at 8:25 A.M. after a full one hour's walk. Immediately upon his arrival there, he again sat down to do his Bengali lession."[14] His secretary Pyarelal reports that, no matter how late the hour or how heavy the pressure of work, the Bengali lesson was never missed.[15] Manu Gandhi's diary entries, precise to the minute, stand witness to the microscopic relentlessness with which the Mahatma imposed on himself and those around him the discipline of calibrated time.

Gandhi's assiduous thrift expressed itself in the smallest and the largest matters. Like Franklin, he went over his accounts daily[16] and would have approved of the entire catalogue of savings aphorisms, from "a penny saved is a penny earned" onward. The ashram rules not only linked cleanliness to thrift but also provided a practical Indian version of the saving-is-earning theme:

> The split twigs used for toothbrushing should be washed well, and collected in a pot. When they dry up, they should be used

11 Gandhi, *Ashram Observances in Action,* p. 147.

12 Mukulbhai Kalarthi (comp.), *Ba and Bapu* (Ahmedabad, 1962), p. 105.

13 Pyarelal [Nair], *Mahatma Gandhi: The Last Phase* (2d ed.; Ahmedabad, 1966), I, 118.

14 February 2, 1947, cited in *ibid.,* p. 44.

15 *Ibid.,* p. 41.   16 *Ibid.*

for starting a fire, the idea being that nothing which can be used should be thrown away.[17]

Gandhi wrote hundreds of important communications on the reverse of old letters and memos. When he began the Natal Indian Congress, he self-consciously avoided the waste and ostentation that often accompanied new organizational beginnings in India. Instead of having receipt books and reports printed he ran them off on a cyclostyle machine in his office, "knowing that in public work minor expenses at times absorbed large amounts. . . ." "Such economy," he instructs the readers of his autobiography, "is essential for every organization, and yet I know that it is not always exercised."[18] In his correspondence with the industrialist G. D. Birla, from whom he extracted vast sums to support various nationalist and service enterprises, a good many letters concern themselves with the saving of bank charges on large transfers.[19]

He worried a good deal about accounting for the public funds with which he was entrusted, beginning in a small way in Natal: "People never cared to have receipts for the amounts they paid, but we always insisted on the receipts being given. Every pie was thus clearly accounted for, and I dare say the account books for the year 1894 can be found intact even today."[20] Returning to South Africa in 1896, he reported in detail to the Natal Indian Congress how he had spent the 75 pounds it had sanctioned toward his expenses, including "Barber, 4 annas; Washerman, 8 annas; Pickwick pens, 6 annas; *Pankha* coolie, 2 annas; Theatre, Rs. 4; Servant Lalu, Rs. 10," and so forth.[21]

Gandhi, who tells us in the first sentence of his autobiography that he belongs to the baniya caste and is descended from shopkeepers, and who spent his formative professional years among Gujarati merchants in South Africa, showed a marked flare for acquiring as well

[17] Gandhi, *Ashram Observances in Action*, p. 151.

[18] *Gandhi's Autobiography, or, The Story of My Experiments with Truth*, trans. from the Gujarati by Mahadev Desai (Washington, D.C., 1948), p. 188.

[19] G. D. Birla, *In the Shadow of the Mahatma* (Bombay, 1953), pp. 1–16, 89, 93.

[20] *Gandhi's Autobiography*, p. 188.

[21] Pyarelal, *Mahatma Gandhi: The Early Phase*, I, 730.

as using money. An incident from the early days of the Natal Congress illustrates his persistence, use of strategy, and sense of timing:

> On one occasion during this money raising tour the situation was rather difficult. We expected our host to contribute £6 [one-fourth Gandhi's initial monthly salary], but he refused to give anything more than £3. If we had accepted that amount from him, others would have followed suit, and our collections would have been spoiled. It was a late hour of the night, and we were all hungry. But how could we dine without having first obtained the amount we were bent on getting? All persuasion was useless. The host seemed to be adamant. Other merchants in the town reasoned with him, and we all sat up throughout the night, he as well as we determined not to budge one inch. Most of my co-workers were burning with rage, but they contained themselves. At last, when day was already breaking, the host yielded, paid down £6 and feasted us. This happened at Tongaat, but the repercussion of the incident was felt as far as Stanger on the North Coast and Charlestown in the interior. It also hastened our work of collection.[22]

Again, in 1919, at a critical point in Gandhi's Indian career, he demonstrated that he recognized the importance of mobilizing financial resources and had the will and the skill to do so. Pyarelal tells us that soon after the Jallianwala Bagh massacre a Congress decision to acquire the park for a memorial to those who had fallen required financial support from the businessmen of Amritsar. Swami Shraddhanand, "the saffron-robed Savonarola of Northern India," told the assembled businessmen that "India's glorious past and her lofty ancient cultural tradition" called upon them to rise to the occasion but his "eloquence produced no . . . results." Pandit Madan Mohan Malaviya, founder and chancellor of the Banaras Hindu University and popularly known as "the silver-tongued orator of the Congress," also cajoled the Amritsar business community, by telling its members that if they would only unloosen their purse strings dharma, artha, kama, and moksha, too, would be theirs, but to no avail. "Finally, Gandhi spoke. . . . In level tones he told them that the target had been fixed.

[22] *Gandhi's Autobiography,* p. 187.

It had to be reached. If they failed in their duty he would sell his Ashram and make up the amount. He would not let the sanctity of the national resolve, to which he had been a party—so had they been too—be lightly treated. . . . The required amount [five lakhs of rupees] was subscribed on the spot."[23]

"I must regard my participation in Congress proceedings at Amritsar," Gandhi confesses, "as my real entrance into the Congress politics." His experience there "had shown that there were one or two things for which I had some aptitude." Not only did he succeed in raising the money to acquire Jallianwala Bagh but he was also appointed one of the trustees to raise and administer an additional five lakhs to construct a national memorial there. Pandit Malaviya had had the reputation of being Congress' best fund-raiser "but I knew that I was not far behind him in that respect." It was, Gandhi adds, "in South Africa that I discovered my capacity in this direction." Malaviya had succeeded by turning to India's rajas and maharajas; "but I knew," Gandhi observes, "that there was no question of approaching" them for donation for the memorial. It was under these circumstances that "the main responsibility . . . fell, as I had expected, on my shoulders." Gandhi turned to the business community of Bombay and was again strikingly successful. "The generous citizens of Bombay subscribed most liberally, and the memorial trust has at present a handsome credit balance in the bank."[24]

Gandhi's ascendancy in the Congress was associated not only with his organizational and idiomatic skills and popular touch but also with his financial capacities. More than any other Congress leader, he had access to the purses (as well as the hearts and minds) of India's business communities, an access he used to generate financial support for Congress even while recruiting merchants, traders, and industrialists into organizations and activities associated with nationalism and social reform. While there was no doubt a conservative political dimension to this support, it is difficult to see how, with public patronage and resources in British hands, the professionalization of Congress politics could have been achieved otherwise.

[23] Pyarelal, *Mahatma Gandhi: The Early Phase*, I, 6; *The Collected Works of Mahatma Gandhi*, XVI, 468.

[24] *The Collected Works of Mahatma Gandhi*, XVI, 596–97.

Evidence of Gandhi's industriousness and productivity can be found in his rigid adherence to schedules; the frequency and pace of his interviews; the volume of letters, reports, petitions, and articles that issued from his pen; the number and scope of his tours; and his leadership and management of literary, reform, and spiritual and political organizations and activities. Ordinarily Gandhi maintained his schedule while on tour, doing his daily writing on trains and in way stations. The collected works, which will run to some one hundred volumes, greatly understate the level of his productivity because speeches and statements that did not enter into the public record and letters that were not directed to officials who filed them or to adherents who saved them will not be recorded there. The enormous volume of replies to unknown or obscure inquirers—Nirmal Kumar Bose recalls that in Noakhali he "refreshed" himself with a six-page letter to an unknown young man seeking his advice on marriage arrangements—and a significant volume of public mail are simply lost.[25] In the busy days of the nationalist movement, many who might have kept records found it hard to do so between jail terms; others were not disposed to keep files. But we do know that it took some half-dozen well-trained assistants to help him handle his daily mail and that he took keeping up with it very seriously.

He did a great deal, and he applied exacting standards of accuracy, clarity, and efficiency to all of it. "His energy," Pyarelal tells us, "was phenomenal. . . . One day I actually counted 56 letters which he had written in his own hand." In the midst of din and disorder, his "remarkable faculty of switching on and off his mind to and from anything at will and to remain unaffected by his surroundings" enabled him to carry on with his usual pace and efficiency. "He had a passion for precision and thoroughness in the minutest details . . . and enforced military discipline and clock-work regularity in his own case and expected the same from those around him. . . . He insisted on his desk being always clear and woe to anyone of his staff who referred to him a letter more than forty-eight hours old. . . . Any reply of more than five or ten lines was as a rule consigned to the waste paper basket. The address was no less minutely scrutinized. Not to know . . . the exact location of an out of the way place in India was re-

[25] From a lecture by N. K. Bose, South Asia Seminar, University of Chicago, Spring, 1965.

garded as a culpable failure. Vagueness about train timings or the exact time it took for the post to reach its destination by a particular route was another cardinal sin. . . ."[26] His public reports, petitions and demands reflect the capacity for orderly clear argument and meticulous care for facts that he had developed as a successful lawyer.[27]

Gandhi's this-worldly asceticism took its meaning in the context of larger motives and meanings. Those who practice it cannot know direct rewards but they remain alert for signs of grace. Gandhi associated his reception by the Indian people with the potency of his charisma and saw it as a visible recognition that his worldly asceticism made him worthy. Public influence was the coin in which he measured his worldly success. "The incomparable love that I have received has made it clear to me that they in whom truth and the spirit of service are manifested in their fulness will assuredly sway the hearts of men and so accomplish their chosen task."[28]

But Gandhi was never certain that he was one of those in whom the spirit of truth and service was sufficiently manifest. Some of the energy that he invested in worldly asceticism must have arisen from this uncertainty. It is in his relationship to *darshan* (view of an auspicious object, such as a temple deity, king, or holy man from which the viewer gains merit or good fortune) that these uncertainties become clear. Soon after his return to India in 1915, Gandhi first confronted his *darshan* dilemma—whether his capacity to give and people's eagerness to receive *darshan* was a worldly sign of his spiritual achievements or whether it was an expression of his vanity and their irrationality. At the Kumbha Mela, a vast religious assemblage of pilgrims and sadhus held once every twelve years, *darshan* seekers did not allow him a minute to call his own. It was then, he

[26] Pyarelal, *Mahatma Gandhi: The Early Phase*, I, 12.

[27] See, for various examples, "Extracts from Minutes of Chamaparan Agrarian Enquiry Committee," *The Collected Works of Mahatma Gandhi*, XIII, *passim;* "Letter to the Secretary, Passenger Grievances Committee, Rangoon, July 25, 1917" (with reference to the bad lot of deck passengers of the British India Steam Navigation Service), *ibid.*, pp. 476–78; and "Report of the Commissioners Appointed by the Punjab Sub-Committee of the Indian National Congress" (1920), *ibid.*, XVII, 114–292.

[28] "Punjab Letter," *Navajivan,* November 11, 1919, in *The Collected Works of Mahatma Gandhi,* XVI, 282.

229

tells us, "that I realized what a deep impression my humble services in South Africa had made throughout the whole of India." And, in almost the same breath: ". . . The *dharsanvalas'* blind love has often made me angry, and . . . sore at heart."[29]

Four years later, as he was establishing his ascendancy in the nationalist movement, Gandhi found, on the one hand, that "the affection that I am receiving from men and women here in Lahore [and throughout the Punjab] puts me to shame," and on the other, that "the unique faith of India and the frankness and generosity of our people enchant me." Not only did "young and old . . . come all day to have *darshan* of [Gandhi]," but also it was impossible for him to go out alone. "I simply cannot check them," he complained. More disturbing was the thought that he knew of nothing in himself that made him "worthy of giving *darshan*"; he found it "intolerable" that they should want *darshan* from a "mere servant." Nor did the people "profit in any way by having *darshan*." "If I keep on giving *darshan*," he commented ominously, "my work will suffer."[30] A month later, in Wazirabad, he had grown tired of *darshan*. ". . . In the end we had to keep the doors closed . . . ; it is not possible simultaneously to work and to give *darshan*."[31]

"No man," he stated flatly, "is great enough to give it." He found that he was embarrassed by the experience and wanted to put a stop to it. But to do so would hurt people's feelings, and he had "not yet found it possible to do this." Perhaps his courage was "inadequate" or his judgment "clouded"; more likely "my principle of non-violence does not allow me to hurt people's feelings." "I do," he protested, ". . . make every effort to extricate myself from this dilemma." But his solution, tentatively stated in 1919 but developed into a habit over the years, was not to choose between *darshan* and work but to try to do both: "At present, even when people come for *darshan,* I continue to write and do other work."[32]

However much Gandhi found himself unworthy of *darshan* and giving it a threat to his work and serenity, he could not escape the

[29] *Gandhi's Autobiography,* p. 475.

[30] "Punjab Letter," *Navajivan,* November 11, 1919, p. 282.

[31] "Punjab Letter," *Navajivan,* December 7, 1919, in *The Collected Works of Mahatma Gandhi,* XVI, p. 325.

[32] "Punjab Letter," *Navajivan,* November 11, 1919, pp. 282–83.

feeling that it expressed in worldly terms some measure of other-worldly approbation, that it was a sign of grace. "Man's instinctive urge to worship," he found "admirable."[33] The test for worship was the worthiness of its object, and Gandhi found it hard to accept that he and those who came to him for *darshan* were engaged in a mutual fraud upon each other. "It is perfectly clear to me that this relationship is the miracle wrought by even a small measure of devotion to truth and service. . . . I am making a prodigious effort to live up to these two principles."[34]

Toward the end of his life, as he was leaving for Noakhali to try to still the communal passions unleashed by partition, the old man in a train was still not certain whether his spiritual virtue and worldly asceticism made him worthy of such attention. But he persisted, mindful of the possibility that he might be and in the belief that effortfulness would make it so:

The journey proved to be as strenuous as many had feared. There were mammoth crowds at all big stations on the way. At places it was like a swarming ant-heap of humanity as far as the eye could reach. The crowd clambered on the roofs of the carriages, choked the windows, broke glass, smashed shutters and yelled and shouted till one's ears split. They pulled the alarm-chain again and again for *darshan,* making it necessary to disconnect the vacuum brakes. . . . Later in the evening, Gandhiji sat with his fingers thrust in his ears to keep out the shouting when it became unbearable. But when it was proposed to him that the lights be switched off to discourage *darshan* seekers, he turned down the suggestion by saying that the simple faith of the masses demanded that he should serve them with the last ounce of his energy. . . .[35]

Gandhi's version of this-worldly asceticism led him to rationalize and extend the organizational bases of Indian political life. Soon after Gandhi returned to India in 1915 he recognized that Congress could not achieve the goals of national mobilization, social reform, and political freedom as long as it depended exclusively on talking

[33] *Ibid.*, p. 282. [34] *Ibid.*, p. 283.
[35] Pyarelal, *Mahatma Gandhi: The Last Phase,* I, 4.

shops by, for, and among the English-educated elite. Legislative debates at the center and in the provinces and the formulation of resolutions at Congress annual sessions could not, by themselves, realize these goals. Until opinion was organizationally related to the aspirations and objective needs of popular social and economic forces, it could be neither legitimate nor politically effective. One of Gandhi's most important contributions to political modernization was to help Congress become a mass political organization, manned by full-time political workers and capable of mobilizing public opinion and bringing it to bear on governmental policy and administration. All that has been said and written about Gandhi's shifting the arena and method of Indian politics from persuasion of the government by elites to direct action among the people has obscured a parallel and equally important shift that he inaugurated, building a political organization.

Gandhi began building political organizations well before he entered Indian politics. Visiting India from South Africa in 1901, he was disappointed by what he witnessed at a session of the Indian National Congress. An association of political amateurs in an era that was ready for political professionals, the Congress provided an annual forum for liberal nationalists to address adherents and sympathizers but found it difficult to translate words into action because it lacked the continuity and specialization that permanent structures and full-time personnel make possible. "The Congress," Gandhi observed, "would meet three days every year and then go to sleep. What training could one have out of a three days' show once a year?"[36] He deplored Congress' slovenly procedures and its subordination of efficiency to ceremony. "I also noticed the huge waste of time here. . . . There was little regard for economy of energy. More than one did the work of one, and many an important thing was no one's business at all."[37] Too many people came and too few had the inclination or the means to take the business at hand seriously. "The procedure was far from pleasing to me. . . . There was hardly any difference between visitors and delegates. Everyone raised his hand and all resolutions passed unanimously."[38]

Gandhi had established his first political organization seven years

[36] *Gandhi's Autobiography,* p. 274.

[37] *Ibid.,* pp. 278–79.   [38] *Ibid.,* p. 281.

earlier, in 1894.[39] The Natal National Congress was a cadre organization, meticulously organized, that demanded of its members a continuous and high level of commitment. At the end of its first year it had a membership of 228 drawn from the prosperous middle-class section of the South African Indian community.[40] Those who failed to pay their subscription or missed six consecutive meetings were struck off the rolls.[41] The subscription was substantial; at three pounds per year (paid in advance) it represented, for example, 1 per cent of the salary Gandhi received in 1894, a salary that enabled him to maintain the style of life characteristic of the white middle classes.[42] A number of middle-class merchants participated in door-to-door canvassing, a labor that Gandhi evidently considered good experience for testing their commitment.[43] The Congress met monthly to discuss policy and pass on expenditures.[44] Its objectices were not unlike those of the caste associations analyzed in Part I: it published and distributed pamphlets on problems confronting Indians as a subject community facing dominant white South Africans; provided legal assistance to indentured Indians; represented Indian interests in legislative and administrative contexts; and worked to upgrade the manners and life style of the community.[45]

Recognizing that political consciousness and organization without political skills inhibited personal confidence and public effectiveness, Gandhi worked to repair the political skills of Natal Congressmen. "People had no experience of taking part in public discussions. . . . Everyone hesitated to stand up to speak. I explained to them the rules of procedure at meetings. . . . They realized that it was an education

[39] Pyarelal, *Mahatma Gandhi: The Early Phase,* I, 435.

[40] *Ibid.,* p. 489. [41] *Ibid.,* p. 436. [42] *Ibid.,* p. 431.

[43] *Gandhi's Autobiography,* p. 186. The group included Messrs. Dawud Muhammed, Moosa, Haji Adam, Mohamed Casam Jeeva, Parsi Rustomji, and Gandhi (Pyarelal, *Mahatma Gandhi: The Early Phase,* I, 437). That Gandhi's early political experiences should have placed him with men who were not intellectuals, who were conservative, merchants, and mainly Muslim, helps explain his later propensity to believe that these groups, in addition to the liberal, Anglicized, intellectual Hindus, could be won over to the nationalist movement.

[44] Pyarelal, *Mahatma Gandhi: The Early Phase,* I, 436.

[45] *Ibid.,* pp. 436, 438.

for them, and many who had never been accustomed to speaking before an audience soon acquired the habit of thinking and speaking publicly. . . ."[46]

The meetings were conducted in Gujarati; if expatriate Gujarati merchants without formal schooling were to participate, there was no other choice.[47] These early experiences contributed to Gandhi's recognition that the use of English inhibited the Indian National Congress and to his optimism concerning the effect the use of regional languages would have on political participation and national consciousness.

Gandhi extended the reach of the Congress by proliferating branches in ten centers outside the territorial jurisdiction of the parent Natal organization.[48] These new structures retained the vanguard qualities of the original organization by being composed of a few, well-placed, committed, and active members.

On his return to India in 1915 he applied the ideas and methods that he had developed in South Africa to the first political organization he joined, the Gujarat Sabha, converting it from an *ad hoc* society that met annually to pass resolutions into a permanent structure whose executive conducted a year-long program of activities.[49] Gandhi was quite explicit about his intention to make politics more professional and to associate it with permanent specialized structures:

> Conferences do not, as a rule, at the end of their deliberations leave behind them an executive body, and even when such a body is appointed, it is, to use the language of the late Mr. Gokhale, composed of men who are amateurs. What we need is men who would make it their business to give effect to the resolutions of such conferences. If such men came forward in great numbers, then and then only will such conferences be a

[46] *Gandhi's Autobiography*, p. 187.

[47] Pyarelal, *Mahatma Gandhi: The Early Phase*, I, 439.

[48] *Ibid.*, p. 442.

[49] N. D. Parikh, *Sardar Vallabhai Patel* (Ahmedabad, 1955), p. 43. It is this program that drew Patel, subsequently one of the Congress' great organizational talents and a man impatient with bodies of a deliberative nature only.

credit to the country and produce lasting results. At present there is much waste of energy.[50]

If the professional revolutionary and the professional politician represent two types of the modern political specialist, the Gandhian professional embodies qualities of both without fully resembling either. The professional revolutionary was first given historical expression in the seventeenth century by the "saints" of the English civil war and subsequently elaborated upon by the Jacobin and Bolshevik of the French and Russian revolutions.[51] The professional politician developed out of the experience with competitive democratic politics in western Europe and America.[52] The Gandhian model of politics as a vocation emerged in the years immediately following his return to India in 1915. Although in its particulars this type was related to the Indian cultural context, it has more general application as an example of the professionalization of peaceable ideal politics. Its concern for spiritual meaning, its emphasis on service, its insistence on non-violent means, and its suspicion of power distinguish the Gandhian from the other two models.

Like professional revolutionaries, Gandhian professionals gave the highest priority in their personal lives and public actions to ideologically defined ends, but unlike revolutionaries, they gave equal priority to non-violent means. Modern political specialists, regardless of type, must attend to the requirements of mobilizing and representing particular classes, communities, and interests. For professional politicians, this task tends to become an end in itself since it is the prescribed means for acquiring power. For revolutionaries, mobilization and representation are options to be used under certain historical con-

---

[50] "Speech at Gujarat Political Conference (Godhra, November 3, 1917)," in *The Collected Works of Mahatma Gandhi*, XIV, 49–50.

[51] See Michael Walzer, "Puritanism as a Revolutionary Ideology," in *Political Theory and Ideology*, ed. Judith Shklar (New York, 1966), p. 64, where he argues that the saints were entrepreneurs, but in politics, not economics. His view of the saints as political specialists is elaborated in *The Revolution of the Saints: A Study in the Origins of Radical Politics* (Cambridge, Mass., 1965).

[52] See Max Weber, *Politics as a Vocation* (Philadelphia, 1965), in which he describes types of professional politicians, particularly the lawyer, journalist, and "demagogue" of the postdemocratic era.

235

ditions. Gandhians used mobilization and representation as a means to help realize certain ideal goals, such as national freedom or social justice, by making their claims more legitimate and effective. Like revolutionaries but unlike politicians, Gandhians placed self-sacrifice above self-assertion and service to the cause and those whom it was to benefit above considerations of personal popularity or advantage.

Gandhian professionals can also be distinguished from both revolutionaries and politicians by their orientation toward power. Revolutionaries must seek and use power if they are to model a new society; it is good societies that produce good men, and power is a necessary instrument for the realization of good societies. Politicians, too, must seek and use power. In establishing their mandate to govern, to realize certain ideal and material goals, and to allocate resources, patronage, and honor, politicians find the pursuit and deployment of power an integral part of their work. For Gandhians, the desire for power, like any other passion (such as sex or anger) destroyed self-control; without self-control neither serenity nor mastery of the environment nor virtue was possible. By aspiring to power, a man demonstrated his unfitness to exercise it. To seek and use power instrumentally, to put it in the service of worthy ends, was possible, but the danger of attachment to power had to be constantly guarded against. The uses of power were, in any case, limited; the cure for the ills that afflicted state or society lay in changing men's inner environment, their hearts and minds, not their laws and institutions. Virtuous men made for a virtuous society, just as virtuous rulers were the ultimate guarantee of good government.

None of these three modern political specialists can admit that the possession and use of power is an end in itself; their legitimacies depend upon its use in achieving objectives that transcend power. Yet revolutionaries and politicians recognize power as an integral and necessary aspect of their role, whereas Gandhians do not. Gandhi managed the incompatibility between the corruption inherent in seeking power and his insistence that organizational power was a prerequisite for political effectiveness by a contingent and temporary relationship to political and other organizations. His example in building organizations, such as the Natal Congress or the Gujarat Sabha, ashrams, service societies, and the Congress itself, and then leaving them to the direction of others, or disbanding them when he thought their goals had been realized (as he attempted to do with the Congress in 1948 after independence had been achieved), set the standard for the relationship of Gandhian professionals to organizational and political power.

When Gandhi in 1920 was able to bring his organizational ideas to bear on the Indian National Congress, he proceeded to make its structure and procedure more rational, professional, and democratic.[53] The nationalist leaders of each province had been drawn from narrow strata of the English-educated whose connections with popular, "vernacular" structures, opinion, and organized interests were tenuous and haphazard. No one was disturbed by the overrepresentation that followed when the host provinces of Congress annual sessions sent more delegates than those more distant. The Congress, Gandhi objected, placed "no limit to the number of delegates that each province could return."[54] Election to the Subjects Committee, then the Congress' highest executive organ, was not based on any explicit principles of representation or procedure; "there was," Gandhi observed, "hardly any difference between visitors and delegates."[55] Most business was settled beforehand by informal gatherings of Congress notables.[56] Gandhi relates the fate in 1901 of his resolution before the Subjects Committee:

"So have we done?" said Sir Pherozshah Mehta.

"No, no, there is still the resolution on South Africa . . . ," cried out Gokhale.

"Have you seen the resolution?" asked Sir Pherozshah.

"Of course."

"Do you like it?"

"It is quite good."

"Well, then, let us have it, Gandhi."

I read it trembling.

Gokhale supported it.

"Unanimously passed," cried out everyone.[57]

[53] At the Congress session in December, 1919, Gandhi was asked to revise the constitution of the Congress (*The Collected Works of Mahatma Gandhi*, XVII, 487, n. 2).

[54] *Gandhi's Autobiography*, p. 598.

[55] *Ibid.*, p. 282.

[56] *Ibid.*, p. 596.

[57] *Ibid.*, p. 281.

Even the battles of 1905–6 between moderates and extremists, battles prophetic of those to come over the conflicting claims of alternate strategies, leaders, ideologies, and regions for dominance within the organization, did not elicit efforts to rationalize representation, procedure, and membership.

Gandhi's draft of a new constitution provided for manageable size, defined procedures, and "scientific" representation. "Without that," he wrote, "the Congress will remain an unwieldy body and we would not be able to carry the weight we otherwise could. . . . I have attempted to give the Congress a representative character such as would make its demands irresistible."[58] Although he was obliged to accept six thousand rather than one thousand as the limit on the number of delegates to attend annual sessions, he did succeed in introducing regular procedures for the selection of delegates and the president by creating an orderly, graduated structure of party organizations with fixed jurisdictions, rights, and responsibilities.[59] He also succeeded in establishing rules for the selection of the Subjects Committee and for voting at annual sessions and in converting the informal committee of notables into a new executive organ, the Working Committee.[60]

The structural core of Gandhi's democratization of the Congress lay in the proliferation of units capable of attracting and channelling a mass membership base. The Subjects Committee, Annual Session, Provincial Congress Committees (PCC's), and District Congress Committees (DCC's) were already in existence, but they were geared to a limited membership.[61] Gandhi expected that "the delegates will

[58] Letter from Gandhi to N. C. Kelkar, July 2, 1920, in *The Collected Works of Mahatma Gandhi*, XVIII, 3.

[59] *Gandhi's Autobiography*, p. ₀13.

[60] The new All-India Congress Committee (AICC) became the Subjects Committee; its procedures were fixed; delegates alone were permitted to vote; and their qualifications had to be ascertained (see articles XXV, XXVI, XII, and XI, respectively, of the Congress Constitution adopted at Nagpur [*The Collected Works of Mahatma Gandhi,* XIX, 190–98]). Article XXIV of the Nagpur Constitution provides for the Working Committee (*ibid.*, p. 197).

[61] Constitution of 1908: Arts. 4, 6–8 (PCC's), 9–12 (DCC's), 24–25 (Subjects Committee), in M. V. Ramana Rao, *Development of the Congress Constitution* (New Delhi, 1958), pp. 13–14.

be elected only through the choice of millions. . . . Every person wishing to join a unit of the Congress is given the right to do so by paying the fee of four annas [about .08 cents in 1920] and signing the Congress creed."[62] The pre-1920 PCC's could not accommodate a mass membership base because their boundaries, which coincided with the administrative boundaries of British India, cut across those of language, with the result that English literacy was virtually a prerequisite for participation. "In so far as Congress is concerned," Gandhi held, "we should re-divide India into provinces on a linguistic basis."[63] His constitution did so, creating twenty-one Provincial Congress Committees each corresponding to a linguistic region. The new PCC's succeeded, although not as much as Gandhi expected they would, in transforming Congress from an elite to a popular organization.[64] Part of the difficulty, then as now, lay in creating structures below the District Congress Committees that could be assigned powers and responsibilities capable of attracting sufficient devotion to insure continuity and effectiveness.[65]

Gandhi also moved to remedy the lack of professional staff and continuous attention to business. "The Congress," he observed, ". . . had practically no machinery functioning during the interval between session and session";[66] "only one of the three general secretaries was a functioning secretary, and even he was not a whole-timer."[67] Gandhi urged that "the secretaries of the Provincial Congress Committees and the District Congress Committees should, so far as possible, be whole-time workers, and may, if necessary, be paid out of the Provincial or District funds."[68] He also provided for the

[62] "Nagpur Congress," *Navajivan,* January, 1, 1921, in *The Collected Works of Mahatma Gandhi,* XIX, 207.

[63] Letter from Gandhi to Chairman, AICC, September 25, 1920, in *ibid.,* XVIII, 289.

[64] "Nagpur Constitution," Article V, in *ibid.,* XIX, 191.

[65] For the party arrangements at the DCC and *taluka* or *tehsil* level (smaller administrative units within a province), see "Draft Model Rules for Provincial Congress Committees," in *ibid.,* XIX, 217–19. The elections to the PCC's and the AICC were to be indirect, DCC's electing PCC's and these electing the AICC (see Nagpur Constitution, Article XIX, in *ibid.,* XIX, 195).

[66] *Gandhi's Autobiography,* p. 597.   [67] *Ibid.*

[68] "Draft Model Rules for Provincial Congress Committees," pp. 218–19.

national and state organs meeting throughout the year; the Working Committee and the All-India Congress Committee (the AICC, which assumed most of the responsibilities of the Subjects Committee) were to meet periodically and the PCC's at least once a month.[69]

Gandhi's reform of Congress in 1920 may not have made it into as popular and representative a political structure as was his intention,[70] but there is no question that he did succeed in changing it from an elite to a mass organization. In doing so he not only changed fundamentally the character of the nationalist struggle for independence but also modernized Indian politics by moving it in a professional and democratic direction and by providing the organizational base, procedures, and habits for national politics.

The Private Origins of Public Obligation

The supersession of private and familial obligations by a public ethic in the conduct of government remains an unfinished item on the agenda of political modernization in India. In the name of such obligations friends and relatives often request public men to use discretion or to bend rules in allocating public resources and places. The dilemma is not peculiar to India; in Britain, too, at an earlier stage of its political development, when bureaucratic norms were struggling for recognition, the principle of "connection" did battle with that of a public ethic. In an era of monarchical and aristocratic politics, a public man's network of relatives, "friends," and dependents expected him to secure places and promotions, favorable rulings, and

[69] *Ibid.*, p. 219.

[70] Gopal Krishna points out that the Congress membership in the high recruitment year of 1921 was only 1,945,865 ("The Development of the Indian National Congress as a Mass Organization, 1918–1923," *Journal of Asian Studies,* XXV [May, 1966], 419–20).

contracts for them. In return he expected them to act in his interest.[1] The standards of British public life that haunt many Indian intellectuals and some of her public men today are the product of a later era, ironically enough, the era during which Britain devised more effective and impersonal means for ruling India.[2] It was not, for example, until 1853, when the Indian Civil Service was established, that appointments to places in India formally ceased to be part of the East India Company's patronage, and even under these changed circumstances, it was some time before they ceased to be governed as much by the requirements of (English) private and familial obligations as by those of a public ethic. And while Americans tend to associate patronage and the more general disposition of the "spoils" of pub-

[1] See nn. 22 and 23 above, Pt. I, sec. 1 ("Marx, Modernity, and Mobilization"), for analyses that examine the principles and practice associated with connections.

[2] The conflict between crown and parliament for control of East India Company patronage and spoils was an important component in the growth of responsible government in Britain; see C. H. Philips, *The East India Company, 1784 to 1834* (Manchester, 1940), the standard work on the company's administration and political management. The Northcote-Trevelyan reforms of 1856, which laid the basis for a modern civil service in Britain, arose out of the establishment of the Indian Civil Service three years earlier in clauses 36 and 37 of the India Act of 1853. Sir Charles Trevelyan and Lord Macaulay, both of whom served in India, were the leading spirits in the creation of the ICS, and Trevelyan along with other public figures who had returned from India played important parts in British civil service reform.

The patronage of the East India Company was in the hands of the members of the company's Court of Directors. The twenty-four members of the court shared in the appointments; in making them, they were required to state in an official document the nature of their relationship with the person being appointed and to swear that they had received no money for making the appointment. Between 1809 and 1850, 54.69 per cent gave "friendship" and 23 per cent gave "kinship connections" (B. S. Cohn, "Recruitment and Training of British Civil Servants in India, 1600 to 1800," in *Asian Bureaucratic Systems Emergent from the British Imperial Tradition* ed. Ralph Braibanti [Durham, N.C., 1966], pp. 103–4). The directors, Cohn concludes, "formed a tight society, bound by culture, economic interest, and social relations. . . . It is likely that from 1840 to 1860 fifty or sixty interconnected extended families contributed the vast majority of the civil servants who governed India" (pp. 109, 111), a situation not unlike that prevailing in India where rajas drew their bureaucrats from particular families within one or more caste communities (see Rudolph and Rudolph, "From Princes to Politicians in Rajasthan: The Political in Social Change" [Cambridge, Mass. (forthcoming)], Chap. 1, "The Rajput Polity").

241

lic office with the establishment of Jacksonian democracy, the practice of aristocratic Britain and of princely India makes clear that honoring private and familial obligations in the allocation of resources and places is by no means confined to democratic regimes.[3]

Whether or not a public or private ethic dominates the conduct of public business reaches beyond the nature of regimes to normative and structural factors that can be shaped by the influence of a great leader. In India, traditional primary-group obligations have been peculiarly compelling. Countervailing obligations to civic virtue or public law, so helpful in the European context in establishing the ascendancy of a public ethic, have found relatively little support in traditional norms and institutions. To establish the idea of public obligations in this setting was a task of considerable proportions. While the norm that Gandhi established has often won rhetorical rather than behavioral adherence, it remains the most significant indigenous statement of civility, paralleling and reinforcing the imported British statement.

The roots of Gandhi's attachment to a public ethic lie in the "first shock" of his adult professional life when he was humiliated by the outcome of an attempt to oblige his brother. The incident brought into conflict two versions of obligation, the one associated with the joint family, the other with norms of bureaucratic impersonality. The incident followed on the heels of Gandhi's failure, upon his return from England in 1891, at the age of twenty-four, to establish himself as a Bombay barrister. He had retreated to Rajkot and the security, dependence, and self-effacement of his eldest brother Lakshmidas' joint family—a position that must not have pleased an independent young man who had been given special advantages as his father's chosen son (to study in England) so that he could lead his family in new directions. The incident's shattering effect on his pride freed him from a course that might have confined him to a far more conventional life; it determined him to leave India for South Africa and strengthened his commitment to public as against familial obligation.

Lakshmidas, head of the Gandhi family after Kaba Gandhi's death in 1886, was suspected by the political agent, E. C. K. Ollivant, of complicity in the unauthorized removal of jewels from the Rajkot

[3] *Ibid.*

state treasury. As secretary and adviser to the young prince, Rana Bhavsing, before he inherited the throne, he was thought to have suggested or abetted the removal. At the least, he was charged with having failed to report it, becoming an acccessory after the fact.[4] The older brother asked the younger to intervene with the political agent on the strength of a passing acquaintance in England.

The request posed a problem of conduct to which Gandhi was already exceptionally sensitive. His return to Rajkot had been marked not only by a sense of failure but also by an awareness that, by meeting his brother's terms, he had sacrificed his integrity and independence. His brother's firm, consisting of two petty pleaders, Lakshmidas and his partner, gave him work drafting applications and memorials. "For this work I had to thank influence rather than my own ability, for my brother's partner had a settled practice."[5] To get this work, Gandhi confesses, "I had to compromise the principle of giving no commission, which in Bombay I had so scrupulously observed." " 'You see,' " Lakshmidas told Mohandas, " '. . . if you refuse to pay a commission to my partner you are sure to embarrass me . . .' "; since he and Mohandas shared a common household, Lakshmidas continued, they would in any case share their earnings. ". . . To put it bluntly," Gandhi writes in his autobiography, "I deceived myself . . ." in agreeing to abandon the principle of not paying commissions.[6]

Lakshmidas' request exacerbated these doubts:

> My brother thought I should avail myself of the friendship and, putting in a good word on his behalf, try to disabuse the Political Agent of his prejudice. I did not at all like this idea. I should not, I thought, try to take advantage of a trifling acquaintance in England. If my brother was really at fault, what use was my recommendation? If he was innocent, he should submit a petition in the proper course. . . . My brother did not relish this advice. "You do not know Kathiawad," he said,

[4] Pyarelal, *Mahatma Gandhi: The Early Phase* (Ahmedabad, 1965), I, 285–86.

[5] *Gandhi's Autobiography, or, The Story of My Experiments with Truth,* trans. from the Gujarati by Mahadev Desai (Washington, D.C., 1948), p. 123.

[6] *Ibid.,* pp. 123, 124.

"and you have yet to know the world. Only influence counts here. It is not proper for you, a brother, to shirk your duty, when you can clearly put in a good word about me to an officer you know."[7]

Mohandas felt he could not refuse his brother. At the same time he knew that he "had no right to approach the political agent and was fully conscious that he was compromising his self-respect." Yet he went, impelled by a sense of family obligation. Once he had stated his mission, Ollivant was immediately on his guard. " 'Surely you have not come here to abuse . . . our acquaintance, have you,' " was the message Mohandas read in Ollivant's manner. Gandhi continued. The political agent said he wished to hear no more; if his brother had anything to say, he should apply through proper channels. Gandhi persisted. "The *sahib* got up and said: 'You must go now.' " Again Mohandas took up his brother's brief. Ollivant, furious, ". . . called his peon and ordered him to show me the door. I was still hesitating when the peon came in, placed his hands on my shoulders and put me out of the room."[8] Humiliated, Gandhi wrote demanding that Ollivant make amends only to be told that "you are at liberty to proceed as you wish."[9] Desperate, Mohandas took advantage of the great Pherozeshah Mehta's presence in Rajkot, sending him a report of the events and seeking his advice. Mehta replied that if Gandhi expected to earn something and have an easy time in Rajkot, he should "tear up the note and pocket the insult."[10]

Gandhi found the advice "bitter as poison . . . but I had to swallow it." He vowed that he would never again place himself in such a false position and "since then I have never been guilty of a breach of that determination." This shock changed the course of his life by strengthening his concern for public as against familial obligation and driving him toward his South African decision.[11]

Gandhi approached the task of establishing a public ethic not only by ceaseless preaching and advice in particular cases but also by his own example and that of his immediate followers. His actions and deeds became anecdotal material for oral and written communication

---

[7] *Ibid.*, p. 124.   [9] *Ibid.*

[8] *Ibid.*, p. 125.   [10] *Ibid.*, p. 126.   [11] *Ibid.*

and for parables that could be recounted to those who would listen as well as those who could read. As usual his wife and sons had to bear the brunt of the Mahatma's construction of models for virtuous action.

The particulars of some of the events involved will suggest their basic themes. When Gandhi left South Africa in 1901, the Indian community of Natal honored him in the customary manner by offering him many gifts, including a gold necklace for Kasturbai worth fifty guineas. After the sleepless night that often accompanied Gandhi's struggles with an uneasy conscience, he determined to convert all the gifts into a public trust. They were, he concluded, a recognition of his public service. Kasturbai resisted this conclusion: "I can understand your not permitting me to wear them. But what about my daughters-in-law? They will be sure to need them." When Gandhi proposed that she ask him for jewels when they were needed, she retorted, "Ask you? I know you by this time. You deprived me of my ornaments, you would not leave me in peace with them. Fancy you offering to get ornaments for the daughters-in-law. You, who would make *sadhus* of my boys. . . ." In the end, Gandhi reports, "I somehow succeeded in extorting a consent from her."[12]

When Gandhi first returned to India and established himself at Sabarmati Ashram, he placed Manilal, his second son, in charge of ashram funds that were the result of charitable gifts. When Manilal heard that Harilal, the unhappy first son, was without money in Calcutta, he borrowed money from the ashram to forward to his brother. Gandhi's discovery of the irregularity occasioned his banishing Manilal from the ashram.[13]

Once, also at Sabarmati Ashram, where a strong rule of simplicity prevailed, a thief carried off various articles, including two boxes of clothes belonging to Kasturbai. "What I fail to understand," Gandhi observed at an ashram meeting called to consider the theft, "is how Ba [Kasturbai] could at all have two boxes of clothes? For, she does not wear a different sari every day." Kasturbai: "Rami and Manu [granddaughters] have lost their mother, as you know. Sometimes they come to stay with me. I kept away all the saris and pieces of

[12] *Ibid.*, pp. 270–72.

[13] Louis Fischer, *The Life of Mahatma Gandhi* (New York, 1962), p. 213.

khadi, given to me as presents from time to time, so that I can give them these things as gifts." Gandhi: "But we can not do that at all. Even the articles, given as gifts, if they are not of immediate use to the person to whom they are given, have to be deposited in the office."[14]

Because the ashram was supported by publicly subscribed funds, Gandhi made it a rule that all visitors, regardless of their connections to persons in the ashram, should pay for the expenses of their stay. This meant that Kasturbai, whose strong sense of family connection and obligation attracted a good many visits, was required over her vehement protests and to her great embarrassment, to ask the manager to render bills to her relations.[15]

Incidents such as these became part of Gandhi lore, spreading from the press, the vernacular pages of *Navajivan* and the vernacular and English ones of Gandhi's autobiography, rippling outward from written sources to tales told in towns and villages by the widening circle of those for whom Gandhi's name and deeds were becoming legend. They illustrated that obligations to family and friends collided with the less familial, more public standard that Gandhi was attempting to erect in their place. Manilal did not embezzle funds for himself but to meet a brotherly obligation. Kasturbai did not want the necklace or the collection of clothes for herself but to maintain the material and symbolic obligations of the family as a community. Her entirely unapologetic protests suggest that she knew her resistance was rooted in the morality of traditional obligations whereas his demands grew out of some alien vision.

The Gandhian norm for the conduct of public business translated this alien vision into a traditional idiom, dramatizing in the context of relations among family and friends what British public law, administration, and civic duty meant and required. By bringing the meaning of public obligation to those outside the small coterie of the English-educated, Gandhi helped place the idea and practice of civility on a more popular footing.[16]

[14] Mukulbhai Kalarthi (comp.), *Ba and Bapu*, pp. 27–28.

[15] *Ibid.*, p. 38.

[16] Edward Shils, "Ideology and Civility: On the Politics of Intellectuals," *Sewanee Review*, LXVI (Summer, 1958), 450–80.

The New Meaning of Old Paths

The ideas and techniques that Gandhi contributed to Indian nationalism were, in some ways, restatements of the truths he learned in his Gujarati childhood. That they were more than that, that they attained national, international, even historical, significance, is related to the nature of his return to them. He did not return unselfconsciously to wallow in the nostalgia of the familiar and the comfortable, the truths of sentiment unleavened by those of the conscience and the mind. Gandhi experienced and knew other alternatives. Many of his countrymen had also been touched in greater or lesser degree by their exposure to alien ideas and ways. He and they found inadequate the life path laid down by birth and family. Gandhi's return to that path, the path of home truths, grew out of his discomfort with the alternatives he tried, with his sense that he could not be himself by following them. This experience, too, coincided with that of many of his countrymen. But Gandhi found that the thoughts and emotions of his early days no longer fitted his sense of himself. Through an alien cultural experience, he won the freedom to choose, rather than be possessed by, the familiar, to reformulate and transform home truths. In settling with his own past, he gave familiar Indian ideas and practices new dignity and moral worth. He spoke to and increasingly persuaded not only those with backgrounds like his but also others that the self-definition and forms of protest and action that he new modeled were more worthy and better suited to them and their circumstances than the path of aggressive self-assertion.

The Gandhi who ate goat meat with Sheikh Mehtab because he envied his spirit and muscle went through a version of an experience common to several generations of Indians. They considered emulating the "mighty Englishman who ruled the Indian small" so that they might regain their dignity and independence. Gandhi, like others of his era, tried to strengthen himself by repairing to another cultural style. Instead of feeling more himself, he felt less so. He learned that for him integrity was tied to the culture of home and homeland, and the attempt failed.

Gandhi's return to vegetarianism, like his slow return from other attempts to acquire English manners and qualities, approximated the experiences of those unwilling or unable to manage the alternative model. When he turned to satyagraha and *ahimsa,* he revived the traditional view of courage, a view that carried with it commitments to non-violence, self-suffering, and self-restraint, qualities Englishmen had perceived differently and identified with cowardice. The path to courage that Gandhi showed his countrymen had fallen into disrepute among those affected by British power and ideas. He now gave it new life and meaning by making clear the exacting discipline it required in action and the kind of sacrifice and self-control it involved. Convincingly demonstrating its moral worthiness and practical worth, he was able to make the path to courage the path to popular nationalism. In the process of mastering his own fear and weakness, he reassured those generations near him that they need not fear or emulate those who had conquered them, that Macaulay and Strachey were wrong in believing them to be cowards. Nehru writes of Gandhi and India: "He had instilled courage and manhood in her people; . . . courage is the one sure foundation of character, he had said; without courage there is no morality, no religion, no love."[1]

Gandhi's political style, too, was a return to traditional modes. His asceticism had autobiographical origins in profound doubt about the permissibility of his masculine assertiveness. Its cultural origins lay in the enjoinment of lustfulness, of the rule of desire, in virtuous men, not least among whom were kings. Asceticism was also thought to bring with it a higher potency, an implication arising out of a theory of sexual hydrostatics reminiscent of Freudian sublimation theory. He who controls himself gains the strength to shape the environment. When Gandhi pursued the political goal of *swaraj* ("self-rule"), he meant to teach himself and Indians that only those who could rule themselves—in the sense of self-restraint—could rule

[1] Jawaharlal Nehru, *Freedom from Fear: Reflections on the Personality and Teachings of Gandhi* (Delhi, 1960), p. 12.

themselves—in the sense of controlling their political universe. His political effectiveness arose in part from the belief of those who observed his career that his self-control did indeed endow him with extraordinary powers. And it rested on the more practical fact that asceticism did bring him peace, not so much from leaping lusts, but from the recollection of the conflict between his own assertiveness and his duty to a father. The serenity he achieved by his asceticism was ultimately among his strongest assets as a leader of a mass movement that sometimes aroused strong feelings and evoked violent hatreds. It lay at the root of his capacity to act sensibly in a crisis, to keep himself from being thrown off stride by other people's hysteria. His serenity conveyed to others, who often were hysterical, the reminder that reasonable conduct could be recaptured in the midst of boundless and irrational chaos. Especially when tested in the communal blood baths of the forties, it lay at the basis of his capacity to make men act as much as possible like men rather than driven creatures.

PART THREE

Legal Cultures and Social Change:
Panchayats, Pandits, and Professionals

You have given India," Secretary of State Sir Samuel Hoare once told his officers, "justice such as the East has never known before."[1] For most Englishmen, having established the "rule of law" on the Indian subcontinent was probably the proudest achievement of the British raj. They believed that they had substituted legal security for disorder, predictability for uncertainty, and impartiality for whim and nepotism. "Under the old despotic systems," James Fitzjames Stephen told his readers, "the place of law was taken by a number of vague and fluctuating customs, liable to be infringed at every moment by the arbitrary fancies of the ruler."[2] Indian nationalists and Britons with a certain kind of cultural sensibility held the contrary view, that law had become less meaningful and useful because of its alien characteristics, inaccessibility, adversary proceedings, and individualistic bias. These opposing judgments highlighted normative and practical differences concerning the procedure, law, and structure to be used in the administration of justice, differences that were rooted in Britain's more modern and India's more traditional society.

[1] Cited in Penderel Moon, *Strangers in India* (London, 1944), p. 48. For help in pursuing problems of Indian law, see C. H. Alexandrowicz, *A Bibliography of Indian Law* (Madras, 1958), an occasionally misleading introduction, and Marc Galanter's review of it in *American Journal of Comparative Law*, IX (Spring, 1960), 303–6, which provides important correctives and additions. See also Charles Szladits, *A Bibliography of Foreign and Comparative Law: Books and Articles in English* (New York, 1955); and W. H. Maxwell and C. R. Brown, *A Complete List of British and Colonial Law Reports and Legal Periodicals* (3d ed.; Toronto, 1937). A suggestive recent effort in the comparative law of new nations is J. N. D. Anderson (ed.), *Changing Law in Developing Countries* (New York, 1963). A more historical approach may be found in Bernard S. Cohn, *The Development and Impact of British Administration in India: A Bibliographic Essay* (New Delhi, 1961).

[2] Leslie Stephen's summing up of his brother's views in *Life of Sir James Fitzjames Stephen* (New York, 1895), p. 285.

Modernity and tradition were more opposed in the context of the law than they were in the contexts of social structure and political leadership. But here, too, there were affinities. The British raj, sometimes by design but more often by inadvertence, advanced the written, more uniform, and professionally interpreted law of the twice-born castes (*dharmasastra*) at the expense of the parochial, diverse, and orally transmitted customary law of villagers even as Anglicization began to supersede Indian legal conceptions and social arrangements. This dual process parallels in the law what has been described in the area of social mobility as Sanskritization and Westernization —that is, lower caste assimilation to high caste norms concurrent with a more diffuse, yet socially separate, establishment of Western values. In the analysis that follows, emphasis is given to the specific cultural and social referents of these processes by examining the Brahmanization and Anglicization of a substantial section of the Indian legal order. These processes tended to establish high-culture and British law at the expense of parochial, customary law and to isolate custom from the official administration of justice. Yet India's dual legal system continues to exhibit three legal cultures: within the parochial system, where most legal behavior is still to be found, non-official tribunals continue to use traditional procedure and customary law to settle disputes, maintain order and regulate change; within the national legal system, the official administration of justice relies primarily but not exclusively on British legal ideas, procedure, and law; and influencing both are the social norms of Brahman high-culture law.

Traditional and Modern Justice

The elements of procedure—the categorization of cases by kind and degree, the concern for jurisdiction and standing, the rules of evidence, and the elaboration of a court system and a legal profession— express the universalism and impersonality of modern Western legal systems generally. As British rule became more firmly established about the end of the eighteenth century, civil and criminal jurisdictions came increasingly under the purview of a graduated court system, conceived on English lines and reaching from the district to the provincial high court. In such courts, to a greater extent in some provinces than others and with variations over time, the elements of Western legal structure and procedure were increasingly asserted.

Within the Western system it is held that procedural correctness is enhanced when tribunals are not part of the context—the village, the caste—in which disputes or crimes arise; fair play then depends upon it rather than upon the knowledge that is available to tribunals embedded in the context of judgment. But the meaningfulness and acceptability of a distant and abstract system are affected, at least in part, by the way in which its tribunals have been separated from their particular contexts. In so far as the Roman and Anglo-Saxon legal systems and their procedures are meaningful and accepted by the people to whom they apply in the West, they are so because they are rooted in historical experience both in their evolution and in their present application. In India, because the procedure of Anglo-Saxon law was evolved in a foreign context and imposed from above and outside in a relatively short time, the moral and social effects were comparable to those of an ideological and revolutionary regime bent on transforming society by imposing its aprioristic conceptions. The effect was, in fact, less than revolutionary since the British had neither the means nor the desire to insist on their "ideology."

Although the British clearly intended to bring justice, their legal system often produced results that were experienced and understood as injustice, not because the British desired or intended such a result, but because most Indians did not appreciate the system's morality and logic.[3] "I do not hold," an Indian anthropologist writes of "Rampura," "that the justice administered by the elders of the dominant caste is always or even usually more just than the justice administered by the judges in urban law courts, but only that it is much better understood by the litigants."[4] This situation resulted from divergent assumptions concerning legal procedure.

[3] See Percival Spear, *Twilight of the Moghuls* (Cambridge, 1951), pp. 94–95; and Penderel Moon, *Strangers in India* (London, 1945), Chap. 3.

[4] Srinivas, "The Social System of a Mysore Village," in McKim Marriott

For Englishmen, the law, if it is to be universal, impersonal, and impartial, ought to be blind, an idea graphically illustrated by the representation of justice as a classically clad, blindfolded woman holding balanced scales. Like Raphael's "Justice" at the Vatican, she adorns the corridors or façades of public buildings in Europe and America. Unable to see differences in men's condition, justice holds all men equal before the law. For Hindu law, the reverse was true; the differences among men in society were central to their legal identity, rights, and obligations. Justice is blind, too, in her incarnation as judge or jury. She may have no relations with the litigants, no contaminating ties of blood, opinion, or interest to color her evaluation of the facts. Blood ties or opinions formed by reading a newspaper account of the case are cause for rejecting jurymen, who are meant to be *tabulae rasae* upon which the adversary proceeding may inscribe its impressions. Like the judge, they are expected to leave behind all previous human ties. A village or caste tribunal, on the other hand, has the most intimate ties of familiarity and kinship with litigants and draws its authority from them. Impartiality is highly regarded in the village, too; the honor and authority of local notables are closely connected with their reputation for detached evenhandedness.[5] But in the intimate little world of the Indian village where judges live among the judged, neither thinks of impartiality in terms of the absence of connections between judges and the judged. "Since the *khandan* (lineage) is localized in part of the hamlet and since there is little that does not take place within earshot of the other households," Bernard Cohn writes in describing a modern Indian village, "the *khandan* leader (the first judge) is aware of the dispute from its inception."[6] When all the lineage heads, joined by the heads of households and interested persons in a kind of *amicus curiae*

(ed.), *Village India* (Chicago, 1955), p. 18. See also his "The Study of Disputes in an Indian Village," in *Caste in Modern India, and Other Essays* (Bombay, 1962).

[5] See the account of leadership in John T. Hitchcock, "Leadership in a North Indian Village: Two Case Studies," in Richard Park and Irene Tinker (ed.), *Leadership and Political Institutions in India* (Princeton, N.J., 1959).

[6] Cohn, "Some Notes on Law and Change in North India," *Economic Development and Cultural Change,* October, 1959, p. 82.

capacity, meet as a tribunal, "everyone who attends will have considerable knowledge of the dispute in question and know and be affected by the chain of relations and disputes which lie behind it."[7]

If justice is not to see anything that will lead her to be less than universal, impersonal, and impartial in her judgment, she must be protected by a strict concern for relevance. Yet there is something faintly comic in the vision of James Fitzjames Stephen, the most coldly logical and least culturally sensitive law member ever to sit in council, presenting the Anglo-Indian world in his *Introduction to the Indian Evidence Act, 1872,* with an elaborate and closely reasoned but irrelevant theory of relevance. Max Gluckman's observation concerning the Barotse of Northern Rhodesia is equally applicable to traditional Indian procedure: "There is no refinement of pleadings," he writes, "in Lozi procedure to whittle a suit down to certain narrow legal claims so as to present the judges with a mere skeleton of the facts relevant to those claims."[8] No one objects when it is found that a tribunal, met to settle one dispute, finds itself adjudicating another that lies behind it.[9] It is assumed that the present difficulty has a relevant history. Village tribunals cannot, of course, escape making judgments on facts even if they can be less concerned about relevance. They must distinguish between direct and hearsay evidence and catch out "tutored" testimony.[10] Yet ascertaining facts, with which procedural safeguards are particularly concerned, is less of a problem for village tribunals than for "Western" courts since most of those involved in a case have direct knowledge of them.

[7] *Ibid.,* p. 83.

[8] Gluckman, *Judicial Process among the Barotse of Northern Rhodesia* (Manchester, 1955), p. 51. As we shall be citing Gluckman's work at several points to bear out the contention that the assumptions of traditional and modern English law differ, it is only fair to point out that Gluckman's purpose is to stress the similarities between African and Western law. His focus, however, is mainly on judicial reasoning, with which we are less concerned here. See especially Chap. 5, p. 224.

[9] Cohn, "Some Notes on Law and Change in North India," p. 86. Gluckman, in "The Case of the Biased Father," in *Judicial Process . . . ,* p. 37, indicates in detail how the tribunal investigates in full all past relations between the feuding parties.

[10] Srinivas, *Caste in Modern India . . . ,* p. 115.

The adversary mode of Western procedure not only isolates the "case" and its litigants from their social context but also is expected to result in a declaration that one side has won and the other lost. Village tribunals, on the other hand, try to compromise differences so that the parties to a case can go home with the appearance at least of harmony and with their dignity intact. British courts in India saw a dispute in terms of plaintiff and defendant, one of whom was right, whereas the traditional tribunals might find both parties at fault. Despite out-of-court settlements and arbitration, which express the importance of compromise and the concern for consensus in Western law, the difference between the two approaches remains significant. The village tribunal, because its members reside among the disputing parties and find their own lives touched by their discontents, is less anxious to find "truth" and give "justice" than to abate conflict and promote harmony. Although the merits of a case may suggest, for example, that the decision should favor a placid defendant who may be satisfied with the appearance of justice and go against an important and aggressive plaintiff capable of stirring up trouble, the tribunal's settlement may make some attempt to satisfy the plaintiff.[11] "In this country," wrote Jonathan Duncan, British Resident at Benares in the late eighteenth century, "the inhabitants have been so long habituated to settle all causes by arbitration, and to terminate all disputes by what they call mutual satisfaction of both parties, that I am persuaded our more decisive and what they would term abrupt mode of administering justice and executing decisions so passed merely upon the proofs exhibited within a certain and fixed time, perhaps by only one of the parties, would not suit the way of thinking of a majority of inhabitants of Benares."[12]

This preference for consensus, probably characteristic of small, morally homogeneous communities,[13] extends in India well beyond

[11] "Eventually a compromise will be suggested, and even though it may be more favorable to one party, as long as it can be defended as a compromise in the rhetorical sense, both parties seem to be satisfied" (Cohn, "Some Notes on Law and Change in North India," p. 86).

[12] Cited in Cohn, "From Indian Status to British Contract," *Journal of Economic History,* December, 1961, pp. 617–18.

[13] Writing on the first civil officer at Tenasserim in 1825, J. S. Furnival noted: "Mr. Maingy was quite unable to fathom the Burmese judicial system. In his

the village to the rhetoric of modern politics.[14] The concern for consensus among contemporary political leaders such as Gandhi may express a residue of village attitudes fated to disappear, or it may express a deeper philosophical commitment touching microcosm and macrocosm alike that will retain for some time its hold on Indian consciousness. Although significant differences between Britain and India existed concerning the importance of procedure and the value of consensus, both traditions recognized the value of the other's system. The high-culture writings of classic Indian lawgivers such as Yajnavalkya contain sophisticated discussions of procedure,[15] and in British courts skilful counsel are able to introduce "irrelevant" material on background, character, and circumstances. Indeed, today, modern legal innovations, going beyond the consensus-oriented procedures of out-of-court settlement and arbitration, have removed justice's blindfold for certain social groups and types of defendants. But even if all of these qualifications are acknowledged, implicit and explicit differences between British and Indian legal procedure remain of great importance for understanding the confrontation of modernity and tradition in India.

The vexations that accompanied the establishment under British rule of a national legal system—expense and delay in the administration of justice, the so-called rise in litigation, and the prevalence of false witness—added to Indian, and sometimes to British, doubts about the validity and usefulness of the raj's justice.[16] "Such agency

---

view legal proceedings were meant to ascertain disputed facts and arrive at a logical decision on them according to fixed legal principle; he failed to understand that Burmans went to court to find a man of wisdom and authority who could help them in arriving at an amicable settlement of their disputes . . ." (*Colonial Policy and Practice* [American ed.; Cambridge, 1957], p. 31). Gluckman reports that judges regularly gave lectures to both sides.

[14] For a full discussion of the problem of political rhetoric in India, including consensus rhetoric, see W. H. Morris-Jones, "India's Political Idioms," in C. H. Philips (ed.), *Politics and Society in India* (London, 1963).

[15] For a discussion, see N. S. Gupta in his *Sources of Law and Society in Ancient India* (Calcutta, 1914).

[16] Philip Mason has written a novel that admirably illustrates the problem: *Call the Next Witness* (New York, 1946).

is too expensive," wrote Sir Thomas Munro, "and even if it was not . . . it is, in many cases, much less efficient than that of the natives. . . . I have never seen any European whom I thought competent, from his knowledge of the language and the people, to ascertain the value of evidence given before him."[17] Hiring a lawyer and getting oneself and one's witnesses to a distant law court—and fifty miles to the district court was and is distant in Indian rural life— there to pay the initial costs of registering a complaint and supporting witnesses, undoubtedly made such courts less appealing than local tribunals.[18] "Justice can be swift and cheap in the village, besides also being a justice which is understood as such by the litigants. The litigants either speak for themselves or ask a clever relative or friend to speak in their behalf. There are no hired lawyers arguing in a strange tongue, as in the awe inspiring atmosphere of the urban state courts."[19]

The alleged rise in litigiousness, generally attributed to the change of system, needs closer investigation. It is often alleged that villagers, torn out of their traditional setting and its social and moral restraints, began to harass one another in a spate of legal disputes. There is some question whether this really happened. Anthropological accounts suggest that litigiousness is not peculiarly modern; the villagers quarrel without the aid of modern courts and there is little reason to believe they were different at an earlier stage of history. The fact that the newly established courts of the nineteenth century were swiftly clogged has been taken as evidence of increased litigiousness, but it need not be. It could as easily be attributed to the movement of litigation from village tribunals to the new system. A

[17] G. R. Gleig, *The Life of Major-General Sir Thomas Munro* (London, 1830), I, 518–19.

[18] Sir Thomas Munro argued, for example, that the separation of the offices of collector and magistrate, rational in terms of a theory of separation of functions, made no sense for the villager's pocketbook, as it forced him to travel twice when once might do. "The *vakils* (agents)," Derrett observes, "who soon became available to represent clients ousted the parties who had formerly appeared in person or through relations or well-placed patrons. The latter acted gratuitously but the former required to be paid and learnt how to protract litigation" (J. D. M. Derrett, "The Administration of Hindu Law by the British," *Comparative Studies in Society and History,* IV [1961–62], 23).

[19] Srinivas, "The Social System of a Mysore Village," p. 18.

thoughtful magistrate at Midnapore, responding to extensive inquiries by Lord Wellesley concerning the nature of British justice, denied that mere quarrelsomeness lay behind the difficulty:

> The complaints of these people are seldom or never litigious. I have seen some conspiracies supported by false evidence; but suits simply litigious, brought forward merely from the quarrelsome disposition of the prosecutor, are not common. . . . Out of one hundred suits, perhaps five at the utmost, may be fairly pronounced litigious. . . .[20]

It seems likely that the "rise" in litigiousness was in part a statistical artifact reflecting the transplantation of disputes to a new location where they were easier to record.

Frederick John Shore, judge at Farrukhabad, believed that "litigiousness of the natives" was more an excuse than an explanation of the courts' inability to cope with the cases that came before them. A magistrate in the first quarter of the nineteenth century knew that "according to the size of his district, from one-half to even three-fourths of the applicants [had] no chance of obtaining redress. . . ."[21] Too few courts and too few magistrates rather than "native litigiousness," he thought, were the causes of the difficulties. Both W. W. Hunter and Sir Thomas Munro perceived a rise in litigation but thought it less a product of the new legal system than a correlate of an increasing man/land ratio and the quarrels arising from it.[22]

But there remains some truth in the belief that English courts encouraged litigiousness. Some individuals regarded the new courts as a way of circumventing the traditional administration of justice if they foresaw that a village tribunal would take an unfavorable view

[20] W. K. Firminger, *Historical Introduction to the Bengal Portion of the Fifth Report* (Calcutta, 1917), II, Append. 10, 592. Strachey, the Midnapore magistrate, provided a more thoughtful and informed reply than the other courts, a reply that contains the raw materials of legal sociology.

[21] Frederick John Shore, *Notes on Indian Affairs* (London, 1837), pp. 238–39.

[22] W. W. Hunter, in his *The Annals of Rural Bengal* (3d ed.; London, 1868), takes strong issue with the "litigiousness" judgment. "If we consider the innumerable sources of dispute which *petit culture,* with its minute subdivision of property and multiplicity of tenures, gives rise to . . . the . . . number is by no means excessive . . ." (p. 340). For Munro's ideas, see Sir Alexander J. Arbuthnot (ed.), *Major-General Sir Thomas Munro* (London, 1881), I, 80.

of their plaint. They also used them as a weapon of harassment against factional opponents. To the extent that people used the new courts to this end, they added to the impression that these courts were devoted to something other than justice. Even now, M. N. Srinivas finds that "taking disputes to the local elders is considered to be better than taking them to the urban law courts. Disapproval attaches to the man who goes to the city for justice. Such a man is thought to be flouting the authority of the elders and therefore acting against the solidarity of the village. The few men in Rampura who take disputes to the urban court are not respected."[23]

Although circumventing the traditional administration of justice may signify mere opportunism, a gamble that the modern court will give a favorable decision, it may also mean that the litigants are searching for a means to escape the disabilities and coercions of traditional village society, that they have turned to the new courts to escape the consequences of low station or membership in the wrong faction.[24] For them, "increase in litigiousness" reflects instead an effort to unravel themselves from the traditional moral and social order.[25]

False witness in the new courts was the despair of English magistrates. In the traditional setting, witnesses were not always trustworthy either, but the village tribunal usually knew enough about the local situation to evaluate what was said. "Ram Singh's" testimony was judged in the context of his known lineage connections, his long-standing dispute with his brother-in-law's family and his past reputation as an upright man. Furthermore, Ram Singh was restrained from undue extravagance in his testimony by his knowl-

[23] Srinivas, "The Social System of a Mysore Village," p. 18.

[24] Harold Levy speaks of a "second strike capacity" in the context of a discussion of how some Punjabis used the British criminal law to threaten disastrous retaliation should the power balance between feuding families be altered by murder. See Harold Levy (Rapporteur), "Report of the Conference on South Asian Law Held at the University of Chicago, May 31–June 1, 1963" (mimeographed; South Asia Area and Language Center, University of Chicago, May, 1964), p. 16.

[25] See F. G. Bailey's account of the means used by Boad outcastes to circumvent the traditional tribunals (*Caste and the Economic Frontier* [Manchester, 1957], pp. 220–24).

edge of the judges' knowledge. These restraints and checks fell away in the new courts. Puzzlement as to what the sahibs wanted made things worse. The judges of the circuit of the second session, 1802, Calcutta, saw the matter clearly: "We cannot," they wrote, "wonder that the natives are aware of our suspicious and incredulous temper; they see how difficult it is to persuade us to believe a true story, and accordingly endeavor to suit our taste with a false one." As a result "they . . . consult upon the best mode of making their story appear probable to the gentleman, whose wisdom, it cannot be expected, should be satisfied with an artless tale. . . ." Because the court "cannot study the genius of the people in its own sphere of action," it is weighed down with "a consciousness of inability to judge of what is probable or improbable."[26]

The prevalence of false witness suggests the strength of kinship relations and the weakness of the impersonal obligations of a public ethic.[27] British procedure disqualifies only the testimony of husbands and wives about each other, recognizing that this tie of sentiment makes truthtelling immoral; the Indian villager, on the other hand, sees the tie of sentiment as much more inclusive.[28] Poverty also contributed to the prevalence of false witness since for many the choice was between hunger and an often ambiguous truth. Finally, the prevalence of false witness reflects the divergence between the

[26] Firminger, *Historical Introduction to . . . the Fifth Report,* II, Append. 10, 648. Bernard S. Cohn reports that between 1795 and 1850 in the Benares region district judges overwhelmingly based their decisions on the official documents that were brought forth, testimony being regarded as invariably perjured ("From Indian Status to British Contract," p. 624).

[27] E. M. Forster, in *Passage to India* (London, 1947), makes clear that if the stakes were high enough false witness could be a two-way street. ". . . At a time like this," District Superintendent of Police McBryde tells Fielding, "there's no room for—well—personal views. The man who doesn't toe the line is lost. . . . He not only loses himself, he weakens his friends. If you leave the line, you leave a gap in the line. These jackals [the Indian friends of Aziz, the accused] . . . are looking with all their eyes for a gap" (p. 179).

[28] The "cheating" scandal at the Air Force Academy in January, 1965 illustrated very nicely the conflict between the moral imperatives of a public ethic and human sentiments by pitting the claims of the Academy's "honor" system against those of not "ratting" on one's friends and classmates. One father publicly defended his son for not "ratting" but was denounced for defending the standards of the "underworld."

inner sense of justice of traditional witnesses and the alien external standards represented by the court, a divergence that divests false witness of its moral opprobrium.

Because some Englishmen saw that the disparity between the old and new legal assumptions robbed the new legal system of authority and comprehensibility, they sought to traditionalize the modern administration of justice by devising forms of official judicial administration that hewed more closely to indigenous proceedings and parochial law. These forms functioned side by side with the unofficial tribunals of village and caste. Thomas Munro in Madras and Mountstuart Elphinstone in Bombay were conspicuous in their concern to create official tribunals that would be in touch with local practice. Munro, by statute, gave new life to village panchayats; both he and Elphinstone encouraged panchayat-like proceedings for cases intermediate between village and district.[29] Elphinstone, to avoid the aridity and impersonality of specialists in code and case law, long supported the union of administrative and judicial functions in collectors with district experience, and in Madras Munro succeeded in having magisterial functions, which had been separated from administrative, returned to collectors.[30] Both favored simple pro-

[29] The court of directors, responding to the criticisms of the Bengal system as it functioned in Madras, appointed Munro president of a special commission to inquire into and reform the judicial system in Madras. He recommended, and the court authorized, among other matters, the transfer of police and magisterial duties from the *zillah* (subdistrict) judge to the collector; the appointment of village officials to deal with petty suits; the authorization of village panchayats to hear suits; and the establishment of panchayats intermediate between village and *zillah* courts (letter from Col. Munro, First Commissioner, to D. Hill, Esq., Chief Secretary to Government, December 24, 1814, in Gleig, *The Life of . . . Munro,* I, 417–23). Elphinstone wrote in 1818: "The judicial business will be managed by Panchayats whose awards are not to be set aside without some glaring impropriety" (Mountstuart Elphinstone to Collectors, July 10, 1818, cited in Kenneth Ballhatchet, *Social Policy and Social Change in Western India, 1817–1830* [London, 1957], p. 106).

[30] Elphinstone put this policy into practice in the Deccan (Ballhatchet, *Social Policy and Social Change . . . ,* pp. 115, 201, and *passim*). For Munro's policy, see Col. Munro to Mr. Cumming, Madras, September 24, 1816, in Gleig, *The Life of . . . Munro,* I, 449.

cedure.[31] Elphinstone expected the members of local tribunals to have prior knowledge of the dispute and of the parties, be responsive to Indian notions of rank and appropriate behavior, and hear evidence that they and those who used local tribunals thought material, regardless of formal criteria of relevance.[32]

In the Punjab, too, the Lawrence brothers introduced judicial procedures that sought to approximate traditional processes by stressing informality, dispatch, and directness in the administration of justice.[33] " 'There was no law in the Punjab in those days,' " Phillip Woodruff quotes John Beames as observing of the years just after the Mutiny. " 'Our instructions were to decide all cases by the light of common-sense and our sense of what was just and right.' " When Beames began a new tour in the Bengal presidency (the province in which rule according to carefully articulated regulations began [and a continuing model of it]), he was often in trouble for his "Punjabi zeal, for his habit of going and looking at things and for 'taking the law in his own hands.' "[34] But the efforts of men like John Lawrence were in fact more substantial departures from panchayat justice than Munro's or Elphinstone's. They retained dispatch, informality, and a concern for compromise and consensus in the settlement of disputes; but the "common sense" and ideas of "justice" arising from John Lawrence's Calvinistic temperament were apt to dictate very different conclusions from those of the villagers in panchayat.

The attempts to recapture or simulate the immediacy of the local customary administration of justice ultimately failed.[35] District collectors and magistrates did not respond favorably to the use of the men or methods of local tribunals even if they had administrative recognition. The tribunals continued to lose ground to the new

[31] Ballhatchet, *Social Policy and Social Change* . . . , p. 201. Munro, for example, opposed the imposition of elaborate checks and forms on the local officials' exercise of judicial powers (Gleig, *The Life of . . . Munro*, I, 448).

[32] Ballhatchet, *Social Policy and Social Change* . . . , pp. 109, 115.

[33] Bosworth Smith, *Life of Lord Lawrence* (New York, 1885), I, 271.

[34] Philip Woodruff, *The Guardians* (London, 1954), pp. 44–45, 51.

[35] John Bradshaw, *Sir Thomas Munro* (Oxford, 1894), p. 160; Ballhatchet, *Social Policy and Social Change* . . . , p. 199; Hugh Tinker, *The Foundations of Local Self-Government in India, Pakistan and Burma* (London, 1954).

courts. The imperatives of time, specialization, and objectivity also took their toll. "Inevitably," Woodruff writes,

> the non-regulation provinces [in the 1870's] came into line with the others and a judge came to be judge and nothing else. . . . The rule of one man had been ideal when districts were first annexed, but a change had to be made. No one who went about the country as much as a district officer ought could have time for complicated civil suits. . . . As a judge in criminal cases . . . [he] could hardly help inclining a little to the side of the police who had taken such trouble to catch and prosecute the accused.[36]

Viceroy Ripon's enthusiasm for local government in the 1880's revived interest in local tribunals.[37] In Elphinstone's old province, Bombay, Sir William Wedderburn pressed for the revival of Maratha village committees to facilitate the settlement of disputes by agreement among the parties: "On the platform under the tree in the village, truth is spoken, but not often in the law courts. . . ."[38] His efforts failed in the face of objections that the memory of the old tribunals had died, that the spirit of the new law courts would infect the proposed tribunals and make them at least as bad as the courts, and that village divisions and partisanship were now so strong that such tribunals would be a positive evil.

Woodruff argues that had Sir Richard Temple, the governor of Bombay at the time, "taken the bold course and agreed with Wedderburn, many years might have been saved."[39] In 1920, village panchayats were introduced in five provinces.[40] The difficulties foreseen at the time of Wedderburn's proposal "proved to be true . . . , but with patience and perseverance," Woodruff argues, "they could be improved. . . ."[41] In the United Provinces, Punjab, and the Central Provinces, these panchayats were vested primarily with judicial func-

---

[36] Woodruff, *The Guardians,* p. 89.

[37] Tinker, *The Foundations of Local Self-Government* . . . , p. 56.

[38] Woodruff, *The Guardians,* p. 162.

[39] *Ibid.,* p. 163.

[40] Tinker, *The Foundations of Local Self-Government* . . . , p. 116.

[41] Woodruff, *The Guardians,* p. 163.

tions.[42] They, like more recent postindependence legislation creating Nyaya panchayats in Uttar Pradesh, were attempts to bring back some features of the traditional administration of justice in the village.[43] Some Englishmen before independence and some Indians after it hoped through these means to restore such advantages of the older tribunals as speed and comprehensibility while retaining such virtues of the new as equality before the law. A combination such as this, bringing together traditional and modern ideas of justice, may be most difficult to realize; however, like recent innovations in the West that stress arbitration or informal and direct procedures that look behind the defendant to his psychological and social circumstances, they may represent creative developments in the administration of justice that transcend traditional and modern categories.

Neither the efforts of those like Munro and Elphinstone who wanted to administer justice in terms of indigenous and parochial ideas and practice nor those of district officers who wanted to administer it directly and on the spot "in the light of a clear mind and a clear conscience" were able to establish an intimate connection with the "judicial" functions of viable village and caste panchayats. The neo-traditional tribunals created by the British raj and Congress governments were and are new constructs with new meanings. Lineage, locality, and caste (jati) had been critical determinants of traditional tribunals. By going behind and beyond these natural associations, the British and Indian creations jumbled together the boundaries and relationships of the traditional arrangements and the jurisdictions and legal standards invented by lawyers, administrators and legislators. The statutory panchayats of Munro and Elphinstone, those instituted under the 1920 provincial acts, and those brought into being after independence encompassed larger geographic units than traditional panchayats, units that were incon-

---

[42] Tinker, *The Foundations of Local Self-Government* . . . , p. 198.

[43] Robert S. Robins, "India: Judicial Panchayats in Uttar Pradesh," *American Journal of Comparative Law*, II (Spring, 1962), 239–46. Mr. Robins expresses concern that *panches* "judge a case on the basis of the parties' character rather than strictly on the facts and the law" (p. 245), a comment that suggests the extent to which traditional judicial presumptions have been successfully recaptured. Much in his article reveals an assumption that these tribunals should attempt to realize modern legal values rather than recapture traditional ones.

gruous with the "natural" geography of village, caste and lineage.[44] Their members were elected locally or nominated by government.[45] For Elphinstone's collectors this meant "persons of respectability, mostly Brahmans" who frequented their offices; for contemporary Uttar Pradesh, it means elected members of *goan sabhas* ("village assemblies") nominated by fellow members and selected by the district magistrate after taking into account the recommendations of Subdivisional (lower-level) officers and consulting with an advisory committee made up of elected and administrative officials from within the district.[46] Neither arrangement captures traditional means of selection nor are the jurisdictional boundaries necessarily congruent with the social relations or moral universes of the localities and groups in which traditional panchayats had functioned and often still do. At least under the British raj, these engineered institutions could not hold their own against the competition of the regular court system. In Uttar Pradesh, where they achieved their greatest measure of success, they never extended over more than a quarter of the rural population, whereas in the Punjab, Bombay, and the Central Provinces they covered in the mid-thirties only one-tenth to one-fifteenth.[47] Their ultimate success in postindependence India remains in doubt; but it is possible that old and new features can be merged in a creative and effective way if they can be made more congruent with the social changes wrought by village decompression, the expansion of symbolic, economic, and social boundaries, and the structural and functional features of paracommunities.

[44] Munro favored, among other bodies, panchayats intermediate between village and *zillah;* see the letter cited on p. 264, n. 29. The Bengal union boards covered an area of some ten square miles and were regarded as representatives of the *sarkar,* not of local interest (Tinker, *The Foundations of Local Self-Government* . . . , pp. 40, 118); the boundaries of Madras' major panchayats enclosed a small town and its surrounding villages; in Uttar Pradesh the single-village principle was quickly abandoned in favor of a five-village union (*ibid.,* p. 201). Uttar Pradesh's postindependence Nyaya panchayats cover seven to fourteen villages (Robins, "India: Judicial Panchayats . . . ," p. 240).

[45] Tinker, *The Foundations of Local Self-Government* . . . , pp. 197–98.

[46] Ballhatchet, *Social Policy and Social Change,* p. 108; Robins, "India: Judicial Panchayats . . . ," pp. 240–41.

[47] Tinker, *The Foundations of Local Self-Government* . . . , p. 199.

The Modernity of Brahmanic Law

The introduction by the British of a national legal system affected the balance between divergent indigenous legal traditions. For the most part, the raj initially disregarded, largely through ignorance, the existence of the orally transmitted customary law of villages, castes, and regions. It identified Indian law with the high-culture, literary law inscribed in the classic texts and in so doing unwittingly strengthened it at the expense of the "popular" law of the peasant society.[1] That it should have done so is hardly surprising. Brahmanic law as Britons understood it bore some resemblance to the law of modern legal professionals; it was available in written texts; although diverse, its cosmopolitanism gave it an air of generality and uniformity that parochial, customary law lacked; and it was interpreted and applied by a class of legal specialists. Its subsequent role as a vehicle of modernization is related to these attributes.

In 1772 Warren Hastings, the East India Company's first governor-general, took an important step in the direction of strengthening Brahmanic law by directing the Bengal courts to administer the laws "of the Koran with respect to Mohammedans and those of the

[1] "At this stage" (after 1772, when Hastings ordered that Hindu and Muslim law be applied in British courts), J. D. M. Derrett writes, "the first misconception obtrudes itself. The relationship between custom and *dharmasastra* was taken for granted." The judges were directed to refer only to the *dharmasastra*. ". . . Hastings and his contemporaries . . . were gravely misled. . . . Non-Brahmans admitted that Brahmans were the expounders of law, and that the Hindu religion required obedience to the *dharmasastra* which the Brahmans alone knew. . . . It was nearly a century before the mistake was generally recognized . . ." ("The Administration of Hindu Law . . . ," pp. 24–25, 28). Elsewhere he observes that Hastings "had obviously been advised that . . . the law of the Hindus must be ascertained from sastric texts . . . , and no steps were taken to collect evidence of local or caste custom" (J. D. M. Derrett, "Sanskrit Legal Treatises Compiled at the Instance of the British," *Zeitschrift für Vergleichende Rechtswissenschaft*, LXIII [1961], 79–80).

Shaster with respect to Hindus. . . ."[2] These texts, which the earliest European students of Arabic, Persian, and Sanskrit were just discovering, were for the English administrators the visible embodiment of Indian law. Hastings was not aware, for example, that most Muslims in Bengal were Hindu converts who often continued to use local Hindu law rather than Koranic and traditional law after their conversion. Nor were eighteenth-century British administrators always aware that the Hindu texts that N. B. Halhead, Sir William Jones, and later, Henry Thomas Colebrooke translated for court use were largely what a later generation would call "Brahmanical" law, that is, law that embodied the morality and interests of the Brahman and other twice-born castes who were the creators and guardians of Hindu high culture.

The idea that there was a dual system of Indian law, one cosmopolitan, encompassing the relatively distinct high-culture law of the classic texts, the other parochial, defined by the diverse custom of the peasant society, although of the utmost importance, must be qualified by an appreciation of the connection between the two. John Mayne's classic *A Treatise on Hindu Law and Usage* supposed that in origin the law of the classic texts was more often the transcription of divergent practice by Brahman pandits than the imposition of new standards. It was the later rigidity of these codes and the sacredness attributed to them by a religious class that increasingly separated them from local custom.[3] Yet the separation was never complete. Pandits influenced local practice by interpreting it in terms of the classic texts. A comparison, for example, of collections of customary law such as Arthur Steele's *Summary of the Law and Custom of the Hindu Castes within the Dekhun Provinces* and Borradaile's *Reports* with classic texts reveals broad areas of agreement.[4] Sanskritization,

[2] Cited in Sir Courtney Ilbert, *The Government of India* (3d ed.; London, 1915), p. 355.

[3] As in the idea that a first son's inheritance was connected with his sacred obligations to his father's spirit and that his inheritance hence fell into doubt if the son was unable or unwilling to perform these duties, an idea that Mayne believed to be a Brahmanic embroidery on a secular idea. See *A Treatise on Hindu Law and Usage,* ed. V. M. Coutts-Trotter, (9th rev. ed.; Madras, 1922).

[4] Sir George C. Rankin reports in his *Background to the Indian Law* (Cambridge, 1946) that divergencies are to be found: the contrast between the great

too, linked them.[5] If local custom was more tolerant of widow re-marriage and gave more freedom to women generally, it was because the tendency for mobile lower castes to emulate higher castes had not yet become widespread.

If the written law of the high-culture classic texts was a clearer expression of Indian "civilization," the orally transmitted custom of local tribunals was more representative of Indian culture. "It is quite true," Julius Jolly told the Tagore Law Lectures audience at Calcutta in 1883,

> that before the establishment of British rule in India customary law used to be given more weight in deciding law suits than the Mitakshara, Dayabhaga [the two most significant high-culture law texts applied by British courts] or any other digest. Most quarrels did not come within the cognisance of the Courts at all, but were decided by private arbitration.[6]

By private arbitration he meant the *ad hoc* caste and village tribunals of the peasant society. It was only when they failed to settle a matter that appeals were made to local notables or rulers who, by using Brahman pandits as jurisconsults, explicitly brought high-culture prescriptions to bear on village practice. It was as much by creating a modern court system and extending its influence into the countryside as it was by bringing Western law to India that the British undermined local tribunals and their law.

---

varieties of castes and sects that exist in practice and the simplified four-varna system of the classics, the small and irregular punishments enforced by the customary caste assemblies, and significantly, the disregard for legal restrictions as to caste in trade and in taking interest (p. 148).

[5] Marc Galanter puts the relationship very nicely when he observes that it is "not that of superior to subordinate in a bureaucratic hierarchy. It is perhaps closer to the relations that obtain between Paris designers and American department store fashions or between our most prestigious universities and our smaller colleges than to anything in our legal experience" ("Hindu Law and the Development of the Modern Indian Legal System" [a paper delivered at the annual meeting of the American Political Science Association, Chicago, Illinois, September 9–12, 1964], p. 7).

[6] *Outlines of an History of the Hindu Law of Partition, Inheritance and Adoption*, Tagore Law Lectures, 1883 (Calcutta, 1885), p. 32.

The new tribunals, innocent of Indian law generally, remedied the situation by surrounding themselves with the classic texts.[7] The Manusmriti (the laws of "Manu"), a compilation, was duly translated. So, too, were more recent glosses and digests based on Yajnavalkya and other ancient law texts. The Mitakshara, a digest of Yajnavlkya's work composed in the eleventh and twelfth centuries, provided the main textual authority for Hindu law throughout India.[8] It was supplemented in different areas by various other texts and superseded in Bengal by the Dayabhaga.[9] Custom was neglected.[10] The Bengal Regulations of 1793, the foundation of the legal system introduced by Britain, did not expressly provide for customary law; and later, the privy council's decision in 1868 that "clear proof of usage will outweigh the written text of the law" was weakened by the fact that stringent common law requirements made such proof difficult.[11]

Until 1864, when their offices were abolished, *maulvies* and *pandits*, Muslim and Hindu authorities on the classic texts, were attached to the new courts to tell judges what the law was. They were encouraged to support their views with citations from the texts. As

[7] For a detailed description of the compilation and translation (by N. B. Halhead) of *A Code of Gentoo Laws, or, Ordinations of the Pundits,* first printed in London in 1776 and reprinted in 1777 and 1781, and the "digest," supervised by Sir William Jones, compiled by Jaganathan (as *Vivada-bhangarnava,* or *Ocean of Resolution of Disputes*) and translated by Henry Thomas Colebroke, see J. D. M. Derrett, "Sanskrit Legal Treatises . . . ," pp. 85–94.

[8] P. V. Kane, *History of Dharmasastra* (Poona, 1930), I, 287–88.

[9] See Mayne, *A Treatise on Hindu Law and Usage* (11th ed.), pp. 44–54, for supplementary authorities.

[10] Elphinstone in western India tried not to ignore custom when in the early nineteenth century he assumed administrative responsibility for Britain's recently acquired possessions there. "Yet even in Bombay," Derrett writes, "the *sastra* under the British made advances over custom, despite explicit protection of the latter." Jonathan Duncan in Malabar also tried to advance custom over the sacred texts of the high culture in the administration of the law. ". . . He believed Brahman pandits of value only in matrimonial and caste cases, and that Codes of *dharmasastra* were useful for checking reports of custom" (see J. D. M. Derrett, "The Administration of Hindu Law by the British," *Comparative Studies in Society and History,* IV [1961–62], 28 and n. 65).

[11] Collector of Madura, 12 Moore's Indian Appeals 397 at 436.

literary men, their inclination was in any case to consult and stress texts rather than custom.[12] Still, because they were closer to their own communities than most British judges and administrators, they knew that in many instances local practice varied from high-culture written law. Mayne believes that Hindu pandits made some attempt to take these differences into account by torturing the classic texts, a practice that had earlier enabled them to absorb and transform non-Hindu practice as well as to sustain the moral connection between the micro- and macrocosm within Hinduism.[13] The British judges, however, were more royalist than the king in their devotion to Sanskritic learning. The pandits' attempts to cover customary practice with in-compatible high-culture law were found out. "Sometimes the vari-ance between the *futwahs* [opinions of pandits] and the texts was so great," Mayne writes, "that it was ascribed to ignorance, or to cor-ruption. The fact really was that the law had outgrown the authori-ties. . . . Native judges would have recognized the fact. English judges were unable to do so, or else remarked (to use a phrase I have often heard quoted from the bench) 'that they were bound to main-tain the integrity of the law.'" The consequence, Mayne observes, "was a state of arrested progress in which no voices were heard un-less they came from the tomb. It was as if a German were to ad-minister English law from the resources of a library furnished with Fleta, Glanville, and Bracton, and terminating with Lord Coke."[14]

The courts of the various Indian presidencies varied in their levels of orthodoxy, from the Bengal court that sought to apply Hindu law to Assamese tribal peoples to the courts of western India that profited from the fact that Mountstuart Elphinstone, an early governor of Bombay, had occasioned Steele's and Borrodaile's compilations of

[12] They also found considerable difficulty in distinguishing between legal and moral commandments, a recapitulation of difficulties experienced in applying archaic law elsewhere (W. H. Macnaghten, *Principles and Precedents of Hindu Law* [Calcutta, 1829], I, vi).

[13] *A Treatise on Hindu Law and Usage* (9th ed.), p. 43. Derrett probably goes too far when he describes the native referees assigned in the eighteenth century to the new courts as "sources of customary law" ("The Administration of Hindu Law . . . ," pp. 24–25).

[14] *A Treatise on Hindu Law and Usage* (9th ed.), p. 44. See also Macnaghten, *Principles and Precedents of Hindu Law,* p. v.

customary law.[15] Still, the main effect of British legal interpretation and administration was to consolidate and lend added authority to high-culture law.

Other factors also contributed to this result. Lower level judges and early incumbents of the modern legal profession were uniformly drawn from the upper castes, particularly the Brahman castes. Their Sanskritic orientation and perspectives colored legal practice.

The main force encouraging Brahmanical law was the need for a legal order with greater generality and reach. The more cosmopolitan and uniform high-culture law was better able to meet the requirements of the times than was the more parochial and diverse customary law of village society. If, from the perspective of Western law, high-culture Hindu law appeared particularistic, from the perspective of customary law, it appeared as it had over the centuries, more uniform. For example, influenced by high-culture texts rather than anthropological sensibilities, the courts tended to assess the rights and obligations of a multitude of caste groups by classifying them under the four varnas mentioned in the classic texts (Brahman, Kshatriya, Vaishya, Sudra) and often further simplified their task by using a twofold distinction between twice-born (regenerate) castes and the rest.[16] The distinction was still particularistic but infinitely more homogeneous than customary particularism. The fact that it was a written rather than an oral law also helped strengthen it against custom, especially under the new circumstances that the raj created. Its relative ascertainability, certainty, and consistency recommended it to those, Indian and British alike, concerned about order and regularity.[17]

[15] See n. 10 above.

[16] William C. McCormack, "Caste and the British Administration of Hindu Law," forthcoming in *Asian Sociological Review*, I, No. 1.; and Marc Galanter, "Changing Legal Conceptions of Caste" (a paper for the Conference on Social Structure and Social Change in India, University of Chicago, June 3–5, 1965).

[17] A comparison between the legal systems of India and Africa, where a parallel diversity of customary law did not shelter beneath an indigenous high-culture law, might suggest the extent to which such high culture law does or does not contribute to the development of a modern legal order. Lloyd Fallers remarks that "at least a dozen distinct customary legal systems exist there [in Uganda, which, he says, is no exception to the pattern in Africa], along with elements of British, Indian, and Islamic law—all under the ultimate juris-

In the 1870's, however, the validity and usefulness of Sanskritic law began to be disputed.[18] Henry Maine, writing from the perspective of historical jurisprudence and experience as a law member of the governor-general's council, observed that "the codified law—Manu and its glossators—embraced originally a much smaller body of usage than had been imagined. . . ." Continuing, he argued that "the customary rules, reduced to writing, have been very greatly altered by Brahmanical exposition, constantly in spirit, sometimes in tenor."[19] Burgeoning Sanskritic research in the second half of the nineteenth century revealed that many classic texts diverged from "official" ones such as the Mitakshara. The Rebellion of 1857, a most dramatic cautionary tale, had already sharply reminded Englishmen of Indian practice and sentiment in all their complexity and diversity. Ethnological research, which also began to accumulate in the second half of the century, escalated sharply after census operations began in 1881 and provided more systematic knowledge of local custom for use in the courts.[20] Finally, the rise of the historical school of jurisprudence had a subtle but discernible influence on the lawyers and judges of the subcontinent.

diction of the superordinate magistrate's courts and the High Court" ("Customary Law in the New African States," *Law and Contemporary Problems,* XXVII [Autumn, 1962], p. 616). See also Max Rheinstein's discussion of "legal problems of pluralism" in "Problems of Law in the New Nations of Africa," *Old Societies and New States,* ed. Clifford Geertz (London, 1963), pp. 222–36.

[18] It had, in fact, been disputed even earlier. F. W. Ellis wrote long ago that "the law of the smritis, under various modifications, has never been the law of the Tamil and cognate nations" (see Sir Thomas Strange, *Hindu Law* [London, 1830], I, 163). A. C. Burnell supported the same proposition and apparently influenced J. H. Nelson's accounts; see n. 21 below.

[19] *Village Communities in East and West* (New York, 1876), p. 52. For a jaundiced view of Maine and his contribution, see J. D. M. Derrett, "Sir Henry Maine and Law in India: 1858–1958," *Judicial Review: The Law Journal of the Scottish Universities,* 1959, pp. 40–55.

[20] A few of the important ones were C. L. Tupper, *Punjab Customary Law* (Calcutta, 1881); E. Thurston, *Castes and Tribes of Southern India* (Madras, 1909); H. H. Risley, *Tribes and Castes of Bengal—Ethnographic Glossary* (Calcutta, 1891); William Crooke, *Tribes and Castes of the North-West Provinces and Oudh* (Calcutta, 1896). Manuals of customary law in the United Provinces and Punjab were issued by government authority and served as evidence in the courts.

J. H. Nelson, a legal polemicist with experience of the Madras High Court, wrote several provocative books attacking its adherence to the Bengal school's Sanskritic orthodoxy.[21] Nelson charged the High Court with having assumed "the self-imposed duty of civilizing the 'lower castes' of Madras, that is to say, the great bulk of its population, by gradually destroying their local usages and customs."[22] Unless he comes into the English courts, ". . . the conduct of an ordinary Chetti, Maravan or Reddi of the Madras Province . . . is no more affected by precepts contained in the Mitaxara than it is by precepts in the Psalms of David."[23] Nelson proposed that the Madras court ascertain and use customary law. His attack and remedy neglected to take into account either the degree to which the so-called Dravidian (that is, non-Brahman) peoples of Madras had adopted Brahman law and practice or the degree to which Madras judges applied customary law. Judges often refused to apply high-culture law when they were requested to do so by litigants from lower castes with whose customary law they were familiar.[24] Nelson may have overstated his case, but he was substantially correct in his diagnosis of attitudes and practice.

"To adopt Mr. Nelson's suggestions," a puisne judge of the High Court wrote the governor in a 110-page "reply," "whether as regards the higher or lower castes, would commit us to chaos in the matter of the Hindu law. . . ." It would require the British courts to abdicate "the vantage ground [they] have occupied for nearly a century . . . ," a ground that will enable them ". . . gradually to remove the differentiations of customary law, and bring about a certain amount of manageable uniformity." Nelson's prescriptions, he warned, would "commit us to investigation and enforcement of an overwhelming variety of discordant customs among the lower castes, many of them of a highly immoral and objectionable character, which if not brought

[21] J. H. Nelson, *View of the Hindu Law as Administered by the High Court of Madras* (Madras, 1877); *A Prospectus of the Scientific Study of the Hindu Law* (Madras, 1881); and *Indian Usage and Judge-made Law in Madras* (London, 1887).

[22] *Indian Usage and Judge-made Law . . .*, p. 7.

[23] *View of the Hindu Law . . .*, p. 147.

[24] Mayne, in the preface to the first edition of *A Treatise on Hindu Law and Usage,* describes such attempts in Malabar.

into prominence and sanctioned by judicial recognition, will gradually give place to less objectionable and more civilized customs of the superior castes."[25]

Nelson, like William Crosskey in the United States, was calling on the courts to reverse and correct several generations' worth of law because it was based on wrong premises.[26] Julius Jolly, in the Tagore Law Lectures, in effect answered Nelson when he observed that "what may have been possible in the early times of the British administration may prove impossible now, after both the legislation and custom itself have been remodelled by a century of judicial decisions."[27] Nelson's essentialist perspective, which held that if the law was to be valid it had to be based on "original" custom, ran contrary to Sanskritization as it affected the law. Social mobility by caste groups usually included efforts to adhere more closely to high-culture law and custom, and sometimes British courts, more often through insensitivity or ignorance than by design, fostered such attempts.

Despite the challenge that Nelson's polemic represented, despite the fact that the courts paid more attention to customary law as it became known and available to them, despite even its recognition in legislation such as the Punjab Laws Act of 1872, the long-run secular trend was in favor of high-culture law. A comparison of the ninth and eleventh editions of John Mayne's classic work marks the triumphal march of what he called "Brahmanization." The English lawyer who edited the ninth edition of 1922 preserves Mayne's cautious view that there is a demand for Brahman law, that such law, without its sacred coloration, captures considerable usage, but that its wholesale substitution for customary law is not justifiable. Mayne himself criticized those judges and pandits who "seem to imagine that those rules which govern civil rights among Hindus, which we roughly speak of as Hindu law, are solely of Brahmanic origin." They admit that conflicting customs exist and must be respected; but, he emphasized,

[25] Cited in Nelson, *Indian Usage and Judge-made Law . . .*, pp. 7, 8. J. D. M. Derrett discusses Nelson's career and views in "J. H. Nelson: A Forgotten Administrator Historian of India," in C. H. Philips (ed.), *Historians of India, Pakistan and Ceylon* (London, 1961).

[26] William W. Crosskey, *Politics and the Constitution in the History of the United States* (Chicago, 1953).

[27] Jolly, *Outlines of an History of the Hindu Law . . .*, p. 32.

"these are looked on as local violations of a law which is of general obligation, and which ought to be universally observed; as something to be checked and put down, if possible, and to be apologized for, if the existence of the usage is proved beyond dispute."[28] Mayne finds it "startling" that the Bengal court, always leery of "heresy" with respect to the validity of high-culture law, should assume "that the natives of Assam, the rudest of our provinces, are governed by the Hindu law as modified by Jimata Vahanu."

Srinivas Iyengar and N. Chandrasekhar Aiyar, however, the South Indian Brahmans who edited the tenth and eleventh editions of Mayne's work, assumed that Brahman law was the norm and custom the exception. Good lawyers, they took account of custom by citing the extant ethnological studies but plainly regarded the high-culture law as that which ought "to be universally observed," a view that they justified in the manner of the pandits by reference to the classic texts. Citing Manu and the Arthasastra as his authorities, Aiyar found that "Sudras also were regarded as Aryans for the purpose of the civil law . . . ,"[29] an observation that in effect extended high-culture law to all caste Hindus. Nowhere do they use Mayne's adjective, "Brahmanic," an adjective designed to characterize not only the content but also the bias of the classic texts. Iyengar and Aiyar, by referring instead to Hindu law, an identification that suggests that the classic texts apply to all Hindus, become themselves agents of Brahmanization.[30] "It may now be taken as settled," Aiyar observes, "that the general Hindu law . . . applies to every Hindu. . . . Special customs have to be pleaded by way of exceptions. Any other view would be to invert the process by which law is ascertained."[31] Supported by decisions since Mayne's time, he is able to argue that Hindu law applies to many social groups, such as Adi Dravidas, Chamars, various Dravidian communities, and Jats, whose legal circumstances were at least in doubt when Mayne first wrote. Even the instance that Mayne found most extraordinary, the Bengal court's application of Hindu law to Assamese tribal people, was confidently brought within the fold. Without citing any anthropological evidence, Aiyar

[28] *A Treatise on Hindu Law and Usage* (9th ed.), p. 1.

[29] *Ibid.* (11th ed.), p. 5.

[30] *Ibid.*, for instance, pp. 5, 87.   [31] *Ibid.*, p. 1.

asserts that "the aborigines of Assam have become Hinduised and are governed by the Bengal school of Hindu law," a statement that has been brought into considerable discredit by postindependence cultural and political developments in eastern Assam.

The role of Brahmanic law in legal modernization arose more from its form and structure than from its substance. Its cosmopolitanism, availability in texts, and cultivation and use by a class of legal specialists, by meshing with the requirements of a national legal system, made it an amenable if somewhat delusive instrument for Britons wishing to find and apply a uniform law to Indians. Yet many of the Brahmanic law's social norms—the sanctity of corporate identity and duties and of social and sexual inequality—were displaced or modified as official law was Anglicized and used to foster social change.

The Anglicization of Indian Law

Traditional Indian law, the sacred texts of the Hindu high culture as well as the spoken law of the peasant society's memory, embodied values that were for the most part antithetical to those found in Western law. (We do not consider in this section Muslim personal law, which has been exempted from official reform in postindependence India.) For traditional Hindu law, the "natural" associations of family, caste, and locality were the units of the moral and social universe, whereas for British law, the individual was valued over the "artificial" groups in which he might find himself. Under traditional law, rights and privileges, obligations and duties, property, and even punishments for crimes varied with an individual's corporate identity. The characteristic form of assets under Indian law was collective and fixed: land inalienably vested in families or lineages and was transferable only by inheritance within the blood line. Under British law, it became individual and mobile: alienable by individuals as well as families, through commercial transactions or by will. Indian law was particularistic, treating castes, communities, and the sexes differently, whereas the law of the British raj was universalistic, in principle treating all men as equal before it. Finally, Indian law, beneath the veneer of uniformity that Brahmanic high culture law gave it, was diverse, differing greatly among regions, whereas British law aimed at uniformity among places as well as persons. These contrasts transcend the cultural and social differences between India and Britain, between East and West, by expressing with considerable clarity the historical differences that Sir Henry Maine, drawing on his knowledge of European feudal society and Hindu social organization, found in the contrasting law of traditional and modern society.[1] Although the dichotomy between tradition and modernity appears to find considerable support in these distinctions, the extent to which British legal values, particularly individualism, succeeded in establishing themselves as the definition of Indian modernity remains an open question.

The change in emphasis in the law from the corporate group to the individual, from the law of persons to the law of place, from particularism to universalism, occurred as much by inadvertence as by design. It is associated with the spread of British power and legal administration, with early efforts to identify and use Indian law in British courts in ways compatible with British conceptions of legal propriety, with subsequent attempts to create a more uniform system of law based on codes, with cautious and selective legislation that incorporated into Indian personal law English conceptions of morality and liberty, and with administrative and legal changes in the revenue system that freed real property from its corporate connections.

New values derived from the law also entered Indian public life and society through the Indianization of the legal profession as it grew into the leading sector of a numerous and influential modern

[1] Sir Henry Maine, *Ancient Law* (Everyman ed.), p. 156. Roscoe Pound (in *The Ideal Element in Law*, Tagore Law Lecture, 1948 [Calcutta, 1958], Chap. 6) deals with related issues in his discussion of the rise of free self-assertion in the law of the seventeenth to eighteenth centuries. His treatment supports the proposition that much that appears to the superficial eye as differences between Indian and "Western" law is in fact a difference of stages. For a recent assertion that the development of law in India is more a matter of historical stages than "East-West" effect, see H. A. Freeman, "An Introduction to Hindu Jurisprudence," *American Journal of Comparative Law*, VIII (1949).

middle class.[2] Indian lawyers came to represent and plead for clients and Indian judges came to sit on high court benches. The influence of the law in its more modern Anglo-Indian manifestation spread well beyond its functional boundaries by profoundly affecting the nationalist movement, whose leaders more often than not were lawyers.

At the same time it must be remembered that the British courts constituted only one part of a dual system, the parochial and the national, and what came to be Anglo-Indian law only one of the wide range of influences that shaped beliefs and conduct. For villagers the administration of justice remained for the most part in the hands of local unofficial tribunals, the panchayats of caste and locality. Here we are more interested in the national legal system where British values were introduced and assimilated than in the parochial system where their effect was more distant and indirect.

The unravelling of the individual from his corporately defined legal definition began and for some time proceeded inadvertently. British courts, established to keep the peace among the East India Company's servants in presidency towns, gradually expanded their territorial jurisdiction to include Indian residents of towns and then of districts. In the late eighteenth century, as the power of the Moghul Empire continued to decline, Governor-Generals Hastings and Cornwallis replaced Indian courts administered by the Muslim agents of the emperor with British courts. When Cornwallis substituted as well English judges for Indian ones at all levels, he did so on the ground that "all regulations for the reform of the [criminal] department would be useless and nugatory whilst the execution of them depends upon any native whatsoever. . . ."[3] Jurisdiction was expanded functionally, too. Crime in the eyes of the prevailing Muslim law was, generally, a private offense. Punishment had become a public responsibility, but complaint, even in serious cases such as murder, remained the prerogative of the affected family, a private and corporate body. If the family of a murdered man for whatever reason did not

[2] See B. B. Misra, *The Indian Middle Classes* (London, 1961), pp. 162–75.

[3] Cited in H. H. Dodwell (ed.), *Cambridge History of India* (1st Indian reprint; Delhi, n. d.). However, Indian legal officers were attached to all courts from the district through the supreme court at Calcutta by the Regulation of 1793.

take the initiative, a court could not take cognizance. In 1792 the British made certain actions, including murder, crimes in the eyes of the state.[4]

The English began with the clear intention of applying, for most purposes, Indian law to Indians. As we mentioned above, Governor-General Hastings in 1772 had ordered that "in all suits regarding marriage, inheritance, and caste, and other religious usages and institutions [succession was added in 1781] the laws of the Koran with respect to Mohammedans, and those of the Shaster [sacred law texts] with respect to the Hindus shall be invariably adhered to."[5] Pandits and shastris (traditional specialists in the sacred texts, almost invariably Brahmans) were assigned as advisers or referees to all courts. British judges and Brahman pandits were to share responsibility for judgments by signing the final document.[6] In "non-listed" subjects such as the law of evidence, commercial suits, contract cases, or civil wrongs, although the shastras did not have to be used nor were pandits required to cosign decisions, pandits were consulted and Hindu law "occupied a large place" in the work of *mufassil* [district], appellate, and supreme courts.[7] Despite these early intentions to use Hindu law "invariably" for the listed subjects and extensively for other subjects and despite a conscious effort to take "care to add as little as possible by analogy or by inference from the known authoritative rules,"[8] British judges and their courts early and continuously in fact transformed Indian into Anglo-Indian law.

As early as 1781 English judges were directed to apply "justice, equity and good conscience" wherever a vacuum of law existed or

[4] Steps were also taken at this time to make the administration of criminal justice more rational and more humane. In 1790, intent rather than the weapon used was made the criterion of offense; amputation as punishment was abolished in 1792 (see U. C. Sarkar, *Epochs in Hindu Legal History* [Vishveshvaranand Institute Publication, No. 8; Hoshiarpur, 1958], p. 348, nn. 6 and 7).

[5] See above, pp. 269–70.

[6] See J. D. M. Derrett, "The Administration of Hindu Law by the British," *Comparative Studies in Society and History*, IV (1961–62), 24; and "Sanskrit Legal Treatises Compiled at the Instance of the British," *Zeitschrift für Vergleichende Rechtswissenschaft*, LXIII (1961), 83.

[7] Derrett, "The Administration of Hindu Law . . . ," p. 41.

[8] Derrett, "Sanskrit Legal Treatises . . . ," p. 41.

was deemed to exist, a directive that was admirably suited to open the way for British legal thinking.[9] "Though justice, equity and good conscience are the law which Indian judges are bound to administer," James Fitzjames Stephen observed, "they do in point of fact resort to English law books for their guidance in questions of this sort and it is impossible that they should do otherwise. . . ."[10]

Anglicization of Indian law took more subtle and covert forms as well. Almost from the beginning British judges tried to free themselves from dependence on their Brahman pandits by gaining direct access to *dharmasastra* texts. Because decisions given on the advice of pandits were to be decisions of a British court, they expected that the rule of *stare decisis* would apply; by the 1840's published legal reports and collections of cases, such as Moore's *Indian Appeals,* had become generally available. But pandits, accustomed to choose and interpret the law according to the needs of the situation and the likely consequences of a decision, did not often offer advice that placed primary emphasis on precedent. As noted previously, this led British judges to suspect their advice and question their motives. The extremely influential W. H. Macnaghten observed in 1825 that if pandits could be restricted in their citations "to a few works of notorious authority, it might have a salutary effect in curbing their fancy, if not their cupidity."[11] As early as 1786, Sir William Jones had had "the pundit of our court read and correct a copy of Halhead's book" (*A Code of Gentoo Laws,* the first and one of the most influential of the "few works of notorious authority") in the original Sanskrit, and "I then obliged him to attest it as good law, so that he never now can

[9] Sections 60 and 93 of the Regulation of 5 July 1781. The regulation was drafted by Sir Elija Impey. For the history of regulations and law in British times, see Sir George C. Rankin, *Background to the Indian Law* (Cambridge, 1946); and Sir Courtney Ilbert, *The Government of India* (3d ed.; London, 1915).

[10] Cited in Sarkar, *Epochs in Hindu Legal History,* p. 378. Derrett observes rather enigmatically that "it is not to be supposed that it [the regulation] was not intended to establish a fundamental source of law" ("The Administration of Hindu Law . . . ," p. 25). See also his "Justice, Equity and Good Conscience," in J. D. N. Anderson, *Changing Law in Developing Countries* (New York, 1963).

[11] *Principles and Precedents of Moohummudan Law* (Calcutta, 1825), cited by Derrett, "Sanskrit Legal Treatises . . . ," p. 76.

give corrupt opinions, without certain detection."[12] Most pandits, of course, viewed the *dharmasastra* more broadly, less literally and more dynamically.

The inadvertent Anglicization of Indian law proceeded in part from ignorance and misunderstanding of the nature and extent of *dharmasastra,* in part from unconscious application of English legal modes of thought. British legal authorities in India failed to explore vigorously the sources of Indian law. In using the traditional law that was at their command, they affected its meaning and the course of its development by applying segments without full regard for their larger contexts, by stating Hindu rules in British legal terms and sometimes following them inflexibly, and quite apart from the conscious application of justice, equity, and good conscience, by reading the logic and substance of British law into questions of procedure, rights, and the interpretation and use of evidence. Jawaharlal Nehru spoke for this critique when he remarked, "The British replaced this elastic customary law by judicial decisions based on the old texts. . . . In the way it was done, it resulted in the perpetuation of the ancient law unmodified by subsequent customs." Yet even one of the most severe critics of the British administration of Hindu law, J. D. M. Derrett, finds that without such importations the Hindu law "could not have been applied effectively or without unjust results."[13]

Digests and texts of *dharmasastra* by British authors gradually replaced the learning of Brahmans as the source of Indian law. As they did so, the courts came to rely more and more on these works and less on the larger range of authorities consulted by court pandits. In 1864, English judges gained that independence for which the work of men such as Jones and Macnaghten had prepared the ground when, dispensing entirely with Indian legal advisers, they assumed full judicial knowledge of Hindu law.

The British came to conceive of their task in India in Roman terms. James Mill, chief administrative officer of the East India Company, characterized the Charter Act of 1833 (which included provi-

---

[12] Sir John Shore, *Memoirs of . . . Sir William Jones* (London, 1804), pp. 276–77, cited in *ibid.,* p. 94.

[13] Nehru's discussion is to be found in *The Discovery of India* (New York, 1946), p. 331. Derrett's critique is in "The Administration of Hindu Law . . . ," p. 44.

sions for a law commission and a law member of the governor-general's council) by remarking that "the state of things at which it aims in prospect is when a general system of justice and policy and a code of laws common (as far as may be) to the whole people of India ... shall be established throughout the country."[14] But if the design was Roman, its immediate origin was Benthamite (although it is not clear that Bentham would have concurred). The Benthamite enthusiasm for codification, which Britain resisted at home with some success, was poured out on the Indian subcontinent. "Here at least," F. C. Montague observed, "Bentham's teachings bore fruit. Had Bentham done nothing more than point out the way in which the law of England could best be applied to the needs of India," Montague adds, seemingly oblivious to the failures and limitations of British law in India, "he would have rendered a distinguished service to his country and mankind."[15]

The common law, as Rankin put it, was transferred to the subcontinent not by reception but by codification. For a good portion of the nineteenth century, a good many Britons interested in the law devoted themselves to the framing of codes. India was considered sufficiently devoid of law that it did not seem anomalous to transfer wholesale large elements of British law. "There is nothing Indian or Oriental about [codification] ... ," C. D. Field remarked in *Some Observations on Codification in India*. What was required was "all in the table of contents of Smith's and Kent's books."[16] After the first and second law commissions had recommended in 1834 and 1853 that civil law be based on English law, the third implemented the idea,

[14] Dispatch No. 44 of December, 1834, by the board of directors of the East India Company, which has been attributed to Mill.

[15] F. C. Montague (ed.), *A Fragment on Government,* by Jeremy Bentham (London, 1951), pp. 56–57. See also the letter from Bentham to Dundas, 20 May 1793, offering his services with respect to Indian legislation; the "Essay on the Influence of Time and Place in Matters of Legislation," in which Bentham considers what modifications are required in order to transplant his system of law codes to Bengal; and other evidence cited in Eric Stokes, *The English Utilitarians in India* (London, 1959), p. 51 and nn. Bentham, however, did not believe that English judicial procedure should be transplanted; see "Essay on the Influence of Time and Place ... ," in *The Works of Jeremy Bentham,* ed. J. Bowring (London, 1843), I, 187–88.

[16] Cited in Rankin, *Background to the Indian Law,* p. 139.

exempting only personal law.[17] The Penal Code of 1860 and a series of civil acts between 1865 and 1872 elaborated the design. By the late 1870's the surge lost its force, but by then codes based on British practice had become a central part of Indian law. It was generally agreed during this great period of codification, however, that the corporately based personal law, which sustained the social structure, primary groups, and morality of traditional Indian society, could be disturbed only at considerable risk, a view strengthened by the Rebellion of 1857.

One realm of law-making that posed relatively few problems of conflict between indigenous and British jural concepts was that concerning business. New laws, although they did help foster the growth of trade and industry, did not conflict sharply with existing practice. When the British jurists remarked that Indian contract law, unlike that touching inheritance or other social practices, rested on "common sense," they were taking note of functional similarities that overrode cultural and social differences. Legal authorities like Colebrooke, Macnaghten, and Strange were all struck by the parallels between British and Indian contract law.[18]

Despite an initial reluctance to disturb personal law because of its intimate connection to the social order, it too was deeply affected, in the first instance by the very directive that ostensibly sought to exempt it from British legal ideas. When Warren Hastings directed that in listed subjects "the laws of the Shaster with respect to the Hindus shall be invariably adhered to," he probably saw himself placing company policy behind the traditional Hindu view that a ruler should apply to each social group and caste its own law. But, as we have pointed out above, that was not the consequence. Rather, he placed Brahman law in a dominant position, converting the high-culture law into territorial law for all Hindu castes regardless of whether they recognized the authority of the shastras. Like others who intended to preserve the legal status quo in the area of personal law, he failed to do so in part because he did not grasp the appropriate means.

Changes in personal law were also deliberately made. The decision

[17] Sarkar, *Epochs in Hindu Legal History,* pp. 351–52.

[18] Rankin, *Background to the Indian Law,* pp. 88–92.

of 1829 in principle abolishing suttee [the practice of widows' immolating themselves on the funeral pyres of their husbands] is the most dramatic example although it affected few people.[19] "When they have been convinced of the error of this first and most criminal of their customs," Governor-General Bentinck wrote, "may it not be hoped that others which stand in the way of their improvement will also pass away."[20] Other acts followed, none decisive in itself, but taken cumulatively constituting a significant breach in the wall that was supposed to prevent British intervention in corporately-oriented Indian personal law. Of these acts, some of the most important were the so-called Freedom of Religion Act of 1850, the Widow Remarriage Act of 1856, various Gains of Learning bills (finally enacted in 1930), and the changes in the provision for wills. Usually of little practical effect, they were rightly attacked by the orthodox as theoretical challenges to the traditional social and religious order.

The Freedom of Religion Act—its unofficial title states as polemic a perspective as does a right to work act—struck not only at the economic sanctions available to Hindu orthodoxy but also at the collective joint family's power over its members.[21] By the mid-nineteenth century, a significant number of Hindus had converted to Christianity. By doing so they not only ceased to be Hindus but also lost the corporate definition on which their property rights depended. They were no longer, for example, Brahmans of a certain subcaste and lineage that held property and regulated succession in a certain way. They had become, in effect, outcastes without legal standing with respect to property rights. The Act of 1850 relieved British judges of the obligation, laid down by Hastings, to enforce the Hindu law that penalized conversion in this way. Any law, the act provided, which "may be held in any way to impair or affect any right of inheritance,

[19] The decision was not easily made. A series of attempts at regulating and rationalizing the practice preceded abolition. Some of these attempts can be followed in Kenneth Ballhatchet, *Social Policy and Social Change in Western India, 1817–1830* (London, 1957); Bentinck's views and the advice that shaped his decision are discussed in Geoffrey Seed, "The Abolition of Suttee in Bengal," *History,* XL (October, 1955), 286–99.

[20] Minute of November 8, 1829. It is conveniently available in D. C. Boulger, *Lord William Bentinck* ("Rulers of India Series"; London, 1892), p. 111.

[21] Caste Disabilities Removal Act is its official title.

by reason of [any person's] renouncing or having been excluded from the communion of any religion, or being deprived of caste, shall cease to be enforced as law. . . ."[22] Individuals who chose a new identity could no longer be materially penalized through the law for doing so.

Ordinarily, property was held by the joint family, not by individuals. Classical law recognized the possibility of partition, but it was rare. When property was divided, it did not necessarily imply the destruction of the joint family, for the part of the family that detached itself continued to be, on a smaller scale, a joint, not a nuclear, family. In the British era, however, those who attended the new English-inspired institutions of higher learning often emerged as professional men earning substantial incomes. Their educational ventures were almost always financed by the joint family, whose head, whether father, uncle, or brother, also took responsibility for the student's wife and children. After he took up his professional career, the family as a matter of course regarded his income, like that from the family lands, as part of its resources. Such was the case, for example, with Gandhi. In 1903, however, twelve years after becoming a barrister and beginning practice, he in effect broke relations with his eldest brother, who had financed his education after his father's death, by suspending the remissions he had been sending from South Africa. That "all future savings, if any, would be utilized for the benefit of the community" did not assuage his brother's sense of wrong.[23] Gandhi, like others before and after him, eventually resisted the presumption that because the family had educated him his earn-

---

[22] Cited in Ilbert, *The Government of India,* p. 358. Act III of 1872 strengthened this trend in that it allowed marriages to be celebrated between individuals of different faiths, provided, however, they in fact foreswore their previous faiths, declaring they were neither Muslim nor Hindu nor Christian. Act XXX of 1923 made it possible for Hindus to contract such marriages without ceasing to be Hindus. But intercaste marriages were not validated until the Hindu Marriages Validity Act (XXI) of 1949. By contrast, Nepal today explicitly bans conversion from Hinduism. The legislation provides that "every citizen, subject to the current traditions, shall practice and profess his own religion as handed down from ancient times," and the state bans conversion (*New York Times,* February 22, 1965).

[23] D. G. Tendulkar, *Mahatma: Life of Mohandas Karamchand Gandhi* (Bombay, 1951——), I, 63.

ings were at least in part permanently committed to it. Most did not resist, at least in part because the courts, following Hindu law, supported the family's claim against the individual. What the effects of such arrangements were on economic growth and social change is neither obvious or settled.[24] Legislatures, too, were conservative in the area of personal law, and it was not until 1930 that a Gains of Learning bill, often before provincial legislatures, was finally enacted in Madras.[25] If legal change trailed behind the most advanced opinion, it supported men who might wish in the future to extricate themselves from traditional collective obligations.

In other areas of the law, increasing mobility and alienability of property, with their consequences for social change, were more evident. The introduction of wills through legal interpretation and legislative acts was particularly important in freeing the individual from the traditional corporate group.[26] Property, particularly landed property, was inherited by blood and kin lines according to prescriptive arrangements. Wills substituted choice, by means of a legal instrument, for birth and particular prescriptive arrangements. Wills began to be effective in Bengal in 1792. In Bombay they were not recognized until 1860, and in Madras until 1862. The Hindu Wills Act of 1870 established a general set of rights and requirements. If the actual effect of wills on property and society was limited, it was in part because the courts applied restrictions that protected joint family holdings and in part because habit and custom were not hospitable to their use.[27] Alienability and mobility of property made further ad-

[24] Whether these arrangements hindered economic growth remains a moot question. There is some evidence that the new professionals favored investment in land, a traditional form of investment that probably had little effect on economic growth. The evidence, however, is still inadequate. Certainly no simple argument that the joint family restrains economic development by smothering individual initiative will do. The joint family units of the business community, by concentrating capital, may often have made risk-taking and entrepreneurial diversification more rather than less feasible.

[25] Hindu Gains of Learning Act (Act XXX), 1930.

[26] Beer Pertab v. Rajender Pertab (1867), 12 Moore's Indian Appeals 137; Act XXI of 1870 (Hindu wills); Act V of 1881; and Indian Succession Act (1865).

[27] Sir Francis Dupre Oldfield, "Law Reform," in H. H. Dodwell (ed.), *Cambridge History of India*, Vol. VI.

vances. Madras in 1855 and Bengal in 1872 permitted creditors to bring to sale debtors' interest in their families' property, and soon after owners themselves were permitted to do the same.[28] Both types of legislation helped bring into being the "liberal" society with its opportunities and pains.

From Cornwallis' time forward, British revenue laws decisively affected the collective nature of landed property. Under the Regulation of 1793, which laid down the permanent settlement for Bengal and provided for revenue procedures, the authorities were instructed to sell defaulting farms and estates when their owners failed to meet the annual revenue demand. These arrangements reversed customary practice by making land salable collateral. Previously, liens on crops had often made agriculturists heavily dependent on moneylenders, but their land had remained at least theoretically inalienable. The effects of the new regulations were often compounded by unreasonable assessments imposed by utilitarian enthusiasts under the influence of the rent-fund theory and the replacement of lax and sometimes humane enforcement by unbending rigor.[29] Turnover in land mounted rapidly, and in 1854 an official inquiry was undertaken to ascertain the causes and remedies. The structure and stability of the old society were weakened and in some places destroyed as merchants with capital and lower level public servants with inside knowledge of revenue arrears and low assessments took advantage of forced sales.[30] "The village communities are decaying . . . ," latter-

[28] Madras in 1862, Bombay in 1873.

[29] Such as Holt Mackenzie's arrangements for the Northwest Provinces or those of R. K. Pringle for Bombay; see *Cambridge History of India* VI, 81, and Eric Stokes, *The English Utilitarians in India*, p. 133.

[30] Villages in northern and western India, for example, collectively held by kinship groups, were particularly hard hit. Some officials, like Byrd and MacKenzie, were aware of this problem and sought to cushion the consequences of the sales law by giving the kin a right to pre-empt defaulting property. See Bernard S. Cohn, "The Initial British Impact on India: A Case Study of the Benares Region," *Journal of Asian Studies,* No. 4 (August, 1960). Cohn's study indicates that in the Benares region about 40 per cent of the land had changed hands by mid-century. See also Thomas Munro's minute against allowing revenue officials to purchase lands sold for arrears at public auction (Board of Revenue, August, 1825, in G. R. Gleig, *The Life of Major-General Sir Thomas Munro* [London, 1830], II, 413–21); the chapter "The Landed

day utilitarian James Fitzjames Stephen observed with considerable satisfaction. "In spite of regrets prompted by various reasons, they decay because they represent a crude form of socialism, paralyzing the individual energy and inconsistent with the fundamental principles of our rule."[31]

The emergence of a new moral and social order that changes in the law helped express and facilitate challenged traditional social arrangements. Personal and revenue law, by increasingly freeing the individual and property from the hereditary prescriptions of traditional society, opened the way for some to shape a more individualistic, egalitarian, and cosmopolitan society. But although most of the structural and normative changes that Britain introduced in the law have been recognized by the constitution of independent India and further developed in case and statute law, their substance and future contain marked ambiguities.

The parochial side of the dual legal system remains pervasive and active. Most recent anthropological studies attribute great vitality to the non-official legal structure of caste and village panchayats, and report continuing bias against using the official legal system.[32] Since anthropologists in India have tended, until very recently, to regard the village as the key unit of analysis, and the sociology of India remains relatively undeveloped, there are few studies of legal behavior in paracommunities such as caste associations and federations. But there is some evidence that one of the services offered by several caste associations is the adjudication of disputes.[33]

Many substantive provisions of the official law, embodying as they do the values of the Anglicized classes and the legal profession, do not affect the conduct of most Indians. The age-of-marriage acts are generally ignored; divorce is rare; the provisions of the Hindu code

---

Middle Classes," in Misra, *The Indian Middle Classes;* and J. W. Kaye, *The Administration of the East Indian Company* (London, 1853), p. 241.

[31] Leslie Stephen summarizing his brother's views in the *Life of Sir James Fitzjames Stephen* (New York, 1895), p. 285.

[32] Bernard S. Cohn, "Anthropological Notes on Disputes and Law in India," *American Anthropologist,* LXVII (December, 1965), Pt. 2, 103–9.

[33] The Nadar Mahajana Sabha (see p. 97, above) and the Berwa Mahasabha (Ruth Simmons, Berkeley, Calif., personal communication, fall, 1966).

with respect to women's rights in property are infrequently observed in villages; and laws penalizing the practice of untouchability have a marginal effect.[34] Some provisions of the official law reflect the persistence of ascribed group identity. Progressive discrimination in favor of scheduled castes and tribes and of backward classes, by associating special privileges with ascriptively defined communities, utilizes traditional social definitions for furthering the modern goal of advancing social equality. Recent official efforts to replace ascriptive with economic criteria will have to overcome a pattern of vested interests committed to preserving and even to expanding the boundaries and the privileges of ascribed backwardness. And the Hindu Code acts, although in general they further Anglicize Indian law, also contain provisions that recognize traditional group definitions, but without progressive discrimination's modernizing goals. For example, one provision, contrary to the intent of the "Freedom of Religions" act of 1850 (when conversion rather than secularity was a frontier of personal independence), imposes penalties for conversion from Hinduism: A convert provides his wife with grounds for divorce, loses the right to give his child in adoption (a not uncommon practice within kin and caste communities concerned to preserve the family line and property) or to be its guardian, forfeits his claims to maintenance, and deprives his children of the right of inheritance from unconverted relations.[35]

[34] For evidence on behavior with respect to the age-of-marriage acts, see William J. Goode, *World Revolution and Family Patterns* (Glencoe, Ill., 1963), pp. 232–36, and K. M. Kapadia, *Marriage and the Family in India* (Bombay, 1958), pp. 138–66. Y. B. Damle, "Divorce in Poona District," in *Society in India* ed. A. Aiyappan (Madras, 1956), and Kamalabai Deshpande, "Divorce Cases in the Court of Poona," *Economic Weekly,* July, 1963, pp. 1179–83, analyze the degree to which legislation providing for divorce has been used. For the degree to which village women have taken advantage of their newly acquired property rights, see Mildred Stroop Luchinsky, "The Impact of Some Recent Indian Government Legislation on the Women of an Indian Village," *Asian Survey,* III (December, 1963), pp. 573–83. The limited effect of laws prohibiting the practice of untouchability has been widely reported; for one perceptive account see T. Scarlet Epstein, *Economic Development and Social Change in South India* (Manchester, 1962), pp. 183–189.

[35] J. D. M. Derrett, "Statutory Amendments of the Personal Law of the Hindus since Indian Independence," *American Journal of Comparative Law,* VII (Summer, 1958), 80, 83–85.

After independence, as before, legal interpretation of personal law and legislative reform of it reflect the persistence of caste and religious particularism, ascriptive group identity, and corporate duties.[36] The dual system of law, the continuing inability of official law to change or control the behavior of most citizens in areas that it is intended to reach, and the infiltration of official law by traditional legal norms suggest the conditions and limits of Anglicization and the special sense in which the term "Anglo-Indian law" should be understood.

[36] See, for example, J. D. M. Derrett, *Hindu Law, Past and Present* (Calcutta, 1957); Marc Galanter, "The Problem of Group Membership: Some Reflections on the Judicial View of Indian Society," *Journal of the Indian Law Institute,* IV (July–September, 1962), 331–58; M. C. Setalvad, *The Common Law in India* (London, 1960), and *The Role of English Law in India* (London, 1967); Harold Levy, "The Hindu Code Bill in British India" (M.A. thesis, Department of Political Science, University of Chicago, 1963). Levy's Ph.D. thesis, in preparation, "The Hindu Code Bill: Social Modernization through Legislation in British India and in Independent India," will provide a comprehensive analysis of statutes designed to reform Hindu personal law.

APPENDIX

TABLE 1

COMMUNITY OF WINNING PARTY CANDIDATES IN KERALA—1957, 1960, AND 1965*

Political Party		Christians 1957	Christians 1960	Christians 1965	Nairs 1957	Nairs 1960	Nairs 1965	Ezhavas† 1957	Ezhavas† 1960	Ezhavas† 1965	Muslims 1957	Muslims 1960	Muslims 1965	Total Seats Secured 1957	Total Seats Secured 1960	Total Seats Secured 1965
Indian National Congress party	Number	20	23	9	9	18	13	11	18	10	3	4	4	43	63	36
	Per Cent	47	37	25	21	28	37	25	28	28	7	6	11	34	50	27
Kerala Congress party	Number	…	…	16	…	…	7			1‡				…	…	24
	Per Cent	…	…	67	…	…	29			4				…	…	18
Communist party§‖	Number	7	2	4	27	13	18	25	12	22	6	2	4	65	29	48
	Per Cent	11	7	8	41	45	37	38	41	46	9	7	8	52	23	36
Praja Socialist party	Number	2	3	1	6	13	9	1	3	3	…	1	1	9	20	14
	Per Cent	22	15	7	67	65	64	11	15	21	…	5	7	7	16	10
Muslim League	Number										8	11	9	8	11	9
	Per Cent										100	100	100	6	9	7
Independents	Number	1	1	2	…	1	…	…	1	1				1	3	3
	Per Cent	100	33	67	…	33	…	…	33	33				1	2	2
Total communal representation	Number	30	29	32	42	45	48	37	34	36	17	18	18	126	126	133
	Per Cent	24	23	24	33	36	36	29	27	27	13	14	14	…	…	…

* Table prepared by Anthony L. Fernandez.
† Scheduled castes have been included with the Ezhavas.
‡ The one candidate of the Kerala Congress party shown as an Ezhava belongs to a scheduled caste (T. Krishnan).
§ The various independent candidates who had specific backing of a party have been included in that party.
‖ The division in the Communist party (left and right) in the 1965 election has been omitted here.

INDEX

Adi-Dravida Educational League, 138 n.
Adversary process; *see* Consensus
Agnikula Kshatriyas; *see* Vanniyars
Ahimsa; see Non-violence
Ahmed, Bashiruddin, 73 n., 74 n.
Aiyappan, A., 38 n., 63 n., 77 n., 126, 133 n., 135 n.
Aiyar, N. Chandrasekhar, 278
Alexandrowicz, C. H., 253 n.
Ambedkar, B. R., 125, 133 n., 137–45
Anderson, J. N. D., 253 n.
Andhra, 67 n.; anti-Brahminism in, 78 n.; politics, 83; Reddis of, 85, 153
Anstey, Vera, 18 n.
Arbuthnot, Sir Alexander J., 261 n.
Asceticism: Gandhi family sources of, 172–73; and courage, 185; Gandhian, 196–200, 209–10, 219–30, 248–49; *see also* Fasting; Self-control; Self-suffering
Ascription, 29, 64–67, 106–11, 130, 292; and political separateness, 66–67; and caste associations, 88; *see also* Caste
Aurobindo Ghosh, 168, 193

Backward classes; *see* Scheduled caste; Untouchables
Baghat, K. P., 73 n.
Bailey, F. G., 32 n., 63 n., 83 n., 102 n., 262
Bakan, David, 215 n.
Ballhatchet, Kenneth, 264 n., 265 n., 268 n., 287 n.
Barber, Bernard, 115 n.
Basham, A. L., 164 n.

Beames, John, 265
Beer, Samuel, 25 n., 26 n.
Beidelman, Thomas O., 31 n.
Bendix, Reinhard, 221 n.
Bengal: and imperialist theory, 162–63; "feminism" of people of, 162–66; nationalism in, 168; Gandhi in, 210, 224; legal system in, 269–70, 277–78, 289, 290
Bengal Regulations of 1793, 272
Bentham, Jeremy, 285
Bentinck, William, 287
Berreman, Gerald, 123 n.
Beteille, Andre, 54 n., 77 n., 83 n., 85, 126–27, 129 n., 135 n., 149 n., 152 n.
Bhakti, 172
Bhangis, 134
Bhatt, G. S., 63 n.
Bhooswami Sangh, 91
Bihar: politics in, 84, 185 n.; Gandhi in, 211; *see also* Kayasthas
Birla, G. D., 225
Black, Eugene C., 26 n.
Bogue, Donald J., 107 n.
Bombay, 67 n.; legal system in, 264–65, 266, 289
Bondurant, Joan V., 67 n., 184 n., 186 n.
Borradaile, Harry, 270
Bose, Nirmal Kumar, 62 n., 112 n., 124 n., 185 n., 186 n., 210 n., 211, 212 n., 214 n., 222 n., 228
Bradshaw, John, 265 n.
Brahmacharya: Gandhi as, 197, 206–7, 209; and control, 198, 214
Brahman law; *see* Law, Brahmanic

Index

Index

Index

Lawrence, John, 265
Leadership: in caste associations, 34; and charismatic responses, 199–200; *see also* Gandhi, Mohandas
Legal order: Anglicization of, 254; Brahmanization of, 254
Legal system: national, 259, 269, 281; parochial, 260, 264–68, 274, 281, 291–92; *see also* Law, customary
Lenin, V. I., 154
Leonard, John, 83 n.
Lerner, Daniel, 102 n.
Leventhal, Doris, 103 n.
Levine, Donald N., 213 n.
Levy, Harold, 262 n., 293 n.
"Life Force," 196–97
Lindell, David, 136 n.
Lipset, Seymour M., 62 n., 65 n.
Litigiousness, rise in, 260–62
Luchinsky, Mildred Stoop, 292 n.
Luillier, Sieur, 164 n.
Lynch, Owen W., 63 n., 80 n., 84 n., 135 n., 136 n., 138 n., 153 n.

Macaulay, Lord, 241 n.
McClelland, David, 220 n.
McCormack, William C., 274 n.
McCully, Bruce T., 18 n.
MacKenzie, Holt, 290 n.
McManners, J., 113 n.
MacNaghten, W. H., 273 n., 283
Macro-institutions, 20–21
Madras: Nadars of, 36–49, 92–97 (*see also* Nadars); Brahmans in, 46 n., 77, 78 n., 84; politics, 49, 85; Vanniyars of, 49–61 (*see also* Vanniyars); "Mukkulators" of, 98–99; Communists and untouchables in, 152; legal system of, 264–65, 276, 289, 290 (*see also* Commonweal party; Congress party; Dravida Kazhagam; Dravida Munnetra Kazhagam; Justice party; Maravans)
Maha Gujarat Parishad, 68
Maharashtra, 193; Brahmans in, 77, 186; *see also* Mahars

Mahars, 137–38, 141 n.; and untouchability, 134
Mahida, Narendra Singh, 101 n.
Maine, Henry, 275, 280
Malaviya, Pandit Maden Mohan, 226, 227
Malkani, N. R., 134 n.
Mandel, Ernest, 66 n.
Manusmriti, 195, 196, 272
Maquet, Jacques J., 66 n.
Maravans, 41–44, 94
Marriott, McKim, 32 n., 47, 62 n., 77 n., 117 n., 139 n.
Maru, Rushikesh, 63 n., 99, 100
Marx, Karl, 3, 8, 17, 21, 154; on peasant society, 17–19; on modernity in India, 21–23
Masani, Minoo, 101 n.
Mason, Philip, 259 n.
Mathes, Dwight L., 152 n.
Maxwell, W. H., 253 n.
Mayer, Adrian C., 83 n.
Mayne, John, 270, 272 n., 273, 276 n., 277–78
Mehta, Balwantray, 217 n.
Mehta, Pherozeshah, 237, 244; as model for Gandhi, 181–83
Mehtab, Sheikh, 176–77, 181, 204, 207, 247
Melting pot creed, 107, 112
Menscher, Joan, 81 n.
Micro-institutions, 20–21
Mill, James, 284–85
Miller, Robert J., 135 n., 141 n.
Misra, B. B., 18 n., 281 n.
Mitakshara, 272, 275
Mitra, Priti, 112 n.
Mitrany, David, 19 n.
Mobilization, 144, 154; horizontal, 36–64, 82–85; of Nadars, 36–49; of Vanniyars, 49–61; vertical, 82–85, 153; *see also* Political mobilization
Modernity, 66, 106–7, 130–31, 240–41; meaning of, 3–14; and history, 12–14; objective conditions of, 17; in law, 254, 280

302

Index

Modh Baniyas, 220; character of, 175; and sexuality, 205–6
Montagu-Chelmsford reforms (1919), 46
Montague, F. C., 285
Moon, Penderel, 253 n., 255 n.
Morris-Jones, W. H., 98 n., 131 n., 188 n., 259 n.
Moynihan, Daniel, 65 n., 108 n.
"Mukkulators," 98–99
Munro, Sir Thomas, 260, 261, 264, 267, 268 n., 290 n.
Murphy, John R., 65 n.
Muslims, 67 n., 165; in Aligarh election, 82 n.; in politics, 140
Myers, Charles A., 19 n.
Myrdal, Gunnar, 123 n.
Mysore: caste rivalry in, 71; anti-Brahmanism in, 78 n.

Nadans; see Nadars
Nadar, Kamaraj, 36, 49, 58, 59, 88–89, 93–94
Nadar Mahajana Sangam, 45, 48 n., 92, 95, 96–97
Nadars, 28, 36–49, 92–97; as Shanans, 36–46; attempt temple entry, 40–41; claim Kshatriya status, 40, 43; Kamudi Temple case and, 41–43; name changed, 45–47; in Madras politics, 48–49; and untouchability, 132–33
Naicker, N. A. Manikkavelu, 55–56
Naiker, E. V. Ramasami, 48, 57–58, 59–60, 93, 125
Naim, C. M., 139 n.
Nairs (Kerala), 71–73
Namboodiripad, E. M. S., 72 n., 74
Namier, Sir Lewis B., 25 n.
Nandi, P. K., 63 n.
Narayan, Jayaprakash, 188 n.
Narayana Dharma Paripalna Yogam, Sree, 125
Narayana Guru, Sree, 125
Natal Indian Congress, 225–26, 233–34

National character (Indian): masculine-feminine distinction in, 162–66; Westernization and, 167
National integration, 111
Nationalism, 166; and impotence fears, 168–69; and Gandhian ideology, 169–70, 183–84; leadership in, 185; and "assimilated" Indians, 192–93; non-violent, 207; Gandhi in struggle for, 216–17, 247–49
Negroes, 109, 137 n., 160, 217–18
Nehru, Jawaharlal, 217, 218, 248, 284
Nelson, J. H., 276–77
Noniyas, 28, 127–28
Non-violence, 184, 198, 203, 248; as Gandhian ahimsa, 191–92, 217; as feminine, 215–16
Novak, Maximillian E., 113 n.

Oldfield, Sir Francis Dupre, 289 n.
Ollivant, E. C. K., 242, 244
Orans, Martin, 119 n.

Padayachi, S. S. Ramaswami, 55 n., 56, 58, 59, 61, 90
Padayachi, Srinivasa, 90
Padmanabhan, Mannath, 73
Pal, B. C., 193
Pallis; see Vanniyars
Panchayats, judicial, 267–68
Pannikar, K. M., 115 n.
Paracommunities, 29, 33–36, 98–99; see also Caste associations
Pares, Richard, 25 n.
Parikh, N. D., 234 n.
Park, Richard L., 29 n.
Patel, Vallabhbhai, 187 n.
Patterson, Maureen L. P., 33 n., 51 n., 77 n., 124 n., 134 n.
Peasants, 17–19
Philips, C. H., 241 n.
Pickett, J. Waskom, 38 n.
Plessy v. Ferguson, 43
Political mobilization: differential, 24, 26–27, 28; horizontal, 24, 25–26, 27; vertical, 24–25

Index

Index

Travancore: Iravas of, 38 n.; riot of 1858 in, 8 n., 39; Shanans of, 39
Travancore, Maharaja of, 39
Trevelyan, Sir Charles, 39, 241 n.
Trevor-Roper, Hugh R., 26 n.
Trow, Martin, 65 n.
Truman, David, 34 n.
Tupper, C. L., 275 n.
Twice-born castes, 120–21; *see also* Brahmans; Caste; Kshatriyas

Untouchability: and pollution, 132, 135; and Sanskritization, 135–37
Untouchables, 132–54; Gandhi and, 123–24; politics and, 140–53; *see also* Ambedkar; Scheduled caste
Uttar Pradesh, 78, 193; Chamars in, 84; vertical mobilization in, 84; legal system in, 367–68; *see also* Bhangis

Vaishnavism, 172, 219–20
Van Buitenen, J. A. B., 21 n.
Vannikula Kshatriyas; *see* Vanniyars
Vanniya Kula Kshatriyas; *see* Vanniyars
Vanniya Kula Kshatriya Sangam, 52–54, 58–61
Vanniyars, 28, 49–61, 81; claim Shatriya status, 50–52; as Pallis, 50–51; in Madras politics, 53–58, 88–90
Varna, 31 n., 116, 117–19
Vegetarianism, 207; Gandhi and, 175–77, 179–80; and courage, 185
Venkatasubbiah, H., 19 n.
Village: system, in Marx, 23; government, 188–89; ideal, of Gandhi,

217–18; law, 254; *see also* Decompression
Vivekananda, Swami, 168
Voluntary association, 29, 33, 35, 88

Walzer, Michael L., 26 n., 235 n.
Watson, Vincent C., 110 n.
Watt, Jan, 113 n.
Webb, Robert Kiefer, 221 n.
Weber, Max, 219–20, 235 n.
Wedderburn, Sir William, 266
Weiner, Myron, 19 n., 68 n., 70 n., 80 n., 82 n., 93 n., 95 n., 99, 100 n., 131 n.
West Bengal, untouchables in, 152
Westernization, 120, 192; *see also* Law; Modernity
Whyte, William H., Jr., 65 n.
Widow Remarriage Act of 1856, 287
Williams, Raymond, 113 n.
Willner, Ann, 19 n.
Wilson, Edmund, 66 n.
Windmiller, Marshall, 68 n.
Wiser, W. H., 31 n.
Wolfinger, Raymond E., 108 n.
Woodruff, Philip, 163 n., 265–66

Yadav, Amrit Lal, 134 n.
Yadav, Lakhan Singh, 84
Yajnavalkya, 259, 272

Zanden, James W. Vander, 109 n.
Zelliot, Eleanor, 63 n., 77 n., 125 n., 134 n., 136, 138 n., 139 n., 141 n.
Zide, Norman, 139 n.
Zolberg, Aristide, 66 n.